'Barbara Pym is one of my most favourite novelists. Few other writers have given me more laughter and more pleasure. I am therefore enchanted that this biography by Paula Byrne captures both Barbara and her writing so miraculously. Best of all, it should bring hosts of new readers to enjoy her work'   Jilly Cooper

'Byrne's book is outstanding . . . Just like a Pym novel, this biography is warm, funny, unexpected and deeply moving'   *Financial Times*

'Byrne is an excellent literary detective, tracing acquaintances directly into the novels. The author seems to have been as fun, clever and kind as her best creations'   Lucy Atkins, *Sunday Times*

'Excellent . . . Although Pym's archive has already been well picked over by scholars and fans, Byrne's book is the first to integrate its revelations into a cradle-to-grave biography'
                                             Guardian, Book of the Week

'Paula Byrne's illuminating biography . . . captures the long, muddled journey of this life beautifully . . . Byrne sees what fun Pym was, how much she liked and was fascinated by people . . . and has done us a great service in exploring this very unusual personality . . . Probably Pym, even at the fairy-tale end of her life, hardly expected to be given such honourable treatment by posterity and by such a well-equipped and sympathetic biographer. This, like its subject's best books, rewards reading and rereading'   *Spectator*

'Both hilarious and heartbreaking . . . Byrne is beautifully savvy about her subject's fiction . . . as a manifesto for her genius, it is gloriously persuasive'   *Daily Telegraph*

'Wonderfully attentive and touching . . . it moves through the necessary facts as smoothly as a spoon through homemade jam. Its greatest achievement, however, lies in . . . her subject's excitable, unbridled heart . . . Byrne's book is such a joy. It refreshes the parts other biographies simply cannot reach' Rachel Cooke, *Observer*

'This was the perfect lockdown treat – a biography that does more than justice to one of my favourite authors'

Daisy Goodwin, author of *My Last Duchess*
and *The Fortune Hunter*

'Paula Byrne has not only succeeded in writing the definitive work on Barbara Pym, she has also – with astonishing skill – pieced together a beautifully nuanced mosaic. Each shimmering piece in this marvellous construct reflects an intricate moment in the life of Pym – the writer who, Byrne argues convincingly, is the twentieth century's answer to Jane Austen. This is biography at its brilliant best'

Charles Spencer, author of *The White Ship*

By the Same Author

*Kick: The True Story of JFK's Forgotten Sister and the
Heir to Chatsworth*

*The Genius of Jane Austen: Her Love of Theatre and Why
She is a Hit in Hollywood*

Belle: The True Story of Dido Belle

The Real Jane Austen: A Life in Small Things

Mad World: Evelyn Waugh and the Secrets of Brideshead

Perdita: The Life of Mary Robinson

Fiction

Blonde Venus

Look to your Wife

www.PaulaByrne.com

@paulajaynebyrne

THE ADVENTURES OF MISS BARBARA PYM

A Biography

Paula Byrne

WILLIAM
COLLINS

William Collins
An imprint of HarperCollins*Publishers*
1 London Bridge Street
London SE1 9GF

WilliamCollinsBooks.com

HarperCollins*Publishers*
1st Floor, Watermarque Building, Ringsend Road
Dublin 4, Ireland

First published in Great Britain in 2021 by William Collins
This William Collins paperback edition published in 2022

1

ISBN 978-0-00-832224-3

Typeset in Adobe Garamond Pro by
Palimpsest Book Production Ltd, Falkirk, Stirlingshire

Printed and bound in the UK using 100% renewable electricity
at CPI Group (UK) Ltd

MIX
Paper from
responsible sources
FSC
www.fsc.org
FSC™ C007454

This book is produced from independently certified FSC™ paper to
ensure responsible forest management.

For more information visit: www.harpercollins.co.uk/green

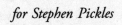

for Stephen Pickles

'No Need for Modesty in a Diary'

Barbara Pym, 9 September 1933

Contents

BOOK THE SECOND:
GERMANY

BOOK THE THIRD:
WAR

BOOK THE FOURTH:
FROM THE COPPICE TO NAPLES

BOOK THE FIFTH:
MISS PYM IN PIMLICO

BOOK THE SIXTH:
THE WILDERNESS YEARS

BOOK THE SEVENTH:
IN WHICH THE FORTUNES
OF MISS PYM ARE REVERSED

PROLOGUE

In which Miss Barbara Pym pays a Visit to Jane Austen's Cottage

It was August 1969, a few weeks after man landed on the moon and a couple of days before the assembled rock stars of the world played the Woodstock festival. The first episode of *Monty Python's Flying Circus* would soon be broadcast on the BBC. An unmarried female novelist, now fifty-six years old, was feeling adrift in this brave new world, so she made a pilgrimage to the cottage in the Hampshire village of Chawton that had been the home of another unmarried female novelist.

That night, Barbara Pym wrote in her diary: 'I put my hand down on Jane's desk and bring it up covered in dust. Oh that some of her genius might rub off on me.'[1]

Like Jane Austen, our novelist had published six well-received novels. She had built a following of devoted fans, including such luminaries as the poet Philip Larkin and the Oxford professor Lord David Cecil. She also had a legion of ardent 'excellent women' who devoured her novels, borrowed them from the circulating libraries and waited expectantly for the next 'Barbara Pym'. She had been hailed as the new Jane Austen.

But six years before her visit to Chawton, Pym's publisher, Jonathan Cape, had rejected Pym's seventh novel. It was 1963 and London was swinging. The decade had begun with the *Lady Chatterley* trial and now the Beatles had just released their first LP, *Please Please Me*. The editors at Cape felt that Barbara Pym's 'cosy' domestic comedies were out of touch, outmoded.

Pym was shocked. She had just completed a draft of what would be her masterpiece. Like the novel she had submitted, it would be considered unpublishable. It was left to languish with her other manuscript novels in a linen cupboard in her shared house in London.

There have been times when even Jane Austen's novels have fallen out of favour. Tastes and fashions change with each decade, each era. But a truly great body of work will sooner or later bounce back: Austen's 'courtship' novels, for instance – which centred on village life, avoiding overt politics and the wider world – are, for all their limited scope, now acclaimed as forerunners of the women's movement because they prioritised female experience in a world run by and for men.

Life had left Miss Barbara Pym emotionally bruised, though few would have known this by her outward appearance and demeanour. To look at her she seemed the epitome of middle-class respectability: perfectly coiffed hair; immaculately dressed; good shoes and handbag. To some, she might seem rather intimidating, redoubtable, even; though there was often a twinkle of good humour in those intelligent eyes. The young women in mini-skirts with beehive hairdos seemed to live on a different planet from Miss Barbara Pym, assistant editor of *Africa* magazine.

'If only someone would have the courage to be unfashionable,' Pym had remarked sadly to her friend Philip Larkin.[2] She feared that her novels would go out of print and she would never find another publisher. Her sense of identity had been founded on her literary status, so Cape's rejection was a bitter blow.

Barbara Pym was a lover not only of Jane Austen, but also of Austen's eighteenth-century predecessors. At St Hilda's College, Oxford, where she studied from 1931, female undergraduates were called by their surnames; Barbara was always 'Pym' to her friends. But she also liked the appellation 'Miss Pym': she frequently referred to herself in this way in her letters, notebooks and journals. In an early (unfinished) novel, she describes the heroine, who is partly based on herself, as a 'perfect eighteenth-century lady'. She loved Samuel Richardson's *Pamela*, but lost interest when Mr B's intentions towards his beautiful maidservant became honourable.[3] (It is a good point: Mr B is a wonderful villain but loses all credibility when he reforms.) It was the racier aspects of the novel that attracted Barbara Pym.

Pym's own diaries are prefaced 'The Adventures of Miss Pym', and later of 'Sandra' and of 'Pymska', in the manner of Henry Fielding's masterpiece *Tom Jones*. Like Fielding's naive hero, Miss Pym spent much of her youth falling in love and – surprisingly in the light of her reputation for provinciality – a considerable amount of it on the road. So it is fitting to imagine her life as a picaresque adventure, with a Fieldingesque narrative: 'In which our heroine . . .'

BOOK THE FIRST

A Shropshire lass

CHAPTER I

In which our Heroine is born in Oswestry

Shropshire is a rural county in the north-west of England, nest-ling on the Welsh border. It is a green and pleasant land, but not far from the city of Liverpool and the industrial shipbuilding town of Birkenhead; it is quiet, slow, rainy and green. The poet A. E. Housman immortalised its 'blue remembered hills' in *A Shropshire Lad*, even though he hardly spent any time there. Oswestry, in the north of the county and close to the border, was the birthplace of another poet, Wilfred Owen. It is an ancient market town dating back to 1190. Its narrow streets conjure up images of its medieval past: 'The Horsemarket', 'English Walls', 'Welsh Walls', 'The Bailey'.

Barbara Pym was born in the family home, 72 Willow Street, near the centre of Oswestry. Across the road was the office where her father, Frederic Crampton Pym, practised as a solicitor; his brass plate 'Crampton Pym and Lewis' is still in place beside the doorway. Barbara was born on 2 June 1913; her only sibling, Hilary, was born in 1916. By then, the family had moved to a detached Edwardian house called Morda Lodge. Set back from the road, it boasted a paddock, a coach house and a spacious garden of three acres. The attic room of the converted coach house was a playroom for the little girls.

During the summer months the garden at Morda Lodge was a riot of colour and fragrance. In a letter written to her Oxford friends, Pym describes the array of spring flowers there: 'primroses, violets, daffodils, scyllas, grape hyacinths, anemones'.[1] In one of her short stories, a heroine, modelled on herself, loves flowers with such passionate intensity that she believes that they have feelings and emotions and worries that they cry when they are cut down. Her diaries too are a record of her passion for flowers, which lasted for all of her life. Many of her happiest moments were punctuated by the gift of flowers, especially when they were brought by lovers – as when one lover once left a farewell note alongside two dozen 'of the loveliest daffodils'.[2]

Pym described her father Frederic as 'extremely good-tempered, undemanding and appreciative'.[3] Every day he would set off on foot for his office in the middle of town and return home for lunch. Sometimes, as young girls, Barbara and Hilary would visit him in his book-lined office, which he shared with his clerk and typist. Fred was a good singer, singing bass in the church choir. He was also athletic and a keen runner. A knee injury kept him out of the First World War, and he took up golf. He enjoyed reading: Rudyard Kipling and the thriller writer Edgar Wallace were among his favourite authors.

A more charismatic and somewhat eccentric figure was Pym's mother, Irena. The daughter of a successful businessman, Irena was from a large, close family. Two of her unmarried sisters, May and Janice, lived next door to Morda Lodge with their mother in a house called Scottswood. The girls would climb over the garden wall to pay regular visits to their aunts and grandmother. Fun and energetic, Irena bought a motorbike to get around during the war, wearing leather gloves and a long leather motoring coat. The Pyms kept ponies and chickens. The girls had little interest in the ponies, though Irena drove one of them, Mogus, around in a trap. Irena would feed the chickens,

Barbara remembered, wearing an old tweed coat – a detail that she stored up and used for a portrait of her mother in the novel, *Jane and Prudence*.

Irena was an avid reader and fond of music. She played the organ at the parish church of St Oswald's and she and Fred belonged to the Oswestry Operatic Society. She was also an active member of the parish and the local Women's Institute. A practical person, in many respects Irena was the epitome of the 'excellent women' that would be at the core of her daughter's novels. She loved to compose doggerel, was a good mimic and had a good sense of humour – a trait she passed on to her clever, lively daughters. She had a font of maxims and favoured quotations, which afforded the girls much amusement. 'It is hardly worthwhile dividing a cherry' was one of her sayings. And she would often quote from hymns: 'God works in mysterious ways' was a favourite.[4]

On cosy evenings, when the family were at home, together with their two cats sleeping in a chair, Irena would declaim: 'Behold how good and joyful a thing it is, brethren, to dwell together in unity.' At other times she would burst into song or quote from Walter Scott. More crucially, in terms of her influence on Barbara, she delighted in fabricating stories about people and their lives: 'See what you can find without *asking*', was one of her maxims.[5] She was sporty – a keen hockey player as a youngster, and later turning to golf – a trait she passed on to Hilary, who also played hockey. Barbara, however, was not fond of physical exercise, preferring to read, scribble stories and pick flowers in the garden for her bedroom.

Barbara loved family jokes and nicknames: Irena was 'Links' – a reference to her love of the golf links; Frederic was 'Dor' and Hilary was Poopa; and she was 'Buddy'. Barbara was extremely fond of and protective of her little sister, her mother often having to scold her, 'What are you doing to Hilary? Put her down.' When Barbara was sent to boarding school aged twelve, Hilary would spend the whole day at the gate waiting in the hope that she would return.[6]

The Pym sisters were close to some young cousins in Hatch End, London, who would come to stay at Christmas and Easter. Hilary recalled sugar mice adorning the Christmas cake and celluloid animals in their stockings. At the age of eight Barbara wrote an operetta called 'The Magic Diamond', which she and her cousins performed at Morda Lodge in 1922.

The Pyms were closely connected to the local church: the girls were friends with the vicar's daughter, Audrey Brown, and they enjoyed Christmas parties at the vicarage. The family would make a habit of inviting the young curates of the parish to tea. Hilary recalled how she fell in love with a handsome young curate when she was fourteen: during a chat with Irena, he had crossed his legs, revealing white combinations under his cassock. This would form the opening of Barbara's first published novel, *Some Tame Gazelle*. It was the kind of detail that the Pym sisters loved; jokes about underwear – 'combinations' for men and 'trollies' for women – were always good value. They were a religious family, but they were never prudes.

The Pyms were typically respectable middle class and had a small entourage of staff: a gardener and several maids – Sarah (who also acted as a nursemaid to the girls), Leah, Emily, Dilys and Marjorie. Two of the maids lived in, occupying tiny candlelit attic rooms (there was no electricity on this floor of the house). The Pym girls were encouraged to help out with household chores, polishing and washing up, but much of the family's life depended upon domestic service.

In her diary, Barbara remembered how 'boring' she found it to show fifteen-year-old Marjorie around the house: the girl's fate as a live-in maid would never be her own. Servants would crop up in Pym's early novels, written during the 1930s, but that changed, as so many things did, after the Second World War. Pym might have felt more sympathy for the young maid had she known about a family scandal that only came to light after her death.

CHAPTER II

In which we learn how a Servant Girl, Phoebe Pym, is seduced by a Gentleman and gives birth to a Baby Boy

Poundisford Park Lodge was a fine English country house in Somerset dating back to the sixteenth century. It boasted large grounds, formal gardens and a medieval deer park. It was home to Edmund Dewar Bourdillon and his wife, Maria. One of their servants was a young girl called Phoebe Pym. She was the second of six children, her father Thomas was an (illiterate) agricultural labourer, and it is likely that her mother, Harriet, worked at the big house.[1] With mouths to feed, Phoebe was sent to Poundisford to work as a maid.

Somehow Phoebe met a handsome young man called Fiennes Henry Crampton, who lived at Sherford Lodge, in nearby Taunton. Fiennes hailed from a connected Irish family from County Wicklow. His ancestor, Philip Crampton, had been Lord Mayor of Dublin. There was a wild streak to the Crampton family, and a history of bigamy and illegitimate children. Fiennes's father, Henry, having married twice, ran away with his housekeeper and married for a third time leaving his young son with his second wife, Blanche. She was a wealthy woman whose family were farmers and small landowners. She and her mother brought up Fiennes at Sherford Lodge.

Fiennes was only sixteen when he met Phoebe Pym, who was nineteen. In 1879, Phoebe gave birth to a baby boy, Frederic Crampton Pym. No father was named on the birth certificate. When the Cramptons heard the news of the baby, they sent their son away to the Royal Military Academy, Sandhurst. It was an all too familiar story of a vulnerable maid impregnated by a man of the ruling classes and abandoned to her fate. So far so Thomas Hardy.

It is unclear how much Frederic Pym knew of his murky past. Hilary Pym recalled that he never spoke directly of his family, alluding only vaguely to his West Country origins. But he seemed to be proud of his 'Crampton' name, which he bequeathed to both his daughters. The brass sign at his office with the double-barrelled 'Crampton Pym' was probably an attempt to confer gentility. Barbara also appeared to inherit the family pride of the Crampton name. She seriously considered writing under the name of Tom Crampton and her Oxford novel was given the title *Crampton Hodnet*.

Phoebe, clearly a girl of energy and courage, decided to emigrate to Canada, leaving her two-year-old son to be raised by her parents. Frederic was evidently a clever boy and was informally adopted by Frank White, a prosperous local manufacturer, and his wife Mildred (who would be Hilary's godmother). He became a clerk to a prominent solicitor in Taunton and was later articled to a firm of solicitors in Shropshire. It was whilst on holiday in Ilfracombe in Devon that he met Irena. On their marriage certificate he gave the name of his grandfather, Thomas, where he was supposed to put that of his father. Though he would keep the truth from his daughters, he seems to have shared the secret of his illegitimacy with his wife.

Frederic's father rose to the rank of brigadier-general. His portrait, showing a very handsome man with a curled moustache, hangs in London's National Portrait Gallery. Although he married in 1901, he never had any legitimate children. There is no mention of Frederic in his will.

CHAPTER III

In which Miss Pym is sent away to Boarding School

When Barbara was twelve, her mother decided that her clever elder daughter should be sent to boarding school in Liverpool. She had ambitions for both daughters: the University of Oxford was the goal she cherished for them.

Founded in 1894, the Liverpool College for Girls in Huyton was a mid-Victorian building set in extensive grounds with lacrosse pitches, tennis and netball courts, a swimming pool and spacious sports hall. It had science laboratories, an art room with a kiln for pottery, a music suite with practice rooms, a domestic science kitchen, needlework room, secretarial training suite, school bookshop and sanatorium. There was also a large school hall with professional stage lighting and a Bechstein grand piano. There was an ample collection of fiction and a large panelled reference library where older girls would study during free periods.

Hilary speculated that Irena may well have been influenced by the boarding school stories of Angela Brazil, with their titles such as *A Patriotic Schoolgirl*, *An Exciting Term*, *The Jolliest School of All* and *A Harum-Scarum Schoolgirl*. Brazil was the first to popularise schoolgirl fiction, written from the point of view of the pupils. Her tales, published in an era of increased literacy for girls, shaped a generation of families, who were encouraged by the Education Acts of 1902 and 1907 to take advantage of better opportunities for their daughters. Between 1900 and 1920, the number of girls at grammar schools increased from 20,000 to 185,000.

Liverpool College was a disciplined school, its motto *Fideliter fortiter feliciter* (faithfully, bravely, happily). The school was divided into six houses named after female saints. Pym was assigned to St Hilda, who was named after a seventh-century Anglo-Saxon abbess who turned snakes into fossils. In preparation, Pym and her mother went shopping for her uniform at the huge department store, George Henry Lee, in the centre of Liverpool. The winter uniform was a blue Harris tweed coat and skirt, especially woven for the girls in Scotland. Pupils wore felt pudding hats and black full-length cloaks, lined in house colours, to keep them warm from the icy Merseyside winds as they ran between houses. St Hilda's colour was a dashing red. In the summer months, the girls wore printed Calpreta dresses and straw boaters with house ribbons.

During Pym's time, the school built its own Gothic chapel.[1] Before then, the girls attended services at the local church. Living in an all-female atmosphere, the students were intrigued by the young curates. As Hilary remembered, 'they were the only men on whom the impressionable girls could exercise their romantic imaginations'.[2] The school chaplain was a tall, handsome man whose visits were eagerly anticipated. Many of the girls were secretly in love with him. Here began Barbara's lifelong interest in creating fantasies about the life of the clergy, which she had started chiefly to amuse her friends.

It was during these school years that Barbara started to write poems and short stories. She enjoyed detective fiction and contemporary novels, as well as her father's beloved Kipling. At school she discovered the joys of poetry: her English mistress, Helene Lejeune, inspired in her 'a profound and abiding love of our greater English poets'.[3] But it was during one summer back at home for the school holidays that she found a book that changed the direction of her life.

Boots Booklovers Library, part of Boots the Chemist, was a lifeline for many readers who lived in small towns or villages. By the early twentieth century there were 143 subscription lending libraries in Boots stores. Irena was a keen reader of modern novels and had decided opinions on the good ones and the ones she disliked. It was in Boots that Barbara Pym picked out the book that would inspire her to become a writer. Aldous Huxley was a newly fashionable young novelist writing in a very distinctive style which made a huge impact on Pym. 'More than anything else I read at that time,' she explained many years later, '*Crome Yellow* made me want to be a novelist myself.'[4]

At face value, Huxley's controversial novel seems an odd choice for the young Barbara Pym. A dark comedy about a group of intellectuals who gather together in a country house – loosely based on Garsington Manor, near Oxford, the home of Bloomsbury socialite Lady Ottoline Morrell – it is sometimes considered to be the archetype of the modern novel. It certainly influenced a generation of writers such as Evelyn Waugh and F. Scott Fitzgerald. Written in the years after the First World War, it perfectly encapsulates the disillusion, disenchantment, moral uncertainty, sexual confusion and intellectual doubt of the 1920s. There are frank discussions about sex, love and spirituality between the characters, who seem to do very little except sit around talking, eating and drinking. The hero is a shy poet called Denis, who is fond of literary quotations, much to the annoyance of one young woman who finds his 'bad habit of quoting' irritating and humiliating. Several of Pym's heroes are given this trait.

Huxley was writing in the great English tradition of the country house, which appealed to Pym. She found the book 'funnier than anything I had read before, and the idea of writing about a group of people . . . in this case upper-class intellectuals in a country house – immediately attracted me, so I decided to write a novel like *Crome Yellow*'.[5]

CHAPTER IV

Miss Pym attempts her First Novel: 'Young Men in Fancy Dress'

Pym's first novel, 'Young Men in Fancy Dress', was about a group of bohemians living in Chelsea. Later, she (laughingly) admitted that Chelsea was a district that she knew nothing about.

The book was never published. It now forms part of the vast Barbara Pym manuscript collection at the Bodleian Library in Oxford. It was written in a blue-lined notebook, which appears to have exactly the right number of pages for her novel. Dated 'August 1929 to April 1930', it is a remarkably confident and assured debut for a sixteen-year-old writer.

The opening is an accomplished parody of *Crome Yellow*. Pym's first sentence is a direct quotation from Chapter 2 of Huxley's novel: 'He took nobody by surprise, there was nobody to take.' She continues with a subtle acknowledgement of the debt:

Denis laid down his pen to consider the words he had just written. He said them aloud and meditated upon their subtle humour with pride. Then a sudden and horrible thought occurred to him. The words seemed familiar. Where could he possibly have heard them before? – no relative or friend of his was capable of saying anything like that.

Like his namesake in Huxley, Denis aspires to be a novelist. He has read all the best modern novels and is not ignorant of the classics. Pym pays homage to the writer who had inspired her novel: 'That afternoon he had read *Crome Yellow* and had enjoyed it immensely. It seemed to him to be as about perfect as a novel could be. Not actually about anything – of course not – the best novels never are – but full of witty and intelligent conversation.'[1]

Pym maintained this view of 'the perfect novel' for all of her writing life. Her own works would reflect this notion – they are novels not really *about* anything, but filled with characterful people and witty conversation. The hero falls in love (twice), contemplates suicide, hangs out in a large country house and in London flats with poets and aspiring novelists, rejects his middle-class parents – 'his father had made money in the sausage trade' is a classic Pym touch. 'It did not seem strange that the son of a sausage king should have an inclination towards novels and poetry.'[2]

At the close of 'Young Men in Fancy Dress', Denis has decided he will start writing his own novel: 'naturally it's bound to be something in the nature of an autobiography – don't you think that first novels nearly always are?' Again, this is an acute observation for a schoolgirl to make. It would be the case for *Some Tame Gazelle*. There are similarities between Denis and Barbara: their stultifying existence in a small English village, boredom with parents, 'hopelessly ambitious' with a desire to be a 'famous novelist'. At school, they are clever but not brilliant. They admire Aldous Huxley and are keen on poetry. Neither one of them wants to get married, though they long to fall in love.

'Young Men in Fancy Dress' shows Pym honing her craft. We

see the young writer experimenting with dialogue, jokes, different kinds of characters – though what unites the young men, convinced by their own uniqueness, is that they are all depressingly conventional. At the end of the novel there is a discussion between a young girl and the hero about the creative process and the interface between illusion and reality. Marguerite tells Denis: 'You can't write about things unless you have experienced them yourself – Love for example.' Denis disagrees: 'I think it's almost harder to write about love when you have experienced it than when you haven't. You realise what a complicated sort of thing it is.'[3] Again, this is a remarkably assured reflection for such a young writer.

Pym had proved to herself that she could write and complete a novel of 267 pages. On a seaside holiday to Pwllheli, in north Wales, she met one of the sons of the local pastor, a young man called Dewi Morgan Griffith and she dedicated her book to him with the words: 'To HDMG, who kindly informed me that I had the makings of a style of my own.'

Her dedication sounds curiously like another fascinating work of juvenilia in the Bodleian, Jane Austen's 'Effusions of Fancy by a very Young Lady consisting of Tales in a Style entirely new'. Though it is unlikely that Pym would have known Austen's juvenilia, her own reveals an affinity with Austen. There is the same love of nonsense and trivia, the same love of wordplay. What she also shared with her literary heroine was a clearly defined confidence in her own literary potential. She wanted to be a writer and she wanted to write in her own way, in a 'style of her own'.

CHAPTER V

In which Miss Barbara Pym goes up to St Hilda's College, Oxford

Pym was happy to fulfil her mother's ambitions to aim for Oxford. She applied to St Hilda's, perhaps in tribute to her own school house. It was still rare for young women to gain a place at Oxbridge, though one of Liverpool College's former head girls had won a place at Cambridge (she was killed in an accident whilst there and in the new school chapel there was a stained-glass window dedicated to her memory).

Barbara Pym's school career, as her sister acknowledged, was not stellar, but by the end of her time at Huyton she was a house prefect, chair of the Literary Society and a member of the chapel choir. Her headmistress wrote that she was thoughtful and efficient, and singled out her 'special literary and linguistic gifts'. Her work, she wrote, was 'original and interesting, showing powers of observation, imagination and independence of thought'.[1] This recommendation helped her to win a place at St Hilda's to read English language and literature.

Pym went up in the autumn of 1931. In her mind, Oxford would always be associated with that season; the smell of woodsmoke and the picking of wild berries. It was also a place to be forever associated with romance, teeming as it was with young men, dressed not exactly in fancy dress, but in scholars' sweeping black gowns.

In 'Young Men in Fancy Dress' the heroine complains of being bored in the company of 'hopelessly stupid' girls, who 'can't talk about anything but dances, or golf, or tennis – they don't seem to have read any decent books and if they have – they can't discuss them with any intelligence'.[2] Whether or not this sentiment echoed her own feelings, Pym certainly was ready to flirt and fall in love. Even before Oxford, she had developed a crush on a young bank clerk in Shropshire. His name was John Trevor Lloyd and she composed two poems in his honour – one of them called 'Midland Bank', dedicated 'to JTL with the author's fondest love (but without his permission)'.[3]

Eighteen-year-old Barbara was a tall, attractive young woman, with an engaging lopsided smile and thick, wavy chestnut-coloured hair. More than one person described her as having a 'Joyce Grenfell' look about her, perhaps because of her height, her ungainliness and her habit of clowning around and making jokes. She was not conventionally beautiful or delicate-looking, but she was always well dressed and well turned out. In one of her early stories, the heroine, Flora, is a thinly disguised version of Pym, described as 'a tall big-boned girl with a fresh complexion and large, bright, intelligent grey eyes'. She has light brown hair with golden streaks and a broad mouth, 'always laughing or smiling'.[4]

When Pym went up to St Hilda's, it was still a small college. She had prepared herself for undergraduate life by reading Oxford novels and the poetry of Matthew Arnold, but none of these was written about the five women's colleges, or indeed from the female perspective. St Hilda's – its motto *non frustra vixi* (I lived not in vain) – had the atmosphere of a girls' private school. Founded in 1893, the college sits on the River Cherwell, over-looking Magdalen Bridge and Christ Church Meadow. Its location in a tranquil nook of Oxford gave it a cosy, intimate atmosphere. The lawn sloped down to the river, where girls could sit in the summer and read – though they were forbidden to place teapots on the lawn (one of many prohibitions in the undergraduate handbook).

Oxford clung to its old traditions and it must have felt to the young girl from the north of England like another world. Then, as now, colleges were the centre of social life and each college had its own identity. There were divisions and cliques within and between the colleges; northerners and southerners viewed each other with suspicion, as did public school and grammar school undergraduates, hearties and aesthetes. In 1931, the year Pym arrived, an undergraduate poet had his rooms trashed and the following year, another student – with 'Oscar Wildish propensities' – had his grand piano smashed up and his clothes thrown on a bonfire.[5]

Rules dated back to ancient times. Black gowns had to be worn, chapel attended, gate hours kept. Most societies remained male preserves. Individual women were allowed to act with the Dramatic Society (OUDS) by invitation only.[6] Male dining clubs flourished and were riotous events resulting in shattered windows, broken furniture and damaged flowerbeds. Undergraduates were treated like grown-up children and lived in an environment that replicated public school life: they were expected to keep to gate hours, allowed to mix socially with the opposite sex only under the strictest conditions and were banned from visits to the public houses. The women were referred to as 'young ladies', the men as 'gentlemen'. Gowns had to be worn when in town, and hemlines were low.

St Hilda's was a particularly strict college, with firm rules about gentlemen callers. Undergraduates were permitted to receive gentleman friends not related to them on Tuesday afternoons only. The gates closed at 9.10 p.m. As late as the 1990s, students had to write down the name of their gentleman visitors, and if they stayed the night that information had to be submitted to the porter's lodge. Women were not free to mix as they pleased. It was not until 1935, after Pym had left Oxford, that a female student could visit a male undergraduate in his rooms unaccompanied by another female, and even then she had to leave before evening hall.

Punishment was fierce for transgressions of rules – particularly so for women. The college authorities had three weapons: fines, gating (being confined to college), and rustication (being temporarily sent home). As late as 1961, St Hilda's expelled a female undergraduate discovered with a man in her bed when her scout came with tea.[7] At St Hugh's, if a female student had a male visitor, the bed was ceremoniously wheeled out of her room and into the corridor.[8] But, of course, when young people of the opposite sex are in close proximity, rules are circumvented, codes of conduct are relaxed, especially when alcohol is added to the mix. Barbara Pym was determined to taste, in Evelyn Waugh's words, 'all the delights Oxford had to offer'.[9]

CHAPTER VI

In which our Heroine might have said *Et in Arcadia ego*

Despite its restrictions, St Hilda's was a warm and friendly college. The dining hall, furnished with long tables and benches, adorned in the evenings with glistening silver and lit by candle-light, overlooked the River Cherwell. Barbara Pym's room was on the top floor, with her own view of the river and the long, sweeping drive. She made friends easily and would chat with her fellow students long into the night.[1] Her closest friends were Mary Sharp, Dorothy Pedley and Rosemary Topping, always referred to by their surnames.

Compared with her schoolgirl days, there were freedoms to be enjoyed: a room of one's own, financial independence, no more school timetables or school uniform. Clothes were an abiding passion for Pym and before coming up to Oxford she had planned a whole new wardrobe. Like many young women of her class and era, she sewed most of her own clothes. Shop-bought dresses were a luxury item.

Pym found Oxford 'intoxicating'.[2] In no small part this was because she suddenly found herself the centre of male attention and, like many girls from single-sex schools, she was ready to enjoy being in the company of young men. As with her heroine,

Miss Bates, in her third published novel *Jane and Prudence*, the male undergraduates beat a path to Pym's door. It was not only the preponderance of men (the ratio was one woman to ten men) that enhanced her desirability, but also the fact that she was so funny and interesting. She was in particular a magnet for homosexual men, who were drawn to her wit and playfulness.

Barbara never forgot the heady days of her first term at Oxford; the city seemed at its most beautiful in the autumn months. In her novel, *Jane and Prudence*, she pays tribute to the feelings evoked by her earliest impressions of the university in the Michaelmas term: 'the new work, the wonderful atmosphere of Oxford in the autumn, the walks up to Boars Hill and Shotover and all those lovely berries we used to gather'.[3]

The first term was spent getting to know her new surroundings, smoking Gold Flake cigarettes and listening to jazz bandleader Jack Payne on the wireless. There was an active social life at Oxford revolving around sherry parties, tea parties, dinners and the theatre. Above all, Barbara loved watching films and took advantage of Oxford's several picture houses: 'the Queener' on Queen Street, 'the Walton Street' cinema, which showed French films, and, up a steep hill, the Headington cinema, where the students cycled, storing their bikes in the yard of the nearby fish and chip shop.

Barbara spent most of her studying hours at the Bodleian Library, a prime place for spotting handsome undergraduates. The oldest reading room, the Duke Humfrey's library on the first floor, was a beautiful room built in the shape of an H. Humphrey, Duke of Gloucester, who was the youngest son of King Henry IV, donated his collection of 281 books to the Bodleian in 1447. At the time, the library had only twenty books and a new reading room was built to house the collection. Readers were compelled to recite aloud a promise not to burn books, a reference to the burning of most of the duke's collection during the Reformation. Pym would have recited the pledge: 'I hereby undertake not to remove from the Library, or to mark, deface, or injure in any way, any volume, document, or other object belonging to it or in its custody; not to bring into the Library or kindle therein any fire or flame, and not to smoke in the Library; and I promise to obey all rules of the Library.'

On the second floor of the Old Library was the Upper Reading Room, which housed the principal collection of printed books published after 1640, in the subject fields of medieval and modern history and English language and literature. The Lower Reading Room housed classics and ancient history, theology and philosophy. It is partitioned into smaller rooms. The central Tower Room had a glass-fronted portrait of Geoffrey Chaucer. Pym used the portrait as a mirror to comb her hair and apply her lipstick – a habit she later gave to the heroine of *Some Tame Gazelle*, though she edited it out of the published version.

Though she allowed undergraduate men to pay court, she developed crushes on the youthful dons, known as 'examination moderators', who set and marked the exams. She invented a game called 'Spot the Moderator'. She nicknamed her favourite moderator 'Fat Babyface'. She loved to stalk him through the streets of Oxford. Another was 'Ruffled Chicken'.

Indeed, Barbara was enjoying life so much that she failed her end of term examinations. It was a shock, and made her resolve to be more diligent and studious. Being home for Christmas only increased her sense of dismay. Oxford was a new world, and back in the wilds of Shropshire she realised that she must not squander her precious gift. She needed to work hard through the holidays in order to resit her exams.

Another resolution was to begin a new diary. Barbara had written a diary as a schoolgirl, which she probably destroyed. From this point on, though, she kept all her diaries. She titled her Oxford diary: 'A Record of the Adventures of the celebrated Barbara M C Pym during the year 1932 (written by herself)' – a satirical nod to the picaresque adventurers of eighteenth-century novels such as *Tom Jones* and *Moll Flanders*.

CHAPTER VII

In which Miss Pym returns North

Pym's first diary entry is short: 'Up at 9.30. No post at all.'[1]

She was hankering for her university friends – just as in *Brideshead Revisited*, hero Charles Ryder sits at home, melancholy, after his first term at Oxford, desperate for a letter from Sebastian Flyte. Oxford seemed a long way away. 'Beginning the year in an excellently one-sex way,' she wrote, in partial relief after the drama of her first term and the excitement of being the centre of male attention: 'Went to Blackgate – no thrills there.'[2]

Life back in Shropshire seemed mundane: eating, sewing, flicks in the evening. She was happy to see her sister and parents, but she now felt the slow pace of home: 'A spot of supper and a domesticated evening. Myself a little desirous of somewhere else.' She felt 'vague' and listless, with a sense of dislocation that was difficult to shrug off. She began to be alienated from her Shropshire friends, who felt that university life was giving her 'airs'. Even her mother noted a change in her daughter, whose heart was back in Oxford.

In another unfinished novel, 'Beatrice Wyatt', Pym wrote about her heroine's disoriented feelings about being back in her old bedroom. She comes home from Oxford for the holidays and wakes up to the same old schoolgirl's bedroom. The pale yellow walls are hung with reproductions of Cézanne and Van Gogh. Her white bookshelves are lined with old novels, such as 'blue phoenix' copies of Aldous Huxley and books that she has now outgrown and is 'partly ashamed' of having once loved. There is a chintz ottoman in the corner of the room in which old essays and stories are stored.

One suspects that Beatrice is also 'partly ashamed' of her dull home life and the mother who tries so hard to please but is irritating and vague, obsessed by her bridge parties. Oxford is far more alluring than the countryside.[3] Beatrice has installed a gas ring for 'private cups of tea' whilst she works hard at her studies, but is interrupted by her mother, who urges her clever, distant daughter to not work so hard, but to listen to the wireless instead.[4]

There is scarce mention of Barbara's family in her journal at this time, other than a passing reference to them taking her to the station. Thrilled as she was to be leaving Shropshire, she was mindful of her precarious position, having to resist the temptations of her active social life and resit her examinations: 'I'm looking forward awfully to going back – but simply must work hard,' she confided. On 12 January 1932 she packed for Hilary term, taking with her her favourite doll, Wellerina – 'made presentable to make her debut at Oxford – may she bring me luck'.[5] Like the fictional Sebastian Flyte's teddy bear in *Brideshead Revisited*, Wellerina seems to have caused quite a stir amongst her Oxford friends.

CHAPTER VIII

In which Miss Pym returns to Oxford

Somehow, at Oxford station, Pym left the train with the wrong suitcase, which belonged to a boy at Lincoln College, a Joyce Grenfell kind of misadventure.[1]

Despite her determination to work hard, she was 'goofy with excitement', her head still full of boys: 'A new term in a new year – golden opportunities (and how!) to get a Moderator, a peer's heir, a worthy theological student – or even to change entirely!' She was determined to find out the name of the moderator who had 'ploughed' her (failed her examination paper). She discovered that it was probably 'G Moore of Magdalen'. Mary Sharp, Pym's best friend, had also been ploughed, making her feel less humiliated. Could G. Moore be her beloved 'Fat Babyface'? She resolved to further her investigations. Her female friends were dismayed by her choice of crush, but she found him chatting to an undergraduate in Blackwell's bookshop, 'Too sweet, in spite of other people's unfavourable opinions.'[2]

Pym kept up her other 'secret passion' for a boy from 'Teddy Hall' (St Edmund's), whom she had spotted at St Mary's, the university church. Rather thrillingly, he was not wearing his gown. She felt he had an 'interesting face . . . I'm sure he must be worthwhile.' Back in her room, she consulted the University Calendar, which provided her with a comprehensive list of all students.[3]

The next day, Pym observed Fat Babyface buying a second-hand record, but it was too late to shadow him. Instead, she went to a Bach concert and on the way home saw her 'pet scholar' from St Edmund's Hall, so she 'traced' him up the Iffley Road in order to discover his lodgings, so she could eventually discover his name. There were men all around who were ready and willing to be flirted with: Teddy, Trevor, Harry, Bill and Gary, Ross and Aidan, John ('his hair so beautifully golden and about twice as long as last term'). 'Ruffled Chicken moderator' turned out to be Herbert J. Hunt: 'He has a Lancs accent and one feels that his H's are more a matter of luck than habit.'[4] She had found out that it was he who had ploughed her: 'I don't think I have the heart to murder him.' Then there was Monkey, 'a funny old darling', whose first comment on meeting Pym was: 'How foul you look.'[5]

And still the men came. A chap called Harlovin asked her for a date. Bill and Stephen walked her back to St Hilda's. After parting from them at the college gates, she went to her room and undressed in the 'dim religious light of two candles'.[6] The next day she spotted her 'pet moderator'. She pondered on whether he was even aware of her existence: 'Really this is the queerest crush ever – I wonder if he has any inkling.' She was thrilled to see the suspicion of a red silk hanky peeping out of his top pocket: 'Who says they [moderators] aren't human!'[7] Much of the thrill was in the chase. Pym was too self-aware not to see this aspect of her attraction to unavailable men.

Teddy often took her to tea at Elliston & Cavell, known as Elliston's, the largest department store in Oxford (later taken over by Debenhams). It was lavishly decorated with a sweeping staircase and a mural depicting deer in a forest glade. The ladies' powder room boasted gold taps and marble basins in the shape of swans. Attendants dressed in black handed out towels. There was even a private entrance for the wives of dons and the heads of house. Though she liked Teddy, Pym still dreamed of the moderators – 'Mad creature that I am!'[8]

She had started attending the lectures of Herbert Hunt, the man who had ploughed her, and confessed to her diary that he was growing on her: 'He used rather a delightful expression – he said, "I haven't finished yet by a long chalk!" – sub human. How mad!' Hunt was on his way to becoming a distinguished scholar of Honoré de Balzac's great novel sequence *La comédie humaine*, which could as well be the perfect title for the sequence of much shorter and lighter novels that Pym would write. At Hunt's lectures, she sat with her female friends and hoped that her male admirers would not mind. Teddy was becoming tiresome and wrote her a letter addressed to 'Darling Barbara'. She decided: 'I've just got to be firm with him.'[9]

The fact was that Pym had not yet met a man in whom she had a serious interest. Those she noted appear to be more fodder for her writing than anything else. A man she spotted in Elliston's called Everard gave her a name for one of her main characters in a novel written years later. Another had 'a sweet face . . . and what a provocative little nose'; another had 'wonderful black patent leather hair'.[10] She was always interested in men's clothes, as well as women's, noting a smart brown suit, or a red sweater, or striped tie. But she admitted to her diary that, despite all the male attention, she had started the term with a 'pure one sex month'.[11]

This state of affairs would soon change. A male undergraduate, Ross, insisted on a kiss (a hard one at that) as a price for walking her back to St Hilda's.[12] She received the good news that she had passed one of her resits. In celebration, she bought a brass cigarette box with a dragon on it. She also purchased a rose-pink cushion. On April Fools' Day, she heard that she had passed her other examinations. Then it was home to Shropshire for the Easter vacation.

Barbara's time there was uneventful and there is a gap in her diary, which is resumed on her return to Oxford: 'On this day I returned to my dear University.' She was looking forward to Trinity (summer) term: although she needed to work hard, she was determined to play hard. This would be the time for punting on the river, picnics, and outdoor Shakespeare plays and concerts in the lovely college gardens. And perhaps for falling in love.

During the Easter holidays, she had been told by her tutors to read the works of the seventeenth-century poet John Donne. He was to be a lifelong passion. His sexy, romantic poems appealed to Pym's passionate nature. Her interest in his poetry ran in tandem with her love affair with a dark, handsome man whom she had met briefly in Michaelmas term. For good and for ill, he would become a very important figure in her life.

CHAPTER IX

In which our Heroine meets a Handsome Young Man called Rupert Gleadow

Pym was feeling her way in Oxford. She decorated her room with a self-portrait by Van Gogh in a gold frame, along with the pink cushion and brass cigarette box. Often, she noted, her room was a fug of smoke when she lit Gold Flake after Gold Flake. At the end of April she had her first punting experience with her friend Dorothy Pedley and Rosemary Topping. The pole got stuck, but they were rescued by a group of 'chivalrous' Teddy Hall men.[1]

On May Day, at 5 a.m., she set off by punt to hear the choristers singing from the Great Tower on Magdalen Bridge. 'May Morning' is a special time of revelry in Oxford; following the dawn madrigals, the church and college bells ring out over the city for twenty minutes. Undergraduates would then decamp to local taverns and restaurants for a May Morning breakfast.

Pym and her friends enjoyed picnics on the riverbank. Oxford was fully living up to expectations. She discovered that Fat Babyface was a theology scholar called Geoffrey Walmsley. 'Oh Geoffrey, how I love you!' she confessed to her diary. There were numerous sightings of him; in the street, on his bike, in Blackwell's bookshop, in St Mary's church. In his plus-fours he comes across as a Mr Toad figure rather than a truly romantic hero, even though Pym later claimed that he closely resembled the actor Leslie Howard. She went walking on Shotover Hill and picked blue forget-me-nots that were the colour of Geoffrey's eyes.

But she also knew that Geoffrey was a fantasy love affair. He had barely spoken to her or knew much about her. And she wasn't entirely serious: 'I'll just forget you when you go down,' she confessed to her diary. She was playing around with the idea of falling in love. This was to change when she became friends with a dashing young man called Rupert Gleadow. They had been introduced in the Michaelmas term, but it was only in the summer that the relationship flourished.

Rupert was in his final year at Trinity College reading classics and Egyptology. He had been educated at Winchester, one of the most prestigious public schools, and had a large and beautiful family home in Surrey, as well as a London home. He was an altogether more sophisticated figure than the men she chased around the ancient streets of Oxford.

In May, Pym spotted Rupert at the cinema. At the Bodleian, he invited her to tea: 'I accepted – wanting to see more of him.'[2] She kept his invitation, scrawled on the back of a tiny library ticket, all her life.[3] He followed up his first message with a second more expansive note, explaining, tellingly, that there was nobody else coming to the tea. His 'digs' were at number 47 Wellington Square, but for the purposes of the tea he would borrow the attractive sitting room upstairs that belonged to his roommate, George Steer. A third note confirmed the invitation, with a hand-drawn map of the house in Wellington Square.[4] Rupert was clearly very keen.

Pym wrote back, expressing some fears about the proctor, who lived in the same house. It was a risk for a female undergraduate to be found alone in the room of a man. Rupert reassured her and told her that the proctor was a good friend and he also thanked her for the 'flattering suggestion' that she had been unable to work since seeing him in the Bod.

When she arrived, Pym was impressed with the room, which was covered with books and decorated with animal skins: 'the leopard skinned couch was to play a more important part later', she wrote mysteriously. She enjoyed Rupert's company immensely and thought him 'far more human' than she had previously thought. His father had died halfway through his time at Oxford and he might well have hidden his grief and vulnerability behind a veneer of aloofness. She was surprised when he took her hand in his and asked her for a kiss; she refused.

Exhibiting a clear tendency to rush into love affairs, Pym decided the very next day that she was in love with Rupert. But she also remained faithful to the idea of Geoffrey, whom she had not yet met alone and who had not shown any signs of reciprocating her affection. She was a young green girl ready to fall in love multiple times over. She noted her 'double-love' in her journal: 'for Geoffrey – very real – and also for Rupert – also very real'.[5] This trait in her character – of rushing into love affairs without really knowing the recipient – would, in the long term, be damaging.

Rupert was making all the running. Another undergraduate called Bill Thacker was keen on Barbara. The notion of a rival enhanced her charms in Rupert's eyes. He wrote letters, begging her to drop in anytime, also writing that he would be keen to see her at St Hilda's, even though he knew that this was forbidden, 'otherwise they'll have all sorts of Don Juans getting in'.[6] Rupert was presenting himself as a Byronic figure and Pym was ready to have fun. He told her that he was unable to concentrate on his Egyptian studies, as she was so much on his mind. Pym had joked about the inferior quality of his sherry and he promised better quality in the future. He told her that he longed for a motor car to take her around the Oxford countryside. There was much talk of his 'wickedness'.[7]

May was rainy and one wet day, Pym and Rupert went for a walk. Soaked through, they stopped off at 47 Wellington Square and drank sherry: 'I remember putting my arms around him and loving him because he was very wet and shivering and looked at me so sweetly.'[8] She still longed for Geoffrey, but it wasn't long before her real affair with Rupert took precedence. A photograph that he sent to her reveals him to be a dark, handsome man, with a lean, angular face of the kind that she found most appealing. He wrote letter after letter in different coloured ink to his 'Darling Barbara', telling her that he dreamed about her, worried that she might still be seeing other men and hoping that she would drop by whenever she pleased. They were the first proper love letters that she had ever received and she cherished them.

Rupert was clearly smitten with this lively 'northern' girl who could hold a conversation and had so many admirers. He found her to be highly original, most unlike any other girl he had met. Her sense of humour and her quick wit made a lasting impression. When one of his eyelashes fell out, she picked it up and granted him five wishes. One of them was to buy his own aeroplane – a wish that was to be fulfilled sooner than he thought.

The pair's pursuits were still largely innocent; tea at Stewart's on Queen Street or at Boffin's, where the cakes and buns were excellent. But it soon became clear that Rupert wanted more from her than an uncomplicated friendship and Boffin's buns. She went on a date with another boy to see a production of *The Constant Nymph*, the story of a girl hopelessly in love with a self-regarding composer, but her mind was on Rupert and the unopened love letter that lay in her bag. She felt 'vaguely depressed and slightly hysterical' when she returned home from the play.[9] It had only been a couple of weeks since the beginning of the relationship, but her feelings were gaining momentum.

Early on the morning of her nineteenth birthday, 2 June, Pym received a letter from Rupert wishing her 'a very happy Birthday and lots of happy birthdays and may they all come after one another as slowly as possible, so as to make you stay young and jolly like ever so – and I do hope I meet you again when we're both far older and I hear that it's all come true'.[10] He took her to Elliston's and bought her an orange and royal blue scarf. Later, his best friend Miles joined them for dinner and then they went to the cinema to watch *Frankenstein*. Miles laughed throughout, so she didn't feel scared and she stole 'surreptitious glances at Rupert's profile'. Miles MacAdam, a large, ebullient man from Worcester College, became part of this close trio. Pym liked the way he talked and the sound of his voice.

The next day, she allowed Rupert to kiss her, though she didn't enjoy the experience. What she did like was the way he considered her thoughts and feelings. One of her male friends told Pym that he disliked Rupert and thought him 'queer' (in the old-fashioned sense of the word), but she was not deterred. They went for a walk on Boars Hill and took shelter under a tree when it began to rain. She expressed impatience with his physical attentions, 'I got a wee bit sick of it – but tried to please him.' He had final exams coming up and she wanted to 'treat him as kindly as possible'.[11]

CHAPTER X

Miss Pym's
Summer of Love

On a lovely June day, Barbara made her first visit to the Radcliffe Camera, the beautiful, circular neo-classical library that stands in the heart of Oxford. Built of golden Cotswold sandstone, it glows in the sunlight and is considered one of the architectural crown jewels of England.

Pym worked in the library, spotting a couple of men, but then on the way out found herself alone with 'heavenly' Geoffrey. She thought of a ruse to grab his attention: 'I longed to crash into him or drop my books – but the incident was over – and became one of those many might-have-beens about which its [sic] so lovely to speculate.'[1] The moment had passed, never to return. These 'might-have-beens' would become a refrain to her romantic life and rich fodder for her novels. She was in love with Rupert and yet she still had strong feelings for the remote Geoffrey. It was the first serious case of her lifelong obsession with unattainable men.

Rupert wrote more affectionate letters, telling her how happy she made him and promising that he was 'quite harmless really'. She consumed his thoughts, making him unable to work; something of a problem as he wanted to achieve a first in his exams.

In between sitting his finals, he saw 'My Darling Barbara' – his *Cara Barbara mia* – whenever he could.

Pym recorded an evening spent in the darkness of 'The Queener' with Rupert and Miles: 'We sat at the back in the corner and I had two arms around me for the first time in my history.' After the movie, *Goodnight Vienna*, they stopped off at a coffee house on the Cowley Road and sipped chocolate Horlicks, toasting one another. This was 'one of the loveliest evenings I ever remember'.[2]

Following a rainy May, the weather had suddenly improved, heralding Pym's summer of love. Her diary records riding on the handlebars of Rupert's bicycle, walking in the woods, kissing in the streets of Oxford. On a hot June day, Miles and Rupert took her punting on the river and then to tea at the Cherwell Gardens: 'much semi nakedness to be seen on the river', she noted. Rupert dropped his watch in the river and stripped off his clothes to dive for it. It may have been the first time Pym had seen so much of a man's body.

There was a sense of sexual awakening in her diary. The next day, she saw Rupert and Miles and they told her the news that they had both won firsts. She was delighted. Now that the boys' exams were over and she had endured her last tutorial, the trio were determined to enjoy themselves. They hired a punt and went on the river, taking a gramophone with them. Pym spotted Geoffrey. He had a beautiful smile on his face and she bade him 'Sweetheart goodbye – Auf wiedersehen my dear . . . I can't believe that I've almost certainly seen his dear face for the last time.'[3] She had another intimate hour and a half with Rupert at number 47: 'the loveliest time I ever remember spending with anyone . . . Oh blessed George Steer and his lovely leopard skin – I hope he gets a first! This kind of a *Private Lives* Love scene was far better in reality than in anticipation.'[4]

These were halcyon days. Rupert had acquired a motor car

and they drove around the Oxfordshire countryside, visiting the lovely Cotswold villages of Great Tew and Charlbury, where they had tea; a nosy maid tried to stop them from kissing, but did not manage to succeed. 'Surely time *spent* so happily cannot be counted as merely wasted.'[5] Rupert, having heard that an undergraduate had been 'progged' (sent down) for the same offence, kissed her in a public telephone box.

Pym had not forgotten her female friends. They went on the river, where Mary Sharp almost fell in. Then had a final tea, with strawberry parfait, at Elliston's. The next day she saw her friends off at the station as they returned home for the long vacation. In the evening, she had dinner with Miles and Rupert at Stewart's; she felt sentimental and sad, especially as the radio was playing 'Auf Wiedersehen'.

On a memorable trip to Boars Hill, Rupert startled her by reciting Andrew Marvell's beautiful and sexy poem 'To His Coy Mistress' ('An hundred years should go to praise/ Thine eyes and on thy forehead gaze;/ Two hundred to adore each breast,/ But thirty thousand to the rest . . .'). He also recited Marvell's 'The Definition of Love', a sadder, more wistful poem about lovers who are parted. Pym was amazed, and touched. She had never heard the poems before and realised that Rupert was more brilliant than she had thought. In the romantic atmosphere, they had what she described as the 'best kiss on record'.[6]

They fetched Miles from a tutorial and went for a picnic on the river. Whilst punting, Pym fell in and was rescued by Miles. She lay on her tummy drying out, Miles's trousers hanging from the paddle. She drowsed in the heat to the rhythm of the punt and was awakened by a gentle kiss from Rupert. They had dinner at the famous Spread Eagle pub in Thame and then drove back to Oxford. Miles's presence inhibited their 'love-making', but Pym didn't seem to mind very much. There was safety in a triangular relationship. Her friendship with Miles and her love affair with Rupert set a pattern that would be repeated.

She and Rupert had a farewell lunch at Stewart's: 'they played *Wien du Stadt meiner Traume*. I heard it for the first time.' Then, on the infamous leopard-skin couch, there was 'a more intimate goodbye' at number 47. Rupert had bought her chocolates from Elliston's. Miles joined them later and saw her off at the train station. The trio held hands tightly and Barbara stared into their 'blue and brown eyes respectively'.[7]

On the train, Pym reflected that her first Trinity term had been so perfect that it had set a 'perilously high standard'. She mused whether any other could live up to the happiness she had felt. Her instincts would prove to be right. A year later, she returned to her diary and wrote: 'My second was bloody.'[8]

CHAPTER XI

Our Heroine returns to Shropshire for the Long Vacation and invites Rupert to stay

Pym's sister Hilary and her biographer, Hazel Holt, played down Rupert's importance in Barbara's story. By their account, he played a minor role in her romantic life and good-naturedly gave her up when she fell in love with another undergraduate. This is not the story of what truly happened between Rupert and Barbara. His letters and her journals reveal a deeply erotic and then traumatic experience, which affected Pym for many years.

In the days following their parting in Oxford, Rupert sent letter after letter to his *Cara Barbara mia*. He described her as his 'darling perfect one' and wrote at length about the lingering glow of those final 'golden days of June's end! Those golden islands of life.'[1]

That summer, Rupert was back in London in his mother's new flat in Holland Park Court and worrying about future plans. He wanted to join the Royal Air Force, but his poor eyesight was a problem. He was also thinking about returning to Oxford for postgraduate studies.[2] Miles was with him in London. They raised toasts to Barbara, and Rupert reminded her in a letter of their 'lovely nakedish times by the Cher'. Like many insecure young men in love with a popular, attractive woman, he felt worried about their romance, concerned that she had feelings for his rival, Bill Thacker. He was also insecure that had she seen Miles first, then she might have favoured him as a boyfriend. There is a risqué hint in his emphasis on the strong bond between the three undergraduates: 'If I'd been told 5 weeks ago how happy we should be three together I should *not* have believed it . . . I think *you* don't mind two at once!'³

Rupert thanked Pym for her part in making his last term at Oxford so charming, sending her a photograph of himself that he thought made him look like an 'angry Italian count'. He even made a bold suggestion: 'Most interesting would be to get married and then see what happens?'⁴ Meanwhile, he had plans for trips to Wales, Ireland and possibly Greece. He also thought of going to Germany but was alarmed by the rise of the Nazis: 'they do seem to be killing an awful lot of people there these days', he wrote.⁵

By mid-July, Rupert had finally achieved his dream of owning a plane. He had taken Miles up for a flight and joked about the difficulty of fitting him into the cockpit. He wrote of how he missed Barbara and their summer together. If he met the River Cherwell in heaven, he said, it would 'still have echoes of you on it – mistily golden echoes of you and Miles and me on the green banks among the willows'.⁶ He assured Pym that his eyes were much better: 'I had no difficulty landing an aeroplane!' Perhaps he could take her for a spin: he must have seemed like a character out of a novel, this clever, handsome fellow who flew his own plane.

Pym invited him to stay at Morda Lodge to meet her family, though she was concerned that her home was not up to Rupert's high standards. Later, he would chide her about her inverted snobbishness. Rupert had kept the news of his love affair secret from his overbearing mother. Mrs Gleadow had been arranging for suitable girls to come to tea. There is a strong sense from his letters that Barbara would not be deemed the *right sort of girl*.

That summer, Rupert began what would be a lifelong interest in astrology and the occult. He had consulted a 'second-sight' woman about his future and had been reading the works of spiritualist writer Olive Pixley. He had also taught himself to read character from handwriting. He studied Barbara's letters and composed a fascinating account of her personality: 'Barbara my dear, you are versatile, original and capable, not always reliable, especially about appointments, but full of variety and you have a sense of humour and some tact . . . you're not very emotional or sympathetic and not naturally optimistic . . . most conspicuously you have a striking and original personality.' Rupert was astute in seeing a hard edge to Pym's character: 'your sympathies do not come flowing out of a soft heart'. He said that they were both 'hard-headed moderns' and also ticked her off for displaying signs of an inferiority complex. 'What on earth or under it made you make yourself out to be such an awful person?' Mrs Gleadow had asked her son whether he had thoughts of marriage, but he had told her advice given to him by Barbara that a man's brain was not ripe until he was twenty-five.[7]

Barbara, meanwhile, wrote to him from that hot summer of 1932 to tell him that she had been sunbathing naked. He retaliated by saying that he was writing to her naked. He was also hoping for some 'alone-time' during their week together in Oswestry. He went on a cruise around the Scottish fjords during the month of August, before heading to Shropshire in September. Barbara met him at the station in a summer frock and yellow jersey, feeling shy and very excited. She thought him twenty times better looking than in his photo. She took him back for tea and he was clearly a huge success with the Pym family.

Barbara was proud of her charming, handsome boyfriend, with a first-class degree from Oxford and an aeroplane. She wrote in her journal: 'Here follows a perfect week which must be recorded and remembered as about the best week of my life.' They were glorious sunshine-filled days, full of long walks and picnics in beautiful, leafy Llangollen and the village of Llynclys. They had a drink at the White Lion pub and then found a secluded spot by the slate stone steps of Jacob's Ladder, where they lay in the grass 'half asleep with our faces close to each other for a long time. We laughed out of sheer happiness.' They walked and kissed and when Pym ran down the hill, he gave her the name 'Atalanta'. They enjoyed 'some moments of raptures, most ecstatic madness'.[8]

Rupert confided to Barbara his feelings about his dead father. He also talked to her about Oxford and his plans, and he asked if she would take the relationship further by going to bed with him: 'We had much fun and a fight about that.' Then, by starlight, they strolled down a lane and she told him that she thought 'the happiness one got out of love was worth any unhappiness it might (and generally does) bring'.[9] Later, Rupert took a bath and Barbara sat in the airing cupboard reciting Dryden. He was about to leave for an excursion to the Lake District with Miles. Barbara was so sad to see him go that she wept and he, too, could barely restrain himself from crying at the parting: 'Even if I hadn't had a carriage to myself I don't think I could have kept back the sobs entirely. It was awful.'[10]

In the Lakes, his head full of Barbara, Rupert kept calling Miles 'Darling' and saying that he wished he was her, 'which he didn't take very kindly'. 'Thank you for making me fall in love with anyone so charming as you,' he wrote to Barbara'.[11]

Though the perfect week had cemented the relationship, Barbara was troubled by Rupert's persistent attempts to have full-blown sex. Often left alone, they experimented sexually. At one moment, she was on all fours, with her dress pushed over her back, revealing her striped underwear. Rupert wrote to her, reminding her of the moment: 'A very touching and pleasing picture you were, even if not quite fit for publication. – (Did you ever find the hole I mentioned in those striped – er – garments?). It was a lovely sight, that!' Their relationship had clearly reached a new level of intimacy: 'My hands send their love to the tropical regions and also to the mountainous regions and my lips send their love to your lips.'[12]

Barbara wrote to Rupert, telling him how foul and miserable she found Shropshire, but he gently rebuked her again, saying that Oswestry was quite fit for her residence: 'To me, Morda Lodge is the centre of a radiating golden star of happiness and it must always be marked in gold on my mental map.' For him, it had been a 'sacred week'. Back in London, he wrote planning a night together before returning to Oxford:

> Oh darling how immoral we are! And what a lot we do take for granted! I feel chary of even mentioning all the lovely things we did together, that is the more indecent ones, in case of any evil accident these letters ever fell into anybody else's hands, who, reading them, would say (quite without justification) 'Barbara Pym seems to have been a rather free and easy young woman.'[13]

Rupert was still vacillating between a DPhil at Oxford, or joining the RAF, or even the intelligence services. He had applied for a fellowship, though he was worried about the academic life as a career: 'all the intrigues about the Readership at Oxford have shown me what to expect there and what sort of people academic people are. So that's not very attractive either.'[14]

Their long talks about going to bed together often resulted in play-fighting and spanking; something they both seemed to enjoy, according to Rupert: 'I note with a thrill how even you, decent as you are, can't write a 2 sheet letter without an allusion to spanking! . . . Sweetheart and most spankable one! You make me all excited.'[15] In October, Pym and Rupert returned to Oxford.

CHAPTER XII

In which Things begin to become a little complicated with Rupert

Barbara was glad to be leaving 'foul' Shropshire. At Banbury, she changed trains, the rolling green hills of the Oxfordshire countryside so different from the grey skies and factories of the north-west.

Philip Larkin, later a close friend and supporter of Pym, wrote a semi-autobiographical Oxford novel called *Jill*. He distilled his own painful undergraduate experience as a shy, lower-middle-class boy who struggles to fit into the Eton-infested atmosphere of the rich Oxford colleges. It opens with a train journey from Banbury to Oxford in mid-October: 'The air had begun to thicken as it does before a dusk in autumn. The sky had become stiff with opaque clouds.' As the autobiographical protagonist sits on the train he notices the transition from the gasometers and blackened bridges of Banbury to the 'little arms of rivers twisted through the meadows, lined with willows that littered the surface with leaves'.[1]

Larkin's hero struggles with the public school hearties who undermine and bully him, whilst retaining their beautiful manners and sense of noblesse oblige. No matter what he does, he simply does not have the 'ease' of the upper classes. Everything is new and intimidating; the black-gowned students, the beautiful quadrangles, the ancient archways with coats of arms and scrolled stones, the Latin at supper and the gilt-framed oil paintings that line the walls of the hall.

Pym had no such fears about fitting in. Her self-confidence, her happy childhood, her sharp sense of humour were all suitable armour for the pretensions, strange rules and poky hierarchies of Oxford. Now that she was returning for a second year, she was determined to enjoy every minute.

Michaelmas term held many beauties for Barbara. Term did not start until October, when the nights were starting to draw in. Her North Oxford novel, *Crampton Hodnet*, recalls the bewitching atmosphere of autumn in Oxford: the smell of fireworks in the air, the lit street lamps and the Victorian Gothic houses, mysterious and romantic in the misty half-light; gardens with monkey puzzle trees and laurel bushes; soft rain pattering on ancient stones and the church bells announcing evensong.

Pym still had thoughts of Geoffrey. She had heard that he had received a distinction in his theology diploma. Rupert had new digs at number 90 St Mary's Road, near James Street, in the east of Oxford. She went to see him as soon as she arrived and they strolled down Aristotle Lane, near Port Meadow, towards the canal, 'talking about life and reminiscing – not contemplating suicide' (they were standing on a bridge). It was, she wrote in her diary, a happy reunion. Miles had also returned to undertake postgraduate studies. They had tea together in his digs and it was like old times. She spotted Geoffrey smiling his heavenly smile. All was well.

Rupert had discovered that there was to be a student pyjama party and wrote to Barbara to say that he could get tickets, so that he could see her in her pink-flowered pyjamas. Once again, he was putting on pressure for them to sleep together. He reminded her of their steamy embraces in Shropshire, 'when your intrepid explorer made such extensive investigations into the mountainous regions', and there was more talk of spanking her lovely bottom and of her tropical regions. She finally agreed that she would like to sleep with him. Rupert was ecstatic: 'I've put down in my diary that you said you'd like to sleep with me! And that document will go down to our posteriors, I mean posterity, as gospel truth, so I'm not the only lascivious one! Goodnight darling and sweet dreams. Make the pillows comfy. If only I could be Jupiter I'd come to you, like Danae, in a shower of gold.'[2]

On 13 October, Rupert's mother and his brother Edmund came to visit, and they had lunch together at the Randolph Hotel on Beaumont Street. Pym was terrified of meeting Mrs Gleadow, but a new fur coat gave her confidence. Edmund she thought less handsome than his older brother, but with 'personal magnitude'. They walked to the Sheldonian and then went to Fuller's cafe for tea. One of Barbara's habits, when she spoke, was to stretch out her hand for emphasis and Edmund amused her by putting things into her outstretched hand – sugar lumps and copper pennies.

Meeting Rupert's mother, whom she liked, and his brother cemented their relationship even further. They had now met one another's families and the love affair was going from strength to strength. The pyjama party seemed to be the designated day and Rupert implored her to wear her pink-flowered ones when she came back to his digs: 'I think you'd better come in those pajamas, or at any rate leave part of them about you. Couldn't you wear the top half of them as a blouse?'[3]

In one of his summer letters, Rupert had told Barbara that he found her especially sweet and vulnerable late at night, when her guard was down. That Saturday evening he was insistent that she should come back to 90 St Mary's for tea. Barbara's diary takes up the record. She wrote that 15 October must be an ever-remembered day: 'Today I must always remember I suppose. Went to tea with Rupert (and ate a pretty colossal one) and he with all his charm, eloquence and masculine wiles persuaded . . .'[4] Here, Barbara has torn out and destroyed pages of her diary, so what happened next must be a matter of conjecture. Nevertheless, whatever did happen caused much damage and pain. How lasting that pain was is difficult to estimate, but the events of this day ruptured the relationship.

Rupert got in touch a couple of days later. Something momentous had clearly occurred. He wrote her an extraordinary letter, in which he admitted that, at the crucial moment, there was a 'complete lack of passion' and that there was bad behaviour on his part. The letter has 'WARNING' scribbled across the top: 'This is a long and philosophical letter.'

Dear Barbara,

I've given you some time to think over events, by not writing – . I said we mustn't write too often – have I been cursed for it? Or have you been too busy? . . . You know our behaviour the other night in bed was really rather extraordinary: such a complete lack of passion! I'm not sure I wasn't rather unkind to *make* you come after all, with that nasty threat, but somehow I couldn't let it all go for nothing when for half an hour I'd used every ruse of science and art to plead as beautifully as I was able. Was I selfish? Say so if you like; that my behaviour was only natural is no excuse. How do you feel about it? I feel at present that if the chance came I wouldn't be so unkind as to ask you to do it again, (partly, of course, that's due to our sexless way of occupying our time there); but I expect if (or when) it comes to the point, I should merely say 'Well, darling, would you like to come to bed?' – and you would probably say no and there would be an end of it. Were you happy in bed at all?[5]

The remainder of the letter is a combination of panicky rambling and rather incoherent musings about their relationship, adverting to their perfect week in Shropshire: 'As it might be, under the cloud-free sun to lie hours long on Lynchys hill in the late summer afternoon; it may be the year 2000 and more before anyone sees us there; but for us it will still be 1932; still we shall be happy and still we shall be young and joyful, to perfection.' He quoted the poet Rupert Brooke: 'Parting, we flung ourselves upon the hill . . . our heaven is now, is won! . . . and laughed, that has such brave true things to say: And suddenly you cried and turned away.'[6] Then he asked her about a romantic time-travel novel with the title *Still She Wished for Company* that she'd started reading but had seemingly lost interest in.

The destroyed pages of Pym's diary speak volumes. It would appear that having written about the day of the pyjama party she did not record anything for several weeks. When she resumes, she appears to be suffering from a kind of emotional amnesia:

October 27th I spent the afternoon with Rupert but can't remember what I did.

Oct 28th Can't remember at present.

Nov 1st Can't remember anything about this day.

Nov 3rd, Went back to Rupert's digs – where we had a pleasant time, I imagine.

Nov 6th, I spent a few pleasant hours with Rupert in his digs . . . Can't remember much else.[7]

Her diary then stops and is not resumed until the following year.

Whatever *did* happen on 15 October, Pym began to withdraw from Rupert. He continued to send affectionate letters and they spent time together, but there was an emotional estrangement from both sides. One of the last happy days was a long walk, where she was 'hatless and Atalanta-esque in blue'.[8]

In November, Rupert heard that he had not been awarded the coveted college fellowship. A letter later in the month is chilly. He says that he doesn't miss Barbara as he ought to and refers to his 'beastly, cold and unsympathetic nature'. He asks: 'Am I really a villain, as well as unscrupulous?'[9]

Pym went home alone for the Christmas vacation. Rupert went skiing in Aspen.

CHAPTER XIII

The End of the Affair

Barbara dealt with the Rupert incident by burying the memory. They both entered into a tacit pact to pretend that she had retained her virginity. He wrote to her at Christmas, discussing presents: 'I'm afraid that we can't add your estimable virginity to the list, as we have agreed that *you* should have that for Christmas!'[1] It was a lie and they both knew it. A month later he wrote that he had seen that in America a man was sent to prison for seduction: 'I shall have to look out, if ever I go there!'[2] Joking about the incident was preferable to open confession and repentance.

Barbara told him that she had been having dreams about being in bed with him and another Oxford friend, she wearing red pyjamas. Rupert asked which of the men was the 'chief attraction?'; later he wrote that if she offered him her virginity for his birthday, he would take it. He told her that he knew a shop in London where he could buy the necessary precautions, and added, 'with the aid of Freud you ought not to have much difficulty in making out the meaning of our periodic bed-going dream'. He finished his letter with a reference to John Donne: 'I must confess "When souls mix, tis an happiness; but not complete till bodies too" etc. Not to mention Marvell and

Herrick and others who knew the value of mistresses. So do I! But it's a difficult art, having a mistress and Oxford is one of the *most* difficult places to practice it in. Hence, darling, your still lasting immunity.'[3]

When Barbara returned to Oxford and resumed her diary, Rupert barely made an appearance. Other men had begun to catch her eye – one in particular, whom she called the 'pale, Magdalen Man'. She had tea with Rupert and indulged in 'some very pleasant caresses . . . but I stuck out against having a real necking party, and got a slight spanking because of it'.[4] By now, Rupert knew that it was all over. He was thoroughly disillusioned with Oxford, describing it as an awful place. He challenged her: 'Have you ever asked your dear father what he sent you to Oxford *for*?'[5] By March, he was complaining that if he were killed in his plane, she wouldn't give two hoots. He added, cynically, 'a woman must keep up her prestige, even at the expense of truth'. He also wrote about how she might regard him in the future: 'There was that poor dear Rupert Gleadow – quite *mad* about me he was, but my dear he really was terribly *trying*, so *lascivious*, never would leave me alone. What did I like him for?'[6]

From then on, their correspondence was sporadic. In April, he asked resignedly: 'Barbara Dearest, Who have you fallen in love with this time?' The following year, he wrote to her saying that his heart was fairly free, though he had had a couple of love affairs early in the year. 'How's your own heart? Pining, I suppose, for some beautiful man, as usual?'[7] He told her that he still remembered their time together in Shropshire: 'That summer is safely gilded in my memory.' And he also dropped a heavy hint that he would like her to destroy his love letters. He found the tone of her letters to him 'colder and more disillusioned'.[8]

By August 1935, Rupert had lost all interest in suppressing

the ugly truth of what had happened between them. He referred to his digs at number 90 and that disastrous night. 'I remember all that too. And that was why I insisted on a second occasion, becos [sic] I felt you had not enjoyed the first occasion and a second would make up for it. Whether I was right I never found out I think you ought to count me among the possibilities – *tho' we both know so well that you did not want it then.*'[9]

Pym did not comment on Rupert's 'seduction', and there is no way of knowing for sure whether she was forced, or whether it happened unexpectedly in the heat of the moment, or whether it was simply a lack of sexual compatibility. Whatever else, she had lost her virginity to him in a disturbing way, which she wiped from her diary, if not her memory.

She kept in occasional contact with Rupert, whose life continued to be touched by tragedy: his photograph, taken in the summer of 1932, is preserved in Pym's papers, alongside a cut-out article from *The Times* announcing his marriage to a French woman. As telling as the torn-out pages of her diary describing that night of 15 October 1932 is the fact that Barbara Pym, who mined her own life for her books over and over again, never based a character on Rupert Gleadow.

CHAPTER XIV

In which we are introduced to 'the Saga of Lorenzo'

Pym expunged the memory of Rupert Gleadow in the most expedient manner: by falling in love with another man. There was to be no bottom-spanking and crawling on all fours in this relationship. Barbara fell deeply and passionately in love and it affected her profoundly. He would be the inspiration for one of her best-loved and most memorable characters.

In Hilary term, Pym had spotted a 'pale, Magdalen man'. She saw him again at a morning lecture on Swift and Pope and then again at another lecture a few days later, where he sat almost in front of her, giving her ample opportunity to observe him closely: 'He languishes over much and has an affected way of leaning his head back. I like his thick curiously-cut bronzy hair and his pale smooth face and hands.'[1] A languid quality and an abundance of affectation were indeed his leading characteristics. Later that day, she went to 'the Bod' and saw him again. One of her tried and tested methods of getting male attention was to stare. She was delighted when he looked back: 'I am convinced he hates me. Our gazes meet and he half smiles – but it is a cynical sort of smile. His affectation intrigues me.' This was the very day after she had refused 'a real necking party' with Rupert.[2]

She called her new man Lorenzo. She may just have liked the romantic sound of the name, but it is more likely that it was a reference to the Lorenzo of Edward Young's epic poem, *Night Thoughts*, written in the 1740s, which she was ploughing through in her studies for the eighteenth-century literature paper. Throughout this rambling meditation on 'life, death, and immortality', the poet addresses his 'Faithful Friend', the dashing and dissipated Lorenzo, admonishing his faults and exhorting him to moral reform. By a curious coincidence (one of many in Pym's life), she later discovered that *Night Thoughts* was one of her very own Lorenzo's favourite texts.

His real name was Henry Stanley Harvey. He was not a Magdalen man, but was at Christ Church, the richest and poshest of the colleges. Henry's tutor was C. S. Lewis: Pym had spotted him at Magdalen because that was where the future author of the Narnia books held his fellowship and gave his tutorials.

Henry was tall and movie-star handsome, with dark hair and hazel brown eyes. He had a fine pointed nose, which only added to his seemingly aristocratic look, and was always impeccably dressed. Like Rupert before him, he was fatherless and adored by his mother. Barbara most definitely had a type. Despite his air of superciliousness and arrogance, she detected a strain of vulnerability. Henry was not quite as dashing as Rupert, with his private aeroplane and Winchester background. He was a grammar school boy, whose father had been a surveyor. He was from a similar social class to Barbara, but as a boy with a doting mother and sisters, along with reckless good looks, there was a spoiled quality to his character. She was to capture this trait to perfection in her fictional counterpart.

She set out to discover more about this mysterious stranger. A good stalking ground was the English lecture room. Sure enough, she found herself sitting next but one to him. Perfect for more detailed observation. Barbara saw from the start a quality of cruelty in his demeanour: 'He doesn't like being observed but often looks at you in his malicious way.' He had twinkling '(but not pleasantly twinkling)' eyes, 'like a duck'. She noted that 'he walks swiftly, in his effortless yet affected manner'. She even took a survey of his small and mingy handwriting, which sloped to the left. He wrote on plain paper. Above all, she was struck by his mouth. 'And what a mouth! He is able to curl it in the most fascinatingly repulsive sneering smile.' She confided to her journal, 'this diary seems to be going to turn into the saga of Lorenzo'.[3]

By the end of the month, Pym had found out his real name and that he was at glamorous Christ Church. She hoped he would be an entry into a new, more sophisticated circle. She stalked him in the Bodleian Library, observing his herringbone tweed grey overcoat and brown leather gloves, lined with lambswool. He made eye contact and passed the occasional sarcastic smile. But no more. She made sure to sit opposite his desk, which was usually littered with books. One of the books was one that she wanted, but she lacked the courage to ask him for it. He had a cold and a cough, 'also a vaguely hectic flush – or was this my over-solicitous imagination?'[4]

During the last week of January, Pym saw a lot more of him in the library, where he was dishevelled and hectic, finishing an essay before rushing out to a tutorial. 'We progress not at all,' she wrote. In February, she saw him at a play in Christ Church, sitting with his friend, Robert 'Jock' Liddell, who was a New College man. Henry looked dashing in black flannel bags and a curious striped coat. She noticed his long, slender neck.[5]

Meanwhile another handsome Henry came into her life. His name was Henry ('Harry') Howard Harker. He was the son of a miner and a clever scholarship man. He was greatly attracted to the ever-smiling, fun-loving Pym and she might have done better to have chosen him. He invited her to tea and was kind and courteous. But her heart was firmly with the other Henry. She had found out that he was in his final year and she needed to move quickly: 'In spite of being very conscious of each other, nothing seems to happen!'[6]

CHAPTER XV

In which Sandra makes her Appearance

Shortly after the Rupert incident, Pym created an alter ego: a sexy, glamorous, free-spirited creature whom she called Sandra, short for Cassandra. Was she named after the Greek goddess who was given the gift of true prophecy, but doomed never to be believed? Or perhaps after Jane Austen's only sister? Perhaps she just liked the name: 'Sexy Sandra' was a very different kettle of fish to Miss Pym.

Sandra wore tight satin skirts and provocative red blouses. She flirted with boys and wore scarlet lipstick to match her nail polish. Miss Pym might have been innocent and 'decent' and unwilling to become an Oxford mistress, but Sandra didn't care a fig about other people's perceptions of her. It does not take a psychologist to see what Pym was doing by splitting her identity. The division between Miss Pym, the good girl, the dutiful daughter, and 'Sandra', the bad girl, was a coping strategy – an effective method, in the short term, of dealing with her sense of dislocation and the fallout from her bad experience with Rupert.

Sex before marriage was still unusual for educated girls in the early 1930s. Most Oxford male undergraduates slept with one another or went to prostitutes or 'fast girls' in London for their kicks, returning to college on the last train (known as 'The

Fornicator'). They took their Oxford girlfriends out to tea at Boffin's. Many of Pym's contemporaries were so-called 'bluestockings'. Very few would dare to be promiscuous. The threat of an undesired pregnancy was a huge deterrent in the days before safe and widely available contraception.

Pym wrote a long poem, 'Sandra to Lorenzo': 'But what of life? – 'tis nothing short of bliss/ When I forget it in Lorenzo's kiss' – and left it where Henry could see it.[1] He continued to say nothing to her, only to return her stares. She poured out her frustration in her journal: 'I love Lorenzo – I mean *love* in my own special way – and I thought I was getting over it – I don't think he cares a damn about me – but sometimes vague and marvellous doubts arise.'[2] She opened the door to the Bod for him and was upset when he didn't express thanks. Then she would send fragments of further poems to Lorenzo, claiming that Sandra was a different person. She asked him to write poems back and deliver them to 'Barbara Pym and she will give them to Sandra'.[3]

Spring was Pym's favourite season, timely for the Lorenzo business: 'Chestnut trees just coming out – pale, almost too good to be true – green blue skies, daffodils and best of all, cherry trees in half and full flower. My attitude to Nature is 18th Century, I know. But oh Marvellous Days.'[4]

Back in Oxford for Trinity term, she longed for more sightings of Lorenzo and managed to catch a glimpse of his profile, 'so divine, his hair is more auburn and his skin lovely, pale brown with a faint flush. What *shall* I do?' Just as she was beginning to lose all hope, Lorenzo finally cracked and spoke to her. He ran after Pym when she left the Bodleian. He seems to have had a profound physical effect upon her: 'I trembled and shivered and went sick.' His first words: 'Well and has Sandra finished her epic poem?' She could hardly contain herself, answering, 'Er – No.'[5]

In her diary – 'Oh ever to be remembered day!' – she professed herself far too excited to write. She was counselling herself, trying to calm down. She quoted Wordsworth: 'Emotion recollected in tranquillity' – a phrase that she would often employ when strong feelings threatened to overcome her rationality. Nevertheless, ever the writer, she still captured Henry's physical aspects: 'He talks curiously but very waffily – is very affected. Something wrong with his mouth I think – he can't help snurging.' Henry asked her if she was still keeping up the dual personality. She was amazed that he knew: 'He had caught me out.' Barbara asked how he knew her. 'Of course I do,' he replied, coolly. 'Everyone does.'[6]

They chatted about mutual friends and then she took the plunge and told him that she had named him Lorenzo and thought the name suited him: 'How awfully flattering,' he replied. Then with a comic Pym touch, she closed the scene: 'He snurged and went on up the Iffley Road.'[7]

In her diary, she mused upon the fact that her love for Lorenzo felt entirely different to her other crushes. She was also prescient in feeling that it would not come to a satisfactory end and that within her personality there was a tendency for self-punishment: 'I had that kind of gnawing at the vitals sick feeling . . . that is so marvellous.'[8]

CHAPTER XVI

In which Sandra has her First Date with Lorenzo and bites him on the Cheek

The tenth of May 1933 was a day that would be forever etched on Pym's heart. It was her first date with Henry Harvey. Two months later she wrote about it in her diary, composing the memory with a degree of self-consciousness, as if she were writing a novel: 'Here follows as faithful as possible a reproduction of the facts of that evening.'[1]

On that 'sultry' day, when 'one expected it to thunder at almost any moment', she had gone along to the library after tea. She paints the picture vividly, even down to her underwear:

> I wasn't looking awfully beautiful. I was wearing (when my body
> was found!) a brown check skirt, yellow short sleeved jersey –
> yellow suede coat – brown hat and viyella scarf – flesh coloured
> fish net stockings, brown and white ghillie shoes (blue celanese
> trollies – pink suspender belt – pink – kestos-white vest) brown
> gloves – umbrella. This all gives the atmosphere.[2]

She stayed in the Bod until Lorenzo arrived. He usually sat in the same seat. Then she waited until the bell rang for closing hour, so that she could walk out with him. Her friend, Mary

Shipley, who was walking alongside Pym, tactfully left the scene, thus giving Henry the opportunity to make his move.

He asked Pym if she wanted a lift. She accepted and as they walked to his car, he asked her if she were an Irish Pym. She said no. He told her that he liked to hire cars and that he shared his (registration YR 4628) with a friend who was a Polish Jew and a count – a man called Barnicot. She didn't believe him: 'He said he liked me and my sense of humour and he thought me (seemed romantic) quite mad.'[3]

Henry drove her to the Trout, a lovely old pub nestling on the banks of the Thames. It was a romantic setting, with mist on the river and the heady fragrance of wisteria scenting the air. She picked some of the lilac-coloured blossom for her room, though Henry rather spoilt the moment by telling her that it would soon wither. It did.

They managed to obtain a private room, where they played ping-pong, had a supper of mixed grill and fried potatoes, and drank beer. He was fussy about greasy chips, so she picked out the least greasy, thinking 'what an awful man to marry!' And yet 'really there's something terribly attractive about the idea'. She was moving very quickly from a first date to thoughts of marriage. After supper, they talked about general things, but Barbara, tipsy, confessed her true feelings for him. She knew that she had said too much, too soon, and it seems things became a little awkward. He clearly did not respond the way she expected. Then she leaned over and bit him hard on the cheek.[4]

What happened next is not clear, but at some point in the evening, things became passionate and he pressed kisses on Pym's 'not unwilling mouth'. In a later diary entry, she recalled his 'cave man squeeze – the sudden narrowing of the eyes as he grew passionate'.[5] He drove her home, she 'still in a daze'. Back at the gate at St Hilda's, she kissed his bitten cheek before returning to her room. Later, she reflected on the evening: 'Words can't bring back the feelings he aroused in me and still does. But there it is. Is there no mode of expression that will crystallise it all into something really worthy which will last? A poem. A sonata?'[6]

Something significant had happened to her, but Pym was too honest not to admit that he clearly did not feel the same way. In some respects, she was still acting the role of a spurned lover in a Renaissance sonnet: 'Oh cruel Lorenzo! . . . cruel Gabriel Harvey.' Henry did, indeed, have a cruel streak, especially towards Barbara. He was a man who liked beautiful, cool girls. He played hard to get. Pym was too open, too guileless and too smitten to enrapture him. This first date set the standard for the relationship between them: she adoring him, he lapping it up and not reciprocating. At the end of her long journal entry, she wrote: 'And so I began to hope – and what a lot of misery was this evening responsible for.'[7]

A few days later, Rupert Gleadow came to see Pym. He wanted a proper kiss, but she refused, 'because the last mouth to touch mine had been Lorenzo's'.[8] She saw little of Henry, but others continued to pay court. The man called Harlovin took her out in his car for picnics, but her head and heart were still full of Henry.

In one sense, her confidence had been boosted by the date with Henry, whom she now called 'Gabriel', after Shakespeare's contemporary, the satirical author Gabriel Harvey. She began to adopt an air of sophistication. At a Keble College musical concert, she wore a black dress 'too charmingly *décolleté* – back and front', accessorised with the 'Pym pearls' and a fur coat. On the other hand, her reputation had begun to suffer. Harlovin invited her to Cheltenham, along with a male friend called Harding, and they teased her about her 'appalling reputation'. Pym's method of coping with this was to deflect onto her alter ego: 'Poor Sandra!'

Harlovin tried to kiss her, but she refused and told him about her love for Henry. He laughed and said he was very attracted to her: 'Damn Gabriel!' Pym had been told that Harlovin was married and so she considered that things could become complicated if she embarked on an affair, though she liked him and the way he teased her.

After dropping off Harding, they had lunch in the car and drank cider, which made her drowsy and she accidentally burnt him with her cigarette. Harding returned and took the wheel. During the drive back to Oxford, she fell asleep on Harlovin's 'very comforting' shoulder. In her diary, she wrote: 'Incidentally, I burnt Harlovin (accidentally) and also bit him – but not so hard as I bit Gabriel.'⁹

CHAPTER XVII

We're having a Heatwave –
a Tropical Heatwave

In June 1933 there was a heatwave. Pym and her girlfriends sunbathed on Port Meadow in backless gingham frocks. On her birthday, 2 June, she noted that she felt no different, but was only 'more and more wretchedly in love' with Henry Harvey. He had raised her hopes when he had taken her to the Trout, but now he seemed to be withdrawing: 'Gabriel lay low.' She imagined him walking around the garden of his digs, naked.[1]

Pym went to the Bod in the hope of a sighting. She heard Jock Liddell 'in his precise little voice' complaining that it was 'dreadfully hot'. Jock was small and blond and delicate-looking. Henry had first met him on a steamer from Dover to Ostend the spring before he came to Oxford, in 1930. Henry thought the boy, aged perhaps thirteen, looked rather lonely and made some friendly overtures. Hoping to give him some ideas for school essays, he began spouting Aristotle and Hegel. Henry's self-deprecating account of what transpired next is testament to his undeniable charm: 'But this little boy was not thirteen. He was 21, already at Oxford and reading Greats. He was two years and 8 months older than I was (18) and knew very much more about Tragedy, Aristotle and Hegel than I did (almost nothing).

So *he* started talking and didn't stop (neither did I) until we got to Aachen early the next morning.'[2]

Pym was attracted to Jock's blond prettiness. She found his babyish looks seductive and noted his waspish wit and 'attractive peevish voice'.[3] Liddell did very little to disguise his campness. Pym's diary makes constant reference to his 'dissipation', and she was clearly in no doubt about his sexual orientation.[4] For his own part, Jock was 'aware of' her before they met. He remembered that she made a friendly gesture whilst he was working as an assistant in the Bodleian's Department of Western Manuscripts, toiling at his draughty desk over the papers of Bishop Percy.[5]

Flirting with other men provided continued distraction for Pym. She and her friend Sharp asked a couple of young men for a light for their cigarettes; this yielded an invitation to tea at the Air Squadron. One of the men took her for a drive in the Oxfordshire countryside, but she still could not stop herself from thinking of Henry. Knowing he had his finals, she wrote Henry a formal note wishing him luck: she told him that she was badly sunburnt – 'absolute agony to touch' – and that it was 'depressing' to have reached the age of twenty. She told him that she thought he'd look 'decorative' in his subfusc – the formal wear required for sitting exams.[6]

When she could bear it no longer, Pym lingered outside 'Schools' (the examination hall), chatting to Rupert Gleadow. When Henry came out, she asked him if he'd enjoyed himself. He did not reply, only grinned 'rather fatuously' and walked off. Rupert thought him 'quite beautiful and merely weak-looking – not vicious'. She saw him again in 'YR' (his car), with Jock sitting in the front seat, 'looking prim and proper'.[7] She waved and was delighted when he turned around and smiled. Seeing him made her feel delirious and she danced happily to the gramophone, though suddenly feeling despondent that

Henry was going down and she would likely never see him again.

Of course she did see him again. He offered her a lift. As she left the car, Henry coolly said: 'Well, I may see you again.' Pym found it all frustrating. 'Thinking of that remark in my miseries that followed, I wondered whether he really meant to be so cruel, because he really did make me feel hopeful and then it all came to nothing.'[8]

Pym worked hard on an essay on the old English poem, 'The Owl and the Nightingale'. The poem details an argument between the two eponymous birds, overheard by the narrator. They argue about their physical appearances and the beauty of their respective birdsong. The nightingale tells the owl that he brings unwanted gloom, whilst she brings joy and reflects the beauty of the world. The owl retorts by saying she only sings in summer when men's minds are full of lechery and that her song entices women to adultery and promiscuity. The nightingale argues that it is in the nature of women to be frail and any sins committed in maidenhead are forgiven in marriage. It is the fault of men, for taking advantage of women. All this seemed apt. Pym, feeling rejected and taken advantage of by Henry, worked hard at her studies and received a good report from her tutors: 'got through with my bright and bluff questions'. She wrote in her diary: 'LOVE! LOVE! LOVE! Do the dons know how much it affects our work, I wonder.'[9]

Pym had been frightened by the intensity of her feelings and the bouts of depression that had consumed her during the summer term. She suffered 'attacks of terrible misery' when she felt that nothing mattered beside Henry and that if she could not see him then 'life didn't hold any more'.[10] She was, despite her bright and cheery disposition, a deeply sensitive girl and there was an obsessive, emotionally charged aspect to her person-ality. She fought bravely against this character trait, always hoping that her good sense would prevail. Many years later, she read the journals of Sylvia Plath and felt a connection with her. She was amazed to find that Plath, too, had a string of male admirers at Cambridge and was a girl who liked a good time, as well as wanting to be taken seriously as a writer.

It had been an unhappy term and, for once, she was glad to leave Oxford to go home to Shropshire.

CHAPTER XVIII

Miss Pym reflects upon Stormy Weather

For many people, the years leading up to the Second World War were a golden age of music. Dance music was at its height, with band leaders such as Jack Hylton, Billy Cotton and Bert Ambrose riding the airwaves. The advent of the wireless set was a game-changer. By 1939, the number of BBC licence holders in Britain was a staggering 8.8 million.[1] The BBC had its own in-house Radio Dance Band, offering light music programmes such as *Band Wagon*, *Monday Night at Eight* and *Music Hall*. On Sundays, though, Sir John Reith, the austere director general, insisted on broadcasting uplifting programmes, leaving his younger audience to tune into Radio Luxembourg to get their daily band-music hit.

On an unseasonably cold summer's day, Pym switched on the wireless to hear the dulcet tones of 'Ambrose and His Orchestra' playing 'Stormy Weather'. 'And the weather is stormy,' she noted in her diary. 'It does nothing but rain (cos my man and I ain't together).'[2] She thought constantly of Henry and when she managed not to think about him, her mind turned instead to his friends, Jock Liddell and John Barnicot.

Nevertheless, she pulled herself together, noting that although she felt 'depressed' she wasn't as 'acutely miserable' as she had been at Oxford.[3] She reflected that although Henry had brought so much unhappiness, he had also been responsible for 'a little heaven and a lot of fun'. She decided she must take control of herself: 'It's really time this diary becomes a real one and stopped being a saga of Gabriel Harvey.'[4]

Her mood improved when her sister Hilary came home from school for the summer holidays. They went for a short break to Ross-on-Wye, driving through the beautiful Shropshire countryside. A trip to London, to visit the cousins in Hatch End, also helped cheer her up. She read in *The Times* that Geoffrey Walmsley had been awarded a first in theology and pondered upon that unrequited but 'happy passion'. An Oxford acquaintance came to tea at Hatch End and Pym was happy to gossip about mutual friends: 'She didn't know Gabriel. Nor did she know that Richard Rumbold was a pervert. Fancy that!'[5] Rumbold was a blond, handsome Christ Church man, who was president of the English Club, where he invited, amongst others, Oscar Wilde's lover 'Bosie' to talk. Rumbold had recently published a highly controversial novel called *Little Victims*, which detailed homosexual adventures at boarding school. Pym's epithet 'pervert' for a homosexual man was not uncommon for the 1930s, though she would modify her language and her prejudices when she became close to men such as Jock Liddell.

Later that evening, Pym went to the cinema at Watford. She was amused to see that the film had a character called Sandra who was 'perhaps even more of a nuisance than I have been to the object of my affection'.[6] She loved London and shopping at Selfridges, where she bought rouge and lipstick and a brown, spotted, silk scarf. Her spirits were raised by her fun-loving cousins.

A trip to Stratford-upon-Avon was planned, to see *Romeo and Juliet*. She bumped into several Oxford people, but not the people she longed to see: Henry, Jock and Barnicot. The actor playing Romeo looked like Henry, she thought, with a similar nose and mouth, and Juliet was very young and lovely. The lovers were intensely passionate and Pym was struck by their parting: '"Thinkest thou we shall ever meet again?" I couldn't help applying those lines to another case. But my answer was not so sure as Romeo's.'[7] She particularly admired the vault scene, with the lovers silhouetted against a dark blue sky with stars.

Pym had enjoyed her time in London and Stratford and was sorry to be going back home to Shropshire. When she returned to Morda Lodge, she tidied her bedroom and swapped her navy blue swimsuit for Hilary's yellow one, which set off her golden suntan. She went out to buy *The Times* and saw that Henry had been awarded a second-class degree. He continued to consume her thoughts: 'How I do want him – where is he tonight? – how is he looking? – what is he doing?' In bed at night, her darkest thoughts emerged and she was subject to another one of her 'attacks of misery':

When I got to bed last night I felt really depressed and just longed for Gabriel – not actually in the lascivious sense. It would have been enough if he'd just been there for me to talk to him. The feeling was the first attack of that terrible misery – (at least it was so to me) that I used to feel last term when nothing else mattered beside Gabriel and that if I couldn't see him nothing at all mattered – life didn't hold any more. Rather a frightening sort of experience – slipping through space into nothing . . . but I just kicked my feet about in dumb misery and went to sleep.[8]

CHAPTER XIX

In which Sandra returns

Ever since seeing the 'Sandra' film in London, Pym's alter ego had been creeping back with a vengeance. The purchase of the dark red lipstick and rouge in Selfridges was a nod to the re-emergence of her wilder side. Her journals were suddenly full of references to Sandra. But there was still a sense of internal struggle.

The pragmatic, sensible Barbara reminded herself of the foolishness of her romantic yearnings: 'I suppose it's really rather funny – I shall probably be amused to read this in later years. How seriously we fools who imagine we're in love do take ourselves.' She took some Yeast-Vite tablets, which she had heard were a cure for a broken heart: 'A slightly unromantic way of curing lovesickness I admit, but I certainly feel a lot better now.'[1]

Sensibly, Pym buried herself in academic work, though her choice of reading material, *All Men Are Enemies* and *The Anatomy of Melancholy*, might not have been the most helpful in her present circumstances. But, as ever, her sense of humour prevailed: 'Perhaps I'm suffering from the spleen too – in that case I may be completely cured by taking a course of our English poets.' Her common sense told her that she should develop a 'whatever is, is right' attitude and 'quite honestly I suppose all this *is* rather good for me – and an affair with Gabriel probably wouldn't be!'[2]

In some ways, she was both cured and cursed by her course in the English poets. Her romantic nature was stirred by her summer reading – Marlowe, Shelley, Spenser and Shakespeare – most of which made her think of Henry. She began knitting a green jumper for him. Her love for him seemed inextricably linked with her fascination with his best friend, Jock Liddell: 'Jockie reminds me of a flower I discovered tonight. I don't know what kind.' For pleasure, Pym was reading Norman Douglas's controversial *South Wind*. Written during the First World War and set on Capri, it anticipated *Crome Yellow* in its focus on the antics and discussions of a motley group of bohemians. Barbara copied out a paragraph that she thought was appropriate for her wild Sandra persona: 'If I had children I would let them run wild. *People are too tame nowadays. That is why so few of them have any charm* . . . Why is everybody so much alike? Because we never follow our feelings.' She added a thought that would prove to be important for her own novels: 'Incidentally people *may* be very untame inwardly – one can seldom know.'[3]

The novel assuaged some of her longing for smart conversation. Her frustration with her dull life in Shropshire is apparent in many of her diary entries: 'I dislike tennis parties – here anyway. Too much small talk with people who are generally bores – sometimes one even dislikes them . . . at 8, Mrs Makelam and Maud came to play bridge. I sat in an armchair like a docile donkey and knitted my green jumper.'[4] Her mother did her best to help, reminding her daughter not to work too hard, bringing endless cups of tea and taking her out for drives around the countryside. She did not know the extent of Barbara's fragility, but offered her comforting sayings such as 'God moves in a mysterious way', and 'It will all work out for the best'.

A family holiday was planned to Pwllheli, where there were beautiful beaches for the girls and a coastline golf course for Links and Dor. Pym was still moody: 'I contended that there was a smell of dead fish everywhere.' Many family friends were on holiday, some of them staying in the same hotel, but she was in no mood to humour them: 'It was very sordid seeing people like the Flemings.' She only longed for '*liebe Gabriel*'. Despite enjoying sunbathing in the glorious weather and swimming in the sea, she thought constantly of Harvey: 'Darling Gabriel, why aren't you here, why can't you write?'[5] In the evening, there was a band and dancing in the ballroom. She danced with a nice young man to 'Stormy Weather'. But in bed later she felt cast down. Pym was growing up and growing apart from her family. Even Pwllheli had somehow lost its charm. The Oxford long vacation was far too long.

Back in Shropshire, the first weeks of September were sunny and beautiful. Pym worked hard on Restoration drama, but enjoyed contemporary novels far more. She read Rumbold's *Little Victims* 'properly' and found it sad. 'I used to laugh at it before I knew one.'[6] 'It' was homosexuality.

A brand new novel about female undergraduate life – *Hot-House* by Gertrude Trevelyan, who had been up at Lady Margaret Hall during the 1920s – made Barbara long to write an Oxford novel herself, but, prudently, she decided that she should wait until her 'emotions are simmered down fairly well'.[7]

It was time to make clothes for Sandra. Pym went into town and bought some red satin to make a Russian-style blouse, which she thought would be plain, but distinctive. She began reading another novel that was hot off the press, Ivy Compton-Burnett's *More Women Than Men*, set in an all-girls school. She was unimpressed: 'saw no point in it – unreal people and not much story'.[8] (Later, she would change her mind and become one of

Compton-Burnett's most ardent fans.) Pym still found herself beset by strange behavioural moods:

> In the afternoon I laughed until I cried, a bad sign – only over a piece of blue georgette too! I wasn't unhappy, I put it down to the length of the vac and depressions of the obvious kind . . . Oh for Gabriel Harvey to press kisses on my not unwilling mouth as he did on that not yet forgotten evening of May 10th![9]

She was preparing herself for the return to Oxford. Hilary went back to school in Liverpool and Pym went shopping, buying a black mackintosh (like Henry's) and a 'chaste green linen bedspread'. She packed her trunk, her books and her hats. Sitting on her bed, she resolved that once back at college, she would not let herself get unhappy about Henry, or his friends, 'or anyone'.[10]

CHAPTER XX

We are given a Glimpse of Sandra's Diary

Pym went up a week early, in order to get away from home, and rented digs until she could move back into her college room – 'very nice, nine bedrooms and no aspidistras'. Oxford was glowing in the autumnal sunshine, 'everything looking swell'.[1] She had tea in Elliston's, noting that they had new china but the same delicious coffee layer cake. The Bod and St Hilda's were shut up, but the Radcliffe Camera was open and there was much shopping to be done.

That term, Pym started a new diary. It was to be a record of the adventures not of Miss Pym, as was her first diary, but of Sandra. Its epigraph was from *Hamlet:* 'Be not too tame either, but let your own discretion be your tutor.'[2] 'Sandra' was determined to fall in love with another man so as to forget Henry. Nevertheless, she traipsed up the Iffley Road and looked into the window of number 252, the room Henry had once shared with Jock.

There was a lot of comfort eating – steak and kidney pie at Kemp Hall cafeteria, whilst looking out for Henry. The only friend she saw there was Jock, who gave her a 'poisonous look, but I didn't mind'. John Barnicot was another of Henry's great friends and she occasionally saw him around Oxford. His eyesight was poor, so she was never quite sure if he was ignoring her or whether he couldn't see her properly: 'I smiled brilliantly but he took no notice – is he afraid, ashamed or merely short-sighted?'[3]

Barnicot, a few years older than Henry, had travelled extensively in the Balkans during the early 1930s on a scholarship. After returning to Oxford he took a job in the Bodleian working on old Slavonic manuscripts. Confusingly, Pym calls him 'the Count' in her journals, whereas the real count in the group was Roberto Weiss. The latter was born in Milan and raised in Rome. There was a legend that Weiss had first gone to Cambridge University, but upon finding he didn't like it, got into a taxi, went to Oxford and persuaded them to take him in.[4] By the time Pym knew him, Weiss was living in the village of Islip, where he worked as a researcher for the novelist, biographer and historian John Buchan.

Pym moved back into St Hilda's and set about decorating her room in the most artistic and aesthetic style she could manage. The chaste green quilt was laid and she had lovely checked cushions (one of them with 'Sandra' embroidered across it). She arranged her selection of books, her bookends and pictures. A fire burnt cheerily in the grate and she had a gramophone to listen to the latest music. On the table in the window alcove she placed a vase of bronze chrysanthemums. From her room she could hear the chimes of the great clocks of Magdalen and Merton. She went to dinner in her black polo jersey to scope out the new female freshers, none of whom she considered beautiful. There were rumours that Henry was back at Oxford, studying for a graduate degree, but she had seen no sign of him. The next day she went shopping for visiting cards and bought red roses for her female friends, noting that if she bumped into Henry, she would give them all away to him.

Pym found that she was starting to enjoy her pose of

romantically unrequited love. She went back to her cosy room and was lying on the bed, listening to the gramophone, when her friend Rosemary burst in with the news that she had seen Henry in town. Pym was so excited and nervous that she could not eat tea. Off she went to Blackwell's in hot pursuit. She wore her black polo neck jersey and a grey flannel suit with a marigold in her collar, giving a pop of colour. She was coming away from Blackwell's for the second time when she saw him. He was with Jock Liddell and there was no escape: 'He took off his hat and gave me a marvellous smile – a slightly mocking bow I thought – but it's difficult to tell with him. I was horribly nervous and grinned, I imagine.'[5] She followed them and glimpsed them at Elliston's and tracked them down St Michael's Street, before losing sight of them. But she was not concerned. Henry was back and she had seen him again.

Lovely Harry Harker was still in love with Pym and paid court, even though she had told him that she was still in love with Henry and that she could not kiss him. He took her out on dates. She knew that being seen with Harry would give a strong message to Henry that she wasn't pining for him.[6]

Sandra was growing in confidence. She bought a fez, the latest Duke Ellington record and henna for her new short hair. She painted her nails a becoming shade of rose pink. But she was also working hard. She enjoyed a lecture by Tolkien on *Beowulf*. She was becoming very drawn to Jock Liddell, whom she saw regularly in the library. She was fascinated by his air of 'dissipation', his disdainful sneer and his sharp dress sense. For the present, Jock found her to be nothing more than an irritating and annoying limpet, who was trying (and failing) to force her way into his circle of friends.

CHAPTER XXI

In which Sandra tries to renounce Lorenzo

Pym was having tea with Harry Harker in Elliston's, when, to her shock and amazed delight, in came Henry with a friend and sat down on the next table. He spoke to her at once, asking her why she was wearing a black mackintosh identical to his own. 'Why, because I think it's so charming,' she answered. They carried on chatting, Pym worried about Harry and what he would think. Though Henry looked very hand-some, his skin deliciously smooth and creamy brown, she felt that her feelings towards him were becoming less intense. Later, he saw her in the library and told her that he was moving into a half-furnished flat in Banbury Road with Jock. He was much friendlier and he asked her to visit him sometimes. Pym was unconvinced by this overture: 'Oh yeh – to use a very un-Lorenzaic expression.'[1]

In the Tower Room, where she applied her lipstick and brushed her hair, she saw Henry looking 'beautiful', with a 'snurg' on his face. She loved the way that he turned his head to one side when he smiled; he gave her another 'snurg' as he left. She was determined not to visit him, but was always pulled back: 'Life is for me a half furnished flat with Gabriel in it.'[2] His friends, the Count and Jock, were becoming more friendly, but Henry ignored her. She thought his returning to Oxford was 'the unkindest cut of all'. She chided herself for feeling depressed – 'Oh Sandra cheer up – you'll forget one day' – and told herself that beauty fades and that there would come a day when she would laugh at her own infatuation, 'when his brown eyes – head on one side – snurge – will cease to thrill', when he would no longer affect 'the open ulcer of my heart'.[3]

Henry had promised to send her a poem that he thought she'd like, but he did not get round to it: 'Oh my cruel Lorenzo, why can't you send me the poem – or be kind to me in some small way? – OH why can't the gods let me meet someone new whom I can love? Why oh Why?' She wrote letters to him, to which he failed to respond. He was never a good correspondent. And although she was still drawn to his physical beauty ('My Lorenzo is *so* beautiful . . . the shape of his face and the line of his cheek fill me with rapture'), she could see his less attractive side: 'He grows more affected – his smile of self-conscious fatuity is sweet – but one day may seem silly.'[4] Sometimes she went into the Bod with the excuse that she needed to sharpen her pencil, in the hope of getting a glimpse of him. Many days, she would go back to her room and weep.[5]

In her second attempt to renounce Henry, Pym let Harry Harker kiss her properly, giving up on the pose that she should not be kissed because her last kiss was from 'Gabriel'. She planned on sending a note to Henry saying, 'thank you for sending me back my heart', but the fates intervened again and she met him in the Bod where he asked her to visit him in his flat the next day. She implied that she would go, but when she got home she wrote him a long letter, pouring out her grief and saying that she would not. He responded by writing to her imploring her to change her mind, told her not to be mean and to please come and see him. She didn't go. By the end of the week, she was once again depressed: 'This evening I reached my lowest ebb of misery for the term – I wish terribly that I'd gone to see Lorenzo . . . why do I make such a mess of things?'[6]

The rest of the term was disappointing. Her spirits were low, only temporarily restored by the news that her sister had been accepted at Lady Margaret Hall. Pym was pleased too that she had also done well in her end of term 'collections' (oral examination and reports from her tutors) and had an especially good report from Rooke, her English lecturer. She longed for a note from Henry, but none came. The day she left for the Christmas vacation to stay with her cousins in Hatch End, she wrote him a goodbye letter. As she left on the train for London, she saw the dreaming spires glowing 'in the twilight of a December evening – romantic time to leave'.[7]

CHAPTER XXII

A Pet Kangaroo

London with the Selway cousins was always a restorative to her spirits. There were the usual cinema visits: Barbara was unimpressed with Mae West in *I'm No Angel* ('fat and unattractive'). She dressed in her fur coat and fez. They went Christmas shopping at Liberty, where she saw 'lovely stuff'. A trip to Selfridges was planned, where she spotted a kangaroo for sale in the zoological department. It had brown eyes and a pointed nose, very much like Henry's, she thought. She stroked its neck and 'it closed its eyes in ecstasy'.[1] She wanted to buy it, but it was already sold – 'anyway what would I have done with it?'[2]

At home, she shopped for Christmas cards and began reading Daniel Defoe's racy novel, *Moll Flanders*. She found it 'simply and convincingly written' and wished she could write a book like it. Shropshire she found as dull as ever: 'one day is almost exactly like the other'. She was honest enough to admit to herself that boredom was part of her problem with men: 'how empty my life would be without a consuming passion'.[3]

Faithful Harry Harker sent her a book for Christmas and the next day, a card finally arrived 'From Lorenzo to Sandra'. On it was a reproduction of Saint Barbara. The card was addressed in Jock's handwriting, so she wondered if it was a joint card, or even Jock's idea rather than Henry's. However, it helped to make for a good Christmas Day. In the morning the Pyms went to church and then unwrapped presents after breakfast. Barbara was given a blue woollen jumper, a pyjama case, silk stockings and a black quilted evening bag with 'Sandra' embroidered across the front in blue silk. It is not clear what her parents thought of her adoption of an alternative name.

In the new year, she decided that she would not make a resolution to renounce Lorenzo, but would just wait to see what happened. Jock Liddell seemed to be playing on her mind too. She vowed to get to know him more when she returned to Oxford. She knew that Jock was homosexual and that he was said to favour men a little younger than himself, such as Bill Ireland, who was descended from the aristocratic de Courcy family.[4] Pym was intrigued by same-sex relationships. The previous November she had attended a lecture on Shakespeare's sonnets in which the lecturer had said 'there was no ignoble sex perversion about Shakespeare's love for Mr W[illiam] H[erbert]'.[5] Her recent reading of Richard Rumbold and Oscar Wilde fed her curiosity. Later, she would write brilliantly about same-sex relationships between men.

Jock and Harry seemed to be inextricably linked, as Miles and Rupert once were: 'I love Gabriel and think about him and Jockie all day and night.'[6] Pym was making Henry a stuffed kangaroo out of pipe cleaners and grey wool. It had brown eyes and a slightly protruding red tongue. She longed to make stuffed animals for Jock, too.

Pym went lingerie shopping in Marks and Spencer in Shrewsbury, and 'bought a peach coloured vest and "trollies", with insertions of lace. Disgraceful I know but I can't help choosing my underwear with a view to its being seen!' She also bought a new red dress: 'crimson jersey – with a collar of red and white crochet which makes me say *Lo the poor Indian,* for

some obscure reason'.[7] The colour reminded her of Gabriel's red
pyjamas, which rather begs the question of how she knew about
such intimate garments. Their relationship may have already
become sexual. There are several torn-out pages in her Michaelmas
diary, which was her habit when recalling embarrassing or
distressing incidents.

Another lasting love affair began in earnest – with Shakespeare.
She quoted Keats: 'I read Shakespeare and I never quite despair.'[8]
Passionate as she was, she felt that Shakespeare inspired a 'hectic
rush feeling'. This was partly a joke, as she was reading him in
a hurry before returning to Oxford, but Shakespeare did indeed
fire her imagination. She was also reading Ronald Knox's *The
Belief of Catholics* and mused 'not yet far enough into it to know
whether I shall become a Catholic or not'.[9]

Thoughts of returning to Oxford were complicated. On the
one hand, melting languor; on the other, misery. 'It means
Gabriel and Jockie and probably some unhappiness – and haven't
I been made miserable enough over this? Anyway, I'm getting
hardened and I expect nothing. I only *hope*.'[10]

CHAPTER XXIII

Sandra returns to Oxford and resumes her Affair with Lorenzo

Pym returned to Oxford, determined to stay away from the Bodleian Library, thus avoiding Henry and Jock. She was thrilled to be reunited with her girlfriends, Sharp and Pedley, but shocked her English tutors by her bright red nail lacquer.[1] Several of the more racy characters in Pym's novels can be distinguished by their red nails.

As usual, Pym was surrounded by admirers, but was still preoccupied with 'the brute' Henry. She tried hard to engage with other men, but in comparison with Henry found them dull in appearance and in themselves. She purchased a stuffed grey kangaroo, which she doted on, and called it Starky.

Pym went on 'beauty walks' with her girlfriends, to windy Port Meadow and Wolvercote, and vowed to cure herself of her sentimental attachment to the Trout, the scene of the passionate embrace with Henry. But her resolution to keep away from the Bodleian didn't last. She saw Jock Liddell, 'looking adorable – his golden curls all ruffled!' But she was in low spirits: 'Coming down the Broad I was struck anew with the hopelessness of this life.'[2]

Harry Harker was still keen and he took her to the cinema

to see the recently released *Blue Angel*. Marlene Dietrich had been discovered in the backstreets of Berlin by the director Josef von Sternberg and he had been instantly mesmerised. His plan was to film *The Blue Angel* in both English and German. The movie was about a repressed, elderly professor who falls in love, becomes obsessed by and is brought down by a crude showgirl. The dazzling Dietrich crooned 'Falling in love again, never wanted to', which would become her signature song. Propelled into box office stardom, she left Berlin for Hollywood as soon as she had finished filming, concerned about her country's new chancellor, Adolf Hitler, who seemed not only power mad, but mad. Hers seemed almost to be a lone voice at the time, as most people in Berlin thought him a saviour. Pym's reaction to the film was lukewarm: 'a horrid, depressing flick and Marlene Dietrich revolting – but it was interesting'.[3] Her reaction to Hitler, however, would be very different from Dietrich's.

After the picture, she caught a glimpse of Henry's back and quickly made her excuses to Harry so that she could tail him, but lost him when he jumped on a bus: 'I still feel the same hopeless desire . . . I must be *sensible* about him.'[4]

Pym continued to hang around the Bod desperate for a glimpse and also stalked him at lectures. She discovered the times of the lectures he attended and then arranged things so she would 'accidentally' bump into him. She timed it all 'beautifully' and was rewarded by the occasional smile and hello. Henry later recalled that she would go to great efforts to stalk him and then be tongue-tied when she finally got his attention. In her diary, she was painfully aware of this and explained that it was because she felt intellectually inferior and wanted to say things that were witty and dazzling. She had always relied on her native wit and sense of humour, but in his presence she was rendered dumb.

Finally Henry cracked, came to sit next to her at the Bod and asked her to tea. When he left, she picked up the scrap of paper he had left on her desk ('it seemed to say will you have tea with me today?'). She kept it amongst her 'Harvey–Liddell relics (of which I now have 3)'.[5]

By the end of January 1933, things had quickly progressed with Henry in ways that not even she had foreseen but that were bittersweet. Pym cut out five pages of her diary. The relationship had now become sexual. Henry's treatment of her, however, was unkind and uncaring and she felt that he was using her for sex. But she could not stop herself from loving and wanting him and, as a result, she suffered miserably.

CHAPTER XXIV

The Saga of Sandra and Lorenzo, continued . . .

Below the cut-out pages of Pym's diary is a sad line: 'I am with him. I'm not happy about it.'[1]

Piecing together the narrative is not easy, with pages of deleted information, but there is a strong sense of bitterness. Lent was about to begin and as Pym was giving up Gold Flake, she smoked her last cigarette. She resolved that from now on she would call Lorenzo by his real name. She still felt low: 'Tired of life – and everything.' She wrote to him, a part witty and part serious letter, but he didn't write back. She was made wretched by the fact that he never seemed to treat her with kindness: 'If only he would just take the wee bit of trouble required to be kind – it's so easy to be nice to people . . . I wish he needed me or wanted me a little.'[2]

In March, there was a student protest in favour of communism. Pym joined the demonstration, though felt a little ludicrous as she shouted: '1-2-3-4 who are *we* for? We are for the working classes. Down with the ruling classes.' The leader was Hilary Sumner-Boyd, dressed in green velvet trousers. Pym thought he looked like a girl; 'somehow one doesn't associate him with Communism'.[3] She also admitted that she disapproved of much that communism stood for.

Her interest in Jock Liddell, meanwhile, continued unabated. She looked up his brother in the Cambridge University Calendar, discovering that he was called Donald.[4] Jock and Donald were extremely close brothers. They had lost their beloved mother to cancer when they were very young. Their father had remarried and their stepmother was cruel and unloving towards the boys. Jock would write about their miserable upbringing in his extraordinary novels, *Kind Relations* and *Stepsons*. He would turn out to be a prolific writer of biographies, poetry, novels and travel books. But for now he was still a young librarian – though admittedly, at one of the greatest libraries in the world. Donald, who would also become a great champion and friend of Pym, was a talented musician.

It seems probable that Henry had confided in Jock about his physical relationship with Pym. Jock, at this time, was protective of Henry and irritated by Pym and her hero worship. She noted that Jock gave her a 'most concentrated look of loathing'.[5] She wrote in her diary of her longing and need for Henry: 'what else is there in life?' Meeting him later, he again asked her to go to tea with him. But she knew what he really wanted and refused: 'I will not be treated in this rude and casual fashion.'[6] Pym wrote him a long letter explaining her feelings. She knew at some level that she was bringing a lot of misery on herself: 'I do seem to mess things up so hopelessly and there is no one to help me.'[7] One day, she cut him in the street and when he came to the Bod she ignored him, but when he left she nearly burst into tears.

In early March, she agreed to go back to his digs for 'tea'. They both knew what was expected, but at least she felt that he was nicer to her than before: 'He took my clothes off by sheer physical force before tea and I eventually had tea clad in his black flannel.'[8] More pages of the diary are scissored. She then wrote an account of Henry flirting with a pretty girl in the library, right in front of her eyes. Pym was livid and felt deeply humiliated. He smiled at her, but she got up and left, with the words: 'Goodbye you hound.'[9]

Agonised, Pym confessed: 'I want him and love him.'[10] She did some research and discovered that her love rival was a young woman called Alison West-Watson. She was very attractive, 'with the same colouring as Henry, though not made up, or particularly well-dressed'.[11] Henry's behaviour towards Pym was caddish. He began comparing her to Alison unfavourably and seemed to enjoy making her jealous. It was cruel, knowing how much she was in love with him. Nor did he ever pretend that he was in love with her.

One day when she was setting out for 'tea', Henry picked her up in his car with Barnicot and another friend, Edward Gardiner. Henry was cruel and teasing and again she felt deeply humiliated. The two friends were charming, but Henry continued being horrid; he talked about Alison and said 'rude things'.[12] Gardiner and the Count left the two of them alone:

> We sat in silence and I was miserable, then into his room where the usual procedure was gone through. He was not kind to me and his attitude towards me was made so cruelly obvious – and he would not stop talking about WW. All the time I was getting more and more unhappy, until suddenly I burst into tears and cried more than I've done for years. It was as if I had felt it coming for days – my love for him, his indifference to me, the mess I'd made of my affair with him and the fact that I was leaving him probably for another woman to have, was simply too much for me.[13]

Henry clearly realised that he had gone too far and was repentant. He promised her that they would be good friends next term and go out on the river together. She began to get dressed and as she did so, Jock suddenly appeared: 'By the time I was more or less clothed and in my right mind Jockie came in. I was terribly glad to see him. His niceness was such a relief and seemed to make up for Gabriel's brutality.'[14]

Jock and Pym made supper, whilst Henry sulked in his room and listened to Wagner's *Tannhäuser* on the gramophone. She felt that although Jock did not seem to have very deep feelings, he was capable of compassion and understanding. During supper, Henry was mutinous, barely said a word and was rude to Pym. She left at 10.30 to go back to St Hilda's to pack for Shropshire. She felt so exhausted that she could barely feel anger towards Henry and his outrageous, callous behaviour. Yet again, she felt used and humiliated.

Pym was correct about Jock's capacity for compassion. Though he could be sneering and catty, he had a deeply sensitive side and an abhorrence of real cruelty – a legacy of the vicious treatment he had suffered at the hands of his German stepmother. Despite his strong friendship with Henry, he saw his flaws and he was distressed by the way Pym was being treated. During the supper preparations, Jock had confided in her about Henry and his faults, telling Pym he knew Henry was a 'terribly difficult person'. She liked Liddell very much; especially his funny turn of phrase and the way he wrinkled up his eyes when he was amused. Jock advised her to drown her sorrows in hard work.

His kindness on this dreadful day went a long way and Pym was deeply grateful. It was the start of what would become one of the most important friendships of her life.

CHAPTER XXV

In which a Very Important Correspondence begins

Henry's dreadful behaviour set the pattern for Pym's relationships with other men: the more badly they treated her, the more deeply in love she felt. The worst aspect of it all was that she knew this and was powerless to stop herself.

Pym had asked Jock to write to her in Shropshire. He had promised to keep her informed of the 'Watson Business'. Pym hereby began a correspondence that would last for the rest of her days. Mary Sharp had already written to Pym to say that Henry had taken Alison out to tea, but Jock, a would-be writer, gave her all the details:

Henry has been staring across at her house and the other night he thought he saw someone at the window and insisted on turning out the light and watching . . . Yesterday he took her to coffee at Fuller's and they sat there from 11.30. She told him

- She always looks up at his window as she passes
- That all the living rooms and her bedroom face off the Banbury Rd
- That she lived alone with an old lady and was lonely.[1]

This was exactly the kind of forensic detail that Pym relished and she was very grateful. Indiscreetly, Jock told Pym that Alison was still 'a maid' (virgin) and that she wanted 'Love', but not with Henry. More importantly, Jock began a long-standing joke that Pym would eventually marry Henry. It gave her much-needed hope, was a source of endless amusement for them both, and made her feel that others were on her side. Both Jock and Barnicot thought Henry would be better off marrying Pym because they suspected Alison 'had shrewish tendencies'. She was delighted to hear: 'You might have her for a bridesmaid.'[2]

Jock revealed that Henry was writing Alison macabre love letters, quoting John Donne and telling her that he was desolate and heartbroken. Henry, too lazy or too heartless to write to Pym himself, scribbled a melodramatic postscript to Jock's letter in his spidery handwriting: 'She doesn't love me. It is the end. Write and comfort my last moments.' Alison had told Jock that the next time she met Pym she was going to 'put out her tongue to you'.[3]

Pym replied instantly and asked for constant updates, which Jock was only too willing to provide. It had not taken Jock long to realise that Pym was rather special. If he had no real idea, at this stage, of the extent of her talent, he no longer considered her as the foolish and annoying limpet. He sent another long and witty letter which was cheering, even though it contained the news that Henry was in love with Alison – mainly it seems because she was playing hard to get and not falling instantly into his arms. Jock was kind and sympathetic: 'Poor dear Pym, I am so sorry that you have wept so many tears over Henry and I wish I could give you more comfort. I am afraid he really is in love with West-Watson.'[4] He added spitefully that Alison would be more expensive to keep than Pym because of her voracious appetite.

Jock captured Henry's idiosyncrasies perfectly: his melodramatic groaning, his laziness, his spoiled manner, his affectation. Pym too would hungrily store up these details and use them later in her novel about Henry. Alison told Henry that she was going to a party in Cambridge, but Jock and Henry spotted a handsome young man at her door. Jock noted how he 'preened' himself before ringing her doorbell. Jock and Henry were just as bad as Pym in spying on other people. The high windows of their lodgings in Banbury Road lent themselves to this habit.

Jock, who had mixed feelings towards Henry, seemed to relish Alison's treatment of him. His letters about the affair are full of malicious wit and spite. He was clearly as fascinated with Henry as Barbara was. He told Pym that he made Henry an apple pudding because of the biblical Song of Solomon's advice: 'Comfort me with apples, for I am sick of love.' Alison had called to see Henry and Jock, acting as chaperone on behalf of Pym, left his sauce to curdle (he was a keen cook). Jock felt sure that Alison disliked him (perhaps homophobically?). This drew Jock and Pym together. Henry added a postscript to the letter, complaining that Pym only wrote to Jock, not to him, and (cruelly) emphasised his infatuation for Alison – 'I have cut my finger and can't write. Why don't you write to me instead of Jock Liddell . . . I am very bored, for the light of my life is going away tomorrow'.[5] He signed his name in his own blood.

All this only deepened Pym's resolve not to write to Henry. 'I am beginning to feel the wee-est bit hostile towards Henry and to think that the glamour of being his doormat is wearing off some.'[6] That day, she listened to a radio production of *The Seagull* and was very taken by its portrayal of unrequited love. She copied out Masha's lines: 'I am in mourning for my life. That is why I wear black. I am unhappy.'[7]

But, despite her Chekhovian leanings, Pym was feeling quietly excited by a plan she had been secretly hatching. She had been learning to speak German and was off to visit Nazi Germany.

BOOK THE SECOND

Germany

CHAPTER I

Miss Pym tours Germany

In the spring of 1934, a young English girl fell in love with Nazi Germany. She was someone with an obsessive nature and she needed a cause. Like many English people, she was deeply impressed by the new chancellor, Adolf Hitler, who was restoring Germany's economy and sense of pride. She set out to stalk Hitler, monitoring his movements and waiting in his favourite restaurant for a sighting. When she saw him, she sat staring, waiting patiently for the moment that he would notice her and notice her he did.

When not in Germany, she lived in a small Oxford village. Here she startled the local shopkeeper and villagers when she came to the village shop dressed in a black shirt and ordered a twopenny chocolate bar, flinging out her arm in the Nazi salute with a cry of 'Heil Hitler!'[1] Tall, blonde and with startling blue eyes, she had been conceived in the village of Swastika in Ontario. Her name was Unity Valkyrie Mitford and she was a year younger than Barbara Pym. Both women were in Germany in the spring of 1934 and both were caught up in the 'heady excitement' of the Nazi regime.

Pym was one amongst many tourists flocking to Germany to witness the transformations wrought by the Third Reich. Writers, journalists, artists and students came in their thousands, responding to Joseph Goebbels's carefully orchestrated advertising machine. He understood the propaganda value of tourism and his aim was to show Germany as a benign, benevolent country. 'Germany Invites You' claimed the Thomas Cook & Son posters showing images of beautiful young people in lederhosen and Tyrolean hats, fairyland castles and mountain ranges framing the background.

Many writers toured the Third Reich in these years, amongst them Samuel Beckett, Thomas Wolfe, Karen Blixen and Albert Camus. In the spring of 1935, a year after Pym's first visit, Virginia and Leonard Woolf drove through Germany on their way to Rome. In contrast to Pym, they were distinctly unimpressed by what they saw. In Heidelberg, Virginia noticed the 'dons and their daughters tripping out to each other's houses with pale blue Beethoven quartets under their arms'. But she described the German countryside as 'pretentious', the scenery 'operatic' and the hills 'high but insignificant'. Leonard noted the grim storm troopers.[2]

Like Unity Mitford, Pym was mesmerised. At Oxford, she had been drawn to German music and culture. 'Auf Wiedersehen' and 'Wien, du Stadt meiner Träume' were her 'Rupert' love songs, and she enjoyed German cinema. She was good at languages and had been learning German at Oxford mainly in preparation for a National Union of Students visit to Cologne. Her St Hilda's friend, Dorothy Pedley, was also signed up. Pym was glad to leave behind the painful and messy affair with Henry.

In fact, Pym was soon to be plunged into another complicated relationship. In her diary on 29 March 1934 she wrote: 'Today was the beginning of a very happy week of my life, which may make a difference to my future.'[3]

At Aachen, the girls were met by a customs officer, who came to look at their books. Only a year before, the German Student

Union had orchestrated a series of public book burnings in Germany and Austria. Enthusiastic crowds witnessed the burning of works by Bertolt Brecht, Albert Einstein, Sigmund Freud, Thomas Mann and Erich Maria Remarque, among other well-known intellectuals, scientists and cultural figures, many of whom were Jewish. The largest of these bonfires occurred in Berlin, where an estimated 40,000 people gathered to hear a speech by Goebbels, in which he pronounced that 'Jewish intellectualism is dead' and endorsed the students' 'right to clean up the debris of the past'.

If Barbara had any reservations about her books being checked, she did not show it – only remarking how satisfying it was to hear German spoken by the customs officer.

By the time Barbara and Dorothy arrived in Cologne, they were feeling exhausted and dirty. They were met by German students who took them by bus to a youth hostel where they had breakfast and then a sleep before lunch. Pym found the other students dull and was starting to regret her decision to travel to Germany. But it was all to change.

Pym was thrilled when she caught sight of 'real Nazis'. One of them was called Friedbert Glück and he was wearing the black uniform of the SS. The other men wore the brown shirts, with the swastika armband, of the Stormtroopers (SA). Pym noted that the men saluted each other 'in the Heil Hitler manner'.[4] She and Dorothy went to luncheon where speeches were made welcoming the foreign visitors. Pym was mesmerised by the handsome blackshirt, Glück:

Friedbert spoke in German – I remember being impressed by him and thinking him a marvellous unapproachable Nazi. What did he look like? Tall with a lovely figure set off to advantage by the black uniform – very dark with smooth black hair and a high forehead-dark complexion and greyish green eyes – (actually I found out most of this later) rather strange looking but undoubtedly fascinating.[5]

After lunch, they toured Cologne and enjoyed looking at the pictures in the museum. Before dinner, she and Pedley shopped for cigarettes, oranges, and Pond's Cold Cream. When she went to bed, Pym thought of Henry: 'I ended up still being in love with Gabriel, however much the Nazis had impressed me.'[6]

Barbara was certainly not unique in being swept up in the excitement of the Third Reich and the way in which the Hitler youth played such a pivotal role: there were marching bands, pageants and rallies, red flags and swastikas, all proclaiming signs of a restored national pride. The Nuremberg rally the previous year had attracted many UK tourists, including Unity Mitford and her sister Diana. By the summer of 1934, Unity had become part of Hitler's inner circle. She also engaged in love affairs with blackshirts, whom she called 'storms'.

Despite the sinister signs in Hitler's new Germany, most tourists were happy to look the other way. As late as 1937, the Duke and Duchess of Windsor toured the new Germany, including a visit to a concentration camp. When the duke asked what it was, he was told: 'It is where they store the cold meat.'[7]

CHAPTER II

In which Fräulein Pym
falls for a Handsome Nazi

By the beginning of April, Pym had entered what she deemed
'a new period of her life'. One evening she attended the opera
to see Wagner's *Die Walküre* (the opera that inspired Unity
Mitford's middle name). She had met a bearded man at the
performance. He invited her into his box and she allowed him
to stroke her arm and her ankle. Afterwards they drank 'lovely
cool hock' in a cafe and then went on to another cafe by the
river, 'a lower class one – where there was real dancing and fat
families swaying in time to the music'.[1] She allowed the bearded
man to kiss her. Perhaps she permitted more than a kiss, as a
half-page of her diary is cut out.

When the narrative continues, we find Pym at a party with
a Nazi called Hanns Woischnik. 'We made much noise and
drank quite a lot. After the party had broken up, Hanns and I
went around the corner and he kissed me several times in the
German way, perhaps "with inside lip", but I did not mind. He
was very sweet and asked me to go to his . . . [deleted lines].'[2]
Hanns would subsequently become a Nazi-approved academic,
with a doctoral thesis entitled 'Júlio Dinis as Novelist and Love
Psychologist'. (Dinis was the pen name of Portugal's first modern

novelist; during the war, Portugal was officially neutral but of great value to Germany.)

The next day, Pym went on a steamboat trip down the Rhine wearing a grey silk scarf that belonged to Hanns, and a summery green dress. She flirted with Hanns, who gave her his address and asked her to write to him when she returned to England. But the man she was really interested in was Friedbert Glück. She got into conversation with him. 'He was looking sweet and he hadn't shaved because his chin was gloriously black and rough.' He wasn't wearing his black uniform, but looked fetching in flannel bags, a brown tweed coat, a flowery tie and an 'exquisite shirt'. Instead of his SS peaked cap, he wore a green Bavarian-style teardrop hat.[3]

The day was hot and the group drank white wine: 'Fancy being nearly drunk in the morning!' They landed at Bonn for a tour of the university and at lunch Pym felt 'excited and hot and couldn't eat much'. They then set off on the steamer for Königswinter, where they boarded the rack railway to climb the mountain of Petersberg. By this time, she and Friedbert were staying close together. 'The district is lovely,' wrote Pym, 'mountains with forests topping them and romantic looking castles. Many cafes and tables outside of course . . . everyone happy and lovely weather.' At the summit, they took tea at a cafe, where the air was beautifully clear and the cakes were 'of a size and lusciousness quite unequalled in England'. Friedbert lent Barbara his green hat to shield her from the sun. After tea, they wandered and looked out at the lovely view. Pym was filled with joy. 'All the time Friedbert was very sweet – why couldn't I have stayed there always – so happy with someone so nice.' Down in Königswinter, they drank a delicious beverage consisting of wine, sliced oranges and herbs. Friedbert told Pym that he wished she could stay in Germany so that they could tour his beautiful nation together. 'It was as romantic as anything could possibly be.'[4] In the next breath, she saw Hanns, who complimented her and held her hand.

On the steamer home, the party drank nine bottles of wine and Barbara felt intoxicated and 'gloriously happy'. Friedbert put his arm around her and kissed her: 'I suppose we didn't behave well – but what did it matter?' By now the entire group was inebriated. Shouting and singing broke out: 'We sang God Save the King and Deutschland über Alles. That rather worried Friedbert although I couldn't understand why. He and Hanns had an animated talk about it in German.'[5] She was clearly oblivious to any political undercurrents surrounding the behaviour of the two young men.

Pym went with Friedbert to the lower deck and they 'close-kissed'. She felt that she was living in the moment: 'An exhilarating sensation too seldom enjoyed.' Pym was simply delighted that a young man was treating her kindly: 'It was so lovely to have someone saying nice things to me after Gabriel's rudeness and unkindness. I at last began to realise that there could be something in my life beyond Gabriel.'[6] It was a little unfortunate that the only man who came close to expelling the memory of Henry Harvey happened to be an officer of the SS.

Pym headed back to England, sad to be parting from Friedbert and Hanns. Friedbert told her that he had singled her out, even before he knew her name, claiming, romantically, that she was like the English song, his 'Secret Passion'. They had a fond farewell; and she felt that she had left her heart behind in Cologne.

On the journey home, she fell asleep and woke up to the unwanted fondling of a fat Frenchman. She bolted and moved away.[7] Other than this unsavoury incident, it was a pleasant trip. As soon as she reached London, she bought herself a German dictionary and Vernon Bartlett's new book, *Nazi Germany Explained*.[8] Pym had indeed left her heart in Germany.

CHAPTER III

In which Sandra returns to Oxford and loses her Swastika Badge somewhere on the Banbury Road

'One important thing seemed to have happened to me,' Pym wrote in her diary: 'My tour in Germany meant that I began to take an interest in Hitler, Nazis and German politics.'[1] She had brought souvenirs home with her, including a precious swastika pin that was a gift from Friedbert. She fashioned a swastika design on a scarlet box. She wrote letters to Friedbert and Hanns. For once, Oxford had lost its allure. She dreamt of Friedbert and being on the Rhine.

Listening to dance music on the wireless made Pym feel nostalgic. 'Let There Be No Heartaches, No More Tears', reminded her of Henry. 'As far as Gabriel is concerned I don't think there *will* be any more,' she added. The next song, 'I'll See You in My Dreams', reminded her of Friedbert, 'and that is probably the only time I shall see Friedbert again'. At this point a double page in the diary has been torn out.[2]

Pym returned early to Oxford and rented a room in Ship Street. She had been reading Samuel Butler's risqué novel *The Way of All Flesh*, notable for its assault on Victorian hypocrisy, its crisis of religious faith and an incident in which a man sexually assaults a young woman whom he wrongly believes to be of 'loose morals'. Pym saw Jock in the library, who she found was his usual sweet self. And she went shopping and bought an 'exciting' red, black and white checked skirt that she considered 'very Sandra'.³ The weather was fine; almond trees in blossom made her think of the Rhine and Friedbert. In the meantime, she had a secret affair with a brother of her friend, Paul Hussey. He was called Bill and she wrote that it was nice to receive admiration and compliments.

It was not long before she had a long letter in German from Friedbert, who also sent a photograph of himself and a copy of one of Hitler's speeches. Pym longed to have the time to translate his letter. In Ship Street, she spotted Henry, following an absence of six weeks. She also saw Barnicot, with 'the real count', Roberto Weiss. The next day, Henry called in at her digs and asked Pym to join him, Jock and Barnicot for supper that evening. Whilst he was there, he translated part of Friedbert's letter ('very satisfactorily!' she noted). Henry was clearly a little jealous of Friedbert's existence.

At Banbury Road, Pym was greeted by Jock, who opened the door in a ravishing paisley dressing gown. At one point Henry pulled Barbara onto the bed, insisting that she lie beside him. Jock and Barnicot left them to it. So far, so normal. For once, Henry was being nice. He said he had a headache and he was kind and gentle and once again, Pym felt her feelings of love revive.

She and Henry were in the midst of an embrace when the other men unexpectedly came back. Henry would not let go of her; there was a struggle on the floor and Pym showed 'most indecent sights' and more of herself than was appropriate: 'I was simply furious and burst into a passionate fit of crying.' Jock and Barnicot were embarrassed and left with Henry so that Pym could have some time to calm her feelings. Henry came back and was solicitous and they all had supper. It was late by the time Pym left and she had to climb through a window to her room. Then, to complicate matters further, Bill Hussey called in whilst she was in her nightclothes and feeling 'distrait'. She was relieved when he left after ten minutes.[4]

Now that Henry appeared to be losing Pym to another man, he was at last showing more interest. He invited her to tea. She refused. He came after lunch and behaved with kindness and courtesy until he ruined it all with one of his cruel comments: 'Oh you are common property.'[5] When he saw how much he had upset Pym, he began to be nice to her again. After Henry left, Pym comforted herself by translating Friedbert's letter, finding many nice things to please her and restore her shaken confidence. It was cruel behaviour. Henry did not want her, but he did not want anyone else to have her attention.

With the start of term, Pym moved back to St Hilda's, into her old room. It felt as if prison walls were closing around her – she missed the freedom afforded by the private lodgings in Ship Street. She bought a frame for her picture of Friedbert and put it on her desk. Her thoughts were consumed by him: she walked to Port Meadow to read his letter in more romantic surroundings.

In the evening, she learnt more German and thought 'much of going to Rhineland again'. She went to the movies and saw Bertolt Brecht's *Whither Germany?* – a love story set in the last days of the Weimar Republic when unemployment and homelessness were rife, and interspersed with left-wing political commentary. 'Affected me deeply,' she wrote.[6] She was also reading *Jew Süss*, a historical novel by the well-known German Jewish writer Lion Feuchtwanger, about the rise and fall of a Jewish businessman. Later, the Nazis would adapt the novel, turning it into a propaganda film and one of the most anti-Semitic movies of all time.

Barbara occasionally saw Henry and Jock, who both asked

her to mend their socks ('I intend to do so and take my wee penknife with me'). She went to their digs in Banbury Road in her (Sandra) scarlet satin shirt and black skirt. As she sat darning seemingly endless pairs of socks, Jock amused her with funny stories, though Henry was rude. Later, he said he was sorry and that he would teach her Chaucer and introduce her to the works of Gerard Langbaine, a minor seventeenth-century author who was one of his favourites. He walked her to the bus stop and asked her to tea. She refused. Back in her room, she looked at her photograph of Friedbert and said, 'Oh my darling – it's you I love.'[7]

Pym had promised to darn more socks for Henry and Jock, so she returned the next evening. She noted that Henry and Jock were arguing and then she had a row with Henry. She was so upset and distracted by this that she lost her precious swastika brooch on the Banbury Road and burst into tears.[8]

Pym was worried, as Friedbert had not written back to her and she felt that she was falling back in love with Henry. Henry came to find her in the library and told her that he and Jock were unable to find her swastika pin, which was depressing. Henry was clearly wishing to resume their sexual 'no strings' relationship, which only made Pym feel used and rejected. On the steps of the Radcliffe Camera, Henry asked her to tea and promised he would not touch her in an inappropriate way: 'But how can I believe him after all the other times he's sworn and promised?' She was surprised that her instinct was to reach out her hand and touch him, realising: 'Deep down in my heart I know that I love him.'[9] She felt her usual hopelessness: she loved Henry, but she could not trust him.

CHAPTER IV

Miss Pym's Final Term

If it hadn't been for Friedbert and the memory of Germany, Pym's final term at Oxford might well have been unhappy. Her on/off affair with Henry dragged on. Jock Liddell came back to their flat in Banbury Road to discover the pair naked in bed reading Milton's *Samson Agonistes*. Pym was penitent for her behaviour and they all had supper together.[1] Later, her friend, Honor Tracy, warned her about Henry and advised her not to continue the affair.

Friedbert and Germany, meanwhile, still held sway over her: a visit to the Ashmolean made her compare the art unfavourably to that of the museum in Cologne. Back in her room, she read the German paper *Die Woche*; it helped her with her German vocabulary and kept her in touch with the latest news from the Third Reich.[2]

On 12 May Pym went to London for a National Union of Students reunion. Several of the people she had met previously on the Cologne trip were there, together with some new Belgian and German boys. The reunion was fun and they watched a cine film and found a photograph of Pym and Hanns aboard the steamer on the Rhine, drinking wine, glasses raised in the air: 'Promoting International Goodwill I called it!'[3] After the reunion Pym went to Cambridge and enjoyed touring some of the colleges, noting that 'there seem to be remarkably few pansies in Cambridge'.[4]

Back in Oxford, Pym tried to buy a new swastika pin, but could only find a gold one, which was too expensive. 'I want so terribly to go to Germany again,' she wrote.[5] She longed for a letter from Friedbert, who seemed to have gone quiet. She read a German play, *Das Mädchen Manuela*, but had to look up almost every word in the dictionary.

Henry, again, joked about Pym's poor reputation and for once she let her irate feelings show, calling him a 'fatuous idiot'. But it wasn't long before she began to feel sentimental about him once more. She was honest about her own feelings, knowing that if Friedbert wrote, then she would have a distraction from Henry. She decided that men often seemed to let her down. 'I have very little faith in Mankind now – although Hope *does* spring eternal in the human breast, especially in Sandra's.'[6]

The next day, Pym wrote Henry a love note and enclosed forget-me-nots. She went with Pedley to a production of Noël Coward's *Design for Living*, a play about a complicated three-way relationship between a woman who cannot decide between her two male lovers and chooses to live with them both. Barbara wondered whether she 'should do that with Henry and Jock'.[7] Evenings were spent improving her German and revising for her final exams. She had a letter from Hanns, claiming that Friedbert had said that she was returning to Germany in June. But still there was silence from Friedbert himself. She noted, sadly, in her diary: 'I suppose the truth is that I belong to a cruel, sweet Englishman called Henry Stanley Harvey.'[8]

On the day before her twenty-first birthday, Pym saw Henry and Jock for supper. Henry remarked that she looked 'blonde and Aryan, like something on the cover of *Die Woche*'. They drank Liebfraumilch and embraced: 'to kiss Henry in a wonderful kiss was the loveliest thing that has happened in years'. Henry tried to take it further, but Pym, and Jock, refused to let him. Henry drove her home: 'Goodbye twenty.' She did let it go further on her birthday itself: 'He was quite sweet really as far as I can remember. The usual proceedings happened of course, then had a bath while I read Spence's Anecdotes to him.' Pym occasionally had pangs of conscience about her sexual activity with Henry; she sometimes felt 'miserable and conscience-stricken' and wept: 'Silly Sandra, but I suppose it was a relief.'[9]

When Jock returned home after work, they had supper and he read Jane Austen aloud to Pym. Jock was an ardent admirer of Austen (later, he would write a very good critical book about her art). Listening to Austen being read aloud was an important lesson for Pym in the art of dialogue and comic timing. It is unclear whether Pym told either Jock or Henry of her aspiration to be a novelist.

That summer term, Henry had a German guest staying. He was called Anton Fendrich. Pym considered him 'nice in a dark Friedbertish way'. She spent her final period at Oxford with Henry and Anton. One beautiful summer's day the men wanted to bathe naked at Parson's Pleasure, so Pym was sent back to Banbury Road with a latch key. She did the washing up and laid the tea things, resisting the urge to poke around Henry's things. By the time the boys came back, she was sitting quietly, reading. Anton had cut his foot and Pym bound it up – acting the part of the 'Hausfrau'. After tea, they all got drunk and drove into the Cotswolds for supper at the Lamb in Burford. Anton flirted with Pym and turned cartwheels in the road. Then he wrapped her in a rug in the back of the car and kissed her. She liked kissing German men: 'How seriously and sensuously they kiss.'[10]

Back in Oxford, they hired a punt to get Pym home to St Hilda's. It was late, and the college was locked up, so Henry helped her over the wall and they walked together in the moonlit garden with the stars filling the night sky. He had been on his very best behaviour and Pym felt 'blissfully happy'. She went to bed hearing the birds singing the dawn chorus.

The next morning, Pym went to Henry's flat clutching a large bunch of yellow and red roses. The boys were still asleep, but they finally awoke to her persistent knocking. Henry was delighted with the flowers. After breakfast, Pym lay on the blue divan and Anton tried to kiss her, but she did not feel up to a German kiss at that hour of the day.

Henry put on the Brandenberg concertos and he gave Pym a last, tender kiss. 'No more need be said about the last morning of my last term at Oxford,' she concluded. But there was one final thought: 'He made the last two days sweet enough to make up for all the unhappiness of the last year.'[11]

CHAPTER V

Night of the Long Knives

Pym waited for her results. She was awarded a second-class degree. Then she firmed up her plans to return to Germany. Friedbert had finally written, suggesting that he could find her a tutoring job, but Pym's mother was not keen that she should go back merely on his recommendation. It was one thing having the safety net of the NUS and quite another to go alone and unprotected.

Back home in Shropshire, Pym signed on the dole and felt very much the same as during any other long vacation. Boredom set in: 'I feel rather comatose.' Another letter from Friedbert arrived, which raised her spirits. On 1 July 1934, she went on a family visit to Bath, but events abroad, 'political and personal', were on her mind. She kept the wireless set on, riveted by the unsettling reports from Germany. What she heard was news of Hitler's purge of the SA in the 'Night of the Long Knives'. His power and that of the SS was consolidated. The brownshirts had been eliminated and the SS became Hitler's personal instruments of terror, loyal to him alone. We have no way of knowing the extent of Friedbert Glück's involvement in the purge, though it would appear from later events that he was close to Hitler.

Pym followed events on the BBC and in the newspapers, while also starting to read Goethe in German. 'Tonight I cut out Nazi Germany cuttings . . . at present my thoughts are most on Germany,' she wrote in her diary a few days after the Night of the Long Knives, on 7 July.[1] That same day, *The Times* headline proclaimed 'Perplexity in Germany. Fate of Brown Army'. Their correspondent reported that the deputy Führer, Rudolf Hess, had given a (carefully stage-managed) address to the national congress of Nazi leaders, in which he stated that the 'merited death of a dozen mutineers averted a fearful bloodshed'.[2] Hess made clear that members of the SS were the 'black-coated executioners' and that the SA must 'resign itself to being a non-military and submissive body always under the eye of the SS'. More disturbing reports followed, emphasising Hitler's severity, the necessity of the 'clean-up', and the importance of the Hitler Youth, who 'looked up to the Führer as [their] idol'. Hess also hinted at the 'abnormal proclivities' of some of the SA leaders: their chief, Ernst Röhm, summarily shot on 1 July, was a known homosexual.

Unity Mitford wrote to her sister, Diana, about the purge:

I am *terribly* sorry for the Führer – you know Röhm was his oldest comrade & friend, the only one that called him 'du' in public . . . It must have been so dreadful for Hitler when he arrested Röhm himself and tore off his decorations. Then he went to arrest Heines and found him in bed with a boy. Did that get into the English Papers? *Poor* Hitler.[3]

If Pym felt anxious about events in Germany, she did not show it. Friedbert continued to occupy her thoughts, as the negotiations for her plans continued throughout early July: 'I still desire passionately to go there and am still trying to acquire more vocabulary.' Plans went awry and it looked for a while as if, rather than returning to Friedbert in Cologne, the only option would be to go with the NUS to Hamburg: 'Today I thought sadly of Friedbert . . . Perhaps it would be dangerous to see him again. I thought of him at the very first lunch in Cologne making a speech in his black uniform. Life is sad but sometimes very romantic.'[4]

In the meantime, Pym returned briefly to Oxford for her viva. She saw Henry, who invited her back to the flat on the Banbury Road. In his usual cruel manner, he talked about a pretty Finnish girl he had met, but that did not stop matters becoming physical between them: 'we proceeded as usual. I felt he was very sweet but my love has calmed down a good deal.'[5] He told her that he expected that they would probably go on having these sorts of meetings in the future. But he was offering nothing more than casual sex.

Pym stayed for supper. Barnicot turned up and Henry opened a letter which informed him that he had got a job as a lecturer in Finland, at the University of Helsinki. Henry got so excited that he thought he was going to be sick, so Pym calmed him down and stroked his head. Later, they toasted his success with whisky (her first taste of it). It was a glorious, 'forever to be remembered' evening. They sang, danced and, to Pym's delight, they spoke German all night. Henry gave Pym a present of a pair of red leather and wool slippers. She painted his mouth with lipstick and then made herself and Barnicot up as clowns. The boys then walked her back to her digs, the happy threesome arm in arm.[6]

The next day, following her viva, Pym had tea with Henry and he accompanied her to the station. It was an emotional parting and the end of an era: 'He said I was part of his background, like Jock and Barnicot, which pleased me – it is what I've always wanted – I love him too, but don't want him for my very own yet awhile.'[7]

CHAPTER VI

Miss Pym returns to Nazi Germany and attends a Hitler Rally

Belinda Bede, the heroine of Barbara Pym's first published novel, *Some Tame Gazelle*, is closely modelled on Pym herself. In the first draft, Belinda is actually called Barbara. In the original manuscript version of the novel, Belinda visits Hamburg in the summer of 1934. She sails, as Pym did, by Russian ship (the SS *Kooperatzi* was the cheapest way to travel to Hamburg). Her heart lifts upon her arrival:

> By this time Belinda was safely up the mouth of the river Elbe and had almost reached Hamburg. She looked out of her porthole and saw the sand and those pretty little homes on the shore. There were petunias and geraniums in the window boxes. Swastika flags were fluttering in the light breeze. *Hast du schon abgestimmt? Denk an deine Stimmpflicht* (Have you voted. Remember to vote).[1]

The juxtaposition of the innocent red flowers and the sinister red flags is entirely lost on the heroine, just as it was lost on Pym.

Barbara would never forget her second trip to Nazi Germany,

particularly as she was in time to witness an important speech by Hitler. President von Hindenburg had died on 2 August and Hitler quickly seized his opportunity. A referendum on merging the posts of chancellor and president was to be held on 19 August. Two days beforehand, Hitler declared a national holiday and travelled to Hamburg to give one of the most crucial speeches of his political career to date. That very same day, Pym arrived in the city. The bright red swastika flags were indeed fluttering, as in the words of the 'Horst Wessel Lied', the new anthem of the Nazi party.

Pym was caught up in the excitement of the day. Hitler delivered his election speech on the referendum for the head of state from the balcony of Hamburg city hall. It was a spectacular event, the Nazi party had pulled out all the stops. Hitler was flanked by SS and SA stormtroopers, and banners screeched *Ja dem Führer* ('Say Yes to the Führer'). The Führer's address was broadcast on the radio, reaching an audience of more than four million Germans.

The swastika flags and the propaganda posters fascinated the fresh-faced British traveller. She noted in her diary: 'There was plenty of publicity etc urging voters to say *Ja* for Hitler. The ones I can remember best were *Führer wir folgen dir, Alle sagen Ja! E in Führer, fin Ja*. At the station – *Reisende! Denk an eure Stimmpflicht*.'[2] Pym found the whole thing 'delightful and more than usually interesting'. Seeing Hitler in the flesh was an added and unexpected boon: 'I thought he looked smooth and clean and was very impressed.'[3] In a passage later deleted from the manuscript of *Some Tame Gazelle*, Pym records the memorable incident: 'Was it not a fortunate coincidence that she had arrived in Hamburg that very day . . . Belinda, who remembered seeing the Führer as if it were yesterday. So nice and clean and tidy he had looked, and of *course* she had heard his speech in the evening, although she had been able to understand very little of it.'[4]

That the referendum was associated with widespread intimidation of voters does not seem to have registered with Pym. Whether or not she made the Nazi salute is not known, although one of the first decisions any traveller had to make when crossing the border in the mid-1930s was whether or not to 'Heil' Hitler. By 1934, the Nazi salute was all-pervasive. One Cambridge University student who travelled to Hamburg the same summer as Pym felt that giving the salute was merely a matter of politeness, like raising your hat in church. Others believed it was a public endorsement of a 'thoroughly unpleasant regime'.[5]

In fact, it became increasingly risky not to raise your arm. A young British woman of only eighteen called Joan Tonge attended a Nazi rally and steadfastly refused to give the salute, standing with her arms by her side 'like an offensive bit of rhubarb'. Immediately a group of stormtroopers came galloping up, shouting and screaming, until they were told she was an 'Englander'.[6] All things considered, it seems very likely that Pym would have Heiled Hitler at the Rathaus rally.

Sometime in the autumn of 1934, Pym wrote to Rupert Gleadow and told him about her summer travels to Germany and her admiration for the stormtroopers in their black uniforms. He wrote back, warning her about her fixation with Nazi men: 'It's good that you have been to Germany and can talk it. Oh but *please* don't admire those *filthy* Nazis in the beautiful uniforms: you won't get a chance much longer, becos [sic] 1936 will just about see the end of Hitler.'[7]

CHAPTER VII

In which Miss Pym returns to England and begins writing a Novel

At the end of the summer of 1934, Pym started a new diary. She called it the 'third volume' of her memoirs. Sandra still featured, though it would also include the adventures of 'Pymska' – a Finnish version of Barbara. During her final term at Oxford, she had begun a novel about Henry, which she later destroyed. But once back in Shropshire from Germany, she was inspired to begin another:

> It is about time I emerged from the silence of the past month and wrote up a little more of my life. Sometime in July I began writing a story about Hilary and me as spinsters of fiftyish. Henry, Jock and all of them appeared in it. I sent it to them and they liked it very much. So I am going on with it and some day it may become a book.[1]

Following a summer holiday, Jock was back at Banbury Road, and beginning in earnest what would prove to be a long and fruitful correspondence between the budding authors. Initially he addressed her as Pym, later she would be 'Cassandra' or 'Pymska'. He was still working as an assistant librarian at the

Bodleian's Department of Western Manuscripts, a position he would occupy until 1938. He sent funny poems to 'Cassandra', warning her against loving 'difficult' Henry. And she sent him pages of the manuscript Barbara and Hilary story.

The original version of the novel that became *Some Tame Gazelle* is markedly different from the published version. Perhaps the most autobiographical of her novels, it drew extensively on her Oxford circle and the experiences she had whilst an undergraduate. The novel was to be 'for Henry', and she confessed that she was able, in fiction, to express her true feelings: 'I seem able to say what I cannot in the ordinary course of events.'[2] The heroine – originally named Barbara, then Belinda, 'keeps looking back to her youth'. Pym thus gave herself 'an excuse for revealing some of my present feelings about Henry': 'No change has been wrought in them, as far as I can see. He remains the only person.'[3]

Pym sets the action thirty years in the future, at a time when confirmed spinsters and sisters Barbara/Belinda and Hilary/Harriet Bede live together in a cottage in an English country village. Belinda harbours an unrequited passion for a man three decades after they had first met as students at the University of Oxford. Henry Hoccleve, tall, dark and handsome, has become, in a stroke of cruel inspiration, a pompous archdeacon. He is married to Agatha, who is, naturally, based on Pym's great Oxford rival, Alison West-Watson. Jock Liddell is imagined as Dr Nicholas Parnell, now head librarian at the Bodley. John Barnicot is John Akenside; Count Roberto Weiss is Count Ricardo Piozzi. Honor Tracy is Hester Carey. Other Oxford friends make cameo appearances, such as Jock's musical brother, Donald Liddell, and Lady Julia Pakenham as Lady Clara Boulding.

Henry and Jock, who were sent manuscript chapters, were stunned by the quality of the writing and highly amused by the in-jokes. It is all there in delightful, assured prose: Barbara's hopeless, unrequited love for selfish, self-dramatising Henry; Jock's quarrelsome, difficult friendship with Henry; Alison's cold-fish superiority and ambition (it is she who persuades Henry to become an archdeacon); Hilary's schoolgirl passion for young curates. Henry and Jock had assumed that Pym's girlish passion for Henry and her sense of subjugation were matters for joking – 'Poor Pym' was their constant refrain. But she had turned the tables on them and revealed how she had stored up every detail and made it into art.

There are, nevertheless, personal jokes galore. Belinda, now a middle-aged spinster, is dressed 'quietly and generally in good tweed', in sharp contrast to Sandra's outlandish and sexy clothes, such as her red satin blouse and black skirt. Jock Liddell's obsession with extensions to the Bodleian Library is satirised, while Henry's penchant for quoting from poetry is much mocked: he is a bore about Middle English, quoting Chaucer and rattling on about the 'Beast fable in the Middle Ages'. Belinda (like Pym herself) loathes the Middle English language and literature studies that were a compulsory part of the Oxford English degree, but she humours Henry. She adores Dr Parnell: 'The two things that bound them together were dear Henry and our Greater English poets.'[4]

Giving her imagination free rein, Pym projected all her worst fears and hopes into a world thirty years in the future. Henry, an only child, has a son who has inherited his father's good looks but none of his charm. Alison, having schemed to 'catch' Henry, has lost her elfin prettiness and has become a shrew, as predicted by her Oxford friends. Barbara and Hilary live together happily in their cottage, knitting and darning socks for the clergy (another joke about Pym's incessant sock-darning for Jock and Henry).

Jock wrote a generous letter, praising her novel in the highest terms:

Henry and I think you are a very great novelist. I implore you
to continue your story – we long to know more about Barbara
and Hilary and the Archdeacon's family and Miss Tracy and Dr
Liddell. Henry thinks you are far greater than Miss Austen: I
don't quite agree, though I place you well above the Brontes.
We have read your story aloud to each other, to West-Watson,
to Mr Barnicot and to Henry's sister Betty. Henry's mother . . .
thought it very clever of the little girl Barbara to think of all
that.[5]

Thus encouraged, Pym wrote on. It was no mean feat to have
the two men, whose intelligence she most admired, comparing
her (at the age of twenty-one) with Jane Austen and the Brontë
sisters. Henry's observation about her similarity, indeed superiority, to Jane Austen was acute. It would not be the last time
she would be compared to Austen.

Jock was soon writing again, begging 'Dear Pym' to send
more chapters: 'I return your story reluctantly – it is one of my
chief consolations in life. I have read it about four times with
very great pleasure . . . you are maintaining the interest perfectly
– and the characters are developing very well. I particularly like
Barbara and Alison in the vicarage garden.'[6] He hoped that her
plans to do a B.Litt (graduate degree) at Oxford were coming
on, joking about being happy to fetch her library books every
half hour. He and Henry had gone to the St Giles's Fair together,
but Oxford was 'cold and dismal'. Jock told Pym that Henry
was 'like the Archdeacon of 30 years on at his worst'. Perhaps,
inspired by Pym, Jock began writing an autobiographical novel
himself, which would eventually have the title *Kind Relations*.
Filled with a new respect for Pym, he sent her some of the
manuscript. He also offered an encouraging message: 'We miss
you so much – my socks are full of holes and West-Watson has
no charms for Henry any more.'[7]

CHAPTER VIII

Pym continues her Novel of 'Real People'

Henry left for Finland on 19 September 1934. For the trio, it seemed the end of an era. Jock saw him off at the station, went to work at the library and when he arrived home found a telegram informing him of his father's death. He wrote immediately to Pym. It is telling that she was one of the first people to be told the news. Jock was a deeply private person, but trusted Pym and confided in her his deep dislike of his stepmother (the subject of his second autobiographical novel, *Stepsons*). He was coming to rely on Pym's friendship. As Henry left, they would draw closer together. Jock told her that he looked forward to seeing her again at her graduation ceremony: 'O Pym, I am so lonely and wretched.' He begged her to continue with her novel: 'So send more story soon, it is my chief pleasure in life.'[1]

Jock was also missing Henry: 'He likes Helsingfors [Helsinki] and seems very pleased with himself for being a lektor' and is 'wildly pro-Finn'.[2] He told Pym about his father's funeral and how he felt curiously detached from his step-family, regarding them as copy for his novel. He was extremely close, however, to his clever, musical brother, Donald. Their early grief, miserable childhood and mutual antipathy towards their stepmother had made them even closer. Don was now living with Jock in Oxford, and playing the piano for five hours a day. Jock wrote that they had settled down 'to a quiet domesticity which is quite restful – a little like your old age with Hilary'. His letter reveals the careful attention he paid to the *Some Tame Gazelle* manuscript. 'Hilary and Barbara could stay at my house on Boar's Hill if my sister were there to be hostess (she is now nearly 17).'[3]

With Jock's encouragement, Pym continued to work hard on her novel. She missed Henry but admitted that 'it is not so easy to be jealous of various vague Finns as of some definite people in Oxford'.[4] Henry did not write to her, so she had to make do with a letter from faithful Harry Harker: 'it would be so convenient if I could love him'. She complained that everyone wrote to her except for the one person from whom she longed to hear. By October, she had snapped, scrawling in her diary that Henry was a swine not to write.

Furthermore, she was bored of her life back in Shropshire. Every day seemed to be exactly the same and she had taken the decision not to get a job, but to concentrate on her novel. Always someone who tried to be honest with her feelings, Pym asked herself whether she really loved Henry or whether what she felt was a 'kind of *sehnsucht*' (yearning or nostalgia). She admitted that part of her longing was 'leading such an entirely sexless life here'. She told herself that 'absence makes the heart grow fonder'.[5] However, Pym confided to her diary, her novel of 'real people' was going on well: 'though not as fast as it ought to'.[6]

Jock continued to send 'the most amusing and charming letters'. He did not patronise or condescend; he gave sensible advice and, above all, took her writing seriously. He thought that the last chapters were even better than the first. Jock told Pym that he was sending on the new chapters to John Barnicot and Henry. For Pym, it was an essential means of contact, as her novel became a vehicle for all her feelings of love and loss.

Pym knew that she could always make Henry laugh – and so she played her pain for laughs. There was enormous fun to be had in the idea that marriage to Alison/Agatha was a big mistake and that Henry would have been much happier marrying loyal and faithful Barbara/Belinda. One wonders what Henry thought as he read her chapters in Finland. Pym, thanks to her diary and sharp memory, had recorded every detail of their relationship, though she did not go into detail about the physical aspects, apart from a joke about Belinda knowing that Henry took a size 38 in pyjamas.

Henry's cruelty is acutely observed. He makes fun of Belinda's appearance, telling her that her eyes are too large for her face; he complains when she turns up uninvited at his door: 'Oh, You!' To which she always replies: 'Yes, Henry dear.' He expects her to knit his bed socks and clean his kitchen, but complains when she cuts the bread badly into thick, jagged slices. He requests that she listen attentively when he reads *Samson Agonistes* aloud in his mannered way (Belinda is not naked in bed when this occurs, as was Barbara in real life), but instead of listening properly, she has 'been thinking how intolerably conceited and sweet he was. He was still both, she reflected.'[7]

Henry had once complained to Barnicot that Pym annoyed him because she always agreed with everything he said. Pym got her own back in her novel:

Dear Henry had once confessed to a friend that he found Belinda boring because she always agreed with him. Belinda had often wondered how it was possible to do anything else but agree with a person whose only topic of conversation were motor cars and the price of travel from Finland to England and who made minute notes on the whole of Spenser's *Faerie Queene* in his second long vacation. What could poor Belinda do but agree?[8]

Like Jane Austen's heroines, the women in Pym's novels know when to withhold their superior intelligence.

In *Some Tame Gazelle*, the Archdeacon loves nothing better than the sound of his own voice, bores his parishioners with his overlong, wordy sermons, and is jealous of his curates. Many of Henry's traits and peccadillos are depicted in this handsome, selfish, petulant, lazy, conceited and not terribly bright man of the cloth: his dislike of olives, his delicate constitution, his habit of lying in bed in the morning, his constant complaints. His Viennese red wool socks that Belinda must forever darn. His black Oxford bags. His blue hat. His habit of leaning his head to one side when he speaks. His melancholy moods. His theatrical sighs . . .

How the real Henry must have blushed at Pym's description of him as 'childishly petulant', a 'sulky child' with an expression of 'sour melancholy on his thin face'. As she writes with a knowing wink: 'If I were to write a book about him people would hardly believe such an Archdeacon could exist.'

Belinda's erotic interests have been fed by her interest in poetry: 'Unsuitable quotations from Donne kept coming into her head at the wrong moments.' There are several jokes about the racy material of Catullus and the 'dear Earl of Rochester'. Just as Jock gifted Pym with an edition of Rochester's poems, so too does Dr Parnell for Belinda's twenty-first birthday. Belinda covers up the filthy *Poems on Several Occasions* when the superintendent of the English Reading Room comes past her desk. And Mr Mold makes lewd jokes: 'fancy ordering dull things like the *Ormulum* when the Earl of Rochester's *Poems on Several Occasions* was in the library'.[9]

Pym knew how much Jock and Henry would enjoy such jokes. And they did. Jock was particularly impressed by the way she wove in literary quotations: 'I think you have a genius for quotation which has probably never been equalled. Not only have you put the culture you acquired here to an extremely effective use, you have also permanently increased your readers' knowledge of English Literature.'[10] As Jock was well aware, Pym's novel was much more than a light-hearted experiment in making her friends laugh. It was a carefully crafted and plotted attempt to be taken seriously as a writer.

Later Pym would tone down some of Belinda's quirky traits, but even in this first version, she is clear-eyed about her heroine's hopeless love for Henry: 'Belinda had always found it most convenient to go on loving the people and the things she had loved at the age of twenty or thereabouts. It had become a habit with her.' The heroine's loyalty to the Archdeacon is as much about her love of her Oxford days, of which he is symbolic. Older and wiser, she sees how difficult her life would have been as his wife and she is content to adore him from afar, to bask in the memory of their gilded youth and to darn his socks: 'Belinda contemplated the Archdeacon, but with the eye of the practised knitter rather than that of the doting lover.' Middle-aged Belinda has finally discovered that it is possible for the heart to become 'the convert of the head'. But there is a poignant sense of loss and waste, a theme that would become Pym's hallmark: 'She had bought the wool, so to speak, and so she must complete the work.'[11]

CHAPTER IX

In which Miss Pym returns to Oxford to take her BA Degree

Life in Shropshire continued to be dull and monotonous and Pym found it difficult to write her diary because 'Nothing happens'. She had heard from Jock that Henry seemed to be settling into his new life in Finland. He had fallen in love with a woman who looked like Greta Garbo.

Pym returned to Oxford in November to receive her Bachelor of Arts degree. The ceremony was 'rather boring', but she was happy to see her old friends. Henry had sent a letter of congratulations. She drew closer to Jock – 'I almost fell in love with JRL – really – and simply adore his company.' She deeply appreciated how seriously he was taking her literary vocation. He sent her detailed criticism: 'Literary allusions: Some cutting is essential . . . and each character could have his *leit-motifs* I daresay.'[1]

Pym decided that she would wait in Oxford for Henry, who was due back for Christmas. She wanted to test her feelings for him and decided that any misery it might cost was probably worth it. When he finally arrived, he greeted her with a derisive laugh and said he was glad to see her. But it was not a happy evening and she ended the night in tears. It appears that she stayed the night with Henry. In the morning things were calmer. 'The intense misery of the night before had given way to a state of "calm of mind, all passion spent"' (her quotation of the final line of Milton's *Samson Agonistes* makes one wonder whether they had read it naked in bed again). Henry drove her down the Banbury Road and on to the station, but there was no parting kiss ('*und keine kuss*', as her diary has it). Pym told herself to live in the present and to contemplate a life without Henry. She was also mindful that he had brought her many friends. Her thoughts turned to the spring of 1933 and the 'divine madness' that afflicted 'the poor Sandra'. She believed that Henry had something special that nobody else had, but then rebuked herself: 'What platitudes for a genius to write! *Die arme Pymchen*' (The Poor Pym).[2]

———

Back at Morda Lodge for Christmas, Barbara reflected that the year had, on the whole, been happy. On 1 January 1935, she awoke from a vivid dream in which Henry was married to a Finn who was 'not beautiful but thin'. They had kissed in the dream and Henry was kind. As she admitted to herself, it was really Jock she missed, with his conversation and good company, 'but I am still enslaved by Henry's baser charms'.[3]

Jock sent regular, gossipy letters. Sensitive to the cold, he complained about the poor heating in the Bodleian and the incessant draughts. He bought a leather jacket to keep himself warm. Much of this made its way into Pym's book. Jock kept her up to date with Henry's news and amused her with 'gay gossip' about a young boy working at the library (just out of high school) whom a French journalist had tried to seduce.[4]

By March, Pym was again in Oxford, visiting friends and her sister Hilary. She sat in Jock's flat, wrapped in Henry's old grey overcoat, and was flooded with memories. The atmosphere of the flat made her yearn for Henry, but she comforted herself with the thought that she would soon be back in her beloved Germany.

CHAPTER X

In which our Heroine goes to Germany for the third time and sleeps with her Nazi

That spring, 1935, Nancy Mitford published a comic novel, *Wigs on the Green*, much to the annoyance and anger of her family. It was a merciless satire of fascism. Captain Jack of the Union Jackshirts was a parody of Diana Mitford's lover, Oswald Mosley, leader of the British Union of Fascists. The heroine, Eugenia Malmains, was modelled on her sister, Unity. Standing on an overturned washtub on the village green, she harangues the local yokels with her fascist declamations:

'Britons, awake! Arise! Oh, British lion! . . . The Union Jack Movement is a youth movement,' Eugenia cried passionately, 'we are tired of the old . . . We see nothing admirable in that debating society of aged and corrupt men called Parliament which muddles our great empire into wars or treaties . . .'

At this point a very old lady came up to the crowd . . .

'Eugenia, my child,' she said brokenly, 'do get off that tub . . . Oh! When her ladyship hears of this I don't know what will happen.'

'Go away Nanny,' said Eugenia.[1]

It was the type of parody that Pym loved. Unity was a fixture around Oxford, where she was often to be seen at the head-quarters of the British Union of Fascists in St Edward's Street. Unmissable, this six-foot girl with the mesmerising blue eyes would sometimes appear with her pet rat, Ratular, perched on her shoulder. She was a school friend of Julia Pakenham, whom Pym knew. Pym mentions Unity Mitford in her journals, though it is unclear whether they met, either in England or in Germany.

By 1935, everyone knew who Unity was. She had managed to insinuate herself into Hitler's inner circle. He was transfixed by the Aryan blonde, who was a cousin of Winston Churchill, who was conceived in Swastika and whose name was Unity Valkyrie. Later, Unity's sister, Diana, was married in Goebbels's house, with Hitler as guest as honour.

In April, Pym returned to Germany with the NUS. It was a smooth crossing during which she devoured a picnic of ham sandwiches, apples and chocolate. Later she sipped coffee laced with brandy and thought about who she would see from her previous trip. By the time the party reached Cologne, Pym was tired but excited. She noted that at the border the guards only asked to see passports and money, not 'books and papers as last time'. Suddenly, she spotted Hanns. Delighted to see a familiar face, they chatted in German, though there was no sign of Friedbert. It was not long, however, before Glück heard that she was back in Germany. Her diary records: 'Friedbert was angelic to me. Such kindness as his one can never forget.'[2]

Pym was certainly not the only young woman at this time to be swayed by a handsome Nazi in black uniform and leather boots: to her he was a symbol of the country that she had come to love. Her feelings were shaped by the romance of the days spent together, gazing by moonlight at the Hohenzollernbrüke (the famous bridge crossing the Rhine) and cocktails ('zwei Manhattans') at the Excelsior, Cologne's five-star hotel with its view of the magnificent twin-spired Gothic cathedral. Pym also remembered vividly an 'evening of love' at 52 Volksgarten-strasse, possibly Friedbert's digs, close to the beautiful public park in Cologne. She had rubbed his Nivea cream on her arm in order to remember the smell of him. By now, it seems, their relationship had become physical. But her feelings were complicated: 'for all these things I loved him and yet I hardly knew him as a person and didn't at all agree with his National Socialism'.[3]

When Pym returned home, Glück was much on her mind. She poured out her feelings in her diary, wondering whether she was really in love with Friedbert, or whether it was 'mostly glamour. His being a foreigner – the little Americanisms in his speech like "terribly" and the way he said "Barbara".'[4]

After Cologne, Pym began reading a lot of German poetry. She also read another novel by Lion Feuchtwanger. *The Oppermanns* details a series of events that take place between November 1932 and the late summer of 1933. A bourgeois Jewish family, the Oppermanns, are confronted with the horrifying realities of Hitler's Germany. They lose their business, their home and their friends, and a son, who commits suicide. There are many shocking scenes, such as when the hero, Edgar Oppermann, a celebrated surgeon who has just successfully operated on an Aryan man, is intercepted by two Nazi thugs who have him removed from the hospital. They force their way into the operating theatre, where the patient is recovering and stamp a message on the man's bandages: 'I have been shameless enough to allow myself to be treated by a Jew.'[5] The family manage to escape Germany, but Edgar returns only to be sent to a concentration camp. He is stripped, shaved and compelled to wear striped prison uniform. Along with the other Jewish intellectuals in the camp, he is beaten and humiliated. The inmates are forced to listen to the 'Horst-Wessel Lied' and are 'educated' into Nazism: 'They marched into the courtyard. The prisoners stood herded together, hundreds of them, in their grotesque, striped clothing. The swastika banner was unfurled. They saluted it in the ancient Roman fashion, shouting "Heil Hitler".'[6]

The novel is semi-autobiographical: like the hero, Lion Feuchtwanger managed to escape to the south of France. The book was banned by the Nazi party and burned. As well as depicting Nazi brutality, it explores those in denial, who refuse to see the danger that is soon to engulf them: 'Their homeland, their Germany had proved false to them. For centuries they had felt secure in that homeland and now everything was suddenly crumbling to bits . . . neighbour spied on neighbour, son on father, friend on friend.'[7]

Pym left no record of her opinion of the book. Her trip to Cologne had reawakened her interest in the German language and she was determined to return in August, despite any misgivings she may have had about Nazi brutality towards Jews.

In June, Unity Mitford sent shock waves throughout England by writing an open letter to the notorious propaganda paper of Julius Streicher, *Der Stürmer*, in which she made no bones about her anti-Semitism: 'I have lived in Munich for a year and read *Der Stürmer* every week . . . The English have no notion of the Jewish danger . . . England for the English! Out with the Jews! . . . please publish my name in full . . . I want everyone to know I'm a Jew hater.'[8] This intervention was widely covered in the British press under headlines such as 'The Girl Who Adores Hitler' and 'Peer's Daughter is Jew Hater'. The newspapers loved to accompany their reports with photographs of Unity, clad in her black shirt, giving the Nazi salute. Unity's parents were furious, with her father, Lord Redesdale, describing the Nazis as a 'murderous gang of pests'. But they still did not prevent her from travelling to Germany and later they visited and met with Hitler, deeply impressed by the way he had united the country and was opposing communism.

Pym was no Unity-style fanatic and she was doing everything she could to educate herself about Germany. But she was also ignoring warnings from her friends about the wisdom of her infatuation with Friedbert. In the manner of Nancy Mitford's *Wigs on the Green*, she began to insert Nazi parodies into her novel. She also wove in her memories of her highly romanticised view of Nazi Germany, something she would later deeply regret.

For now, Pym turned a deaf ear to the alarm bells. She returned to England and headed back to Oxford where she knew Henry was expected, as he was signed up for a teaching course. Jock told her that Henry was dangling two Finnish girlfriends, including the one who looked like Greta Garbo. She was called Brita; the other was a woman called Elsie Godenhjelm. Pym was determined to see for herself. Despite her 'evening of love' with Friedbert, she still wasn't quite ready to give up on Henry.

CHAPTER XI

An Untoward Incident on the River

Pym wandered the streets of Oxford in the hope of seeing Henry. Luck was on her side. After an absence of five months, he seemed genuinely pleased to see her and teased her about her pink polished toenails, telling her to hide them as much as possible, preferably under a table. This she proceeded to do when he took her to Fuller's for coffee.

Jock had duly reported back to Pym that Brita was 'vulgar, coarse and plain', and was not in the least like Greta Garbo, as Henry had led them to believe. He did not mention Elsie.

Henry was being pleasant. It seems that he had been taken aback by Pym's novel and was beginning to see her in a different light. That evening, in his flat, he embraced her: 'He took me in his arms, called me darling and kissed me three times sensuously and passionately, during which I experienced again all the love I have ever felt for him. "There is no more future, there is no more past".'[1]

Later they went out to dinner with Jock, just like old times. The boys bickered in their usual manner. This time it was about Jock leaving Oxford and cutting himself off from it entirely. Pym noted that Jock paid for dinner. Henry was not known for his generosity and he had the impudence to tease her for her greediness: 'It's no use looking at those strawberries Pym. You won't get any.' She had actually been contemplating a lobster. Back at the flat, Pym sat on Henry's knee, in her suspenders, which she remarked loudly was 'so sordid'. Jock, as ever, was the willing audience and played 'Holy, Holy Holy' on his recorder. 'A strange combination of circumstances,' she noted. 'I suppose I imagine that I must be more interesting and intelligent than the other unwanted lovers of this world.'[2]

The relationship with Henry was back on, but he was still evasive whenever she pressed him to commit. 'I want so much to know how things *really* are between us.'[3] She agonised over whether or not she could be happy just being friends or hold out some hope for romantic love, even marriage. Barnicot told her that there was no hope at all and friendship would be of no use. But she comforted herself with the thought of her novel, which she believed connected them:

> I don't mind being part of the furniture of his background or even hanging over him like a gloomy cloud, as he said at tea one day. He himself has admitted that I have a special place in the little world he has built for himself and of which presumably J is the centre. And I suppose too that he feels this is so in the novel where I have brought us all together in our later years.[4]

However, her novel had shown Henry that she had read his character acutely and that she was certainly not blind to his many faults.

Pym was rudderless and still in love with her world at Oxford, even though so many of her set had moved on. 'But at the present moment it seems as if this world is falling to pieces – so what becomes of me then?' She developed a German persona. On her dyed blonde hair, she wore a Tyrolean hat ('it looked like a kind of parson's hat or dish'), even to the library. She peppered her words with German phrases and expressions, such as '*selbstverständlich*' instead of 'of course'. She would quote German poetry and sing loudly the 'Horst Wessel Lied'. Her favourite wine was Liebfraumilch and she carried around her weekly copy of *Die Woche*. By now, she was fluent in German. Jock and Henry seemed to find her antics hilarious, not yet seeing where it was leading.

There was a nasty incident with Henry on the river. Pym recorded the event carefully in her diary. Henry, Pym, Barnicot and Jock went on the Cherwell to a riverside pub, the Victoria Arms. It nestled on the edge of Marston village and had a foot ferry for passengers. Jock left by the foot ferry, leaving Henry and Pym alone together, where Henry proceeded to get very drunk. They were sitting next to a group of male undergraduates, one of whom made a pass at Henry. He repeatedly asked Henry to sleep with him and, Pym reported, Henry 'rather getting the worse of it in the wit combat, diverted attention to me'. As she wryly commented: 'From then on I was for it.'[5] Henry told the boys that Barbara was German and she played along with it, with none of them suspecting she was English. One of the young men was Jewish.

They left the pub with the undergraduates – Henry by now exceedingly drunk – and decided that it would be a good joke to put Barbara in the punt that belonged to the young men. When she resisted one of the other men helped Henry to deposit her in the boat. Barnicot, she noted, 'was silent'. At first she was enjoying herself, but as the punt, by now filled with a gang of drunken male strangers, moved away, she began to panic. She was far from her own group and the punt began to fill with water. She kept up the deception of being German to the bitter end, as she was far too embarrassed to admit that she was English and had once been an Oxford student: 'I should have felt very much ashamed of myself but I wasn't really, especially as it was all H's fault.' The five men then forced her to kiss them all, 'and the Jew boy (who was the leader) tickled my bare legs somewhat unpleasantly I thought'. Eventually, Pym was rescued and taken to Jock's flat. She felt that she ought to have been more angry with Henry for acting like a 'complete cad'. Jock pretended to be shocked, but Pym thought that he was secretly amused. Her humiliation complete, she should have stormed out or remonstrated with Henry, as she once might have done, but her behaviour was strange. 'I was feeling very loving to him and sprawled all over him on the sofa and kissed him as much as I could.'[6]

Later, as if ashamed for his conduct, Henry kissed her goodnight and in the morning she went back to his flat and spent a lazy, sleepy morning with him. That day he asked her to go with him to Basingstoke to pick up a car. They took the train together, smoking Finnish cigarettes. She marvelled at the thought that she was together with Henry on a train. 'The most ordinary things done with someone one loves are full of new significance that they never have otherwise.' Catching a glimpse of their reflections in a shop window, she thought that she and Henry looked like two comic characters out of a musical comedy – Barbara wearing her German hat and Henry a blue one: 'There's always something faintly ludicrous about Henry's hat with him inside it.'[7]

At tea, Henry told her that if he were rich, he would buy her a cottage in the country, but no wireless; he disliked the wireless. Pym also insisted on an establishment in Oxford. For once, they seemed to be getting on very well. She loved driving back to Oxford with him in the Bentley, with the roof off, but when it started to rain, they stopped to put the roof on and she hurt her finger. Henry made a fuss of it: 'It was nice to be poor Pymed at intervals.' She could not help but be transfixed by his beauty: 'I found myself wanting to gaze at Henry's divine profile,

particularly those lovely hollows in his cheeks which delight me
so.'

In the evening, Pym went riding with Henry, Jock and
Barnicot in the Bentley, but Henry's good humour had worn
off. He told her that he was bored with her and made nasty
comments in response to whatever she said. Barnicot sat Pym
down to tell her once more that there was no hope at all as far
as Henry was concerned. He advised her to be a bit rougher
with him. Then, she and Henry went to the Botanical Gardens,
where she chased him around with a stick. Later, they had a
meal at the Union and Henry was cruel about her crooked teeth,
'which always makes me unhappy'.[8]

Pym, like many would-be-writers, usually wrote with an eye
to posterity and a view of her future biographers: 'Now I've seen
Henry again I must make myself write. Otherwise his biographers
(or mine) will be disappointed at the break in the otherwise
continuous account of my acquaintance with him.'[9] Still uncertain and unhappy about the state of their relationship, she headed
back to Germany, where she was sure of receiving better treatment at the hands of her blackshirt boyfriend.

CHAPTER XII

'An English Gentlewoman can never come to any Harm'

Pym left no record of her trip to Germany and Budapest of the summer of 1935, though there are later references to her love for Budapest: her unfinished novel *Adam and Cassandra* is partly set there. On 3 August, Rupert Gleadow wrote telling her how his 'heart leapt up when I beheld your writing'. He felt jealous, he said, that she had travelled to the Hungarian capital: 'I've been wanting to go there for some time . . . you seem to have reached a very pleasant stage, travelling about promiscuously to Cologne and Budapest and various other places and as you are a woman and have no work to worry about I suppose you'll go on doing so.' Pym had clearly seen Friedbert, telling Rupert that she was in love with Glück and with Henry. Rupert insisted that it was simply not 'possible to truly give your heart to two people'. He remained deeply concerned about her interest in Nazi men. He warned her again: 'And of course one can NOT under any circumstances love a *real* Nazi. Yours I'm sure must only be a pretence. The real ones (and I've been arrested by them!) are all sadists and keep their women brutally in order.'[1]

Later, Henry told Pym that he did not think Friedbert was a true Nazi and that he would recant. Pym was not convinced.

Glück was becoming closer to Hitler and was now involved with the organisation of the 1936 Summer Olympics. In *Some Tame Gazelle*, Helmuth (closely based on Friedbert) gives Belinda a framed photo of himself 'chatting with the Führer in Berlin'. It seems possible that Pym began to consider an engagement to Friedbert Glück, a detail she used for her novel, which she finished that summer of 1935. Her mother was, not surprisingly, dead set against it.

Back home in Shropshire, Pym invited Henry, Jock and Barnicot to stay. It was an emotional visit, as Pym knew that Henry was leaving for Finland on 11 September. Henry, she recorded, was 'absolutely at his best'. He was wearing a grey flannel suit, a bright blue silk shirt with a darker blue tie and blue socks.

> He looked beautiful and took me in his arms in the bathroom and in the bedroom. He wanted me to return to Oxford with them so that we might do again those things we used to do when I was an undergraduate and he a graduate living in 86b Banbury Road. I wanted it too, but I felt somehow that were I with him like that again, I should not be content with half measures.[2]

She wanted much more than to be his sexual plaything. 'So it is better that I remain here, thinking lovingly of him, with more real fondness than before.'[3]

A photograph dating from that time shows the genuine affection between the group, as they sit in deckchairs in the garden of Morda Lodge. Pym, looking girlish and pretty in a white summer dress with bows, gazes adoringly at handsome Henry, who lights her cigarette.

When they left, Pym focused her efforts on her writing life. Although she disliked the genre, she wrote two short stories, believing that it was a useful stepping stone to getting published. Titled 'Unpast Alps' and 'They Never Write', she sent them to the *London Mercury*. She was also beginning to think about a plot for a new novel: 'Possibly another me, in the character of an undergraduate this time!'[4]

She was making a concerted effort to be more positive – cleaning her room, writing letters, darning socks, and pulling up some 'aggressively dead' zinnias in the garden: 'Last sad signs of summer.'[5] And she was reading a lot. Her current novel was Dorothy L. Sayers's *Gaudy Night*, a murder mystery set in an all-female Oxford college. Inevitably, it made her think of her St Hilda's. 'Pleasure and pain in an agreeable mixture. That's what I think of when I think of Oxford and my days at St Hilda's.'[6]

Jock wrote thanking her for the wonderful stay. He told her that he'd met Elsie, who was very nice and pretty and adored Henry. He was sure that Henry would break her heart. Brita, he confirmed, was 'hideous'. As ever, Jock urged her to find consolation in her writing.

By the end of the summer, Pym had finished her novel about Belinda and Harriet. She had the manuscript, divided into two volumes, 'nicely bound in soft yellow covers and green backs', receiving it back on Armistice Day. She was still unsure about the title, torn between 'Some Tame Gazelle' and 'Some Sad Turtle' – 'But somehow it reminds me rather too much of turtle soup . . . I am alternately cheerful and depressed about it.'[7]

CHAPTER XIII

Omit the Nazis

Barbara was twenty-four years old, studying in Munich and had obtained a Nazi soldier for a boyfriend, whom she described as 'absolutely moulded into his uniform'. He was handsome, with 'closely cut chestnut hair, a straight little face, white teeth and a darling, wide smile. His cap tilted over one of his green eyes was a sight.' He was sporty and strong: 'very sensitive, very amusing, very affectionate, could sing and play the guitar beautifully, was an expert shot and skier'. He was a dead ringer for Friedbert Glück, but his name was Karl Maier. His American girlfriend, Barbara Rucker, found him 'fascinating'. 'Karl was a typical soldier of the very best kind – quick, clean, brave, proud and believed infinitely that Germany should be *wieder gross und stark* [once more big and strong]. He didn't want war, but said if it came he'd fight until he was killed.'[1]

Barbara Rucker, who hailed from Cambridge, Massachusetts, where her grandfather had been president of the Massachusetts Institute of Technology, was a music scholar, but interested in politics. Initially she had been sympathetic towards the Nazis: 'At first one does incline to be, particularly when one sees how relatively more secure and hopeful the people feel.' But she soon realised her mistake: 'Slowly but surely I've grown to be a great

enemy of National Socialism.' She tasked Karl on the Jewish
question and he admitted that he knew some nice Jews and that
in theory communism had some good ideas. As the historian
Julia Boyd says: 'It is a curiously touching portrait and a reminder
that in 1936 not every young German wore a uniform to beat
up the Jews.'[2] A year later, Barbara wrote to her sister to say
that she had had an encounter with Julius Streicher and that
any illusions she had about Nazi achievements had been
destroyed. She was 'shaking with anger' at hearing his 'unbeliev-
able lies':

> That there's no such thing as a decent Jew in the world, that
> they all have a certain bacillus in their blood which gives diseases
> to 'white' people; that they caused the world war, the downfall
> of Rome and heaven knows what else . . . I really looked
> desperately around the room for one sane person who wasn't
> believing it all – but with the exception of Klaus, who, although
> a National Socialist, was also disgusted, they were all hanging
> on his words.[3]

By the end of 1936, the rabid anti-Semitism of Nazi Germany
should have been apparent to everybody. Yet there was a stubborn trait in Barbara Pym and a refusal to believe that Friedbert
was capable of being cruel. She could not separate him from
his beliefs.

Jock, who had read Pym's novel in instalments, offering useful
advice and criticism, had one serious objection: 'Omit the Nazis.'[4]
Eventually, Pym acceded to his wish. That the Nazis were ever
included might come as a surprise to readers of the published
edition of Some Tame Gazelle. But the typed version in its
original green binding is perfectly preserved in the Bodleian.

With the benefit of hindsight, it is easy to judge. Pym was
possibly blinded to the true nature of Nazism by her love affair

with Germany: she was drawn to the language, to the magical and romantic landscapes and the poetry of the great German writers. Friedbert's adoration came at a time when Pym was badly damaged by Henry Harvey's callous behaviour. Nevertheless, friends and family (in particular her sister Hilary, who was vehemently anti-Nazi) repeatedly warned Pym about her relationship with a blackshirt who just so happened to be a rising star in the Nazi party. There were no invitations issued to Friedbert to come and visit Shropshire.

Pym felt herself to be in love with Friedbert and fascinated by modern Germany: in the Ur-*Tame Gazelle* Belinda honestly admits that her interest in Nazi politics is due entirely to her infatuation with Helmuth. Pym was also, at some level, trying to hurt Henry and to show that she could be adored by another man. Henry certainly responded to women who played hard to get and who aroused his jealousy.

Pym continued to pour out her love for Germany and for Friedbert in her novel. Belinda, now in middle age, is a romantic who frequently lapses into daydreams about her days in Germany. Like Pym, she spends time in Cologne as a student. She is blonde and Aryan, speaks German, loves German poets and, in her youth, had a penchant for Nazi stormtroopers:

> Liebfraumilch always reminded Belinda of the Rhineland, which she had visited in the spring just before she was twenty-one. The Nazis had been young and arrogant then and she had hardly known which she liked best, Kurt or Helmuth. Although it had been April she could not help thinking of Heine's 'Im wunder-schönen Monat Mai' as being symbolic of her first visit to Germany.[5]

In Pym's imagined world, set thirty years in the future, the Nazis are now exiled to Africa, following a revolution in the 1950s.

There has been no world war. How could she have anticipated such a war in 1935? Kind Belinda knits socks and vests, not for her boyfriends, but for the 'poor Nazis'. She insists on using expensive wool, 'but she always excused herself by saying that after all the Nazis were rather *special* people. Helmut had been a Nazi.'

Though Belinda is still in love with Henry the Archdeacon, she lives mainly in the past.

'Dear Helmuth,' she murmured, rolling her eyes . . . gently stroking the unfinished vest. A set of confused German memories now came into her mind. She saw herself at Bonn, – or had it been Königswinter? – walking along the narrow streets with Helmuth, while he explained the meaning of *Dampfschifffahrt*. And a band was playing 'Warum kuszt mich dein Mund so heiss?' Or the 'Horst Wessel Lied'. One of the two; it didn't really matter now, for after the terrible revolution of the nineteen fifties and all the dear Nazis in exile in Africa, things like that were of no importance. What a good thing Belinda had taken her good mother's advice and had not become engaged to Helmuth! Otherwise she would probably have been in Africa now and one heard such *dreadful* things.

Whereas Archdeacon Henry is selfish and rude and barely notices Belinda, 'Dear Helmuth had been most appreciative'. Pym uses the detail from her Oxford diary – when Henry described her as being 'like something off a chocolate box or the cover of *Die Woche*. Belinda at twenty-one had thought all this rather delightful, although she knew that it was not intended as a compliment and she had always rejoiced in being blonde and Aryan.' Belinda now says, 'Of course' – whereas in her youth, she would say '*selbstverständlich*'. Page after page is filled with Belinda/Barbara's memories:

Belinda's thoughts began to wander from Sunday's joint to the happy times she had spent in Germany. Through a blur of sentimental memories she saw herself in Berlin (or had it been Hamburg) in a place where they drank a lot of beer and stood on the table and danced. And dear Helmuth had told her how important it was that one should be a good leader, like the Führer.

Expecting the new curate to visit, Belinda considers wearing her swastika: 'She was wondering whether to wear her little swastika brooch or not. Dear Helmuth had always been so pleased at this sign of presumable sympathy with the Nationalist Socialist party.' In her house, on her mantelpiece, Belinda proudly displays a framed photograph of dear Helmuth, 'chatting with the Führer in Berlin. She kept this for sentimental reasons and pointed it out to visitors. "You can understand how I feel about these poor Nazis" she would say.'

The Archdeacon is compared with Hitler. His wife Agatha has allowed moths to spoil his suit and Henry leans out of the window to rant, as Hitler leaned out of the balcony in the Rathaus:

The voice went on calling. It seemed that the moths had got into his grey suit and why had Agatha been so grossly neglectful to let this happen? The tirade was audible to anyone in the garden or in the road beyond.

It was like the Führer's speech in Hamburg, thought Belinda, although the Führer had been more important than poor Henry and what he said had been of significance to a whole country.

In Pym's fictional world, it is Hilary/Harriet who is the voice of reason, urging Belinda to forget about the Nazis. Harriet has never been to Germany and dislikes people 'reminiscing about how lovely the Swastika flags looked in the street'. In a long scene, later deleted, a German couple, now in exile, appear at the village. Harriet is horrified, whereas Belinda is thrilled:

> But of course Belinda felt differently. How delightful it would be to see if she could still speak German! How she would enjoy remembering with them their lamented Führer! Why they might even have known dear Helmuth or dear Kurt, though perhaps that was rather too much to expect.

Belinda thinks that the refugee 'Herr Niersteiner' looks like one of the Nazi leaders:

> It was too late in the day to say *haben Sie gut geschlafen*, so she contented herself with nodding pleasantly from time to time, taking in the full details of their appearance. Herr Niersteiner was a stout man of middle age, rather like General Goering, or was it Goebbels? The names were so alike that Belinda always muddled them up. He was wearing a brown shirt which looked like a relic of his Nazi days, if a shirt can be expected to last twenty years.

On and on the references go. Belinda breaking into German songs; Helmuth's green hat (like Friedbert's); the beer garden in Königswinter where they had that lovely drink; the Hohen-zollernbrücke in the moonlight; Helmuth's dislike of Heine.

> 'Well I thought a young girl in love if she read German at all would surely be fond of Heine,' said Belinda. 'Or at least *some* poetry. But especially Heine, although dear Helmuth didn't really like me to read him,' she mused rather sadly.
> 'Oh, of course he wrote against Hitler, didn't he?' said Harriet complacently.

'Oh no dear,' replied Belinda in a shocked voice, 'Heine was a long time before the Führer. I don't quite know *why* dear Helmuth didn't like him. I think he said things against Germany,' she murmured vaguely. And anyway, she thought, I expect Helmuth wouldn't have approved of *Jenes Land der Wonne, Das seh' ich oft im traume*. Such things didn't exist in Nazi Germany and he had always disliked anything that was too *romantisch*.

Heine was not only Jewish, but also a pioneering left-wing political radical who deeply influenced Karl Marx (and famously wrote 'where they burn books, they will ultimately burn people as well'): little wonder that Friedbert was sceptical.

In Belinda's middle age she wonders what has happened to Helmuth. 'It would be so very nice to send a sum of money sufficient to keep him in beer and *heisse wurstchen* all his life. Or perhaps he was dead. She hated to think about that, she who had once been his *liebe kleine Belinda*.'

Jock, who knew and understood that Pym's novel was a love letter not only to Henry, but also to Friedbert, was wise in advising her to 'harden her heart' and to omit the Nazis. Nancy Mitford later regretted *Wigs on the Green* and refused to let it be reissued; satirising Nazis was no longer a mere tease. Pym was not alone, during the thirties, in treating the Nazis as a bit of a joke. At the time, she did not take Jock's advice. But when *Some Tame Gazelle* was finally published after the war, in 1950, every single reference to Germany and the Nazi party was deleted.

CHAPTER XIV

Pymska

With thoughts of Henry in Finland, Pym began to learn Finnish and created a new persona. She was to be known as Pymska. She kept herself busy in Shropshire, learning to drive and sending *Some Tame Gazelle* to Chatto & Windus. Her thoughts were turning to her new novel, *Adam and Cassandra*, which would reflect her love for Budapest.

Jock was regularly in touch. He was still living in 'North Oxford' with his brother, Donald, but seriously contemplating a life abroad, possibly Cairo. Jock and Don were devoted to their landlady, Mrs Trew. They had witnessed a shocking turn of events, which had troubled them deeply. Mrs Trew was a rather lonely and sad figure, widowed and devoted to her only daughter, Christine. Whilst Christine was at Somerville College, Oxford, she met an aristocrat who was at Christ Church. His name was Edward Pakenham (brother of Julia, whom Pym knew). They married, Christine thus becoming the Countess of Longford. Christine established herself as a novelist and a play-wright and she and her husband set up a theatre company. They lived in Pakenham Hall Castle in County Westmeath in Ireland, where they had country house weekends with writers such as Evelyn Waugh and John Betjeman. However, Christine cruelly neglected her mother because she was ashamed of her lowly origins.

Mrs Trew's deepest fear was to die in a workhouse. When she fell ill, her daughter refused to take care of her and did indeed leave her to die in a former workhouse in Oxford, now a public assistance institution, but to all intents and purposes still a workhouse, where vagrants and prostitutes were left to die.[1] Don and Jock, who visited her regularly, could never forgive the heartlessness of Christine Pakenham. One day, Jock vowed, he would write the story and wreak his revenge. He told Pym all about the tragedy.

Pym also heard from Jock that Henry was returning to Oxford in December, as he had the year before. This time she vowed to keep away. A few days later, she changed her mind and packed for Oxford. The city seemed changed, with nobody she knew in her old haunts, Elliston's, the Bodleian, Cornmarket. Most of her friends were long gone, 'everywhere is full of strange, young faces'. She had dinner with Jock and they looked at photographs of Henry in his photo album. Pym was surprised, as Jock's relationship with Henry had fragmented over the years: 'I was so moved that my eyes filled with tears, whether from love, memories of the past, regret of the present or anticipation of the future I don't know.'[2]

Oxford was full of ghosts. Barbara dressed in her new guise of Pymska, a more sophisticated person than Sandra. She wore a turquoise dress, a black fur cape and high heels. When she called on John Barnicot he was impressed that she looked so elegant. His new friend, Meurig Davies, called in and they all sat together in the dark, listening to music from Budapest on the gramophone – 'which always makes me a little melancholy' – and sharing stories of unrequited love: 'Mr B in love with Honor, Meurig with Ann Sitwell and Pymska with Henry.'[3]

In December, Pym heard that Chatto had rejected her novel.

She was comforted by Barnicot and Jock. Five days before Christmas Day, she heard that the *London Mercury* had rejected her short stories, but 'in the bustle of Christmas shopping I seemed not to care overmuch'.[4] She looked forward to 'cutting and improving' her novel and took heart that the editor at Chatto said kind words: 'I had a style which is a pleasure to read.' Lonely as she was, she also felt 'there is a world elsewhere'. Returning home to Shropshire for Christmas seemed a time for reflection. She felt that every time she went back to Oxford, it seemed to be a little sadder: 'A slow wrenching away indeed.'[5]

CHAPTER XV

In which Pymska is involved in a Tragic Accident

'The King died tonight at 11.55 pm. It was a very peaceful ending,' wrote Pym on Monday 20 January 1936. It snowed heavily in Shropshire and the Pym family huddled around the wireless to hear the popular Prince of Wales being proclaimed as King Edward VIII.

Barbara had 'vivid and lovely' dreams about Friedbert. She wrote to Jock to say that she was enjoying the snow: 'Everything looks romantic. One only wants Friedbert and his fine pair of skis for everything to be perfect.'[1] They exchanged news about the fate of their respective novels. He said it was a great pity that they both failed to get recognition. 'You are undoubtedly "the finest comic writer of the age", though still, perhaps a little too diffuse.' Jock, as always, read attentively: 'I am inclined to think that a great deal of the blackberry episode might be cut short – the interest seems to me to flag a little just there.' He also advised her to cut all the personal references and jokes and to be more general about Oxford and the Bodleian. 'More disguise – Bodley may be Bletchley University, perhaps.' He also tried once again: 'Omit the Nazis.'[2]

There were exchanges of news and book recommendations.

The truth of the matter was that Jock and Pym had far more in common than Henry and Pym. Jock had become fascinated by the novels of Ivy Compton-Burnett and thought she was a better novelist than Henry James. Pym vowed to give her another go and in time would become just as devoted to her novels as Jock. He, meanwhile, confirmed that Henry had developed a new respect for Pym since reading her book, but knowing that she was still hurt by him he did his best to present his friend in the worst possible light, hoping that it would alleviate some of Pym's suffering. He wrote witty, sometimes malicious letters that would have made Barbara laugh out loud: Henry being chased by an angry bull; boring on about Wordsworth and the Lake District; roasting mutton 'in the Finnish way', which involved pouring hot coffee over the meat ('it makes no appreciable difference', he noted drily). Jock composed and sent hilarious epic poems addressed to 'Cassandra', urging her to forget Lorenzo. 'In Oswestry, as once on the Ilian plain,/ Apollo woo'd Cassandra . . . The gaunt Archdeacon stalks into our view.'[3] They both carried on the pretence that one day Henry would come round and marry her. He joked about their future children, Cassandra Barbara Crampton Harvey and Lorenzo Gabriel. Jock and Pym began what would be a long-cherished habit of referring to Harvey as 'poor Henry' and ridiculing his oft-used phrase 'remarkably fine'. It was affectionate teasing, though Jock's attitude towards Henry would harden over the years. He told Pym that Henry would 'surely wear out more than one wife'.[4]

Pym wrote to Henry, telling him that her novel had been rejected and that she needed to shorten it, though she would always keep the full original version in its two volumes: 'If you can't have Pymska in Oxford, you can at least have her novel, which you will like much better as it doesn't have to be kissed, or taken out to dinner, or to Basingstoke.'[5] She told Henry that she was now at a stage in her life where she was looking for a suitable husband. She also told him that she was making a serious attempt to become an author.

At Oxford that winter, Pym met a man called Brian Mitchell who was very keen on her and, according to her sister, proposed marriage. She rejected Brian, as she had rejected Harry Harker. She could see the advantages of a single life and so far only Friedbert had come close to expunging Henry's memory.

Jock returned her novel with his latest edit. She had decided to follow his advice and 'cut out the Nazis', adding 'lately I've been thinking the story would be better without them and I don't think I was ever very keen on them'. She thanked him and told him that her father was buying her a much-needed portable typewriter. She was deeply grateful to Jock: 'If the book is published your name should appear with mine as joint authors I think.' Jock replied that she was 'wise to remove the Nazis'. He had also suggested that she cut the passage about 'Belinda and Henry's trip to Basingstoke, Pusey street etc'. Pym confessed that she had written this because she was upset with Henry: 'All this part was written in a wave of anger against Henry, because he told Mr B that I was boring and always agreed with everything he said. It is to be omitted.'[6]

In late January, Pym and her mother were involved in a serious car accident. Irena was driving when two motorcycles came roaring round the corner. There was a head-on collision, hurling the bikers into a hedge. Barbara and Irena were only bruised, but when they extricated themselves from the car, which was a write-off, they saw two young men covered in blood and lying unconscious on the road, their motorcycles beside them. An ambulance was called and a crowd gathered round, though there had been no witnesses to the accident. The motorcyclists both had fractured skulls – helmets were not usually worn in those days; one died as soon as he reached hospital, the other was in a critical condition.

There was to be an inquest, though it seemed clear that it was the fault of the motorcyclists. Pym appeared to be remarkably calm about it all – almost indifferent to the gravity of the situation:

> If it hadn't been so tragic it would have been very amusing making statements to the police and hearing them read out in that marvellous stilted language, but as it is I keep seeing those poor boys lying there with the blood pouring from their heads – although that picture is becoming mercifully less and less real.[7]

It is possible that she was in shock. She repeatedly said to Jock that her mother was not to blame for the accident and there was nothing that they could have done to prevent it. She later told him that straight after writing to him she had been violently sick.[8] Though he could be malicious, Jock was a very sensitive man and sent his deepest sympathies to Irena: 'I am very glad that you are so strong-minded about it, I am afraid I should be haunted very badly about such a thing.'[9]

Barbara told Jock that the young man's funeral had taken place and that the Pyms phoned the infirmary twice each day for news of the other critically ill biker. He was only nineteen and after two operations it seemed likely that he might pull through. Eventually he recovered, though with a large scar on his forehead.

Pym repeated to Jock (somewhat unconvincingly) that she was no longer in love with Henry. She was hurt that he had failed to write to her. Even Friedbert had 'spared a moment from the organisation of the Olympic Games to send me a beautiful postcard'.[10] It was the first time that the Olympics had been televised and radio broadcasts reached over forty stations. In order to outdo the Los Angeles Games of 1932, Hitler had built a new 100,000-seat track and field stadium. But his attempts to use the games to prove Aryan supremacy were foiled by African-American Jesse Owens, who won no fewer than four gold medals.

Pym was told that she was not permitted to leave Shropshire until after the inquest. Part of her was relieved. She told Jock that she knew she was a great comfort to her parents and, with her new portable typewriter, she was throwing herself into her work. Jock admired her fortitude and wrote that he too must emulate her strength and mind and 'occupy myself with the trivial round, the common task'.[11]

CHAPTER XVI

In which Jock and Pymska draw closer together . . .

Jock and Pym continued their correspondence, advising one another on literary agents and editing one another's work. Pym sent detailed notes on Jock's novel, *Kind Relations*. She advised him to change the beginning, so that it was from the point of view of the small children. She also suggested chapters that might be cut and tightened.

For the time being, despite a job offer from Cairo, Jock decided to stay put in Oxford. He agonised over the decision and longed for Henry's counsel. When a letter finally arrived from him, Jock described it as 'wretched, like a blow from a blunt instrument'. Henry was never very good with other people's problems, preferring to focus on his own. 'Is not Henry an unhappy creature when his letters are so full of misery that it needs a prolonged convalescence after each of them?' wrote Jock.[1]

Liddell was grateful to Pym for her own consoling letter and was beginning to look forward to staying in Oxford, even in the 'Arctic cold' of the library: 'I dare say I should only sit in front of blank pages in Cairo and squash mosquitoes on them.' He regaled her with hilarious library gossip, including an account of an American looking for Shakespeare. And when she talked of being busy with spring cleaning, he told her a story of his prep school days that had her hooting with laughter:

> Never shall I forget a short drama enacted by the domestics of my preparatory school on 17 June 1922 called 'Mrs Mulligatawny's Spring Cleaning'. The cook began, regularly letting her voice rise and fall on alternate words: 'Now girls, do hurry up, or we shall never get the spring cleaning done before Aunt Maria comes.' And someone sang a moving song about charring.[2]

Another of Pym and Jock's favourite jokes was to pretend that one day their manuscripts and papers would be read and studied in the Bodleian Library. In response to his playful suggestion that their correspondence would be of immense value to the Department of Western Manuscripts, she replied: 'All my love letters – no young woman should be without 50 of these. Could I deposit them in Bodley and order them when I felt inclined to reread them?'[3]

Jock always remembered to ask about the injured young motorcyclists in his letters. Pym told him that the inquest was imminent. She was wondering what to wear: 'I daresay it will be my old blue costume and a beret. In films, fox furs are the correct wear, but then they cost – decent ones – anything up to half my yearly allowance.' She had revisited the scene of the accident, as part of the pre-inquest: 'I am glad to say that I felt no other emotion than curiosity. And I don't really think I'm hard hearted – just lucky I suppose.'[4]

CHAPTER XVII

The Inquest

On the day of the inquest, Pym was shaking with nervousness. The hearing lasted two hours, with the opposing lawyer doing his utmost to make Irena and Pym appear to be culpable for the accident. The young man who had survived, Grainger, was too badly injured to make it to court. It was all far more distressing than Pym had anticipated, she confided to Jock.

Liddell had recently finished his autobiographical novel, *Kind Relations*. It was the first of a remarkable trilogy, which would be completed with an Oxford novel about the brothers and Mrs Trew, *The Last Enchantments*. It is among the best books about Oxford ever written. Pym found *Kind Relations* brilliant and moving, especially because it corresponded with so much of what Jock had told her about his early life: the death of his beloved mother, his absent father, the way he and his brother were passed like parcels between relatives. 'I am curious to know how many of them are true and how many are made up. Perhaps they are all true because they seem so very natural.' She urged Jock to begin his second novel, *Stepsons*. She wanted to know more about the dreadful stepmother, Elsa: 'You give quite enough of her to make her a horrible prospect.'[1] She also said that she was thinking of writing her own Oxford novel.

Pym told Jock that she wasn't in love with anyone, though 'this state of affairs can easily be rectified by Friedbert'. There was more fantasy talk of marriage to Henry. They just couldn't help themselves from bringing Henry into the conversation. The truth was that they were both still more than a little obsessed by him and, though driven mad by his arrogance, were drawn to his physical beauty. 'I am so glad that you are resigned to marriage with dear Henry, he is your fate you know,' wrote Jock. 'I don't doubt that you will be a most useful wife to him – though he himself is fond of painting furniture, so you need no accomplishments of that kind.'[2] Pym, knowing that this was a delicious but increasingly painful fantasy, played along:

> Money is the chief objection and lack of affection on Henry's part the second. I want a platinum wedding ring, also one set with diamonds and perhaps a sapphire engagement ring, too . . . perhaps it is a pity that the wedding cannot take place but I am fortified by the information contained in my horoscope which Rupert Gleadow did for me some years ago. He prophesied that I should make a *profitable* marriage – otherwise my husband's description coincided with Henry's.[3]

Jock and Barnicot's banter about a future marriage between Pym and Henry had been meant kindly, but it had raised false hope: 'Please give my love to my future husband and tell him that if he can find a rich Finn to marry first, so much the better,' she wrote.[4] Pym still clung to the hope that Henry had thought differently about her ever since reading her novel and seeing that she was a talented writer. She wanted him to come and stay with her so that her mother could 'knock some sense into him': 'I often ask myself (as a kind of test) whether I would rather be loved by Henry or have my novel accepted; at the present moment I feel I would like *both*, but perhaps if my work were published the rest would follow.'[5]

Jock, having had an emotionally stunted childhood blighted by his stepmother, had a tainted view of marriage. In the manuscript version of *Some Tame Gazelle*, Belinda and Parnell often discuss the state of love and marriage and Parnell's views are Jock's: 'After all the emotions of the heart are very transitory or at least so I believe. I should think it makes one happier to be well fed than well loved.' Jock begged Pym to return to Oxford, but although 'literally pining to come to Oxford again', she seemed to be coming round to his view that, 'perhaps a pleasant, uneventful existence is happiness after all'. She told him that she planned to return to Germany in the summer, adding: 'I'm assuming there won't be any war or anything like that.'[6]

But then, in May, Henry wrote Pym a hurtful letter, telling her that they had 'never been real to each other'. She penned a long response, which was a testament to her candour and self-knowledge. She told him that she was tired of writing 'gay flippant letters to you and expecting you to see that I didn't really feel that way'. She was 'fed up' with their sporadic meetings, his promises to write, his excuses, his inability to 'improve' as he got older, 'of having my peace disturbed for no reason'. Henry tried to put some of the blame on Jock and his inability to take their relationship seriously, but Pym was having none of his lame excuses: 'it is really because you haven't been sufficiently interested in me to make much effort about it'. She was drawn to triangular relationships – as we have seen from her relationship with Rupert and Miles – but she was not prepared to betray Liddell: 'however much Jock may be responsible for the state of affairs between *us*, I can never forget that he saved me a great deal of unhappiness by his way of looking at things, which I adopted too, at least in our correspondence and conversation'.[7]

Pym tried desperately to explain the two sides to her personality – 'Sandra' and Barbara, the 'real' side and 'the flat one' – but she ended up confusing herself: 'I'm finding it rather difficult to explain myself clearly, but I hope you'll see what I mean?' In the end, she fell back on what she felt was her winning shot as far as her relationship with Henry was concerned: 'Did I tell you I started a new novel? I am just beginning to get into form, although at first I found it something of an effort.'[8]

What she didn't tell Henry was that, once again, it was a novel based on her relationship with him.

CHAPTER XVIII

Miss Pym begins her Second Novel in the Summer of 1936 and returns to Oxford to be Henry's Amanuensis

One of Pym's favourite authors was Elizabeth von Arnim (Mary Annette Beauchamp), who wrote under the pen name 'Elizabeth' and had achieved a huge success with her autobiographical first novel, *Elizabeth and her German Garden*. Depicting a cruel and domineering husband (whom she calls 'The Man of Wrath') and struggling to fit into high-class German society, the central character takes refuge in her garden and in her writing. After the breakdown of her first marriage (her husband was sent to prison for fraud), the author Elizabeth embarked on a three-year-long affair with H. G. Wells. Her 1921 novel, *Vera*, drew on her disastrous second marriage to Earl Russell (brother to Bertrand) and was described as '*Wuthering Heights* by Jane Austen'.[1]

Pym was reading 'crowds of novels', she told Jock, 'often a little jealously, as I think mine is so much finer and more delightful than so many of them'.[2] Her discipline was to write at least one page a day. She again encouraged Jock to begin his second novel, telling him that it might help him to look back on that part of his life without it being painful for him.

Jock's dislike of his German stepmother was given full rein in *Stepsons*. Elsa's jealousy of her stepsons, her sour resentment, her prioritising of the needs of her own dull daughter, Joan, her stupidity and lack of humour, spill from every page. Liddell was on his way to becoming a fine writer and Pym was indispensable in giving him support and encouragement. She typed manuscripts for him on her new Remington portable and explained that she was altering his style and editing as she typed.

In May, Macmillan rejected *Some Tame Gazelle* and Pym turned to Jock for advice. Undaunted, she planned on sending it out to Methuen or Dent. She told Jock that *Adam and Cassandra* was not as literary as *Some Tame Gazelle*, but hoped that it would find a readership. 'Cassandra is a perfect wife,' she said. 'Adam is sweet but rather a fool.'[3]

As usual, Henry was not far from their minds. Jock continued his tease about Pym and Henry's nuptials. He had promised her a fish slice and a saucepan, but the joke was beginning to wear thin: 'I am a nice girl and have some new clothes, but what's the good of all that without money?' She told Jock, with her usual honesty, that she knew she was no catch, 'a poor frog without a log on which to hop'. She'd heard from a friend that Henry was looking 'ravishingly beautiful', but added, tartly, 'it is to be hoped that his disposition and behaviour will suit his appearance'.[4]

At the heart of Pym's novels are a troop of 'excellent women' who are the bulwarks of their menfolk, propping them up mentally, cooking sustaining food and typing up their papers as unpaid secretaries. It was a theme she knew well.

In June, Pym returned to Oxford. She had agreed to become Henry's secretary. He was back from Finland, writing up a thesis on Gerard Langbaine, the seventeenth-century English dramatic biographer and critic. He was particularly interested in an 'amorous novel' that Langbaine had translated from French called

The Gallant Hermaphrodite. Pym, with her portable typewriter and newly acquired typing skills, took dictation from Henry. It was a time she would never forget; she felt like they were living as man and wife. She was in Henry's company night and day, making tea, typing, checking references. In exchange, she was paid 'thirty shillings a week and a few caresses'.[5] The Oxford B. Litt. dissertation survives in the Bodleian Library; it formed the principal source for the *Oxford Dictionary of National Biography* entry on Langbaine.[6]

Whilst typing for Henry, Pym also made time for her own novel. She channelled her fantasy of what marriage to Henry might look like if she ever succeeded in winning him over. Living in such close proximity gave her excellent copy. She had marvellous fun portraying him as the handsome but rather dim Adam and herself as Cassandra (Sandra), the perfect wife who is tempted to have an affair with a foreign stranger.

The day Henry returned to Oxford was the first time Pym had seen him in nine months. She was wearing her turquoise dress and, for once, Henry complimented her on her appearance. He had bought a new Morris car and took her and Jock out in it to see Barnicot and Count Weiss. Later, after dropping Jock back to his digs in the Banbury Road, he took Pym for a drive in the countryside. They stopped at an old ruined nunnery, a romantic spot on the banks of the Thames, where they 'made love' (which probably meant no more than kissing and fondling). She had not been kissed since Budapest, so she was happy to be intimate with Henry, but she also felt that somehow he was a stranger to her. When she tried to explain her feelings, he merely responded: 'Oh dear.'[7]

Another outing did not go so well. Pym, Jock, Barnicot and Henry visited some 'lovely, gracious and unspoilt' Oxfordshire villages. Pym was in a quarrelsome mood and 'lowered the tone' with her talk about dance music: 'I think I did this because I felt intellectually inferior to them all, especially Henry, who always makes you feel it more than the others do. I felt they were all against me.' She knew that she was making things worse by her obstinacy, but for once she was tired of their condescending manner towards her: 'I felt resentful of being dominated by them and not being allowed to be myself at all.'[8]

Nevertheless there were better times. A row ended with a kind apology from Henry, 'standing in the room in the early hours of the morning, looking like an unshaven Russian prince with a turquoise coloured scarf around his waist'. The next day, Henry fetched Pym in the car to listen to a record of a reading by James Joyce, with whom he was obsessed. But he was morose and bad tempered. Pym, tearful and upset, wondered why he bothered coming for her, only to be rude and obnoxious, but then his mood turned as she made to leave and he said a gentle farewell: 'I often think that Henry is never so nice as when he's standing at the door of the flat saying goodbye.'[9]

One day, when Henry was out, she discovered on his desk a half-finished love poem that he had written for Elsie. He remembered that it was written in 'bad mock-heroic'. When he returned he found that Pym had finished the poem in good mock heroic.[10] Jock had sent her a photograph of Elsie. She was a beautiful young woman with a heart-shaped face and long flaxen hair. It was a painful moment, seeing the poem, but Pym made a joke of it, whilst also showing Henry her superior writing skills.

Pym worked ceaselessly, typing Henry's manuscript. On the last day, she sat at her Remington all through the night and then had two hours' sleep in Henry's bed. She enjoyed taking care of him, making endless cups of tea and tucking him into his armchair with a rug around his knees. It was a 'playing at' domesticity: 'I have been given a taste of how lovely things *could* be with Henry.' Later she reflected: 'My own little love – at that time he really *was* mine and nobody else's.'[11]

CHAPTER XIX

The Story of Adam and Cassandra

Back in Oswestry, Pym once again felt depressed. She confided in her diary, listing all the reasons for her misery:

a) because I missed Henry
b) because I loved him and could see no hope for the future
c) because I couldn't get any of my works accepted
d) because Oswestry was so frightful after Oxford
e) because it was a dull day.

She knitted, got a new haircut and went shopping for new trollies ('a peach and pale yellow') before going on the annual Pym family holiday to north Wales. As usual, Henry never replied to her letters, even to send a postcard. She took solace in her writing: 'I must *work* at my novel, that is the only thing there is and the only way to find any happiness at present.'[1]

Good news came in August with a letter from the publisher Jonathan Cape saying he was interested in publishing *Some Tame Gazelle*, 'if I would make some alterations'. She told Jock, who was delighted and not at all envious, though he was having no success in getting his own novel published. He told Pym that he believed Henry would be jealous of her success.

Pym was anxious to tell Henry the good news, still believing somehow that success in the literary field would enhance her charms. 'I daresay Jock has told you about Jonathan Cape and my novel . . . I am greatly cheered about this, but only vaguely hopeful.' She joked about being able to type 'frightfully fast after doing Gerard [Langbaine], but find that instead of being able to type words like Archdeacon and Belinda I want to type Langbaine and Architypographus'. Nevertheless, she worked hard and by July had written a hundred pages. She was also correcting and editing *Some Tame Gazelle*: 'so wearying to do'. She told Henry that she no longer pined for him, 'I mean my eyes don't prick with tears every time I think of you as in July.'[2]

In early September, Henry, Jock and Barnicot came to Shropshire for a flying visit. They visited Portmeirion, 'a very charming, very Henryish place with pink and blue and yellow Italian villas and statues all about in odd corners. Henry was very nice and it was all very pleasant.' Henry was returning to Finland, but Pym felt that she had a part of him that was hers alone. 'I envy Elsie Godenhjelm – after all I love him too!'[3]

By October, she had almost finished *Adam and Cassandra*. Pym's new novel was heavily influenced by Elizabeth von Arnim, just as 'Young Men in Fancy Dress' was influenced by *Crome Yellow*. She had been reading *The Enchanted April*, a story of four gentlewomen who escape to Portofino in Italy. She draws on the same themes: the submissive, downtrodden wife who finds herself rejuvenated in the company of strangers and the beauty of her surroundings; the dull, unappreciative husband who is transformed by the magic of abroad. Pym loved the premise of the novel, which begins with an advertisement in *The Times:* 'To Those Who Appreciate Wisteria and Sunshine. Small mediaeval Italian Castle on the shores of the Mediterranean To Be Let Furnished for the Month of April.'[4]

She sets *Adam and Cassandra* in the small Shropshire village of Up-Callow. As with *Pride and Prejudice*, the novel begins with the arrival of a new tenant of the big house, Holmwood. Stefan Tilos is Hungarian, wealthy and handsome. Before long, he falls in love with Cassandra, who is neglected by her spoilt, selfish husband. She goes to Budapest, leaving her husband to the village gossip that she has run away with Tilos. Adam, the husband, follows her abroad and rediscovers his love for his wife. The dialogue is more confident than in *Some Tame Gazelle* and there is a first-rate comic chapter centring on a sermon by the rector, Rockingham Wilmot, in a style that would become trademark 'Pym'. The pompous rector visits an old lady for tea. During their conversation, he praises her embroidery. She tells him that 'some people don't put in enough stitches', which is the starting point for the sermon:

> 'Some people don't put in enough stitches,' repeated the rector, in a slow emphatic voice. 'Isn't that true of many of *us*?' He leaned forward. 'Aren't our *lives* pieces of embroidery that we have to fill in ourselves? Can we truthfully say that we always put in enough stitches? Are there not in all our lives some patches that look thin and not properly filled?'[5]

Adam, meanwhile, bears more than a passing resemblance to Henry Harvey. Smug, vain and complacent, he likes being mothered by his wife; her needs are subsumed to his. 'Only Adam was allowed to have any nerves. Cassandra had learned to keep hers in dutiful subjection.' Pym wrote to Henry: 'Adam is sweet but very stupid. You are sweet too, but not as consistently stupid as Adam.'[6] There are some acid touches too in Cassandra, who resents the way that she is perceived as a good wife:

Cassandra being an excellent wife did what was expected of her
. . . 'Do remember that, after all, I'm not much more than a
faithful wife and an excellent housekeeper.'

'Well, that's something,' said Adam. 'I'm not sure it isn't a
great deal,' he added thoughtfully.

'Yes it may be,' agreed Cassandra. 'Anyone can be both those
things with a little practice, though. They are essentially the
attributes of a stupid woman.'[7]

Adam's 'thoughtfully' is a delicious barb.

Pym used her experience of travelling to Budapest to good
effect, but she felt dissatisfied with the book. The problem was
that she was too often copying someone else's style, instead of
fully developing her own voice. Jock wrote to say that he thought
Adam and Cassandra more mature in style than *Some Tame
Gazelle*, but without something of its peculiar charm.

Nevertheless, by the summer of 1936, Pym had reached a
crucial moment. Later, she paid tribute to the importance of
Elizabeth von Arnim's works on her early development: 'Such
novels as *The Enchanted April* and *The Pastor's Wife* were a
revelation in their wit and delicate irony and the dry, unsenti-
mental treatment of the relationship between men and women
which touched some deep echoing chord in me at that time.'
It was at this moment that Pym made the decision as to the
kind of novelist she wanted to be: 'these novels seemed more
appropriate to use as models than *Crome Yellow* – perhaps even
the kind of things I might try to write myself'.[8]

CHAPTER XX

Jilted

In September, Pym heard she had been 'jilted' by Cape. They had decided that they were not able to take her on and give the novel the attention it deserved. Jock was outraged and sympathetic: 'With all my bitter experience of the falseness and cruelty of publishers I never expected anything quite so heartless as Mr Cape's conduct to you.' Still toying with his own plan to leave Oxford, he had been learning modern Greek and a recent holiday there had been a huge success. He was always able to say the right thing: 'We are, I think, entirely right-minded authors – we write, not perhaps because we like it, but because we are not satisfied if we don't . . . we should probably write on a desert Island if there was no possibility of publication.'[1]

Pym told him that her next step was to try and find a literary agent, though Jock thought she could do just as well on her own. She was taken on by the Pinker agency. James Brand Pinker had been the leading agent of the early twentieth century, representing everyone from Oscar Wilde and James Joyce to H. G. Wells, Arnold Bennett and D. H. Lawrence. He had especially close relations with Henry James and Joseph Conrad. After his death in 1922, the agency was taken over by his two sons, and its prestige diminished. Pym was not, however, propelled into print.

It was helpful that Jock and Pym were in the same boat – desperate to be published authors and wholly committed to a writing career and the discipline that it required, as well as the tenacity. Jock advised Pym to read Stevie Smith's debut, *Novel on Yellow Paper*. She took his advice and loved both Smith's prose and her poetry.

Jock enclosed a letter from Henry in which Henry had denounced Barnicot, who had travelled to Finland for a visit: 'To begin with he STINKS. He wears his light new brown suit and sweats into it and has not had a bath since I don't know how many days before he left England.'[2] Henry could be extremely vicious when riled. He complained that Barnicot's shoes were mouldy, his socks and feet black with dirt. He found it 'horrible to be alone with him, or even to look at him'. Henry ranted on for four pages, pausing only to write wonderful things about Elsie. Jock advised Pym to keep Henry's letter; 'I'm sure H would like all that eloquence to be left for posterity.'

Jock also confided in Pym that he had had another altercation with his stepmother, after refusing her invitation to visit his sister Betty in London. 'We expected an outburst and even considered if that woman would not perhaps drop down dead from the shock of being opposed.'[3] In the event, she allowed Betty to visit her brothers in Oxford. Betty was a cause for alarm; she was feeble-minded and oppressed by her domineering mother.

Pym was making plans to visit Henry and Elsie in the summer of 1937. In the end, she changed her mind and decided that she would rather return to Germany. 'Tonight I have been drinking beer to get into practice for the large quantities we shall consume there.'[4] Pym seemed to be accepting that Henry and Elsie were becoming serious. There were jokes about embroidering a fire-screen for their forthcoming nuptials and she had taken to calling Elsie 'dear sister'. Jock seemed convinced, however, that the relationship would not last. He had been to stay with them in Finland and sent photographs: 'My dear sister has a sweet little face, I think. What nice people Henry seems to get hold of! Because I have a beautiful nature, although opinions vary about my face.'[5] Pym, in return, joked about her availability as a companion for Elsie's mother: 'I am twenty-four, a gentlewoman, cultured, a good needle woman, very clean and pleasant-tempered. I speak English, German, French, Swedish, Spanish, Hungarian and Finnish.'[6]

It was around this time that Pym, having reread and enjoyed Ivy Compton-Burnett, began to write brilliantly amusing letters in the same style. She and Jock soon became obsessed by Compton-Burnett's novels. Jock found her address in London and was thinking of writing to her to request a meeting.

CHAPTER XXI

An Introduction to
Miss Ivy Compton-Burnett

Ivy Compton-Burnett became well known with the success of her second novel, *Pastors and Masters*, published in 1925 and hailed by the *New Statesman* as 'a work of genius'. It was the first work to introduce the clipped, precise, staccato dialogue – like the plays of Harold Pinter but long before their time – for which she became famous.

When Jock first read her novels, he said the hair on his head stood on end, 'like that of Henry Tilney in *Northanger Abbey*'. The Compton-Burnett themes were family relationships, unconventional sexuality and power struggles between the sexes. But for Jock, there was only one theme: 'Here was someone who knew all the horror that can lurk behind the facade of the respectable, upper middle-class English home.'[1]

Given his wretched upbringing, Jock identified strongly with this world. Like Pym, he was at first bemused by the strange writing style, almost entirely in dialogue, but he was soon converted by the precision and subtlety, proposing that 'she wrote better than anyone else'. He introduced his brother to her work with the exclamation: 'It's about us!' Jock's admiration was bound up with what he saw as Compton-Burnett's hatred of family and her mastery of dialogue. She is especially brilliant on despotic fathers:

> 'And who has been spilling water?' said Horace, on a deeper note.
>
> There was a pause.
>
> 'Answer me,' said the father, striking the table.
>
> 'I have,' said another boy in an uneven tone.
>
> 'And why were you playing with water? You know that is forbidden.'
>
> 'I was pouring some into a saucer, to see if it would freeze.'
>
> 'You know better than that. We are not at the North Pole.'[2]

Jock claimed that he introduced Pym to 'ICB', as they called her, but in fact she had read her first, two years before, and it was Pym, not Jock, who began their habit of writing comic letters in the ICB style. The dark subject matter and black humour made Jock suspect that Compton-Burnett had suffered 'a profound and horrible experience'; how else could she have written so powerfully about cruel family life? He was determined to find out.

The ghastly truth was discovered in the basement of the Radcliffe Camera, where the back numbers of *The Times* were stored. 'With trembling fingers', Jock read the shocking story of the double suicide of Ivy's younger sisters, Baby and Topsy. Ivy had been called as a witness to give evidence. Thirty years later, Hilary Spurling, Compton-Burnett's first biographer, revealed the multiple tragedies that had unfolded. The family suffered at the hands of a bullying, unhappy mother. Two of Ivy's brothers died young (one in the Great War), and Baby and Topsy killed themselves in a suicide pact on Christmas Day in 1917. Another half-brother had killed himself. Ivy never spoke of her sisters. When Jock got to know her sometime later,

Compton-Burnett claimed that, other than one friend, she had never known anyone to commit suicide.

Pym and Jock adopted ICB's turn of phrase and locutions, such as 'I do not wish to be speaking of it', and 'in all the ways that don't go into words'. Henry Harvey also remembers Pym and Jock's 'Ivy' conversation style: 'What could be my meaning?' and 'I would not tolerate it'. They particularly loved the phrase: 'I think tea should go through all its proper stages.' They 'tried to make life produce enough dialogue to satisfy the needs of Ivy imitation'.[3] Henry was not a fan and felt left out.

More Women Than Men became one of Pym and Jock's favourites. Set in a girls' boarding school, it revolves around the formidable and manipulative Mrs Napier, who conceals her true nature beneath a facade of gentility and amiability. Her elderly brother, Jonathan Swift, is engaged in a long-standing homosexual love affair with one of his former pupils, Felix Bacon. There is no question about the nature of their relationship. When a friend told Compton-Burnett that some people felt the relationship between Swift and Bacon to be 'improper', she retorted: 'Oh, it was meant to be improper.'

> Felix danced towards Jonathan and took a seat on his knee, the older man moving his arm as though accustomed to the position.
>   'What would your father say, if he knew all our life together?'
>   'I don't think he uses words about everything.'
>   'He deserves to be more respected than I am.'
>   'Well, I think he gets what he deserves.'[4]

Felix eventually marries, to uphold his ancestral family seat, believing that he can still maintain his homosexual relationship with Jonathan.

When Jock finally met Compton-Burnett, she confided in

him that she had written a more explicitly shocking homosexual scene that she had been advised to omit: 'One cut out one scene because one didn't want trouble.'[5] Pym was entranced by the novel, telling Jock that he had to read it, if he hadn't already; she particularly wanted to know what he thought of the character of Josephine Napier. It was a name she stored up to be used for one of her most memorable characters.

One of Pym and Jock's running jokes was that phrase from John Keble's hymn 'New Every Morning is the Love' – 'the trivial round, the common task, will furnish all we need to ask'. In her 'Finnish' novel, Pym explains: 'to no other life can these words be better applied than to the everyday activities of an English country Parish'.[6] It became a mantra for the two aspiring novelists, who were both fascinated by ephemera and the importance of the trivial. The platitude appears in several of Pym's novels, so it must have come as something of a sign when she read the quotation in the first chapter of Compton-Burnett's *More Women Than Men*. Compton-Burnett was showing the way to an art of writing that concealed cruelty and transgression beneath the calm surface of English provincial life.

'Of course I couldn't help being influenced by her dialogue,' Pym wrote later: 'that precise, formal conversation that seemed so stilted when I first read it.'[7] In Barbara Pym's archive is Compton-Burnett's first letter to Jock, which he bequeathed to his friend, who loved 'relics'. He eventually got the meeting he had asked for. One of the first critics to acknowledge her genius, Jock Liddell was rewarded with a friendship that would last for many years.

CHAPTER XXII

Pymska writes a Finnish Novel

In July, before she left for Germany, Pym wrote a chatty letter to Jock in which they planned a rendezvous with Henry. It was the first one she wrote in the style of 'ICB', which delighted Jock, but it also revealed her despair at the idea of losing both Henry and Liddell:

Anyway, it will be nice seeing you both – quite like the old days you might say.

'No,' said Barbara, in a low, harsh voice, 'it is not like the old days. You know it is not. Why do you wish me to believe a lie? Elsie was not with us then and now she is a wife to Henry and a sister to you. She has taken my place with you both. You do not need me now. No, Henry, there is no need to make such insincere protestations – I had my uses last summer, but a year has passed since then.'¹

Jock responded in ICB style:

'You must copy out my letter,' said Jock. 'Miss Pym wishes it to be returned to her. I do not know what can be her motive.'

'You need not always be speaking of it,' said Henry in a flat tone. 'It shall be done some time or other. It hardly matters when it is done.'

Jock also hinted that Henry and Elsie were becoming more serious. Writing in this jocular fashion was a way of telling Pym that she must prepare herself: '"Marriage is a great responsibility," said Henry. "I do not wish to be thinking of it."'[2]

Pym was perhaps preparing herself by writing her 'Finnish novel' in which she, Henry and Elsie featured. It was called *Gervase and Flora*. As in *Adam and Cassandra*, she was using her novels to convey to Henry those words she found so hard to say in real life.

Gervase Harringay, the hero, is a lecturer at the University of Helsingfors in Finland. Gervase is pursued by his old love, Flora, who has followed him from England. But Gervase has fallen in love with a beautiful Swedish girl called Ingeborg. She has a 'thin, delicately modelled face and long straight flaxen hair'. In her 'hearth-rug' fur coat, she looked 'just like Garbo'. As with Elsie, she has a difficult relationship with her mother. Flora is described as 'a tall big-boned girl with a fresh complexion and large, bright, intelligent grey eyes'. Like her creator, she has light brown hair with golden streaks in it and a broad mouth 'always laughing or smiling'. Of all her heroines, Flora is the one who is most physically like Pym. She is handsome and comely, rather than pretty; she is 'energetic and cheerful, a jolly girl'.[3]

Gervase finds Flora 'alarming' and goes 'hot and cold' at the idea of marrying her, as his friends wish him to. He feels 'a net was closing around him'. When he sees her again, Flora is reproachful about the fact that Gervase never answers her letters:

'Oh, Gervase,' she said, keeping her hand on his, 'why didn't you answer any of my letters? You could at least have sent a postcard of the Hauptbahnhof if there is one.'

'Oh yes, indeed, it's quite celebrated. But you know that I'm a bad letter writer,' he said lamely. Could one also claim to be a bad postcard writer? He wondered.

'It would have been much nicer coming here if I had thought you wanted to see me,' persisted Flora.

'But I *do* want to see you,' said Gervase, putting his arm around her shoulders. 'You know I do.'

'Well, perhaps you do.' Flora did not sound convinced, but then neither had Gervase.[4]

Flora's friends are keen to see her settled in marriage, but each suitor that presents himself is perceived as 'not good enough for their dear Flora'. She is rather bitter about this: 'Is there anyone who is good enough for me? I feel that there may not be. I feel that I may be condemned to keep myself to myself all my life.' Another character, Mr Boulding, tells Flora: 'I thought your generation with all its education rather looked down on men.'[5]

Pym poured out her hopeless feelings for Henry in her portrayal of Flora, who has been suffering from unrequited love for seven years: 'She had been in love with Gervase for so long that she could not imagine a life in which he had no part.' At night, he fills her mind, 'her night thoughts, generally less noble than Young's'. She could not resist a joke about Henry's love for the gloomy eighteenth-century epic poem *Night Thoughts*. But Flora is also sensible and clear-minded about her conflicted feelings towards Gervase. 'Nor, on the other hand, could she imagine a life in which he returned her love. That would somehow spoil the picture she had made of herself . . . Noble, faithful, long-suffering, although not without its funny side, it was like something out of Tchekov.'

There's a new sophistication in Pym's writing in *Gervase and Flora*. Belinda Bede's unrequited love for Archdeacon Hoccleve is depicted in a jokey, warm manner in the unpublished version of *Some Tame Gazelle*, but Flora's feelings are rendered with more depth and feeling: 'She wanted to cling to Gervase's arm – a thing he hated her to do – and say, "Not yet, please, not yet. Let us stay the same for a little longer. Let me stay in the unhappiness I'm used to rather than start a new one which may be even worse."'[6] Gervase is a colder, more hard-hearted figure than Henry Hoccleve. He tells Ingeborg, unkindly, that Flora was never really in love with him – 'it was simply an over-developed imagination and the boredom of being a girl in an English country vicarage. She always dramatises herself and sees herself as leading a life of absorbing interest . . . I know Flora far better than you do. She can just as easily fall in love with somebody else – it's her nature.'[7]

Flora, knowing that she is defeated by Gervase's powerful attraction to the more beautiful Ingeborg, is angry when Gervase tells her that they will always be friends:

'Friends? What's being friends?' said Flora, turning her head away.

Gervase gave a barely perceptible sigh. 'But have we ever been more than friends?' He asked. 'Very good friends, I admit, but not more than that.'

'You don't understand,' said Flora desperately. 'I can't ever make you understand, I can see that. You're too afraid of facing any sort of finality, even if it doesn't touch you. You haven't the courage to put me out of your life as I would put you out of mine.'

'But Flora,' said Gervase in a puzzled, exasperated tone, 'it isn't necessary. Why should I face things I don't have to face? All this putting each other out of our lives,' he added with an indulgent smile. 'Darling child, you take things so seriously. We can always be friends. Now kiss me and show me that we can.'[8]

Here there is a note of maturity in the writing that is absent in Pym's previous work. The dialogue is fluid and convincing. She is finding her voice. When Flora retires to bed, knowing she has lost Gervase, she is comforted by the thought that her feelings might not be permanent: 'Perhaps if she put her misery away at the back of her mind and left it there she might one day be able to bring it out into the light and smile at the idea of its ever having the power to hurt her.'

Pym sent chapters of her work to Jock and Don Liddell, who proclaimed themselves delighted by the results. They both thought the chapters 'excessively funny' and Jock admired her for the 'full lives' she was giving to her characters. 'I wonder how Miss Ivy Compton-Burnett would enjoy it?' he wrote. He saw the debt: 'From your work and my own I detect another Compton-Burnett source which I had not discovered before – viz the Russian dramatists. But I really wonder whether she did not hit upon her style by accident in the first place. Is it not easy and delightful to write like that? I wish we had thought of it first.'⁹

In print, Pym was imagining the very worst: marriage between Gervase and Ingeborg. Somehow, she believed that if she could fictionalise her worst fear and make fun of it, then it would be a preparation for it as an eventuality.

But then reality struck and it was nothing like what she imagined. On 6 December 1937, Jock posted a letter to Hilary Pym. He typed the address, so that her sister would not recognise his distinctive writing and open the letter:

Will you please break the news to your sister that the marriage has been arranged and will take place in about a week's time (quietly in the English church at Helsingfors) between Lektor Harvey and Froken Elsie Godenhjelm? I had not the courage to tell her – besides, I thought it would come better from you and in Oswestry. I hope she will resign herself to be a kind stepmother to Elsie's children.¹⁰

CHAPTER XXIII

Paavikki Olafsson and Jay

It was 3 December 1937. Pym had gone back to Oxford to visit friends. She did not know that Henry and Elsie were in the final stages of planning their wedding. She was not, at this time, looking for love; she was entirely focused on her writing. And then she met a young Balliol man who would become hugely important to her, both as a lover and a muse. More than anyone, he would expunge the memory of Henry.

Pym was in Oxford with a friend called Denis Pullein-Thompson. Her latest reincarnation was as a Finnish woman called Paavikki Olafsson. Vikki was the name given to one of Gervase's students in her novel – a sexy girl in her manuscript – and to compete with Henry, Pym was learning Finnish and trying to pass herself off as a student. Amused, Denis played along. They had lunch in Stewart's, one of her old student haunts, where Pym was introduced to an undergraduate friend of Denis. The young man walked over to their table. Pym was a little hungover from a sherry party the night previous. The man was of singular appearance: 'He was about my height, slight and dark with a quizzical, rather monkey face. He wore a camel coat and a spotted tie and looked sleek and nice.' At the top of her diary she wrote and underlined his name, as if somehow she recognised his importance: 'Julian Amery' and in German, she wrote, quoting the Romantic poet Heinrich Heine: '*Neuer Frühling gibt zurück*' (new spring returns). She also noted that he was an Etonian whose tutor was Henry's brother-in-law.[1]

Denis introduced Pym as Paavikki Olafsson, and then left to go to a drama rehearsal, leaving Pym and Julian chatting. There was an instant attraction. By then she had dropped the pretence of Paavikki. They talked about her writing.

Julian invited her back to his rooms in Balliol which looked over St Giles' and the Randolph. His room was untidy, with papers and letters strewn all over the table. Though he didn't smoke or drink, he lit her a Camel cigarette and then took her hand to read her future. She was shocked when he suddenly kissed her. 'It was the first time anyone so much younger than me had done such a thing, for he was only eighteen and I twenty-four.'[2]

Later Pym mused how desperate she felt for affection and how charming Julian was, 'with a kind of childish simplicity combined with Continental polish that was most appealing'. He stole her paisley handkerchief as a love token, refusing to give it back. He played German and Hungarian records on the gramophone and, when she left, he walked her to the bus stop in the rain, their fingers interlocked: 'I was happy.'[3]

The next morning, Pym took the train back home to Shropshire, her head full of Julian. They conversed in German and he made her promise to say '*auf Wiedersehen*', not '*adjö*' and said he wanted to see her again. She read German poetry on the train home: the wheels of the train appeared to be repeating Romantic verses.

Despite his youth, Julian Amery was already a rising star. He was the son of Conservative politician Leo Amery, whose mother was of Hungarian-Jewish descent. When he was eleven, Julian was taken to the House of Commons where he met Lloyd

George. He asked the boy what he wanted to do when he grew up, and Julian said that he wanted to go into the navy. 'Why the navy? There are much greater storms in politics, you know. If you really want the broadsides, walking the plank and blood on the deck, this is the place.' Julian recalled that from this moment on, the scales fell from his eyes.[4] He told Pym that he wanted to be prime minister. He was a determined young man, clearly going places.

Though he was so much younger than Pym, she was mesmerised by Amery's confidence and striking dark looks. Short and stocky, he was the physical opposite of the tall, angular Henry Harvey. Unlike Henry, he was utterly sure of himself. He was an altogether more glamorous figure than anyone Pym had previously encountered, with skiing holidays to St Moritz in the winter and summers spent in the south of France. He lived in salubrious Eaton Square in Belgravia, where he was brought up in 'imbibing the atmosphere of politics', conversing with Churchill and other leading politicians who were friends with his father.

That year, before coming up to Balliol, Julian had been sent to Vienna to learn German (he was already fluent in French). He had 'flirted with' national socialism, attending one of Oswald Mosley's meetings, but he was repelled by anti-Semitism and thought that the blackshirts and the Roman salute were 'ridiculous'.[5]

The day after meeting Pym, Julian sent his '*liebe Vikki*' a lavender-blue handkerchief for 'drying her tears' whilst reading Goethe's *Werther*. Pym kept this relic all her life, though little did she know how useful an extra handkerchief would soon be.

Julian was clearly very keen. He had been to a ball at the Austrian legation and said he wished that Pym had been there too. He was full of questions: 'When am I going to see you again? When do you come to London?' He teased her about her personae: 'Will you be a Shropshire spinster? A Finnish Student? Or just a novelist up to see her publisher?'[6]

But then, shortly after receiving Julian's letter, Hilary broke the news to her of Henry's marriage to Elsie. Heartbroken and close to emotional collapse, Pym scrawled her misery onto the pages of her diary. Unable to find sufficient words of her own, she resorted to a string of quotations:

> My pen's the spout
> Where the Rain-water of mine eyes runs out
>
> (Cleveland)

1937

On 12 December – a Sunday – Henry Stanley Harvey married Elsie Beatrice Godenhjelm in Helingsfors at the English Church.

So endete eine grosse Liebe

> Now if thou wouldst, when all have given him over,
> From death to life thou mightest him yet recover
>
> (Michael Drayton)

> When killed with grief Amyntas lies
> And you to mind shall call
> The sighs that now unpitied rise,
> The tears that vainly fall:
> That welcome hour that ends this smart,
> Will then begin your pain,
> For such a faithful tender heart
> Can never break, can never break in vain (The Earl of Rochester).

Josephine turned to the woman and hurried her words, as if anxious to get the matter behind. 'Simply the deepest widow's mourning that is made.

And of good quality and no definite date. Shall wear such things for a long time.'

'Well, you must have your own way,' said Elizabeth.

'It is not my way. It is my character and has nothing to do with me. I have no way in the matter. It is settled for me from within, as it were behind my back.'

(I Compton-Burnett)

Herz, mein Herz, sei nicht beklommen,
Und ertrage dein Geschick,
Neuer Frühling gibt zurück,
Was der Winter dir genommen.
Und wie viel ist dir geblieben,
Und wie schön ist noch die Welt!
Und, mein Herz, was dir gefällt
Alles, alles darfst du lieben!

(Heinrich Heine)

THE END[7]

CHAPTER XXIV

Liebe Vikki

Jock gave Pym time to absorb the news and then wrote a long letter in the style of Ivy Compton-Burnett. In many respects, he was as emotionally wrought as Pym. Writing in this vein kept things at a safe distance for them both.

'Tell me all,' said Barbara in a harsh hurrying tone. 'I can bear it. I hope there is much to tell.'

'It's known that I like discovering other people's business,' said Jock. 'But there are things that I am not at liberty to divulge. My lips are sealed.'

'Oh,' said Barbara in an eager tone. 'You do not mean . . .'

'No, I do not,' said Jock in a firm even tone. 'I mean something very different.'[1]

Elsie was not pregnant and it was not a 'shotgun' wedding. Jock told Pym that he had been authorised to tell her in Oxford, when they had supper together, but he 'dared not'. He felt some guilt but took comfort in black humour: 'I expect they will be quite comfortably miserable ever after in the Russian manner.' He reported that Henry seemed to dread being alone with his bride on their honeymoon and had asked both Jock and Barnicot to join them in the Alps. Jock tried hard to make her laugh: 'I had imagined terrible scenes at Morda Lodge':

'She's dead,' said Mr Sagar. 'What a loss to letters!'

'Do you remember who was sitting in that chair a minute ago?' said Aunt Janie.

'Perhaps Heinemann will issue a memorial edition?' said Mr Sagar in a hopeful tone.

'Bring me burnt feathers,' said Mrs Pym. 'She has fainted, merely that.'

'My daughter is restored to me,' said Mr Pym. 'I shall go back to my work on *Pym v Harvey*.'

'Leave me with my sister,' said Barbara in a feeble tone . . . 'We shall always be together now.'[2]

ICB was their go-to voice in times of crisis. Pym responded in similar style and bought herself an expensive black lace dress – her version of widow's weeds.

Nevertheless, the new year of 1938 started 'peacefully' for Pym. On 1 January she wrote about eight pages of her Finnish novel, which had now reached page 256. She was reading lots of contemporary novels and some modern poetry, including W. H. Auden and Louis MacNeice's travel book in prose and verse, *Letters from Iceland*: 'a good book for bad days'. She went shopping in Liverpool to cheer herself up and bought a pale blue jumper, gold bracelet and a lining for a waistcoat.[3]

On 26 January the first snowdrop came out and she received a letter from Elsie Harvey. Jock sent letters on writing paper with black edges, because when writing letters of condolence after a bereavement it was tactful to use mourning paper. He told Pym that Elsie had received her letter and considered it very brave. Elsie was kind and sympathetic and determined to be friends, expressing the hope that Barbara would be like a sister to her.

Pym's flirtation with Julian Amery was proving to be a godsend. Julian spent Christmas in Kitzbühel, before returning to Oxford where he met Hilary Pym at a sherry party (he heard the voice of a woman saying that she wanted to meet Julian Amery). Hilary thought him a curiously small man but rather intriguing. For Julian, seeing Hilary and hearing her voice, so like Barbara's, made him think of the older sister and he wrote to Pym asking her to visit him in Oxford:

> I am angry with you. You have been in my mind all day and stopped me concentrating on Louis XVI – I simply can't believe that I have only seen you once for an hour and a half. What will it be like when I see you again . . . write to me and tell me what you are doing and thinking and don't forget to tell me when you're coming.[4]

Pym confided in her diary her gratitude towards Julian for taking an interest in her when she 'was still feeling rather unhappy and lost about Henry's marriage'. Rather than ridicule Pym's love for all things German the way that Henry had, Julian called her '*liebe*' and wrote endearing messages in German. Hearing Hilary's voice, he said, gave him a 'serious attack of *sehnsucht*' – a lovely, untranslatable word meaning 'yearning or craving'. He signed off with the title of a recent German song, '*Mein schönes Fräulein, gute Nacht*' (Goodnight my pretty lady).

Pym found out all she could about Julian Amery. She learned that he was a speaker at the Oxford Union and was writing for a political newspaper called *Oxford Comment*, which was edited by Woodrow Wyatt. He was friends with Randolph Churchill. She was determined to return to Oxford to see him.

In *Gervase and Flora*, the heroine knows that the only way of getting over her hopeless love for Gervase is to fall in love with someone else. Pym went to Oxford at the end of February, excited but also worried because Julian had failed to answer her latest letter. She tossed a coin to decide whether or not to leave a message and then left a note at Balliol, telling him of her arrival and address. After tea and shopping, she returned to her lodgings and saw a light on in her room. She walked in to find Julian with his back to her, wearing a camel hair coat. He turned around, holding out his hands. Pym was nervous. Julian told her that he thought perhaps she was disappointed in him. It was only their second meeting. But, as Pym recorded, they soon had their 'arms around each other and I knew it wasn't so'.[5]

CHAPTER XXV

A Trip to the Botanical Gardens

Pym was convinced, from the outset, that Julian Amery was going to be someone very special in her life. For him, in turn, it was the 'first experience of true love'.[1]

The next day, she found him again waiting in her rooms. He was wearing a brown suit and a red spotted tie. He walked her to St Giles', where she was meeting friends, and they made plans for the evening. Pym went to his rooms in Balliol, where there were three blond Etonians 'like teddy bears'. Two of them were probably Julian's close friends, Simon Wardell and Sandy Hope. When they left, Julian kissed her with such force that he hurt her nose and 'made it crooked'.

They had supper at Stewart's, where they ate chicken and fish and drank wine. Julian was charming, showering her with compliments and kissing her fingertips throughout supper. Afterwards, they went on to the Oxford Playhouse to see a production of Ibsen's *Ghosts*. The play – about incest, illegitimacy and venereal disease – seems an odd choice for a romantic date. Pym wrote that 'it was the most terrifying play she had ever seen'. In the interval they talked about their life ambitions. She hinted about her relationship with Henry and her unhappiness. Julian told her that he 'couldn't bear to die without having done something by which he could be remembered'. Then they returned to the play. Its horrifying conclusion left them both feeling 'frightened and distressed'. Back in Pym's room, they shared a bottle of wine, before Julian headed back to his rooms at Balliol. She wrote him a love poem and felt grateful for the happiness she felt. The next morning, she wrote him a 'Stevie Smith' letter, which she posted in the Broad, feeling 'intensely happy'.[2]

Pym had arranged to see Jock in his Banbury Road flat, but he was critical about her Finnish novel, which left her feeling depressed and tearful. Seeing Jock in his flat brought back painful memories of Henry, 'my own life seemed pointless and just a waste of time if I wasn't even going to be able to write'. She went back to her digs and cried, thinking there was nothing to live for and feeling more miserable than ever. Jock's criticism had hit her hard. The next day, she pulled herself together and thought about writing a new novel or getting a job.[3]

She went to a pacifist meeting in the town hall, where she spotted the Liddell brothers and Julian Amery in the audience. Afterwards she ran after Julian to ask if he were going to sign the 'Peace Pledge'. He took her hand and asked if they could go back to her rooms. She felt happy, looking at his 'dear little face'; he told her that she was looking very sweet. They walked back arm in arm, stopping at the Randolph to buy a bottle of Niersteiner wine. Pym told him all about her Finnish novel, which he asked to read. Back in her room once again, they 'drank wine and talked and loved'. She confessed that he was just what she needed: 'To have Julian say in his young, intense voice – God, you are so sweet! *So ist das leben – und die liebe – und so bin ich!*[4]

Pym recalled making a half-hearted attempt to convert Julian to pacifism, but he told her that he thought there were worse things than war, and 'if he thought all Beauty was going out of his life he would simply shoot himself'. She put her arms around him at the top of her staircase and they kissed. She wondered what Henry and Jock would make of it all, but decided that they would not understand.

She and Julian met again the next morning outside the Ashmolean. They looked out at the Randolph Hotel and the bright blue sky behind. Pym was carrying a notebook and *Continual Dew*, the new poetry collection by John Betjeman. Julian was also holding a book and she asked if it was interesting: 'It's not now,' he replied, charmingly. 'We were like two people having a coltish flirtation.' He bought her a bunch of violets and she gave back six – 'one for every occasion we had met'. She told Julian how much she loved the Botanical Gardens and the orchids in the hothouses. Then he left to write an essay.

Inspired by her reading, Pym wrote Julian a poem in the style of John Betjeman.

Oh the sky is blue behind it
And the little towers of stone
Of the Randolph Hotel will still be there
When this present day has flown.

When Jay has quite forgotten
That one early closing day
He leaned against the wall with me
And I would not go away.

And I went back to my lodgings
And there I made a shrine
Of *Oxford Comment* and violets
And the bottle that once held wine.

And I took a glass I had used before
And filled it to the brim
And I thought as I drank of the night before
When I had been with him . . .[5]

The fifth of March 1938 was a glorious hot day in Oxford, 'full of sunshine and happiness'. Pym went to lunch with Julian in his rooms at Balliol, 'eggs with cream on the top, chicken and chocolate mousse'. They drank their favourite Niersteiner wine and she was flooded with joy: 'the sun was shining all the time when we were eating and drinking and kissing'. During an afternoon walk, the pair discussed going away together for the weekend, to the Cotswolds or even Italy. They visited the Botanical Gardens, where they lay down on the grass under a tree by the river. There were bunches of mistletoe in the branches, so they kissed and kissed again. Julian told Pym about his older brother, John, whom he described as 'more charming and more cruel than he was'.[6]

John Amery was a troubled young man. From his earliest years, he had displayed signs of disturbing behaviour. His relationship with his younger brother was difficult. When Julian was a baby, John had thrown a lighted match into his pram and tried to poison his milk bottles by washing them in liquid polish. When he first saw the new baby he had a screaming tantrum, upending his breakfast and storming out of the nursery. Nanny Mead found him 'not quite normal' – which would prove to be an understatement.[7]

John always carried around his large teddy bear, taking it to restaurants and buying it drinks and comic magazines. He also had a fixation with his overcoat and would buy an extra seat for it in the cinema or at the theatre.[8] He was sent to Harrow, his father's school, but disliked rules and ran away to become a car mechanic. He was found and returned and sent to a renowned psychiatrist who came to the conclusion that he had 'no moral sense of right and wrong . . . no sense of remorse or shame'.[9] He was sexually precocious and during his teenage years contracted syphilis. He claimed that he was selling his body to homosexual men for money.

By the time Julian was in Summer Fields prep school in Oxford, John had married a woman called Una Wing. She was a prostitute, frequenting London's West End, and considered her husband to be a 'sexual pervert'. He continued to sell his body to men for money and paid prostitutes to beat him. He also liked to force his wife to watch whilst he had sex with other women. Leo Amery and his gentle wife, Bryddie, who doted on John, were at their wits' end.[10] Their latest worry was that John, who was a staunch anti-communist, had come under the influence of the French fascist leader Jacques Doriot. Under his tutelage, John travelled to Austria, Italy and Germany to witness fascism for himself.[11] Even then, no one could have anticipated the consequences of his actions.

Back in the Botanical Gardens, Barbara and Julian talked about Budapest. She lay on the ground with her head on her arms, willing herself to 'capture and hold the happiness of that moment'.[12] The day only improved. They went into the hothouses to look at the fish and palms: 'Julian kissed me by the orchids and stole a spray of three for me . . . they were pinky mauve with purple centres like velvet.' She liked the sweet smell, though he thought they had the whiff 'of the tomb'. She quoted Andrew Marvell: 'The grave's a fine and private place/ But none I think do there embrace.'[13] She said she would prefer a marble vault together than a house in North Oxford, or a farm in the *puszta*. Then they wandered down Rose Lane and into Balliol – where they had tea and peppermint creams – and Pym kissed him, smearing lipstick on his forehead. He seemed to have none of Henry's aversion to lipstick.

The next morning, Pym went to the English Reading Room

and wrote Julian a letter, in part to dispel the 'unhappy associations' of the place.[14] The next few days were warm and sunny, and filled with Julian. Lunch in his rooms consisted of 'fish, duck and green peas, fresh peaches and cream, sherry, Niersteiner and port'. After his scout had cleared the dishes, they sat looking out of the window: 'There was one long, happy embrace which was so lovely that I would gladly have died there and then.' Julian then had to see his tutor. As he stood at the mirror, combing his hair, Pym sat at his desk and wrote him a farewell note. He came up behind her, kissed her and said 'Servus'. Julian was on his way to Spain, with two of his Oxford friends, to report on the civil war there.

Pym recorded, rather melodramatically, that this was the last time she saw him. In fact, she would see him again, but not ever at Oxford. For that she was grateful, as she wanted to preserve, in a place she loved, what had been an unclouded and perfect love affair.

She inscribed a postcard of the Swiss artist Arnold Boecklin's *Die Insel der Toten* (the Isle of the Dead) with their initials and the dates of their first meeting and their last, and '*Neuer Frühling gibt zurück*'. She thought the new spring a perfect leitmotif for their relationship: 'He and the spring have given me back what the winter took from me.' As she left, Pym took a red anemone from her buttonhole and left it on top of Julian's pale blue pyjamas. Then she walked around his rooms, touching things and kissing the mantelpiece. She walked slowly out onto St Giles', in a happy daze. Pym went back to her digs to change for a dinner at St Hilda's. She wore a green chiffon dress and pearls and diamonds. As she left her room, she saw two huge bunches of daffodils in the hall and a card written in German from Julian saying that, although he had to go away, he thought of her: 'I felt it was the perfect ending to what had been one of the happiest episodes of my life.'[15]

CHAPTER XXVI

An Old Brown Horse

Barbara Pym sat by the fire in the drawing room of Morda Lodge, smoking a cigarette and listening to the wireless. Her Aunt Janie was knitting a white jersey and they sat together in companionable silence.

Pym was in high spirits from her 'spring reawakening'. She had written to Julian, who was on his way to Spain, wishing him good luck in his exam results. He posted a warm and loving letter from the 'gloomy' Lord Warden Hotel in Dover, which reminded him, he said, of the Randolph. 'Darling,' he wrote. 'If anything in the world could have got me through Pass mods, they [her letters] would have.' He told her that it was all to no avail as he had forgotten to attend his French unseen examination. But he was so excited to be travelling to Spain that he hardly cared about Oxford. 'If I never come back, well you can remember that at least I cared [about you].' He told her to say a prayer for him on his birthday and buy a bottle of Niersteiner to drink his health: 'Meeting you Darling has been one of the big pieces of luck in my life and if I've mended your heart, well that is more than I ever dared to ask.'[1] He asked her to visit him in London when he returned.

Julian was rather enjoying the pose of young man going

off to war, leaving behind his sweetheart, but he was too kind and too honest to lead her on: 'I cannot promise that I will always be faithful to my little Finn, but I can promise you that she will have to be a very charming woman to gain my heart now that I have at least your memory.' He also told her that if 'Wien' (Vienna) was now a 'concentration camp', she should remember that the 'Danube does flow through Budapest as well'. He told her to 'be happy and smile when you think of Julian'.[2]

Pym was aware of the worsening situation in Europe. On 12 March 1938, Hitler's troops marched into Austria and on the fifteenth the Führer himself arrived in Vienna in a triumphant blaze of glory, cheered by 200,000 German Austrians. His speech at the Heldenplatz announced that annexing Austria was his 'greatest achievement'. Friedbert had recently been in touch.[3] He had been posted to Dresden and wrote to say that it was *schade* (too bad) that she was not in Germany 'to experience these so great events which have shaken the heart of Germany'. He was clearly referring to the Anschluss. Pym wrote a 'very cautious' letter in reply, justifying it to herself on the grounds that she did not 'like to be rude to a dear friend who has been always so kind to her when she was *allein in einer Grosstadt* [alone in a big city] like Marlene Dietrich in the song'.[4]

Her heart was still full of Julian. In Pym's diaries, she reflected on their relationship. He was soon to turn nineteen and she twenty-five, but she felt that five years and ten months did not seem to make much difference to their relationship. She had only spent a total of twenty hours in his company, but none of that mattered. It was the intensity of the romance and the happiness it brought her that mattered. She didn't care if she never saw or heard from him again – and indeed she felt that 'it might almost be better so'. The brief encounter had been the perfect antidote to her misery over Henry: 'Nothing can take away what has been and in my heart there is so much more than I could even write here. Harold Julian Amery – Barbara Mary Crampton Pym.'[5]

She was reading two writers who would be an important influence on her writing and were inextricably bound up with her love for Julian. The first was John Betjeman, whose latest poetry collection she had been carrying when she met Julian outside the Ashmolean. In a 1978 BBC radio interview for *Finding a Voice*, Pym cited Betjeman: 'His glorifying of ordinary things and buildings and his subtle appreciation of different kinds of churches and churchmanship made an immediate appeal to me.'[6] 'Ordinary things' would be her theme, too. The best-known poems of *Continual Dew* were 'The Arrest of Oscar Wilde at Cadogan Hotel' and 'Slough', in which Betjeman mocks the industrialisation of the town where 'there isn't grass to graze a cow' and everything – from fruit and meat to milk and beans to minds and breath – is 'tinned'.[7]

The second writer was Stevie Smith – particularly her 1936 *Novel on Yellow Paper*. The book is structured as the random typings of a bored secretary, where she discusses death, life, sex, relationships, even Nazism. Here she is discussing sex, which in retrospect seems risqué for a novel of the 1930s:

> Now this, brings us slap up against that mighty ogre Sex that is a worse ogre to the novelist than those families histories I so cleverly avoided a few pages back. But oh how I have enjoyed sex I do enjoy myself so much I cannot pass it over . . .
>
> Cenobites just can't take sex as they find it, it has to be conflict and frustration and really so-o-o important in a way it isn't really important, though it is important in the way if it wasn't there it would be a pretty punk world. But you could never say of a cenobite that he enjoyed sex, no you couldn't hardly say that, not that he enjoyed sex, oh no not to say enjoy.[8]

In the spring of 1938, Pym wrote a joint letter to Jock and the newlywed Harveys, whom Jock was staying with in Helsinki. It was self-mocking – a parody of herself in the manner of Stevie Smith:

> Now it is spring and the garden is full of beautiful flowers, primroses, violets, daffodils, scyllas, grape hyacinths, anemones, *und so weiter* (and so on). And Miss Pym is looking out of the window – and you will be asking now who is this Miss Pym and I will tell you she is a spinster lady who was thought to be disappointed in love and so now you know who is this Miss Pym.
>
> But this Miss Pym, although she is, so to speak, a maid, is not dancing in a ring, no sir and she is not frisking, no buddy, no how. She is seeing an old brown horse which is walking with a slow majestic dignity across this field and she is thinking that it is the horse she will be imitating and not the lambs.[9]

Henry later recalled 'how beautifully, delightfully, cleverly, deliciously, inventively dotty Pym's letters to Finland were'.[10] What he failed to see, then and before, was the very real pain that lay beneath the humour.

In the summer of 1937, Jock had gone on holiday with the Harveys to France and Italy. He wrote to Pym in the style of Compton-Burnett:

Ladies and Gentlemen

'Ah, very fine,' said Elsie. 'These hills are like Alps and perhaps there is skiing. It is like dear Finland – but there is no lake. It is a pity.'

'No Elsie, I do not think it is very like Finland,' said Henry. 'In Finland there are no such mountains. In fact, there are no mountains at all.'

'True, but the nature is like,' said Elsie.

'You must not say "nature" when you mean "scenery",' said Henry, 'and I do not think you have brushed your teeth today and I fear you have not been to the lavatory. We should not like to be constipated, should we Jock?'

'No,' said Jock, 'I suppose we should not. And I daresay that she should not like it either and it is known that women have different tastes to men. Why do you not let her decide?' . . .

'Here is an hotel,' said Henry. 'Shall we stop here?'

'It is well recommended,' said Jock, 'that is something.'

'Let us drive round and look at other hotels,' said Elsie. 'Let us choose after full consideration.'

'Let us make haste,' said Jock, 'there is thunder and lightning and much rain.'

'Ah, thunder is so dangerous,' said Elsie.[11]

It was Jock's way of showing Pym that she had made a lucky escape from Henry's controlling and pedantic behaviour. Pym responded in kind, though her highly tuned parody is more effective and more comic than Jock could deliver:

'Those flowers were some I picked in the garden of St Hilda's in the spring of five years ago . . . So dear Lorenzo, would you like these poor flowers that have waited five years to be given to you? No? It was what I thought. You would not wish me to be deprived of any sentimental token that would give me pleasure.'

'No,' said the Herr Lektor in an emphatic voice – 'I should not wish it.'

'I think Miss Pym is not quite herself today,' said Mr Liddell, in a nervous, hurrying tone. 'This talk of pressed flowers and sentimental tokens is not good' . . .

'Oh fancy if all passion should not be spent!' said the Frau Lektor in a high, agitated tone.

'Oh, do not speak of it. It is more than I can bear,' said her husband sinking down on to the couch and taking a glass of schnapps.

'Well, well,' said Miss Pym, coming into the room. 'Two old men bearing an imaginary burden, that is what I see' . . .

'Oh, do not say any more. My head is reeling. I cannot keep up with this,' said Mr Harvey, in a low, groaning voice . . . 'we do not wish to be hearing about these dreadful people she is associating with.'

'Oh, fancy that the Herr Lektor should end a sentence with a preposition,' cried Mrs Harvey in a delighted tone.[12]

Pym bravely embraced Elsie as a necessary part of her friendship with Jock and Henry. She also let Henry know that she was not pining away. She told Jock, Henry and Elsie about her 'dear little young boy friend, Mr J', who was now in Spain, and she wished Henry and Elsie well: 'Miss Pym is asking tenderly after Herr Lecktor Henry and his beautiful wife . . . and she is hoping to see dear Henry and darling Elsie if they come to England in the summer and she is hoping that marriage has improved dear Henry and that he will not any more be rude to her.' She told them that she was reading *The Christian Year* and *Don Juan*, as well as Rainer Maria Rilke and the *Daily Mirror*, 'and the so nice poems of John Betjeman, which remind her of standing looking up at the Randolph on early closing day and having a coltish flirtation with a young man'. Jock had not liked Julian and found him unprepossessing. She joked that it was not true: 'For Jock has not seen him in his pretty blue suit, looking like a handsome little boy out in the East End.'[13]

Well, now, what is she doing, this Miss Pym, what has she to tell her new friends in Finland . . . You will perhaps be more interested to hear that Miss Pym has written 60 pages of her new novel in her lovely marbled notebook. Now this is not so much because during this week she has been doing other things. Yes, she has been sewing and buying new clothes . . .

Miss Pym is praying every day for Mr J. in Spain and she is writing him a beautiful poem for his birthday and it is in heroic couplets and it is such a clever poem because it spells his name down the side and it is not sentimental, no sir, it is most unique . . .

And she is happy again now because she has had another letter from that so kind, nice Mr Liddell out of Helsingfors. And she is so especially, so *immensely* pleased with the photograph of her dear sister Elsie, who is so charming and can speak Finnish, which is the most difficult language in the world . . . so cheerio chaps says this Miss Pym.[14]

Pym could not stop thinking about Stevie Smith's brilliantly innovative *Novel on Yellow Paper*. For all its bright humour and inventiveness, there were also darker themes. The heroine is forced to address her own subconscious anti-Semitism, fostered and encouraged by her German boyfriend, when she confronts the reality of the Nazi persecution of the Jews:

Oh how I felt that feeling of cruelty in Germany, and the sort of vicious cruelty that isn't battle-cruelty, but doing people to death in lavatories. Now how I remember how Karl said, No . . . No, Karl said, Germany couldn't be so cruel like they said at the beginning of the war . . . But then see what they did this time to the Jews and the Communists . . . in the latrines, and the cruel beating and holding down and beating and enjoying it for the cruelty.

Oh how deeply neurotic the German people is, and how weak, and how they are giving themselves up to this sort of cruelty and viciousness, how Hitler cleared up the vice that was so in Berlin, in every postal district some new vice, how Hitler cleared that up all. And now look how it runs with the uniforms and the swastikas. And how many uniforms, how many swastikas, how many deaths and maimings, and hateful dark cellars and lavatories. Ah how decadent, how evil is Germany to-day.[15]

As with *The Oppermanns*, it is clear that Pym was familiar with novels exposing Nazi brutality and anti-Semitism. But there is only silence. Her 'Stevie Smith' letters are peppered with German poetry, song lyrics and expressions. Beneath the humour, her resentment and barely suppressed anger broke through the calm facade:

For this Miss Pym, this spinster, she is getting to a good age now and she is got very touchy like and crabby . . . And then everyone is angry with her because she says these things and is not behaving like the old brown horse I was telling you about, but she is not minding that everyone is angry, no not at all . . . Oh you want to know everything, you old people, with your wagging fingers . . . well you will never know now, because this Miss Pym, this old brown horse spinster, is all shut up like an oyster or clam. And now she is an old stuffed-shirt is this *gnadiges Fraulein* . . . no sir, no how, but she is a devoted friend, Oh yes, she is so devoted.[16]

Pym's letters in the first part of 1938 have a tone of increasing desperation. With Jock in Finland visiting Henry and Elsie, and Julian in Spain, she felt even more isolated and hopeless. It is clear, too, that her pro-German sensibilities were causing concerns at home: 'And Miss Pym is reading the newspapers and listening to *Wein du Stadt meiner Traume* on the wireless. But it is not that any more. No it is Deutschland. *Ein Reich, Ein Führer – Heil Hitler!* That is what it is.'[17]

She was also anxious about Julian. She scanned the newspapers for news from the front in Spain: 'I look every day in the papers to see if he is dead yet.' What she really wanted, despite her protestations, was to be 'imparadis'd in Mr J's arms in Balliol'.[18]

CHAPTER XXVII

In which our Heroine sees Friedbert for the Last Time

Pym wrote to Jock again in the style of ICB explaining her alienation from her family and their disputes about her German feelings:

'What do you think about Austria and Germany?' asked Aunt Helen.

'Well, I always like the Germans,' said Barbara.

'Oh, Barbara, surely you do not like the Germans,' said Aunt Helen.

'The ones I have met have been very nice,' said Barbara in a firm, level tone. 'I have a friend in Dresden . . .'

'Ah, I expect it is a young man,' said Aunt Helen in a triumphant tone, 'that is what it is.'

'Well, yes,' said Barbara, 'it is a young man, but that is not why . . .'

'Oh Barbara, you surely would not marry a German?' persisted Aunt Helen.

'No, I have no intention of marrying a German,' said Barbara firmly.

'Well it would be something to talk about if Barbara married
a German, would it not?' persisted Aunt Helen.[1]

Pym had, at Jock's suggestion, deleted her portrayals of Hanns
and Friedbert from *Some Tame Gazelle*. They were rather crude
caricatures of the men she had known, but she had not wholly
given up on them. In *Gervase and Flora*, the heroine consoles
herself after Gervase's rejection by enjoying a flirtation with two
'Finnish' students, Torni and Ooli. Torni is fair and handsome
and kisses first gently and then fiercely, muttering endearments
in his own language. In the end, she chooses black-haired Ooli,
who, like Friedbert, has eyes the colour of the Dover–Ostend
sea on a calm day. 'Then I don't make you sick,' he quips. It is
Ooli who restores Flora's confidence.[2]

For her portrayal of the two Finns, Pym (who knew nothing
of Finland) drew on her memories of Hanns and Friedbert. The
fact that Ooli frequently lapses into German is something of a
giveaway. His funny broken English phrases, such as: 'You are
not in the right state of condition' are Friedbert's. Flora picks
up a photograph of Ooli – 'so stern so handsome' – and thinks
he looks like something out of a 'German spy film'. His catch-
phrase is: 'Get Knowledge, Get Understanding'. He confesses
to Flora that 'we have no humour as a race'. He wants a lovely
English mistress, but more than this, would prefer an English
wife. He speaks of Goethe's *Werther*. Pym's attempt at drawing
Finnish men was a disaster and no doubt one of the reasons
Jock disliked the book.

Friedbert's recent letter reminded her of their passion and,
despite the worrying European situation, Pym was determined
to travel back to Germany to see him. Her parents were not
unusual amongst the British middle classes in having been willing
in the mid-thirties to send their offspring on visits to Nazi

Germany. But by the spring of 1938, few could believe that Hitler's aim of defeating communism and restoring his country to greatness was all that he intended. What is more, this time Barbara was not returning to Cologne with the National Union of Students, but was making a personal trip to Dresden, intending to stay for a month. Aged just twenty-four, she was going unchaperoned to visit an SS officer who was close to Hitler. It is not clear that Dors and Links fully grasped the situation, however.

Pym left for Germany on 3 May. She had missed Friedbert's twenty-seventh birthday on 11 April, though had made a note of it in her diary. Friedbert met her at the station in Dresden, took her to her accommodation and then they had lunch. In the afternoon, he had a sore throat and was feverish, so after dinner they parted and she slept well in her digs. Friedbert was busy with work during the day, so they established a pattern. Pym would spend the morning sightseeing, Friedbert would come for lunch, return to work, and then they would meet for supper.

Pym's diary for this period reveals little of Friedbert's life as an SS officer, though it is clear that there were tensions in some of their conversations. She does not record why Friedbert was stationed in Dresden. However in 1936, the Dresden Gestapo fused with the criminal police under the umbrella of the SS. By 1938, the Gestapo had moved their headquarters into the former Continental Hotel, just across the street from the city police station. Disturbingly, from 1936 the Nazis used the Münchner Platz as a 'special court' where alleged traitors were put on trial and executed. The site used for the killings was the courtyard between the courthouse and the prison complex; the instrument of execution was the guillotine. It is estimated that over six thousand Dresden Jews were persecuted, deported or executed between 1933 and 1945.[3] At the end of the war, the Dresden

Jewish community numbered just forty-one people. By 1938, Jewish shopkeepers were prohibited from trading; soon it would be announced that Jewish doctors were no longer permitted to practise medicine.

How much Pym knew of these developments is unclear, but during her month in Dresden she spent many hours at the Eden Hotel, where she drank coffee and had access to English papers. For the first four days of her holiday, she saw little of Friedbert. On 9 May they had lunch together, then tea and supper. In the evening, they went to see *Olympia* – Leni Riefenstahl's newly released Nazi propaganda film of the 1936 Olympic Games – in which Friedbert had taken part. 'Very good' was all Pym noted in her diary.

Friedbert introduced Barbara to two of his friends, a young woman called Inge and a man called Walter Naumann. 'We drank a lot – Rhine wine and cocktails.' They then went on to the Regina Palast where they drank champagne and danced until three in the morning. 'Not much sleep that night,' Pym wrote in her diary.[4]

They planned a trip to Prague at the weekend. In a letter to Jock, Pym confessed that things hadn't gone as well as expected. It was hot on the train and she and Friedbert made 'waspish' comments to one another. A handsome Czech began talking to Barbara during the journey, which made Friedbert jealous. He had never visited Prague before and did not seem to share Barbara's excitement.

'Oh the Golden City, I kept saying, the Golden City.'
'No I do not think it is Golden,' he said.
'To me it is Golden, it will always be Golden.'[5]

Sitting in a beer garden on her return to Dresden, Pym wrote to Jock telling him that she was educating Friedbert in the poems of John Betjeman. Friedbert would read the poems aloud to her, 'which is a treat'. She confessed, hilariously, that he found some of the lines difficult to translate, such as: 'The incumbent enjoying a supine incumbency.' Friedbert got his own back by translating long passages out of the Nazi party newspaper, the *Völkischer Beobachter*. There is something chillingly incongruous about the juxtaposition of Pym and Betjeman with the Nazi and his propaganda paper.

Of course Pym put a comic spin on it all. Friedbert, she told Jock, had a disconcerting habit of 'asking me things I feel I ought to know and don't':

F. Let us talk about Cromwell.
B. (in an interested, condescending tone) Cromwell? What about Cromwell?
F. (in a firm, direct tone) What was the influence of Cromwell on Milton?
B. (in a high, nervous, hurrying tone) The influence of Cromwell on Milton? Did you say the influence of Cromwell on Milton?
F. (giving the word its full meaning) Yes.[6]

Back in Dresden, they reset a pattern for their days: lunch and supper together during the week, more time at weekends. Sometimes after lunch, they would both fall asleep. Pym joked about Friedbert going back to the 'Büro', but it seems that he was doing more than office work. She joked in a letter to Jock: 'Supper has been brought in and I am waiting for dear Friedbert to come: it is all so domesticated. I feel I should say "The Master has to go to Pirna today – he will not be here for lunch." And then in he comes – the hasty husbandly kiss.'[7]

Pym's playing at being married to an SS officer had a very dark side. It is impossible to know how much she really knew about his working life, though she must have known about the worsening political situation. In Prague, she had joked about sending John Barnicot a postcard from the cafe where he had been shot – a reference to a plot line in *Some Tame Gazelle*. And she had also, at the same time, read a letter that Barnicot had sent to *The Times* about the Sudeten Germans. Following the Anschluss, Hitler's next ambition was the annexation of the Sudetenland. Perhaps this is the reason why Friedbert did not approve of Pym's enthusiasm for the 'Golden Land' of Czechoslovakia.

Pym's joke about the Master being in Pirna is also highly dubious, but, again, ignorance may have played a part. On 26 May, Friedbert took her for a brief sightseeing trip to Pirna, a medieval town on the Elbe, about twelve miles from Dresden. They had tea and then climbed the rocks at Rathen which revealed a wonderful view into Bohemia, but there were tensions. After supper, back in Dresden, they had 'a long, long talk and cleared up many things and ended up very happily'.[8]

What the 'long talk' was about, we will never know. But Friedbert's trips into Pirna reveal a dark and ugly twist to his story. In Pirna, the Nazis were preparing a part of the huge mental asylum at Sonnenstein Castle, overlooking the town, to convert it into a 'euthanasia' killing centre for the disabled. A gas chamber and crematorium were installed in the cellar there. This building was a trial run for the techniques later rolled out and refined for use at Auschwitz, Treblinka and the other death camps. Between 1940 and 1942, over fifteen thousand people were gassed in Sonnenstein.[9] Many of these killings took place before the Wannsee conference of January 1942, during which the 'Final Solution' to the Jewish question was agreed.

CHAPTER XXVIII

In which Pymska returns briefly Home to England and Vikki Olafsson goes to Poland

Pym's relationship with Friedbert Glück was nearing its end. Though the matters that needed 'clearing up' are unknown, it could be that she was finally having doubts about her boyfriend's politics. On 27 May, they had lunch and a walk in the Grosser Garten. Friedbert went back to work and then they met again for a late drink. 'Came home, had a talk and parted friends.'[1]

The pair met again over the next few days. On Pym's final day, Friedbert was working, but he came to supper at her digs, before leaving to write some letters. She went along with him to his room. Then they went to the Weindorf in Pragerstrasse: 'very nice. The mock turtle soup at the station.' Presumably, this is where she saw Friedbert for the last time. There is no record of their final meeting, only that it ended in typical Pym fashion: 'I chased my hat down Uhlenstr[asse].'[2] She left Dresden on Henry's birthday, the day before her own. On the train home there were many soldiers: 'all nice to me'.[3]

Julian sent 'Darling Vicki' a charming birthday letter, telling her that he had returned safely from Spain: 'I have not forgotten

BARBARA MARY CRAMPTON
PYM
(b. 1913)

HILARY CRAMPTON PYM (b. 1916)

DUNKERY 1921
J. & T. Hare, F. & J. Pym, M. Hodgson, E.J.S. Price,
F. White, M. White.

Miss Pym's family album

Dor and Links on
their wedding day

Miss Pym as a child

Sisters

Schooldays: somewhere among the bonneted girls of Liverpool College, Huyton, at the dedication of the new school chapel in 1927

Young Men in Fancy Dress
A novel by
Barbara Pym

To H.D.M.G.
who kindly informed me that I
had the makings of a style of my
own.

August 1929 · April 1930

Miss Pym, aged sixteen, writes her first novel, with 'the makings of a style of [her] own'

Miss Pym applying lipstick
and hanging out with friends

A Shropshire Lass

Miss Pym towers over her friends at St Hilda's College, Oxford

[Admit to the Camera also.]

BODLEIAN LIBRARY

I hereby *of my personal knowledge** recommend

(Applicant's name) † Miss Barbara Pym

(Applicant's college or address) St Hilda's College

as a fit person to be admitted to the privilege of using the Bodleian Library for purposes of study.

The main subject of the applicant's study will be

English Literature

(Recommender's signature) S. W. Rooke.

(Recommender's status) M.A.

(Date) May 3rd 1932

* The Librarian particularly requests that the recommender, when he has no adequate personal knowledge of the applicant, will cancel the above words and state separately the ground of his recommendation.

The recommendation should be signed by some one in a responsible position in Oxford or elsewhere. Ordinary cards of introduction or letters which merely state facts, but do not amount to a personal recommendation, cannot be accepted as sufficient.

† It is necessary that the recommender himself should fill in the name of the applicant.

(Applicant's signature) Barbara M Pym

[P. T. O.

Miss Pym gains admission to the Bodleian (left) and begins to flirt with many young men

Rupert Seeley Gleadow (left), whose love affair is captured in 'A record of the adventures of the celebrated Barbara M C Pym'

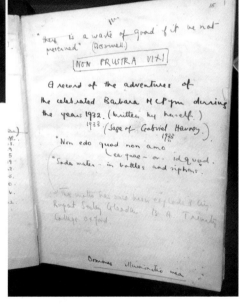

Miles and Rupert

The object of Miss Pym's enduring affection: Henry Harvey, a.k.a. Gabriel Harvey, a.k.a. Lorenzo, the model for the Archdeacon in *Some Tame Gazelle*

The triumvirate: Pym, 'Jock' Liddell, Harvey

Henry's evocative pencil sketch of Miss Pym

Summer vacation: with Barnicot, Liddell and Harvey at
Morda Lodge – all became characters in *Some Tame Gazelle*

Julian Amery addressing the Oxford Union in a debate on conscription,
April 1939. Miss Pym clipped this photograph from the pages of the
Oxford Mail and kept it on her mantelpiece beside a vase of flowers

that tomorrow is your birthday, may you have as many more as you gave me minutes of happiness and, contrary to the normal rate, may they make you, if possible more beautiful.' He told her that he was poor and could only give her love and that he had returned from Spain a little greyer and more wrinkled and that he hoped he would see her again. He also seemed to know about her trip to Germany, asking: 'Have you married a German?' He told her that he had his back to the Randolph, as she had recalled in her John Betjeman poem, and that thoughts of her interrupted a serious conversation about the Sudetenland. He ended on a romantic note: 'Will you come and see me one day, just walk up to the front door of 112 Eaton Square, bang twice with each bronzen knocker and walk down the long marble corridor to the room where Julian walks, endlessly dictating to a battery of tired secretaries. He might stop for a moment to kiss you, as he does not on your birthday.'[4]

Pym would see Julian again, but almost as soon as she got home to England she made plans to return to Europe. Once again, she was demonstrating a political naivety or recklessness. Once again, Dor and Links failed to intervene on the plans of their headstrong daughter. Pym's intention was to be an English governess to a family who lived in Katowice, southern Poland.

Before she left for Poland, Pym saw the married Harveys in Oxford. She made no record of the meeting, but she clearly liked Elsie and they began a correspondence.

On 25 August 1938, she wrote in her diary:

I'm really starting a new life today, but I won't make it more significant than it is by turning over the page. Why shouldn't it be near Julian? I want it so straight on from there, with him still in my mind and the remembrance of the hours I spent with him as something warm and comforting to draw about me like a camel hair coat when I'm lonely and frightened and uncertain.[5]

Ahead of her trip, Pym went shopping with her mother and Hilary in Liverpool, buying black lace for an evening gown, some turquoise wool, a white lace blouse and a white and gold evening bag. Irena treated her to a long fur coat for the cold Polish winter.[6]

On 29 August, Pym arrived in Poland: 'country flat with factories – poor looking'. She settled in well with the family. Her pupils were Ula and Zuza, the daughters of a Jewish doctor, Dr Michale Alberg. Pym was also expected to teach English to his wife. She went sightseeing with the girls, enjoyed walking the family dog and eating fried potatoes with yoghurt. With her novelist's eye, she hoovered up local details. 'Saw a large animal like a wolf hanging up outside a provision shop . . . went into the market and saw many curious mushrooms, fungi etc arranged on the stalls.' More 'thrillingly', she went for an evening walk and saw 'Polish prostitutes and thieves being taken away in a horse-drawn van. The street lamps shining on wet pavements gave me a momentary *Sehnsucht* for England.'[7] On 31 August she noted in her diary that a Sudeten German delegation was negotiating in Prague.

In Poland, she adopted her Finnish persona, dressing in her 'Vikki Olafsson mackintosh and a battered Austrian hat'. The weather had become wet and cold and Mrs Alberg took Pym to Częstochowa, a city on the Warta river, in her car: 'Forests and barefooted peasants. Saw a wonderful church – turquoise marble, pink, grey, dark grey, white fawn, green crochet work around the pulpit and altars in green and puce. Virgin Mary picture with gold door sliding over it. And music.' The town was famous for this shrine to the Virgin Mary, known as the

Black Madonna, housed in the Pauline monastery of Jasna Góra. The family took Pym on outings to Bielska and a forest belonging to the Prince of Pless. She loved the wonderful mountain scenery and the 'dark romantic forests'. But she was lonely for English company.

Things improved when she went to the vice-consulate to meet the British consul, Mr Thwaites, whom she found 'easy, intelligent and amusing'. She met him again the following day and they walked in the woods: 'Talked all the time of Modern Art, poetry, America and Spain. I couldn't believe I was in Poland. It felt just like Oxford.'[8]

Now that her relationship with Friedbert had cooled, Julian was much on Pym's mind again. Hearing any English news reminded her of him. Pym's mood had darkened. One night she had a nightmare that Julian was dead. She met a doctor friend of Mrs Alberg, 'a jolly little Jew', and read *Pride and Prejudice* in the evening, but even Jane Austen didn't seem to charm: 'In the evening Vikki [Pym] was temperamental – but after cigarettes, some Mozart and a Brandenburg concerto felt better and went for a walk with the dog Bianco.' She saw Mr Thwaites again and spent two hours in his flat looking at 'modern pictures' and listening to music. Then they went to dinner in a German restaurant and took another long walk: 'Oh the delight of English conversation and pleasant company.'[9]

Just as Pym was beginning to settle in, however, the political situation deteriorated, with the genuine possibility that war might break out and she would not be permitted to cross the German border. The annexation of Sudetenland was expected immediately. At a rally in Nuremberg, Hitler made his intentions clear. A few days later, Neville Chamberlain flew out to meet the Führer. The world was watching to see what would happen next. Dr Alberg was extremely concerned, though Pym did not seem to understand his anxiety. Back at home, her parents were also worried and wanted their daughter home and safe. Pym later confessed that in Poland 'everyone was terrified'. None more so than Jews such as the good doctor and his wife. Pym was potentially living the reality of that prescient novel she had read a few years before, *The Oppermanns*. Her failure to comprehend this suggests that she was in denial about the Nazis and the nature of the regime.

CHAPTER XXIX

Miss Pym leaves Poland in a Hurry, whilst there is still Time

In the early hours of 16 September 1938, Barbara Pym left the home of the Albergs. She had been given 'enough food to feed myself and numerous Germans all through Germany and still have a lot to bring home here'. She made her way to the car, where the family chauffeur was waiting. As a last gesture, Mrs Alberg grabbed a bunch of gladioli out of a vase and thrust them into Pym's hands.

Dr Alberg bravely and selflessly accompanied Pym all the way to Beuthen, the German frontier station. He was very nervous in the car, giving her instructions 'not to speak at all at the frontier but just to show my passport and money and not to speak to a soul in Germany'. She was a little anxious, but relaxed when she finally left Poland after an eight-hour journey, 'because of course Germany seemed just as usual. Naturally, they knew very little about the crisis and I talked to so many people and everyone was very kind to me.' She even found time in Berlin to see the famous Unter den Linden and to walk along the Wilhelmstrasse: 'felt disappointed that it didn't show signs of feverish activity. It was so dark and silent.'[1]

Somewhere along the way, Pym lost half of her luggage. She

began to feel alone and tired, with a splitting headache. She sat at the Friedrichstrasse station smoking a gold-tipped Polish cigarette, 'feeling as I used to feel when I came back from Oxford and sat waiting at Snowhill station Birmingham that my whole life seems to be spent sitting on stations all over Europe leaving people I love'.[2] She wrote this account of her travels two weeks after she had arrived back in safety to England. The day she returned, Parliament approved Chamberlain's plans to meet Hitler's demands.

On 30 September, Pym wrote: 'And now we are here with seven gas masks in the house and Mr Chamberlain is safely back in England and thanks to him there isn't going to be any war.' That was the very day that the Munich agreement was signed, approving cession to Germany of the Sudeten German territory of Czechoslovakia. 'Peace For Our Time' shrieked the headlines, echoing Chamberlain's words.

The Union Jack, the Tricolour and the Swastika flags fluttered together in the streets of Munich. But not everybody was convinced. On 5 October, Winston Churchill made a powerful declaration in Parliament, denouncing the Munich agreement:

We have suffered a total and unmitigated defeat . . . you will find that in a period of time which may be measured by years, but may be measured by months, Czechoslovakia will be engulfed in the Nazi regime. We are in the presence of a disaster of the first magnitude . . . we have sustained a defeat without a war, the consequences of which will travel far with us along our road . . . we have passed an awful milestone in our history, when the whole equilibrium of Europe has been deranged and that the terrible words have for the time being been pronounced against the Western democracies: 'Thou art weighed in the balance and found wanting.' And do not suppose that this is the end. This is only the beginning of the reckoning. This is only the first sip, the first foretaste of a bitter cup which will be proffered to us year by year unless by a supreme recovery of moral health and martial vigour, we arise again and take our stand for freedom as in the olden time.[3]

There was another man, known to Pym by association, who vehemently opposed appeasement – and that was Leo Amery, Julian's father. When Chamberlain announced his flight to Munich to the cheers of the House, Amery was one of only four members who remained seated (the others were Churchill, Anthony Eden and Harold Nicolson). He was the man who demanded that Chamberlain should 'Speak for England'.

Pym's mention of gas masks is telling. Despite hopes that Chamberlain had avoided war, it was becoming increasingly obvious that this was not so. As well as the distribution of gas masks, trenches were being dug in London's parks in preparation for German air attacks.

Meanwhile, desperate for 'Something To Do', Pym made plans to live in London with Hilary, who had signed up for a secretarial course. Pym's hope was to continue her writing. She told Elsie Harvey: 'I honestly don't believe I can be happy unless I am writing. It seems to be the only thing I really want to do.'[4]

CHAPTER XXX

We rummage in the Lumber Room

Back in the spring of 1938, Pym had begun a new novel. It was a tribute to Julian and a farewell to Henry.

In *Gervase and Flora*, Pym had dramatised their frequent quarrels. Gervase criticises Flora for being 'ridiculously romantic' and overdramatising with her capacity for suffering: 'I believe you almost like it,' he explains, not unreasonably. He is a chauvinist, telling her that women are peculiar; they don't know what they want. 'Women and their interests and their conversations are always so trivial,' he complains. But Flora, like her creator, knows exactly what she wants. And, as in all Pym's novels, the apparently trivial conversations of women reveal a strength of character singularly lacking in the feckless men.

Now that Gervase is finally married, Flora knows that she must let go, that he was never really hers to begin with: so why should she mind that he is now Ingeborg's? She decides how she will resolve her problem. She will lock away her feelings. In a discussion about jumble sales, Pym revealed Flora's, and her own, new philosophy:

'On tidying the box-room lumber room you might come across an old governess which the children had outgrown.'

'Yes,' agreed Flora, 'just as one looks back in the lumber room
of one's mind and finds there old loves that one has outgrown.'[1]

The metaphor of the 'lumber room' of one's mind and past
memories stayed with Pym. For the title of her new novel, she
alternated between 'Beatrice Wyatt' and 'The Lumber Room'.
She bought a handsome marbled notebook and inscribed in it
an epigraph from Betjeman: 'Of marble brown and veined/ He
did the pulpit make.' On the front page, she wrote: 'begun
March, 1938'.

Writing to Jock and the Harveys with renewed vigour, she
told them that she was starting a new novel: 'there are no Finns
or Swedes or Germans or Hungars'.[2] Pym did not mention that
the character based on Henry was a widower whose wife had
recently died.

Her novel was about two sisters, Frances and Beatrice Wyatt
(Beatrice was Elsie Harvey's middle name). They are spinsters
in their mid-thirties. Beatrice, the younger sister, is an Oxford
don. Frances lives at home with their mother in the little country
town of Middle Eaton.[3] Mrs Wyatt, a widow, longs for her clever
daughters to get married, but this is becoming increasingly
unlikely. Her husband, William, died twenty years ago: 'The
realisation that she might never see him again – for her religious
views were hazy – had aroused in her fondness for him which
she had never felt when he was alive.'[4] So far, so *Pride and
Prejudice*. Frances and her mother's lives revolve around the
parish. The vicar is married to a clever Somerville girl called
Jane Cleveland (later Jane Otway). The vicar's son, Gerald
Cleveland (later Lawrence/Hughie Otway) is in his first year at
Balliol.

Beatrice is on her way home to her village of 'Middle Eaton'
for the long vacation. On the train back to Shropshire she bumps
into Gerald, who begins a flirtation with the older woman.

Beatrice has seen changes in Oxford since she was an under-graduate. Then it was all cocktail parties and bad behaviour, aesthetes and hearties. Now it is sherry parties, political meetings and men with long hair wearing teddy bear coats and suede shoes. Gerald/Hughie is closely modelled on Julian Amery. He is thin and dark, with a 'childish mouth'. Like Amery, he wears a sharp suit under his camel coat. Beatrice notices that he has come from Schools (examinations), as he is wearing a white bow tie and a salmon pink shirt.

Beatrice buries her head in her book to avoid having to spend the journey with him, but he engages her in conversation with the words: 'Good afternoon Miss Wyatt, you look so forlorn', in his distinctive, drawling voice. He insists on them sharing the carriage, offers her Russian cigarettes and says that, with those cheekbones, she looks like a blonde Russian. Despite herself, she is drawn in by his confidence and self-assurance and his intense stare. He tells her that one day he will be famous and that his birth town will be remembered as the place where Gerald Cleveland was born.

Unconcerned that she is several years older, he begins to flirt, feeds her sherry and tells her that women of his own age are boring: Oxford female students drink cocoa and talk loudly in the hope of being overheard and written about in *The Isis*, he says. He invites Beatrice to lunch, tells her that she's beautiful, and holds out his hands and takes her fingers. He has 'conti-nental polish' because he has spent time in Vienna. So far so Julian Amery.

Beatrice feels displaced. Her neighbours think that she's too clever for them and resent that she appears to talk down to them. Her mother fusses over her, bringing her breakfast in bed, which she doesn't want, and has a habit of popping her head around the door to ensure that her daughter is not working too hard. And yet in Oxford, she cannot relate to the 'bluestocking' women who wear clothes that nobody would donate to a jumble sale and might look terribly clever, but never seem to say a word for themselves.

Pym poured out all her feelings of the boredom of being at home in Oswestry, with endless games of bridge and parish teas. Beatrice, like Pym, listens to the wireless, reads the papers and hears about the worsening crisis in Europe. The women 'talk about the situation'. Frances Wyatt, closely based on Hilary Pym, is vehemently anti-Nazi and thinks Hitler's invasion of Austria is 'sickening'. The not-so-bright parish women believe the situation will 'blow over'. Mrs Wyatt, her usual vague self, is confident that there will not be a war on rather spurious grounds: 'Mr Eden has such a nice face and then Lord Halifax is a good man too.'[5]

When Beatrice returns to Oxford, she goes to tea at Elliston's and trembles with excitement when she overhears Gerald's voice. He bluntly asks her out to lunch. She notices every detail about him, a scratch on his chin, his dark red tie, his black hair and hazel eyes. The effect overall is 'of brightness'. They begin a romantic affair. Beatrice is not at all troubled by having a relationship with an undergraduate; her only concern about the age gap is what other people, especially her outspoken sister, will say.

But there is another man in her life. An Oxford don called Henry Grainger. He is an old flame, whose wife, Eve, has recently died. When Henry married Eve, Beatrice bought herself an expensive black lace dress, her widow's weeds. But now he is free. There is little need to point out the wish fulfilment in Pym's story.

Henry takes Beatrice out to dinner. She forgoes cosmetics because Henry doesn't like women who wear too much make-up. She thinks back seven years to the 'uncomfortable rapture' and unhappiness of their nights together. In those days, the chaperone rules were strict for women and Beatrice broke many of the rules in order to meet Henry. When she recalls the fun of those days, Henry is surprised. He thought their affair had caused her unhappiness. Then he adds, sourly, that women, especially intelligent women, 'adore suffering' and are masochists.

After dinner, they go to the Oxford Union where Gerald/Hughie is giving one of the speeches. He is an impressive political speaker and Beatrice is drawn back to him. But then Henry asks her out for a late night drink at the Randolph and she hesitates. He accuses her of acting immaturely, but she is afraid of opening Pandora's box:

> 'My dear girl – it's very little after half past nine – you're not a second year student with an essay to write. You're grown up now – a don and a respectable woman.'
>
> 'The two aren't synonymous,' said Beatrice.
>
> 'No.' Beatrice could not see his expression in the dark, but his voice sounded surprised and pleased. 'That means that I might suddenly come across the Beatrice of ten years ago.'
>
> 'No it doesn't,' said Beatrice firmly. 'The door of the lumber room is kept locked and all the past is shrouded in dust sheets.'[6]

Pym was telling herself that even if Elsie Harvey died, she would not return to Henry's bed. Later, towards the end of the novel, Beatrice indulges in a daydream about the two men she has really loved. Here we see the makings of Pym the mature writer:

> Most women had somebody in their life, she supposed. The skeleton in the cupboard, the owl in the attic. Her own heart or memory or wherever it was that past loves were stored away must be like a kind of lumber room – full of old pictures, with their faces to the wall, broken chairs, stuffed birds and in one corner there might be an object shrouded in a dust sheet, so

that one couldn't see it or think about it any more. Like Henry when he had married Eve. Or Hughie. And then years afterward one might lift a cover of the sheet and discover that one could fling it off quite carelessly, finding underneath it only mild, kindly looks and spectacles – nothing to be afraid of any more. That had already happened with Henry. And one day it would be the same with Hughie. The Lumber room, like death, was a great leveller.[7]

The novel is unfinished, but Julian Amery would continue to be a model for several literary heroes and, moreover, the embryo plot of a love affair between a young man and older woman would continue to intrigue Pym, culminating in her masterpiece written many years later.

———

That autumn, Pym and Hilary moved into 27 Upper Berkeley Street, close to Hyde Park. Barbara had a 'minute little room at the top of the lodgings house'. She always liked to write at high windows. She wrote to 'sister' Elsie: 'It is such a pleasant life – I don't think I've been so happy since I was a young girl at eighteen in my first year at Oxford.'[8] She reported that she had finished *The Lumber Room* (omitting all mention of the dead wife sub-plot) and that she was writing a new novel about North Oxford and its inhabitants.[9] She was feeling better than she had felt for a long time: 'I am very happy and don't need comforting which is something new! The only thing is to work at something you like and that you feel is worth doing, even if it's only a novel that doesn't get published. I suppose it's all good experience, anyway and while I'm doing it I'm perfectly happy.'[10]

In this new novel, she eschewed the more experimental approach of her previous attempts and returned to her old style.

She told Elsie Harvey that it would be a comic novel in the manner of *Some Tame Gazelle*. It was a good decision. She would later say that the world that she evoked would seem a million miles away from the cruelty and misery in the real world. Pym was also excited to be in close proximity to Julian in London. She had not forgotten his invitation to walk up to the door at 112 Eaton Square.

CHAPTER XXXI

We go to Crampton Hodnet

Crampton Hodnet is a lie. It does not exist outside the imagination of a deceitful clergyman called Stephen Latimer. He has been caught out walking with a single woman on Shotover Hill, near Oxford, when he should have been at evensong. Not wishing to be discovered in an indelicate position, he pretends that he has been to visit a vicar friend who lives in the imaginary Oxfordshire village of 'Crampton Hodnet'.

Latimer is young, good-looking and unmarried, and resents being considered marriage fodder for every available spinster. He is described, unforgettably, as 'a handsome, complacent marmalade cat'. His lie about his whereabouts seems to grow bigger with the telling. Jessie Morrow, with whom he had been walking, is astonished and appalled in equal measure: 'Miss Morrow listened to this story in amazement. She wondered if it showed in her face, for she had never before, as far she could remember, heard a clergyman telling what she knew to be deliberate lies. And what a hopeless story! she thought pityingly.' The problem with his lie is that it has put him in Miss Morrow's power. He is horrified when she proposes a toast to 'your friend, the vicar of Crampton Hodnet'.[1] She is not going to let him forget his fabrication.

He has been weak and foolish and now has to find a way out of his mess.

Francis Cleveland, an Oxford don, is having a midlife crisis. His academic research is going nowhere (he has been working on his thesis for twenty-eight years); he is bored by his kind but dull wife and unappreciated by his only child, Anthea. When he is asked to teach a brilliant and good-looking undergraduate, he is ripe for the taking. Barbara Bird, 'a tall, dark girl with beautiful eyes', has written a good essay on John Donne, which encourages Mr Cleveland to take an interest in his new student.

> He was completely taken aback. At one moment she had been no more than one of the better-looking young women, who had just read him an extremely good essay and then suddenly he found her beautiful dark eyes looking at him in such a way that he was startled into asking himself how long it was since any woman had looked at him like that. He thought of his colleagues in the Senior Common Room at Randolph: old Dr Fremantle, Lancelot Doge, Arthur Fenning, Arnold Penge . . . One couldn't imagine a woman gazing at any of *them* in such a way.[2]

Barbara Bird and Francis have tea together in Fuller's, in the direct gaze of the nosy inhabitants of North Oxford. When he arrives home and his wife asks him about his whereabouts he also tells a deliberate lie.

> 'I had tea with Killigrew,' he said defiantly. It was the first time, as far as he could remember, that he had ever told his wife a deliberate lie. It made him feel fine and important, a swelling, ranting Don Juan with a dark double life, instead of a middle-aged Fellow of Randolph College, ignored or treated with contempt by his wife and daughter.[3]

Of course Francis Cleveland and Barbara have been spotted and become fodder for North Oxford gossip. Miss Doggett, Cleveland's formidable aunt, holds Sunday afternoon tea parties for undergraduates in her large Victorian house on the Banbury Road. Tittle-tattle and teacups circulate freely in her drawing room, where she reigns supreme. It is not long before the rumours about her nephew and his pretty student reach her and cause her to get involved. What Miss Doggett does not know is that her companion, Miss Morrow, has a secret of her own.

The novel is peopled with the kind of Oxford types that Pym knew well and characterised with acuity: the flamboyant Eton aesthetes, Michael and Gabriel; the dull, dry master of Randolph College, Dr Fremantle (Balliol is reinvented as Randolph because it lies opposite the hotel); the camp assistant Bodley's librarian, Edward Killigrew. Pym suggests that North Oxford is its own village. And like the villages of Jane Austen, it is a place that could be described as 'a neighbourhood of voluntary spies'.[4]

Pym depicts, with a razor-sharp scalpel, the toxic insecurities of Oxford academics, the petty squabbles of the Bodley's librarians, the bitchiness of the aesthetes and the callousness of the female undergraduates. The worlds of North Oxford and Randolph College are riven with petty jealousy, muck-raking and tale-bearing. Clever people, she notes, are inclined to be fond of spiteful gossip and intrigue.

The heroine, Jessie Morrow, is described as thin and used-up. She buys a lovely dress, the colour of tender green leaf, which she hides in her wardrobe for fear of damping remarks and disapproving raised eyebrows. It does not do for a lady's companion, who is regarded as little more than a piece of furniture, to aspire to romance. She wears a shapeless grey cardigan and is ignored by most of the important Oxford worthies, but is nevertheless a woman of 'definite personality', who is able to look upon herself and her surroundings with detachment.

Miss Doggett's character is perfectly expressed in her opening words: 'Miss Morrow, Miss Morrow. Where are the buns from Boffin's!' She is a busybody with a muckrake: 'Her chief work in life was interfering in other people's business and imposing her strong personality upon those who were weaker than herself.'[5] Though she has no connection with the university, other than her nephew's position as a don, she keeps her finger on the pulse and invites an assembly of odd bods to her teas: 'Where but in a North Oxford drawing room would one find such a curiously ill-assorted company? thought Miss Morrow. The only people who really seemed at ease were Michael and Gabriel, but then they were old Etonians and Miss Morrow was naive enough to imagine that old Etonians were quite at ease anywhere.'[6] Michael and Gabriel ('two giggling pansies on the sofa') are two of Pym's finest comic characters. It is they who inform on Francis Cleveland when they bump into Miss Doggett and Miss Morrow in the University Parks:

'Oh Miss Doggett, what a *delight!*'

. . . 'Why Michael and Gabriel,' she said, 'what are you doing here? You quite startled me, leaping about like that.'

'We feel we must express ourselves in movement,' said one of them.

'We've been playing Stravinsky's *Sacre du Printemps* all day and we're simply shattered by it.'

'Michael wants to leap into that pond with one glorious leap,' said Gabriel.

'Wouldn't that frighten the ducks?' said Miss Morrow prosaically . . .

'Do you think we ought to tell Miss Doggett?'

'Tell her what?'

'What we saw in the Physick Garden?'

'He means the Botanical Gardens,' explained Michael. 'Of

course it *was* the Physick Garden in the seventeenth century, wasn't it? We always like to use the old names.'

'What are you talking about?' asked Miss Doggett indulgently.

'Well it's *rather* naughty,' Michael giggled.

'But it may be our duty to tell,' said Gabriel piously. 'Think how frightful it would be if we failed in our duty.'[7]

As Pym would report to Jock, there were several excellent comic set pieces of this sort scattered through the novel. Mr Latimer's proposal has a similar comic pomposity and underlying self-centred pragmatism to that of Mr Collins's proposal to Elizabeth Bennet in *Pride and Prejudice*. Mr Latimer does not love Miss Morrow, but he believes that 'he might do worse than marry her . . . how pleased she would be'. When his proposal comes, it is deliciously absurd:

'Oh, Miss Morrow – Janie,' he burst out suddenly.

'My name isn't Janie.'

'Well, it's something beginning with J,' he said impatiently. It was annoying to be held up by such a triviality. What did it matter what her name was at this moment?

'It's Jessie, if you want to know, or Jessica, really,' she said, without looking up from her knitting.[8]

It's a marvellous touch that even as he forgets her name she doesn't bother looking up from her knitting.

The set piece of Mr Cleveland's elopement with Barbara Bird is equally impressive. A weekend in Paris, which seemed so romantic in principle, is thwarted by a missed boat to Calais and a rather sordid hotel in Dover, rather like the one Julian Amery stayed in. Barbara runs away from the hotel and Mr Cleveland is left feeling more relieved than jilted. 'After all, everything had happened for the best. Things generally did. Margaret always said so and wives were usually right.'⁹

There are glimpses of Henry and Jock. Francis Cleveland, the handsome Oxford don and failed academic, owes something to Henry Harvey, with his love of the poet Cleveland and academic interest in Gerard Langbaine. His midlife crisis affair with a young undergraduate called Barbara is a sly joke in which Pym pokes fun at her younger self, who 'had cherished many impossible, romantic passions for people she scarcely knew, or had perhaps seen only once'. Edward Killigrew, assistant librarian, wears a leather jacket and mittens to keep him warm in the freezing Bodleian Library, just as did Jock. The only reference to Friedbert is a green Tyrolean hat.

Pym was relying less on in-jokes for her friends. She was honing the skills for which she would be celebrated. Her characters work better because they are more fully rounded, not just the caricatures of her first attempts at fiction. Above all, the novel is uproariously funny, as Pym intended: 'There are no sick people in North Oxford. They are either dead or alive. It's sometimes difficult to tell the difference, that's all.'¹⁰

Pym had been encouraged to hear that Jock had found a publisher for his novel, *The Almond Tree*. He was to be published by Jonathan Cape, the publisher who had shown initial interest in *Some Tame Gazelle*, but had ultimately not accepted it. Pym had been upset at the time, jokingly calling Cape 'falser than false Cressid' but, inspired by Jock's news, she wrote to him asking for a meeting.

Pym asked Mr Cape if she could have a job in publishing, but was told there wasn't an opening. However, he was encouraging about her work and advised her to keep on writing. Cape invited Barbara and Hilary to a cocktail party at his flat: 'He is a charming man and so amusing.' Pym's agent, Ralph Pinter, advised her, in her writing to: 'Be more wicked if necessary.'

She found Pinter 'kind and helpful', but was not entirely sure about this advice: 'Can you imagine an old spinster, frowning anxiously over her MS, trying to be more wicked? Or rather, trying to make her people more wicked? It is difficult to imagine is it not?'[11]

CHAPTER XXXII

Introducing Mr Simon Beddoes

Just as Julian Amery was the inspiration for Gerald – the younger man from Balliol with whom the heroine falls in love in *Beatrice Wyatt or The Lumber Room* – so in *Crampton Hodnet* we meet Simon Beddoes, with whom Anthea Cleveland is deeply in love. We first meet him kissing her passionately in the family library.

Like Julian Amery, Beddoes is an Etonian and now at Balliol. He hails from a political, titled family and wants to be in politics like his father. He is short in stature, but huge in personality. When Anthea first meets him, he sweeps her off her feet with his glamour, but, deep down, she knows that his political ambitions take precedence. Like her creator, Anthea would like to be in the enviable state of 'calm of mind, all passion spent', but she is in love. She decides that rather than spending her time kissing Simon, lying on the sofa, she will show him that she is 'intelligent': 'We'll really talk about something. She wasn't sure what – perhaps the Foreign Policy of His Majesty's Government, she thought, stepping into a puddle and splashing her stockings.'[1]

Anthea visits his rooms in Randolph College, pausing for a moment at his staircase and looking at his name painted over the door; 'knocked, went in and the next thing she knew she was in his arms'. He has turned out all the lights: 'except for the glow of the fire, for Simon understood the value of a romantic atmosphere'.

Pym both evokes and mocks the romance of love-making in the room of an Oxford undergraduate on a rainy December evening:

> At this hour time seemed to stand still . . . The Salvation Army went on playing half-recognised hymns, the rain fell softly but steadily and from different parts of Oxford came the sound of the various bells calling people to evensong . . . Lights were turned on to reveal the happy lovers blinking like ruffled owls, the honey toast lying cold and greasy on a plate in the fireplace, the tomato sandwiches curled up at the edges and the Fuller's walnut cake a crumbly mess because it had been roughly cut by inexperienced hands.[2]

The pair hold hands, staring into one another's eyes. When Simon hears one of his friends calling his name from under his window, he takes great care that his friends see him kissing Anthea's hand: 'He was the only one of his set who had a young woman in love with him.'[3]

Beddoes likes being the centre of attention and likes the sound of his own 'caressing' voice. Men like him, but women are less sure. Jessie Morrow realises that he will never marry Anthea: 'He wanted to do things that people would remember, great things and making a woman happy could hardly be called that.' She sees with a flash of 'worldly insight' that Simon wants a fine romantic love affair to 'fill in the time when they were not busy with more important things, like making speeches or writing clever political pamphlets'.[4]

Anthea looks out of her bedroom window and blows kisses in the general direction of Balliol/Randolph:

Simon was not thinking of her. He was lying happily awake in his college bedroom, going over a speech he hoped to make at the Union debate on Thursday. Of course he adored Anthea, but 'Man's love is of man's life a thing apart', especially when he is only twenty and has the ambition to become Prime Minister.[5]

The men in *Crampton Hodnet* are, on the whole, weak and spineless. Jessie Morrow spurns Mr Latimer's declaration of his 'Respect and Esteem'. She knows that he does not love her:

It had been such a very half-hearted proposal . . . poor Mr Latimer! She smiled as she remembered it . . . 'I respect and esteem you very much – I think we might be very happy together.' *Might!* Oh no, it wouldn't do at all! . . . For, after all, respect and esteem were cold, lifeless things – dry bones picked clean of flesh.[6]

The phrase 'Respect and Esteem' was one that Henry Harvey had written to Pym when he was trying to explain his feelings towards her. (Henry may well have been quoting from Jane Austen's *Sense and Sensibility*, since these are the words that Elinor Dashwood chooses for the way she feels about Edward Ferrars – terms of affection strongly rejected by her more romantic sister.) Now, in her Oxford novel, the lukewarm words are put to work by being described as dry bones picked clean of flesh. The same metaphor recurs in a diary entry written a few months later, in which she recalled her romance with Julian Amery: 'Respect and Esteem, the dry bones picked clean of flesh. To one who has known Oxford in the spring with Jay they are not enough.'[7]

Faithful wives are expected to turn a blind eye towards marital infidelity. Mrs Fremantle, spouse of the master of Randolph College, endures her husband's affairs. Old Mrs Killigrew feels that it is her 'duty' to report to his wife that Mr Cleveland is having an affair with his student, Barbara Bird. Mrs Cleveland's first impulse is to laugh. Her second is to squash down the stiff straw hat that Mrs Killigrew is wearing, and tear off the stuffed bird before flinging it into the fire – the bird symbolism is clear. But there is sympathy, too, for the men imprisoned in dull marriages: 'The walls had closed round him again. There was no escape.'[8]

Pym worked hard at her novel over Christmas and into the early part of the new year. Elsie had written to Pym to tell her that Henry had decorated the Christmas tree with his own hands. Pym wrote back: 'things like that make me want to cry'.[9] She told Elsie: 'The best piece of news from London is that spring has come . . . There was that unmistakable feeling in the air that sends people mad, particularly old spinsters like your sister Pym who is already rather queer in the head.'[10]

Her intense love of flowers always made her happy. The shops were full of them: daffodils, narcissi, tulips, blue irises and of course lots of mimosa. On Julian's birthday, 27 March, she placed red roses by the photograph of him that she had on her mantelpiece.

Pym was feeling that she might never be married. Her old Oxford friend, Mary Sharp, had married and moved to America. Pym told Elsie: 'I think you would be shocked if I were suddenly to marry, for instance. But there seems to be no chance of that.' Part of her was enjoying her single status, visiting exhibitions with Hilary, including 'one of pictures and drawings by Man Ray, which I didn't understand or like very much'. The other exhibition was of work by the contemporary Surrealist artist, Wolfgang Paalen, which she thought more interesting. The first thing they saw was an umbrella covered entirely with sponges, which she thought was a waste of expensive sponges.

Pym resumed her diary in March 1939. She kept the anniversary of the time she first met Julian Amery. On 15 March she noted grimly: 'Nazis in Prague'. On 17 March: 'Sat on a peach-coloured sofa in Grosvenor House in the afternoon and waited for Dr Alberg. International situation serious.'

Dr Alberg was making arrangements to bring his family out of Poland. Mr Thwaites's family had already been evacuated from the country; Pym met his wife in London: 'Things seem to be about as bad as they can be there – she and the children have come back to England and see no prospect of returning to Poland yet and the Embassy and Consulate in Warsaw have sent all their women and children home.'[11]

If she felt any guilt over her affair with Friedbert, she had locked it away in the lumber room. On 11 April Pym noted: 'Friedbert 28 today'.

On 27 April there was an Oxford Union motion on conscription. Pym wrote in her diary that it had been proposed by Julian Amery. In May, conscription was indeed introduced for men aged between twenty and twenty-one. 'I don't know what Jock would say to these views, if he is still a Pacifist,' she wrote to Elsie Harvey. She told Elsie that she was training for a first-aid certificate, 'which ought to be useful even if there isn't a war'. She went every week and enjoyed it: 'Fancy me learning how to make splints and bandages!'[12]

Pym began to loiter around Julian's house in Belgravia. On a sunny day in May, 'the air soft and warm and lovely, trees in leaf and red hawthorns in flower . . . a nostalgic smell of churches and new paint', she wandered through Mayfair and ventured to 112 Eaton Square. The aroma of a Sunday dinner rose up from the basement:

His house is newly painted in cream and royal blue and a window box next door has petunias in it. How all things are in tune to a poor person in love. A fine, sunny afternoon in May, Beethoven and German Lieder. I go to my irises, thinking to throw them away, but find that each dead flower has a fat bud at the side of its stem. And so I take off the dead flowers and the new flowers begin to unfold. The photograph of him at the Union stands on the mantlepiece and in front of it a spray of dead roses – but they are artificial ones from Woolworth's.[13]

A couple of weeks later, Pym watched the movie *Love Affair*, with Charles Boyer and Irene Dunne, which made her feel very emotional. She walked in the park and then back to 'the deserted streets of Mayfair' for a sighting of Julian: 'Such of the aristocracy as still lives here is away for the weekend.' She continued: 'One day you will really go and see what it is. But not yet. You must go back and read your new *Vogue* and wash stockings – for that is an essential part of a lonely weekend in London.'[14]

In *Crampton Hodnet*, Anthea goes to London and stalks her beloved's Belgravia house, hoping for a glimpse and worrying that, 'Lady Somebody might be giving a dance for her horrid debutante daughter and Simon was very eligible.'[15] It is July and she scours the newspapers to see if the Beddoes have left for Scotland, or the countryside, or abroad. When she arrives in Chester Square, she sees that the house is shut up: 'She could hardly have had a greater shock than if the house had been in ruins. She had been so sure he would be there.' Pym harboured similar nightmares and daydreams about Julian.

On her twenty-sixth birthday, Pym met Jock for a walk in Hyde Park and then had lunch with him at the Queen's Head in Chelsea (known as the Old Lady of Tryon Street, it was indeed a celebrated watering hole for 'queens'). With the prospect of war imminent, Pym was in a thoughtful, reflective mood. Julian Amery was much on her mind. He had sent her a birthday letter: 'Darling, a line to wish you many happy returns of the day and to tell you that I have never forgotten you and that I never will.' He said that so much had happened since they last met that they probably wouldn't recognise each other. ('I think I would,' she said to herself.) He told her that he had been in Spain, in France and in Switzerland and that he was learning to fly an aeroplane. He remembered their time in Oxford when 'we drank Niersteiner and spoke with our eyes'. He said that he wished he was having a birthday party with her and asked her if she would 'write a special novel' for his next birthday. He asked her to reply to his letter and sent a message in German: 'God greets you a thousand times.'[16]

Pym began a new notebook-diary, entitling it 'Reflections by Barbara Pym concerning herself and Julian Amery', which she preserved along with a pressed flower and one of his blue hand-kerchiefs. She wrote lyrically about her love:

What is the heart? A damp cave with things growing in it, mysterious secret plants of love or whatever you like. Or a dusty lumber room full of junk. Or a neat orderly place like a desk with a place for everything and everything in its place.

Something might be starting now that would linger on through many years – dying sometimes and then coming back again, like a twinge of rheumatism in the winter, so that you suddenly felt it in your knee when you were nearing the top of a long flight of stairs. A Great Love that was unrequited might be like that.

Some Solemn Thoughts – That so many places where one has enjoyed oneself are no more – notably Stewart's in Oxford – shops are pulled down, houses in ruins, people in their marble vaults whom one had thought to be still living. One looks through the window in a house in Belgravia and sees right through its uncurtained space into a conservatory with a dusty palm, a room without furniture and discoloured spaces on the wall where pictures of ancestors once hung.[17]

She wondered if Julian knew how deeply he was beloved: 'Suddenly it occurs to me that as at no other time somewhere in the world, somewhere in England probably, a young creature very beloved is still alive and going about his independent life, which touched one's own for twenty hours.' On 4 July, she got her wish: 'I met one I loved and had not seen for more than a year.'[18]

CHAPTER XXXIII

A Peek into 112 Eaton Square

It is highly probable that Pym engineered a 'chance' meeting at the traffic lights in Portman Square. She was nothing if not persistent. Julian invited her back to Eaton Square and she was delighted finally to be inside his curious home, with its oil paintings and smell of incense.

Pym was introduced to Julian's mother, thinking her a splendid character for a novel. Florence Amery, known to her friends as Bryddie, was Canadian. She was a striking woman with a strong intellect. She was a graduate of another St Hilda's College, part of Toronto University. Julian was unashamedly devoted to his mother and always had been, even at prep school. Like Pym, he was a lover of nicknames and had christened his mother 'Porick'. His father was 'Coco'. In his letters home, he called his mother 'my Sweetheart' or 'my Angel'. In the face of John's appalling conduct, Leo impressed upon Julian the importance of being a good son to his mother. He was.

Pym was fascinated by Bryddie and she would appear several times in her novels. It is possible, too, that Pym met Leo. A week later in her diary, she quoted a phrase made by 'Leopold Amery': 'Family Life is founded on sex. Today's great thought.'[1]

Pym only went this once to Eaton Square, but the visit gave

her a mine of memories. After she left, she returned later in the evening and observed Julian through a window, dressed in white tie, tails and wearing a red carnation.

It seems probable, from later writing, that she knew that he had lost interest. He was making many conquests at the time, but no commitments. With war imminent, everyone's future was uncertain. Barbara knew that Julian was ambitious and would not throw himself away.

She returned home for the annual family holiday to Pwllheli – 'a carefree fortnight' – while the international situation grew worse. Hilary was working for the BBC, and, with war now inevitable, left London for their emergency quarters at Evesham, while Barbara returned home. Soon Pym was recording the news of Hitler's invasion of Poland in her diary: 'Heard on 10.30 news that Hitler had taken over Danzig and invaded Poland – bombed many towns including Katowice.'[2] She had been living there with the Albergs only a few months before.

The third of September 1939 was a gloriously sunny day in Shropshire. Pym wrote in her diary: 'We gave Hitler until 11 a.m. to withdraw from Poland and at 11.15 Mr Chamberlain spoke to the nation and told us that we are now at war with Germany.'[3] Like almost every family in the nation, they huddled round the wireless to hear the prime minister's broadcast.

Pym, with her heart full of Julian, felt the comfort of their brief encounter:

But now when the world is in this sad state, when one hardly dares to look ahead into the years, all this is a warm comfort. All this . . . the remembrance of meetings, letters, a photograph, all the little relics, all the jokes, everything that did happen and didn't quite happen and might still happen. Twenty hours – but perhaps twenty years of memories.[4]

In her diary that night, she told of how, with the declaration of war, such irrelevant memories of 'past happiness' came into her mind. Oxford and its libraries, cocktail parties, country pubs and punts on the river seemed a very long way away.

BOOK THE THIRD

War

CHAPTER I

Operation Pied Piper

The same evening that war was declared the 'Birkenhead refugees' arrived in Oswestry.

By the end of the first week of September, 8,500 children, parents and teachers from Liverpool and Birkenhead had been evacuated to rural areas and small towns in Wales, Cheshire and Shropshire as part of a national scheme known as Operation Pied Piper. Liverpool and Birkenhead were targets for the Luftwaffe because the Mersey estuary was a significant port in the north. One of the most powerful propaganda posters of the time depicted a mother with young children, with a spectral figure of Hitler standing over her, telling her to 'Take them back' to the cities, where they could be bombed. 'DON'T do it, Mother' screamed the poster, 'Leave the Children Where They Are'.

Pym's war journals and stories offer unique insights into work on the home front. In the run-up to the outbreak of conflict, new voluntary groups mushroomed. Women were at the core of this enterprise. The government expected women to help the war effort in a number of ways. One, for instance, was on the domestic front: caring for the family, managing rations, growing one's own vegetables, mending clothes, 'making do'. Another was to help the government in war work. Two of the main groups in which women were involved were the WVS (Women's Voluntary Service), set up in 1938, and the ARP (Air Raid Precaution). Alongside the British Red Cross, these organisations played a vital role in wartime community service.

Pym had already joined the WVS in London, where she practised making bandages. Now that she was back home at Morda Lodge, she prepared to welcome the evacuee children. In Pym's short story 'Goodbye Balkan Capital', the autobiographical heroine Laura Arling recalls the police car which had come round 'on a dreadful Sunday evening' to tell the family that 500 evacuee children had arrived at the local station.[1] In her wartime diary there is little sense of Pym's emotional response to the plight of the evacuees, so far from home. Instead, she notes the extra amount of housework they brought that left her exhausted. In her fiction, however, she is more expressive. Laura remembers with pity 'the sad little procession dragging through the garden gate, labels tied to their coats, haversacks and gas masks trailing on the ground'.[2]

Pym started work on a new novel about the home front, writing as events directly unfolded. Jane Palfrey (based on her mother, Irena Pym) is moved to tears when she first sees the evacuees: 'The children all carried gas masks and an assortment of luggage, satchels, little cardboard suitcases and cretonne bags and Jane felt a sudden pricking of tears in her eyes.' Her daughter, Flora, sees them as an 'invading army'. Both mother and daughter 'never quite believed the children would come'.[3] With Hilary working for the BBC in Evesham, it was left to Irena and Barbara to look after the children. The Pym family, with their comfortably sized detached house, could be expected to take at least four children. In the event, they took four and one mother from Birkenhead, who refused to be parted from her children.

Before the evacuees arrived, Barbara spent the day making blackout curtains for the bedrooms and dining room. 'Everyone cheerful,' she observed.[4] One aspect of the home front which Pym captured so well was the way in which many women were energised and invigorated by the war effort. The women of the host families had to deal with all of the problems that came with the children, such as lice infestation and dirty clothes. Most of the Birkenhead children were from working-class backgrounds and had barely left the confines of their own town before. In Pym's novel, Flora, less sentimental than her mother, thinks it is 'bad enough talking to children of one's own class, but the lower classes were even more difficult'.[5] She is amazed to find the children hail from a family of nine. 'I expect the father's unemployed, too,' she thought, very prim and social and birth control clinic.'[6]

At Morda Lodge, Irena's first thought was to take the four evacuees to the lavatory. Jane does the same in Pym's home front novel, as does Janet in 'Goodbye Balkan Capital': 'Janet had been so splendid. She had taken them all to the lavatory, which was just what they wanted, if only one had been able to think of it, for after that they cheered up and rushed shouting about the garden until it was time for bed.' Which is precisely what happened to the children billeted with the Pyms, who were delighted to find a large, private garden at their disposal.

Pym, with her acute eye, was surprised to see how people like her mother, whom she often describes as 'dreamy' and 'vague', took up the challenge. In her home front novel, spinster cousins Agnes Grote and Connie Aspinall are asked to take in a mother and two children. When Connie finds head lice, she is determined to send the children away – 'no one could expect to have children who were not clean in the house' – and is roundly reprimanded by Agnes:

'*Send them away!*' Agnes stood in the middle of the room, a magnificent figure with a newly lighted cigarette jutting aggressively from her mouth. 'My dear Connie, this is wartime. Go and get the Lysol out of the bathroom cupboard – I shall wash the children thoroughly in the scullery and their clothes must be dealt with too.'[7]

Agnes bakes the evacuees' clothes in the oven to rid them of the lice and gives the children a thoroughly good clean, as though she is washing a family pet. Pym is brilliant at showing the immediate sense of purpose and meaning that the war brings to the lives of women whose lives hitherto have been rather quiet and dull. All of a sudden, they are needed. Agnes makes plans to dig up the garden to plant vegetables to feed the children and even mild-mannered Connie feels the excitement of change: 'Oh God . . . don't let there be a war. But at the back of her mind was that a war might be rather exciting. It would certainly make a difference to the days that were so monotonously the same.'[8]

The day after the children arrived was gloriously sunny; Barbara had a dull time, mostly telling the children *not* to do things. The fine weather made it difficult to believe that England was at war with Germany. Pym would wake every morning with feelings of happiness before the realisation of being at war suddenly hit home. One of the effects of war was that young women who were previously in domestic service often left for service or factory work. Dilys, the family help, did stay on but the Pyms were permanently anxious that they would lose her to the munitions factories.[9]

Nonetheless it was hard work running Morda Lodge with the extra lodgers and everyone in the house had to pull their weight. The first few days were exhausting. Pym's diary is full of references to washing, ironing, bed-making, washing-up, mending, sewing curtains and sheets – 'sides to middle'. One of Barbara's jobs was to draw the curtains at night: it was a job she took seriously as the 'Air Warden Officer', who came to do the checks, was also the grocer, with whom she was not yet registered. Rationing would begin a few months later in January 1940.

After just three days, Pym expressed her hope that the war would soon be over. It was wishful thinking of the highest kind.

CHAPTER II

In which we meet Mrs Dobbs of Birkenhead and Lady Wraye of Belgravia

Morda Lodge's first evacuees only lasted for four days. The children's mother was 'breaking her heart to go back' to Birkenhead.[1] Evacuation was a voluntary process, and it was often hard for families, especially those in close-knit communities, to be torn apart from their extended relations. This was especially true for pregnant and nursing women and mothers of young children, who refused to be separated from their little ones, and then found it difficult to settle in the countryside, far from home. Some said that they would rather be bombed by the Nazis than be bored to death in the country.

Pym gives no description of the Birkenhead mother in her journal, but in her novel there is a rather savage portrayal of a feckless young mother, Mrs Dobbs, who has a bold face and brassy bleached hair which could do with a 'good brushing'. She lies in bed all morning, wearing a 'slightly soiled' pink shiny nightgown, lavishly trimmed with artificial lace, smoking and dropping her ash onto the carpet. Agnes commands mild Connie to get Mrs Dobbs out of bed to help with the children:

'Yes, I was just having a smoke,' said Mrs Dobbs, producing a hand from underneath the bedclothes and revealing a cigarette, which she had evidently hidden on hearing Connie's knock. 'I thought you was the other one,' she said with an ingratiating smile.

'Wouldn't you like some breakfast?' Connie began, not liking to say what she had to say straight out.

'Well, that's an idea,' said Mrs Dobbs brightly. 'It would be ever so kind of you. A nice cup of tea and a bit of toast and I daresay I could fancy a nice boiled egg. You get nice fresh eggs in the country.'

'Well, if you like to get up, you can go down into the kitchen and cook yourself something,' said Connie ineffectually.

'Rightyho, dear, just as you like,' said Mrs Dobbs, settling herself comfortably among the pillows and with obviously no intention of getting up.[2]

Mrs Dobbs is unconcerned that her children's heads are crawling with lice, as all the rest of the kids have got them. She saunters down to the kitchen for a cup of tea, tucking her cheap satin blouse into her skirt. Agnes makes sure that she is not given the best china. 'I only came for a bit of a holiday,' Mrs Dobbs explains to the startled spinsters and tells them that she expects she will go back home soon. She trots off to Woolworths to meet the other mothers. Meanwhile the children run wild and complain about the home-made country food. What they would like is fish and chips, but there are no fish and chip shops in the countryside.

Pym was unfamiliar with working-class characters, knowing few people outside her own class, but, as she says in the same novel, the war is a leveller. It was the first time in her life that she had spent time in the close company of people outside her social sphere, other than their Welsh maids. Almost as soon as the original children, and their mother, left Morda Lodge, three more young children arrived to take their place: Billy, Ronnie and Gordon. 'They look very sweet,' Barbara noted, 'but are reputed to be naughty.'[3]

The weather was hot and she felt 'tired and worn – washed and ironed'.[4] One of Pym's many duties was to do the shopping. Then, once back home, she usually did the children's washing up and made supper for the adults, after which she felt absolutely exhausted. Later, she was responsible for getting the children ready in the morning, before they went off to do their schooling with the other youngsters and their teachers.

After a month, Pym was not only exhausted but depressed. She was finding it tough being at home and the children were driving her mad, 'running about like bears in the kitchen'. Feeding them was like being at the Mad Hatter's tea party, she noted. 'Billy screamed all day about something or another.'[5] Another evening, a frightened Ronnie and Gordon woke her up in the middle of the night. She got up and took them back to bed. One morning she awoke to hear them cheerily singing 'The Lambeth Walk'.

Whenever she could, Pym escaped into her writing. Visiting Julian's family in Eaton Square, just before the outbreak of war, her novelist's mind had been richly stimulated. Fascinated by Lady Amery, she knew that she would make a great character in a novel and so she would prove to be. The unpublished manuscript of Pym's home front novel begins with a prologue about a character called Mandy Wraye – this is omitted from the fragment of the novel published posthumously in *Civil to Strangers*. It is dated early July 1939: the time when she was rejected by Julian Amery.

Pym's depiction of Lady Wraye draws deeply on Julian's mother (flip the W to an M and you have an anagram of Amery). She is thin with a long face, solemn eyes and a melancholy expression. Pym knew that Bryddie had much to be sad about, given the anxiety about her eldest son, but neither of them could predict the tragic consequences of John's delinquency. Pym, sensitive to sadness, perceived a profound loneliness in Bryddie. Like her, Mandy Wraye is married to a busy politician whom she barely sees, is lonely at her home in Eaton Square and has a son with political ambitions:

> He had been such a dear little boy until he went away to school. And now he was a nice young man with charming manners who called her by her Christian name and made fun of her in an affectionate way and didn't need her anymore. Nobody does, she thought wistfully, not even Lyall. Certainly not Lyall, she added to herself as he got up purposely from the table. 'I have work to do and I don't want to be disturbed.'[6]

Her Belgravia home smells of incense, as did Julian's. The smell of cooking drifts up from the basement kitchen. The house has been freshly painted and petunias grow in the window boxes. All of these details were used from Pym's diary, as she walked the streets of Belgravia in the hope of a glimpse of Julian. There is a 'church-like' atmosphere to Belgravia on a sunny Sunday morning, but there are also the telltale signs of war: trenches are dug into the square: 'A wave of desolation swept over her and she now saw Eaton Square a mass of mouldering ruins. Would they all crowd into the trench of sodden clay, like a newly dug grave.'[7]

Lady Wraye returns to her home in the country to help with the evacuees. Her loneliness is assuaged by children from Birkenhead. Flora Palfrey (the heroine based on Pym) describes the boys as 'little beasts', who let the chickens escape from their coop and wet the bed. But Mandy Wraye is charmed by the children, as her cold, snobbish sister-in-law, Lady Eleanor Nollard, is repelled:

'Oh, I can hear the children,' said Mandy, her face lighting up. 'Eleanor, can you hear?'

'I could hardly fail to,' replied Eleanor with a shudder.

'I *love* Saturday morning when they don't go to school. I like to hear them laughing and singing about the house.'

'I doubt whether you'd be quite so enthusiastic if you had to look after them yourself,' observed Eleanor drily.

'But I *do* look after them. I take them for walks and give them their tea and bath them and put them to bed. And I always say goodnight to them. They are so sweet – it's almost like having Edward a baby again. Better, really, because Nanny never let me do anything for him.'

'All this evacuation will only make them dissatisfied with their own homes,' said Eleanor severely. 'There was certainly no obligation on your part to purchase clothing for them.'

'It wasn't an *obligation!*' Mandy said. How could she convey to Eleanor that one of the happiest moments of her life had been the one when she had taken the children shopping in the nearest large town. She had bought coats and shoes and trousers and dresses and berets and all the other clothes they needed and even some that they didn't need – just for fun.

'Do you realise,' she said 'that Jenny had never had a *new* coat before. Always something handed down or from a rummage sale! Imagine!'

But, of course, Eleanor could not imagine and Mandy was only just beginning to do so.[8]

This exchange between the two ladies is a masterclass in its economy of style and strong characterisation. Lady Nollard does not have the imagination or sympathy to comprehend anybody outside her own narrow social class and not even the war will change that. But Lady Wraye is a character for whom the war has been transformative: 'She went out of the room humming what anyone but Lady Nollard would have recognised as a rather silly song about the Siegfried Line.'[9]

CHAPTER III

Miss Pym reads a Government White Paper about Nazi Atrocities

On the day that war was declared, a young Englishwoman who was living in Munich drove to the beautiful Englischer Garten, on the banks of the river Isar. It was a place she loved and where she walked her dogs under the willow trees and along the winding pathways, before letting them off their leads to run free in the open spaces. A few weeks earlier, she had found new homes for the dogs. Today, she was alone. She took out a small pearl-handled pistol from her handbag, put it to her right temple and pulled the trigger.

The woman was Unity Mitford. Unable to bear the thought of war between her beloved Germany and England, she shot herself, leaving suicide notes for her parents and a sealed letter for Hitler. She failed in her mission: the bullet lodged in her brain, leaving her in a coma, but it did not kill her. It was the first of the war casualties for the Mitford family. In 1940, Diana Mitford was arrested and incarcerated in Holloway Prison without trial; her closeness to Hitler and the British Union of Fascists was enough to have her detained. It was an indication of how serious it was to be involved with the Nazis and fascism.

Pym would not yet have known of Unity's fate. It would be

many months before the story got out. Pym was restless at home and bored by the mundanity of domestic duties. The first months of the war seemed an endless round of housework, punctuated with the odd moments of pleasure, such as planting hyacinth bulbs, going to the cinema and writing her novel. The first time she went to the pictures since the start of war meant taking her gas mask with her, which made her feel 'rather silly'. She had heard from a friend that Julian was now in Egypt, which only enhanced his glamour.

On 18 September Pym noted in her diary that the Russians had entered Poland. She did not know if the Albergs had managed to escape. On 1 October she listened to Churchill giving a 'fine and inspiring' speech about 'Herr Hitler and his group of wicked men'.

In mid-October, Pym heard from Don Liddell that Jock and the Harveys were trying to leave Finland. 'Flight from the Bolsheviks in an open boat. Somehow, though it's serious, I can't help laughing.'[1] Henry and Elsie had cleared their flat and were escaping the bombs by moving to Elsie's aunt's home outside Helsinki. Henry burnt his papers, 'suitcase after suitcase', including the majority of Pym's love letters, a decision he later greatly regretted.[2]

The wireless was a lifeline and Pym devoured letters from friends. But it sometimes seemed that everyone else was having a more exciting time: 'This is a war diary, but this seems to be our life.'[3] In late October, she had upsetting news about her favourite Aunt 'Ack', who was diagnosed with cancer and was facing surgery. It was turning out to be a bad month.

Then, on 31 October, Pym wrote a grim entry in her diary: 'Government white paper on Nazi concentration camp tortures.' If she still entertained any doubts about the brutality of the Nazis towards the Jews, that could no longer be the case. The White Paper reported that the treatment of prisoners in German concentration camps was reminiscent of 'the darkest ages in the history of man'. A former prisoner from Buchenwald concentration camp spoke of filth and mud and beatings on the slightest pretext, such as asking for a drink of water. The men lay on straw sacks and were not allowed to sleep on their backs. Sentries were ordered to use their rifles without warning. Some prisoners pretended to escape so they could be shot, putting an end to their misery. Hitler himself had given an order permitting flogging up to sixty strokes for Jews.

> Flogging and torture were the order of the day, and it was common knowledge that the National Socialist movement was taking a terrible revenge on those who had the temerity to oppose it . . . the violence and brutality of the Nazis did not spare . . . British subjects, including a member of the staff of His Majesty's Embassy, were wantonly assaulted in the streets by uniformed S. A. men on duty.[4]

Extracts in the daily newspapers made for harrowing reading. Pym had not heard anything from Friedbert since the outbreak of war in September, when he sent what she believed would be his final letter. Now she was filled with horror and guilt. Everything she had read about German brutality towards Jews and the concentration camps in *The Oppermanns* was proving to be true. The warnings she had ignored from Rupert and Hilary were now vindicated. Her romantic disposition had led her into dangerous territory. Now she was alone and had no one in whom to confide or express her remorse.

CHAPTER IV

Our Heroine is rejected Again

Pym was making good progress on her wartime novel and was close to finishing her North Oxford novel, *Crampton Hodnet*. She had not written down the details of her meeting with Julian at Eaton Square in June 1939, but it was clear that he had effectively ended the relationship. She recreated this rejection in different scenes in the two novels she was working on and in doing so, managed to process some of the pain.

In *Crampton Hodnet*, charming Simon Beddoes, who is too ambitious to marry the daughter of a vicar, rejects Anthea with a pompous letter, telling her that he has fallen in love with someone else: '"I think you will agree that it has been evident for some time that we were growing rather weary of each other's company" . . . the curious, parliamentary phraseology seemed to her infinitely pathetic.' Beddoes is dismissed (somewhat bitterly) as someone who would 'avoid the truth at all costs', and who was therefore well suited to politics: 'the Secretary of State for Something, answering questions in the house'.

In the home front novel, there is a face-to-face rejection in Eaton Square. Flora has sensed that Edward, the character based on Julian, has gone cold on their relationship. He stops returning her phone calls; nor does he answer her letters. Flora knows that

Edward wants to become prime minister and knows that he is too ambitious to throw himself away. She also knows that he is bored of her and she is nothing but a fun diversion. Edward is kind-hearted and does not like hurting women, but there is little time for love in his carefully planned-out life. And she knows that he will make a 'suitable marriage' when the time is right. 'Oh Edward, once upon a time last Easter . . . and now he is bored!'[1]

When he ends the affair in his room at the top of the house, he 'does what is expected of him' – puts his arms around her and kisses her affectionately several times, 'but now his bright hazel eyes were looking out over Flora's head, while one hand played absently with her golden hair'. He is already thinking of another more suitable girl and his next term back at the varsity and whether he will be head of the Oxford Union.

Edward offers Flora a glass of sherry, but she refuses and says she needs to go back to her aunt's house in Bayswater. One can sense his relief. She has become an impediment. Flora, sensing that she will never be in his room again, takes a final look: 'the books, the desk littered with papers, the white horses on the red curtains and Edward standing there in his grey suit'. She quotes two lines from a hymn, because she can't help herself and because she has a religious background: 'By many deeds of shame we learn that love grows cold.'[2] Flora feels that she will burst into tears and run down the three flights of stairs in a 'grand' gesture, but she remains composed and dignified and walks quietly to the front door. On the way down, she sees Lady Wraye, who notices the tears in Flora's eyes and is full of pity: '[P]oor girl, if only I could say something comforting to her, make her see that in twenty years, ten years, even one year, it won't matter at all.'

Pym was humiliated and hurt when she was rejected by Julian. Even Henry Harvey had never found her boring. Julian had asked Pym to write a novel for him and so she wreaked her artistic revenge in the characters of ambitious but weak Simon Beddoes and Edward Wraye.

Later, when Flora meets Edward again, before he is about to go off to war, she notices his flaws: 'Surely he was not as *tall* as she had always thought him.' He had a spot on his forehead and his manners, which she once thought of as charming, she now finds affected.[3] Flora realises that Edward wants to go to war knowing that somebody back at home will be thinking of him. He gives her a signed photograph and she tries to summon up the romantic feelings he had once inspired. She is momentarily touched by his childish manner and his black hair, which reaches to a point at the back of his neck, but things are not the same as they once were. He gives her a violent kiss by a cabbage patch, but she is unimpressed and wonders if her lips are bleeding.

Flora delivers a final blow. She knows that deep down the reason that she is in love with him is that 'there was really nobody else to be in love with'.[4]

CHAPTER V

Miss Pym begins a Novel in Real Time

With Julian's rejection temporarily expiated, Pym threw herself into work. Closely observing and being part of the women's war effort would give her one of her great themes, though she was scarcely aware of it as yet. She was writing her home front novel as she was living it, giving her fictional world a sense of vivid immediacy. As always, there were good jokes.

The preface completed, Pym begins her novel in earnest 'somewhere in England'. Canon Palfrey is returning home to the vicarage. He is unsure about what he will find as it is the evening of the Red Cross lecture, but not even he expects to be confronted by an elderly spinster in her underwear:

> He remembered the first occasion very vividly and his shock at seeing a skeleton dangling in front of the large still life oil painting in the Dutch manner . . . but this evening an even more alarming sight met his eye. Miss Connie Aspinall was lying in a bed in his drawing room . . . Miss Heves and Miss Beatrice Wyatt began to roll the clothes off the bed, leaving Miss Aspinall exposed to full view, her hand furtively pulling down at her shapeless grey flannel skirt, which had slipped up to reveal an inch or two of mud-coloured celanese knickers . . . her helpless

body was rolled from side to side while Nurse Stebbing briskly demonstrated different ways of changing the sheets.[1]

Having demonstrated bed-changing, the lecture turns to bandage practice. The home front was expected to be prepared for casualties when Hitler's bombs struck. Curate Michael Randolph uses the opportunity to flirt with Beatrice Wyatt. He'd like one of those 'elaborate cap things', but she responds crisply: 'I shall do you a broken jaw,' said Beatrice seriously. 'Sit down here and shut your mouth firmly.'[2]

The home front women complain that the men are not doing enough for the ARP. It is the women who seem to do all the work, whilst the men stand around and mock, note Agnes and Beatrice as they prepare dark curtains and buckets of water for incendiary bombs and fit up the cellar as an air-raid shelter. Agnes, as seen deploying her brisk competence with the child evacuees, comes into her own during the war, making blackout curtains and removing lightbulbs where necessary, even in the lavatory. Beatrice Wyatt and her invalid mother take in a schoolteacher, whom Beatrice dislikes, but somehow the houseguest manages to amuse her querulous mother. The war keeps surprising people and brings out their best and their worst.

The vicar, who is watching the women busily preparing for the war, is impressed by their activity, though too lazy to help: 'Excellent Women, thought Canon Palfrey idly, always busy doing something.' His curate notes: 'There's something very soothing about watching a lot of busy women . . . like reading Jane Austen.'[3]

The novel is extraordinary in the way in which it captures Pym's own thoughts and feelings as events unfold. Flora knows that Edward will go to Egypt when the war begins (as Julian Amery had), and she is terrified for his safety, even though he has ended their affair. But she is also frightened for all the men she has loved:

> There was nothing that could save them now. How long would it go on she wondered? Oh years and years. All the men I know, all the men everywhere will be killed. Edward will be killed. Edward whom she loved or had loved, it wouldn't matter in a year or two that he didn't love her any more . . . She would never marry or have children now. This war was the end of everything.[4]

Flora, lying in her bath, becoming drowsy, is startled by her mother knocking on the bathroom door, reminding her of 'Aunt Bella', who fell asleep in the bath and drowned. Flora thinks that drowning in one's own bath is a rather nice way to die, 'rather inconvenient for other people, but peaceful. Not bloody or violent like dying in a war would be.'[5]

When news of the war is announced, Mandy Wraye feels deep compassion for Chamberlain, whereas her husband, Sir Lyall, blames him for his policy of appeasement. Pym knew about Leo Amery's intervention in Parliament, denouncing Chamberlain with his infamous 'Speak for England' remark. The prospect of war appears to divide the long-married Wrayes rather than unite them. Sir Lyall reprimands his wife for her 'undignified' weeping alongside her servant, Rogers, but Mandy knows that war binds womenfolk together: 'When Mr Chamberlain started to speak, the tears pricked Mandy's eyes and soon Rogers had turned away her face too and they were just two ordinary women like all the other ordinary women over England crying because there was going to be a war.'[6]

CHAPTER VI

The Shadow of the Swastika

In the summer of 1939, Julian Amery was staying with family friends on the Dalmatian Coast. On 31 August, war impending, his father sent him a telegram advising him to leave at once and head for Egypt, via Bosnia and Belgrade, to report to the Air Ministry. He packed his belongings into his car, draped it with the Union Jack, and drove off.

Pym, meanwhile, was writing his character in Edward Wraye: the young man hoping to gain a first in his finals, win the presidency of the Oxford Union, become a barrister and then prime minister. But under the spectre of war, the intrepid Julian had no thought of going back. He may have been a charmer, 'compliments flowing easy from his lips', but few could doubt his courage and thirst for adventure. He did not return to Oxford, gain a first or become president of the Union. He went to war.

At Belgrade, Julian was persuaded to stay on as an assistant attaché to Stephen Lawford Childs, the embassy diplomat in charge of press relations. He founded a magazine, the *Britannia*, whose sole purpose was to circulate as much pro-British propaganda as he could muster. Amery's gift for languages and his charismatic personality won him many friends (and a few enemies). Later, he would meet a spy called Sandy Glen and his career would take a different turn.[1]

Pym kept a close eye on Julian's movements and her attitude began to soften as his exploits in often dangerous Balkans territory were reported and applauded. She was often alarmed for his safety. In her scrapbook, she pasted clippings of his war adventures. Pym felt a sense of pride that she was part of his romantic life and that he had once loved her. Meanwhile, she sat quietly sewing and listening to radio plays on the Home Service. This was a new BBC national radio service – the former National Programme and Regional Programme had been merged on 1 September 1939. It offered news items, updated war bulletins and light entertainment, often of a morale boosting or anti-Nazi kind (in 1967 the Home Service became Radio 4).

Pym tuned into a play called *The Shadow of the Swastika*, a six-part series about the rise of Hitler. The voices of ordinary people were dramatised, as well as the fanatical and paranoid – those in fear of being toppled by their enemies. One of the most chilling moments in the script is when a father criticises the Nazis and then is terrified that his son (a member of the Hitler Youth) might report him to the authorities. Pym remained silent.

Each day seemed to bring bad news. On 30 November, the Soviet Union invaded Finland and bombed Helsinki, where Henry and Elsie had lived before they were evacuated. Two hundred civilians were killed and once again Pym was distraught that she could do nothing to stop such terrible things. The only good news was hearing from Dr Alberg that the family was safe and well in London. It was a reminder of her lucky escape. In her home front novel, she ponders on why it is men who fight wars:

If only women ran the world . . . there wouldn't be any wars.
No, thought Jane, because if they had their houses to look after
as well they simply wouldn't have time to annex countries and
break treaties. Hitler and Stalin and Mussolini hadn't got enough
to *do*, that was the problem. They would soon give up thinking
of Lebensraum if they had a handful of evacuees to feed and
clothe.[2]

By Christmas, to Pym's great relief, most of the evacuees had
returned to their homes. In what had become known as the
'Bore War' (later the Phoney War), no bombs had dropped and
yet food shortages, conscription and transport difficulties led to
a strange mixture of discomfort and anti-climax. In December
there were warnings issued by the prime minister about the
dangers of not taking the war seriously enough. Pym wrote:
'One can live only from day to day – the future is full of frightening uncertainty.'[3]

On Christmas Eve, she picked stocks and primroses from the
garden and spent the day peacefully reading Jane Austen's
Mansfield Park. On Christmas Day, the Pyms had good food
and Barbara was given Elizabeth Arden beauty products and a
red leather writing case. On Boxing Day, she slept late and was
roused by a crowd of militia marching past her window. On
New Year's Eve she finished *Mansfield Park*: 'a comforting book
with which to finish 1939'. She wrote to Jock Liddell: 'A Very
Happy New Year to you and may it not be quite as bad as we
expect and even bring the end of the War in sight.'[4]

CHAPTER VII

Food Glorious Food

The year of 1940 in Shropshire started cold, with heavy frosts. The snow began to fall, which froze the pipes in Morda Lodge, leaving the Pyms without hot water in the upstairs rooms. On 8 January rationing began, with bacon, butter and sugar top of the list.

Propaganda poster campaigns, aimed especially at women on the home front, cried out: 'Use less water', 'Grow your own food', 'Plan and grow for winter', 'Carrots keep you healthy and help you to see in the blackout', 'Every available piece of land must be cultivated' and 'Eat in moderation: a clean plate means a clean conscience'. The Pyms, like everyone else in her town who had gardens, were growing vegetables and cultivating chickens for meat and fresh eggs. Even so, when rationing came in on the heels of a bitter winter, times were hard.

Barbara kept up her correspondence with Jock. The winter had never seemed so long or so cold; she had chilblains for the first time. All she could do was hold out little hopes and take pleasure in small things such as getting letters, sewing a blue tweed jacket, watching her bulbs sprout and flower, and imagining that one day she would see her friends again. Hunger pangs were hard to bear. Once at church she became convinced that she could smell rabbit cooking and hallucinated that the altar was a celestial Aga. Pym had always enjoyed good fare and her novels are full of references to food, often carrying symbolic value. Wartime rationing made her even more aware of its value.

She told Jock that she had heard nothing from Friedbert, which was just as well as he was now an 'enemy alien'. By 2 January, Pym had done with Nazi Germany and all it stood for, and began 'expurgating my 1933–4 diary!'[1] As fervently as she had once admired the Nazis, she now turned against them with equal vigour.

Nevertheless, Pym was still counting her blessings. She had gathered Christmas roses and was now sitting in a comfortable chair with a blazing fire: 'there is much writing and reading to be done'. She told Jock all about her novel, which she had now almost finished, believing that it might be exactly the sort of novel that 'some people might like to read at a time like this' because it was set in a world far from the war. Here she was referring to the one which she was finishing, not the home front one she had just begun. 'It is about North Oxford and has some bits as good as anything I ever did . . . Mr Latimer's proposal to Miss Morrow, old Mrs Killigrew, Dr Fremantle, Master of Randolph College, Mr Cleveland's elopement and its unfortunate end.' She agreed with Jock that the influence of Compton-Burnett was 'powerful once it takes hold'.[2]

For a time there seems to be no point in writing any other way, indeed there seems not to *be* any other way, but I have found that it passes (like so much in this life) and I have now got back to my own way, such as it is, but purified and strengthened, as after a *rich* spiritual experience, or a shattering love affair.[3]

At the end of the month Pym fell ill with measles and was confined to bed. Snow continued to fall: 'Thick snow and a sad,

sad world.'[4] When she recovered, she saw the first blatantly propagandistic film, *Confessions of a Nazi*, starring Edward G. Robinson. Part of the plot was based on a real-life espionage case. This may have inspired her to begin taking notes for a spy novel.

February was cold and dull. She read Jane Austen's *Persuasion* and knitted balaclava helmets for the airmen and stockings for the WAAFs working the barrage balloons. Thinking of Julian, it struck her that the troops in north Africa would not need warm headgear. She had assumed that by now he was in Egypt, though he was still in the Balkans. She wrote to him and got no reply.

Finally, the weather improved and Pym was able to pick snowdrops in the garden. One morning, she awoke from a vivid dream about Julian: he was standing in the dining room and she begged him not to disappear. She continued to keep a note of his birthday, remembering that he was twenty-one on 27 March. She drank his health with burgundy and lit a candle in front of his photograph: 'I wish I knew where he was.' The candle was lit because she did not have a reading lamp, but the light and shadows gave a pleasing aspect: 'As it was there was a beautifully religious effect in my room at night – a single candle before his photograph lighting up his lovely, sparkling Russian eyes. Like an ikon – he would have appreciated it.'[5]

Julian was now living in the heart of Belgrade with Sandy Glen. He held a twenty-first birthday party at their flat with Gypsy musicians borrowed from a local cafe. The wine flowed into the early hours and glasses shattered against the wall, as was the custom.

Pym was determined to finish her North Oxford novel, settling on the title, *Crampton Hodnet*: Crampton for her middle name and Hodnet being a village in Shropshire. She made notes in her diary, which give a revealing glimpse into the narrative methods: 'A scene in which Mr L[atimer] says he does not care what her father is or did. Make Barbara more strikingly beautiful so that F[rancis] expects more than she is able to give. Make Mr L less feeble. Bring Barbara affair [with] Mr Cleveland sooner – naughtier . . . mildly sexual!' The memory of her love affair with Julian continued to inspire her and kept her from brooding too much:

> But *I remember, I remember* . . . I was never more happy in my life than with him in the Spring of 1938. I am sure that I truly loved him and do still. I put this in writing so that in the years to come I may look back on it and reflect about it (as poor Friedbert would say) and smile and say 'No, no it was only a passing infatuation' or 'Yes, yes, you *did* love him'.[6]

A radio broadcast by Leo Amery on the Balkans made her reflective. One morning, she found an old box, 'walnut with black and yellow inlay and a brass crest on the lid'. She polished it up and filled it with all her Julian Amery relics:

> In went all the letters, pressed flowers, Niersteiner corks, handkerchiefs . . . If I were to die tomorrow I should either have it sent back to him or buried with me (probably the latter) . . . People who are not sentimental, who never keep relics, brood on anniversaries, kiss photographs goodnight and good morning, must miss a great deal.[7]

Pym was in a pensive mood. Her days passed pleasantly and uneventfully, and she felt that she was not accomplishing very much. 'I have done so little writing this year. But writing is not now quite the pleasure it used to be. I am no longer so certain of a glorious future as I used to be – though I still feel that I may ultimately succeed.' The dullness of her days was not helping her writing and she longed for 'some shattering experience to awaken and inspire'. But how to get it? 'Sit here and wait for it or go out and seek it? Join the ATS and get it peeling potatoes and scrubbing floors?'[8] (The ATS was the women's territorial army.)

She still longed to fall violently in love, 'which is my idea of experience', but admitted that even that did not help much in the way of writing. She mused: 'Perhaps the war will give me something.' She was thinking about whether she could be happy not being a writer and be content with domestic life. However, clear-eyed as usual on such matters, she knew that she would grow restless and dissatisfied:

> But women are different from men in that they have so many small domestic things with which to occupy themselves. Dressmaking, washing and ironing and everlasting tidying and sorting of reliques. I think I could spend my whole day doing such things, with just a little time for reading and be happy. But it isn't *really* enough, soon I shall be discontented with myself, out will come the novel and after I've written a few pages I shall feel on top of the world again.[9]

CHAPTER VIII

Oxford Revisited

Pym was twenty-eight. Many of her Oxford friends had settled down, married, or were living seemingly glamorous lives with the new opportunities provided by the war. At the end of April 1940, she sent *Crampton Hodnet* to Jock, who was back in England. He replied immediately, saying that he was impressed with the novel and asking whether Hodnet was named after Hodnet in Shropshire, the sometime seat of the Percy family.

As so often, when she was feeling listless and low in spirit, Pym returned to Oxford. For once, the city did not work its magic. 'In Oxford once more and it is melancholy, because I know absolutely nobody except the Liddells – and they are charming in their way, but it is not in a way which fits all my moods.'[1] Jock gave her a copy of his new novel, *The Gantillons*.

Pym was becoming less emotionally self-indulgent: 'How differently one behaves now though on a melancholy evening! Instead of the abandonment of tears and the luxury of a good cry one thinks philosophically about what is the best thing to do – to smoke, get ready for bed, read a nice light novel and then sleep a long sleep.' As ever, her musings gave rise to thoughts about writing: 'It would be interesting for a novel to trace one's development . . . in matters of emotional restraint.'[2] Pym did the conventional Oxford things: walking on Christ Church Meadow, evensong, a sherry party with Jock, afternoon tea. She was sad to find that Stewart's, the setting of many a love affair, had been replaced by Marks and Spencer. On the whole, though, Oxford appeared to be unchanged, except for the people walking around carrying gas masks. Many of the college gardens had been dug up and planted with potatoes and beetroot. But it was still hard to believe that Britain was at war. Within days, all this was to change.

On the way home from Oxford, Pym sat in a blacked-out train reading Jock's novel by low light. Changing trains at Birmingham, she had a cup of tea at Snow Hill station, noting stained-glass windows in a tree design. It was one of her last moments of peace, before the war began in earnest.

On 7 May, Julian's father stood up in the House of Commons and called for new leadership that could 'match our enemies in fighting spirit, in daring, in resolution and in thirst for victory'. He was thinking, of course, of his friend Winston Churchill. He ended his speech by addressing Prime Minister Chamberlain directly: 'Depart, and let us have done with you. In the name of God, go!'[3]

Three days later, Germany invaded Holland and Belgium, pushing on into France. The phoney war was over. 'Of course the first feeling was the usual horror and disgust and the impossibility of finding words to describe this latest *Schweinerei* by the Germans,' wrote Pym. The sudden realisation that the war 'was coming a lot nearer to us – airbases in Holland and Belgium would make raids on England a certainty'. As a major port, Liverpool was a main target for bombing and the people in Shropshire rightly feared that German bombs would be dropped over the countryside on the way back from air raids.

Reactions to hostilities differed. 'People were either gloomy (Mr Beauclerk, the electrician and Mr Cobb, the wireless shop), slightly hysterical (Miss Bloomer) or just plainly calm like Steele.' Pym felt frightened, 'but hope I didn't show it and anyway one still has the "it couldn't happen to us" feeling'. That evening, Chamberlain went to Buckingham Palace to tender his resignation to the king. The sound of his voice on the wireless was, for Barbara, a reminder of how he had tried so hard to attain peace: 'there is no more courageous man in the government or indeed anywhere, I'm sure of that'.[4]

Churchill was immediately asked to become prime minister and form a government of national unity. Hilary, always less naive than her sister, welcomed the change of leadership. She believed that Churchill 'will be better for this war . . . he is such an old beast!' Pym was forced to agree: 'The Germans loathe and fear him and I believe he can do it.'[5]

The tenth of May, now an historic landmark, was always a significant personal anniversary for Pym as it was the day she had gone on a date with Henry. Seven years on, in a new and terrifying world, she looked back: 'Imagine a lovely summer evening at the Trout with the wisteria out and the soft murmuring of the water. And my heart so full of everything. And now, emotion recollected in tranquillity . . . dust and ashes, dry bones.'[6]

CHAPTER IX

Miss Pym joins the ARP

Where once Pym's diary was full of dates with boys, and shopping and travel, now it recorded the news on the wireless:

16th May, Fierce fighting in France and Belgium. Duff Cooper. Very Good talk . . .

21st May, Grave news from France . . .

23rd May, The Germans have Boulogne.

On 26 May there was a day of national prayer. Pym attended church services both morning and evening. Despite the bad news, she remained optimistic. The sermons were first-rate and the church was packed: 'I thought, Friedbert against this, you haven't a chance!'[1]

Jock Liddell took a darker view of the events in France: 'If Herr Hitler wins, I hope you will marry Friedbert and then do your best for us all.'[2]

Liddell had written to Pym in March to tell her that his sister Betty had suffered a nervous breakdown. Both he and his brother Don believed it had been brought on by their stepmother, and events would prove them to be correct. The news had been kept from the brothers, but somehow Don discovered the truth and they went immediately to the hospital in Clifton where Betty was being treated. They learned that she had had three bad breakdowns. Their stepmother had insisted she had been suffering from the flu. Betty Liddell was a pitiful sight and begged not to be sent home to her stepmother. The doctor told the brothers that, although she was very ill, it was not necessary to incarcerate her, provided kind people could be arranged for her care. Jock insisted that she should be kept away from her stepmother and if necessary a family intervention could be staged if the woman made trouble.

On 29 May, Pym noted: 'Desperate fighting on the Western Front.' On 10 June came the news that Mussolini had declared war on Britain and that France had fallen. The French government departed that day and on 14 June the Germans were in Paris and the occupation had begun. Two days later, she wrote: 'France is in desperate straits. We must prepare for the worst knowing in our hearts that we shall win in the end.'[3]

Many people, including Jock, believed that England would be next on Hitler's list. He hoped that when the English occupation took place that he would be in Oxford. He wrote to Pym: 'I am amazed at your confidence, convinced as I am that before the end of the month the swastika will be flying over St Oswald's church.'[4] Pym was having none of it: 'The country is lovely, honeysuckle in the hedges. How dare the Nazis think they could invade it.'[5]

That month, she joined the Oswestry ARP.[6] Her role was to help man a first-aid post set up to deal with casualties from air raids. One of her initial tasks was to practise picking up imaginary casualties. When the air-raid sirens wailed, she had to rush to the post. In her short story 'Goodbye Balkan Capital', Pym channelled her experience into that of Laura Arling. Night-time duty was especially daunting. Every time Laura hears the siren wailing in the evening, her stomach turns over:

> Still, it was eerie when it went at night and one never knew for certain that the planes were just passing over on their way to Liverpool. Sometimes they sounded as if they were right over the house and, as the Head Warden had said, not without a certain professional relish, two or three well placed H. E. bombs could practically wipe out their small town.[7]

The Blitz began on 7 September 1940. London was systematically bombed by the Luftwaffe for fifty-six of the following fifty-seven days and nights. The Liverpool Blitz was no less horrific. The first major air raid took place in late August, when 160 bombers flew over the city in a single night. This assault continued over the next three nights, then regularly for the rest of the year. There were fifty raids on the city during this three-month period: some of them minor – a few aircraft dropping bombs and incendiaries over a few minutes – others comprising up to 300 aircraft and lasting over ten hours.

Pym heard the bombers as they passed over Shropshire on the way to Liverpool. The Luftwaffe jettisoned bombs in the countryside on their way back to their air bases. The sirens would go off and they would dash to the shelter, returning home in the early morning when the all-clear was given.

Like her heroine, Laura Arling, Pym was given an ARP badge, an armband and a tin hat, serving as a makeshift uniform:

> She came downstairs carrying her gas mask and a neat little suitcase, in which she had packed her knitting, *Pride and Prejudice*, some biscuits and a precious bar of milk chocolate. On her head she wore a tin hat, painted pale grey and beautiful in its newness . . . Going out like this and not knowing when

she would return always made her feel rather grand, almost noble, as if she were setting out on a secret and dangerous mission. The tin hat made a difference, too. One felt much more *splendid* in a tin hat. It was almost a uniform.[8]

Pym was also given a torch, with strict instructions to hold the beam downwards. The bulb was swathed in tissue paper and tied as on a pot of jam so that she wanted to write on it something like 'Raspberry 1911', as her mother used to do.

In the story, Laura's eyes soon become accustomed to the dark and she can hear the 'sinister purring sound' of the planes overhead. Her tin hat is heavy on her head, 'like a flower on a broken stalk'. When she finally arrives at the shelter, she hears a woman saying: 'Liverpool again.' Laura wishes for something adequate to say, but there is nothing: 'It was of no consolation to the bombed that the eyes of women in safe places should fill with tears when they spoke of them. Tears, idle tears were of no use to anyone, not even to oneself.'[9] Pym's war journals are bald and factual, whereas this moving short story is evidence of her very deep feeling and compassion for the pity of war.

In Pym's writing, however, compassion is always leavened with good humour and cheerfulness. Once everyone is gathered at the shelter, there is an air of bustle, efficiency and brisk jollity. People have their jobs to do. Stretcher-bearers dressed in dark blue boiler suits fill water bottles and collect blankets. An efficient girl mans the telephone. The doctor is stout and reassuring.

One of the boons of the war was the way in which classes and ranks mixed. 'The most unlikely people were gathered together, people who otherwise would never have known each other.' In the darkness of the shelter, conversation is animated: 'horrible stories of raid damage, fine imaginative rumours, tidbits about the private lives of the Nazi leaders gleaned from the Sunday papers'. They sit drinking tea and sharing their food;

biscuits, rare blocks of chocolate 'broken up and shared like the Early Christians'; thickly cut bread and margarine with a smear of fish paste on each slice. 'No banquet was ever more enjoyed than this informal meal at one o'clock in the morning.'[10]

All of these details were gleaned from Pym's real-life experiences, recorded in her diary. One night, they all stood around listening to aeroplanes and looking for them amongst the stars, hearing the thud of bombs in the direction of Wrexham. 'The Surrealists have nothing on us for odd situations!' Pym noted, grimly. So too, her heroine Laura observes the 'smoky room crowded with silent men and women, lying or sitting on beds, chairs or the floor, some covered with dark army blankets . . . there was nothing in Dali and the Surrealists more odd than this reality'.[11] Pym's experience of war, collated in her observational journals, is transformed into her fiction, an alchemy that was becoming crucial to her art.

CHAPTER X

In which our Heroine works for the YMCA in an Army Tented Camp

Almost as soon as war broke out, the YMCA set up mobile canteens to feed the troops. In 1939, an army tented camp was erected on the outskirts of Oswestry. In July 1940, Pym volunteered to help out. There was a great sense of excitement about the camp and the soldiers.

Her first day was enjoyable: 'Great fun and very busy.'[1] The next day, Pym made herself a fetching overall of blue checked gingham. She now had a bike and so she cycled to the camp. Her principal duties involved handing out food and drink, working on the cash desk and, most importantly, chatting with the soldiers and keeping up morale.

Pym found some of the work exhausting, but it was fun talking with the other women and flirting with the soldiers. She was delighted when a Scotsman called her a 'wee smasher'. She discovered a 'beautiful pre-Raphaelite Lance Bombardier' and a theological student called Harry. She thought it was amusing when one of the sergeants asked her if she would darn his socks – it was a world away from darning Henry's in Oxford. Despite working all day and often in the air-raid shelters at night, she never complained.

The Pyms were still able to enjoy their family holidays at the Welsh seaside resorts of Pwllheli and Abersoch: 'many pretty boats and a glorious view'.² Pym also took a city break, visiting Hilary in Bristol, where she had relocated with the BBC. The sisters had a day excursion in Bath, a city made famous by Pym's literary heroine, Jane Austen. It was another heavenly day when the war suddenly felt a long way away: 'Sunshine and Jane Austen.'³

Back at the tented camp, she met a nice gunner called Desmond Green. They made a pact to meet for a rendezvous on the Isle of Skye in 1944.⁴ Desmond, 'all violet-brillatined', rode her bicycle around the field outside the camp. He took off her magenta chiffon scarf and put his identity disk in its place. 'And now I wear it.'⁵

In late October, the camp was packed up: 'Down to the camp to find mud and desolation, everything being packed up – said many goodbyes.'⁶ Pym's life went back to its usual routines of dressmaking, cycling around Shropshire and occasional shopping trips to Shrewsbury. She missed the buzz and camaraderie of the camp. Things looked up in November, when she was assigned to a new camp in Park Hall, a former army barracks. Her duties were much the same and she met many more soldiers, though she continued to write to Desmond. She also helped out at the local food office: 'I stamped 700 ration cards three times each. Aching in every limb.'⁷ Again and again, she noted the sound of distant bombing as Liverpool was targeted by the Luftwaffe.

Back on duty in the air-raid shelter, she read Jane Austen's *Emma* to pass the time, sitting on the shelter stairs.⁸ The shelter was hot and stuffy with so many people crammed into a small space. So hot that she longed to be inside a gas mask, 'with its cool rubbery smell'. In 'Goodbye Balkan Capital', Laura describes the lethargy after the main meal and before settling for sleep:

The women knitted rather grimly and the men, already tired after a day's work, dozed and smoked. The room was very hot and people were seen dimly through a haze. Laura thought longingly of rivers, pools and willows, of her own linen sheets, of plunging one's face under water when swimming, even of the inside of a gas mask, with its cool rubbery smell and tiny space of unbreathed air.[9]

When the all-clear is sounded, there is sudden activity:

A beautiful note sounded through the room, piercing and silvery as the music of the spheres must sound. It was the All Clear. In a surprisingly short time the blanket-covered shapes became human and active, everything was put away and they walked out into the sharp, cold air, their voices and footsteps ringing through the empty streets.[10]

Pym describes the feeling of 'the glow of virtue which comes from duty done'. No matter that there are no bombs and no casualties, 'but they had been standing by. They had missed their night's rest so that if anything *had* happened they would have been there to deal with it.'[11]

As Christmas drew close, Pym finished *Emma* and looked forward to Hilary's return from Bristol. At the end of the year she wrote: 'I have met many charming people. May 1941 be as nice and bring us closer to VICTORY!'[12]

CHAPTER XI

A Sketch of Miss Ivy Compton-Burnett

By now, Jock was in Athens with the British Council. Before he left he had managed to procure a meeting with his literary idol, Ivy Compton-Burnett. He was planning an article for *Horizon* about her genius, but wanted Compton-Burnett's approval first: 'It would be a pity to make mistakes about a living writer who was there to correct them.' Ivy invited him to tea at her home, Braemar Mansions in Kensington – and thus began a friendship which would endure over a quarter of a century. Liddell later wrote a book about his friendship with Ivy and another novelist whom he greatly admired, Elizabeth Taylor.[1] At the time of his meeting Ivy, he sent Pym detailed letters of the kind he knew she would enjoy:

> I called on Sunday at 3.30 and she let me in. Miss C.B. is a small, upright woman in the fifties, plainly dressed in a well-cut black silk dress. Her hair hangs low in a fringe on her forehead . . . it is reddish gold, little streaked with grey . . . in spite of keen blue eyes, she has generally a peaceful expression.[2]

It was a great moment for Jock and he greedily absorbed every detail, the sparsely furnished room with grey walls, scattered with rugs here and there. He sat on a plain black velvet Empire sofa and they talked. Ivy told Jock that she liked his piece and hoped it would be published, as she was so little known.

Tea went 'through all its stages' (a phrase lifted from the novel *More Women Than Men*): watercress sandwiches, cheese straws and home-made gingerbread. With Ivy was her life partner, Margaret Jourdain, whom Liddell felt was a most impressive figure. She was a great expert on English furniture and was the younger sister of Eleanor Jourdain, the principal of St Hugh's College, Oxford. Eleanor was famous for her 'adventure' at Versailles, where she and her friend Annie Moberly claimed that they had been transported back in time and seen the ghost of Marie Antoinette at the Petit Trianon. The women wrote a book about their experience, which was a cause of great controversy. One wonders whether Pym's adoption of the appellation Miss Moberly as the name for a cantankerous old lady might have been a tribute, or whether it was a coincidence.

Liddell and Compton-Burnett talked about publishing – she complained about her publishers and said the only one of her novels that had sold well was *Brothers and Sisters*, because it was about incest. To his evident delight, Ivy told him that she was passionate about Jane Austen and liked *Mansfield Park* the best – she was 'devoted to the Crawfords'. She 'thought she would go mad' because Jane Austen never finished her novel *The Watsons*. Jock remembered that they talked too much of the Marie Antoinette vision: 'we wished to be speaking of other things', he noted.[3]

Knowing Pym's fondness for relics, Jock attached to his letter a paperclip belonging to Compton-Burnett. He told her: 'You had better keep this letter for use by literary researchers in better days, who will know all about that great writer.' He also told Pym more about the ongoing crisis with his sister and step-mother. It looked to the Liddell brothers that Betty's doctor was going to betray her back into her stepmother's hands, so they headed straight to Clifton, with suitcases, to carry her off to Cornwall. They managed to convince their sister's doctor that living with their stepmother was the cause of all her mental suffering. But as they left the clinic, Don opened the front door to reveal, to their horror, the most unwelcome sight of their stepmother: 'It was one of the great moments of one's life.'[4] After an awkward exchange, they escaped to the station, laughing with relief and anxiety.

Pym's life in Shropshire seemed slightly monotonous by comparison. At Park Hall camp, she befriended a Scottish gunner called Stewart. As she had learned German for Friedbert and Finnish for Henry, she began to learn Gaelic for Stewart. They went to the pictures 'holding hands, eating ice-cream and being generally childish'. It was January and there was snow on the ground; Pym was bitterly cold despite her new fur-lined boots. She painted her nails 'thistle' and had Stewart to supper: 'poached eggs, spaghetti and mince pies'.[5] He gave her a lesson in Gaelic, until they were disturbed by the sirens going off, forcing them to decamp to the air-raid shelter.

At ARP training there were make-believe casualties for practice: 'very macabre and surrealist'. Pym also had a new job at the baby clinic in town: 'I'm learning quite a lot about babies and their feeding.'[6] She had a very amusing letter from Private D. S. Liddell, Jock's brother, now in the army. Both Liddell brothers continued their regular correspondence, though she rarely heard from Henry.

Later that month, it was time to say goodbye to Stewart, who was about to leave for the war. Pym felt melancholic. She thought of him getting up at 4.30 a.m and going off to fight the Germans. After lunch, she read a new novel by R. C. Hutchinson called *The Fire and the Wood*, a story of decency and oppression in the early years of Nazism, centred on the incarceration of a Jewish doctor. The incongruity of reading its concentration camp scenes whilst listening to Beethoven's Emperor Concerto led her to declare in her diary: 'Oh Germany.'[7]

Many of the British soldiers whom Pym befriended had now left for active service. When she went to Park Hall later on, she was saddened by the air of absence, though one of the remaining soldiers caught her eye: 'A ravishingly handsome second lieutenant poured into an exquisitely tailored overcoat came in, but he studied his book of "Gas Drill", rather than me.'[8]

It snowed for most of January and into February. Her friend Rosemary Topping's London flat was bombed in the Blitz and Rosemary was buried in the ruins, though survived unharmed. Pym was deeply impressed by the courage of her friends: 'Now we have heroes and heroines for friends who before were just ordinary people.'[9]

CHAPTER XII

I Married a Nazi

'Went to the clinic,' Pym noted. 'I am gradually learning to pick up a baby with a nonchalant air.'[1] This was all well and good, but in the new year of 1941 she felt that there might be more challenging work she could undertake for the war effort: 'Busy in the house and wondering (as I sometimes do) whether I ought not to be doing other things – leading a fuller life.'[2]

There were no more small luxuries such as cigarettes and chocolates. Within a few months, the government announced clothes rationing. Each person received a ration book of sixty-six coupons, which had to last for a year. Every item of clothing had a coupon value attached to it. Coats needed sixteen coupons, a jacket thirteen, trousers eight, a shirt five, shoes seven and underwear eight coupons. Clothes had to be adapted to suit every season. But at least the cinemas were still open. Pym had loved the pictures ever since her student days in Oxford. Her war journals list all of the films she saw, many of them war propaganda movies.

In May, Pym saw a film that had many resonances. *The Man I Married* (sometimes known as *I Married a Nazi*) was a powerful anti-Nazi film. It tells the story of an American art critic, Carol, who has married a handsome and genial German man, Eric.

They have a young son. Despite the protestations of their American friends, they visit Germany in 1938, where Eric becomes caught up in the Nazi movement. Initially, Carol is enthusiastic about the Nazis and believes that Hitler has restored pride to her husband's nation. 'I gather you're one of those people who pride themselves on being fair to the Nazis,' says one of the Jewish characters, who is unimpressed by her naivety.[3] But once she is in Berlin, she is horrified to witness the violence of the Nazis against the Jews.

Meanwhile, Eric becomes indoctrinated after hearing Hitler speak at Nuremberg. He falls in love with a blonde Aryan fascist called Frieda. Carol befriends an American journalist who tells her that making a joke about Hitler is a crime. She is horrified by the transformation of her charming husband into a cruel and heartless Nazi. He asks her for a divorce and, when she refuses, he threatens to tell the Gestapo that she has insulted Hitler – a crime that gives grounds for a man to divorce his wife. When Carol tries to flee to America with her son, he refuses to allow the child to travel, claiming that he needs to stay in Germany, where he will eventually become part of the Hitler Youth. The day is saved by the intervention of Eric's father, who is deeply troubled by the events in his country and wants his grandson to live as an American citizen. He tells Eric that his mother was a Jewess – a revelation that causes Eric to break down in tears, much to the disgust of his wife.

The film caused Pym to reflect once more on her troubled relationship with Germany. She had become close to being engaged to Friedbert and it was a frightening reminder of the vulnerability of her position. At one point, Carol is taken by the Gestapo for helping a Jewish family and is only released by the intervention of an American journalist. Pym thought that the film was 'very good'. Inevitably, her thoughts turned immediately to her Nazi boyfriend: 'Oh, if I had married poor

F[riedbert].' There is a whole wealth of meaning in that sentence. Sassy, straight-talking Carol's fate might well have been Pym's own. The transformation of handsome, clever, cultured Friedbert, in his green Tyrolean hat, into a Jew-hating Nazi was all too close to the bone. Her joke in *Some Tame Gazelle* about the 'poor Nazis exiled to Africa' could have cost her much if indeed she had married poor Friedbert.

Nevertheless, Pym was happy to 'hear German spoken'.[4] Her fluency in the language would come in handy by the end of the year, when the government decreed that unmarried women and all women from the ages of nineteen to thirty were required to register for war work, and the Ministry of Labour sent Pym details of a job in the Censorship Department (German Division). She began brushing up her German by reading Friedbert's letters. 'Even if there are things to regret and even be ashamed of, one cannot forget happiness and kindness.'[5]

CHAPTER XIII

Miss Pym returns to her 'Sentimental Journal'

Pym reported her impressions of the war: the frightful bombing, sirens blasting and the distant rumble of bombs over Liverpool and Birkenhead. She endured long nights at the first-aid post, getting through by smoking, knitting, talking, eating and trying to sleep in the stuffy air, covered with a scratchy army blanket. She also worked hard in the YMCA canteens at the tented camp and at Park Hall.

Early in 1941, Pym rummaged in search of a notebook in which to keep a record of her dreams. She found her recollections of Julian Amery, describing it as a 'sentimental journal' in contrast to her pocket diaries in which she recorded 'everyday happenings'. This was where she reflected on past loves, future hopes and momentous events. She actually described it as 'a sentimental journal or whatever you (Gentle Reader in the Bodleian) like to call it', which suggests a degree of confidence that she would become a published author and posterity would want her archive.[1]

The spring made her think of Julian yet again: these were 'his months'. She had been temporarily in love with Stewart, but 'it has all passed now and my heart is quite free again with Jay's memory warming it'. She had accepted that her love for Julian was a fantasy and that he was a useful muse: 'I hear no news of him – I don't write.' She was improving her mind by reading Walter Scott, Samuel Johnson and Jane Austen. She also read *Vanity Fair* after hearing it as a serial on the wireless: 'That marvellous Waterloo chapter was especially appropriate this summer although I had nobody in France or at Dunkirk.'[2] Pym's writing in her sentimental journal was sensuous and lyrical: 'Here it is – summer and at least the dream of flowers has come true. In my room delphinium, sweet williams, roses and sweet peas . . . Afterwards picking flowers I thought of "Go Lovely Rose" and "How small a part of time they share/That are so wondrous sweet and fair".'[3] She was self-reflective, too:

> It is extraordinary how the slightest emotional disturbance (like hoping to have a little German conversation with a Czech officer) can put all other ideas out of one's head, making one stupid and unable to concentrate on anything intelligent . . . it is humiliating to discover that one has not grown out of this sort of thing, but enlightening too, a useful experience and happily it passes.[4]

Pym was still trying to discover what kind of writer she wanted to be. Writing short stories for magazines was a useful way to be published, but her heart was in writing novels. After reading Tolstoy's *Anna Karenina* that summer, she considered writing something 'nostalgic, faintly Russian and true . . . it seems that the best stories nowadays are more atmospheric than anything else'.[5]

She had also been reading Virginia Woolf's *To the Lighthouse*. She had encountered Woolf before, but this was the first time she took note of her 'special technique'. Though at face value it is difficult to imagine more different writers than Virginia

Woolf and Barbara Pym, Pym was acute in sensing their mutual interest in small things and events and in the creation of mood. Less concerned with plot, in favour of philosophical introspection, Woolf's novel reads more like a series of observations and thoughts. It was a style that appealed to Pym:

> It is one that commends itself to me – I find it attractive and believe I could do it. Indeed, I already have, in a mild way. Sitting by the kitchen fire drying my hair, a cat, a basket chair and a willow tree and Mr Churchill and President Roosevelt meeting in the middle of the ocean to discuss War and Peace Aims.[6]

Woolf's *To the Lighthouse* recalls childhood experiences and emotions which, combined with her experiences of the evacuees and in the nursery, gave Pym a new interest in children. Home help was increasingly difficult to find in 1941 and the Pyms hired a grandmother, Mrs Morris, who brought along her granddaughter, Dorothy. Barbara's sharp eye took in every movement:

> Dorothy follows you about or if you are sitting in the garden stands and peers at you through the trelliswork by the back door. One morning when I was washing up the breakfast things she came and stood with her hands at the draining board staring at me . . . We are embarrassed when children stare at us – there is something unnerving about it.

She toyed with the possibility of writing something about a child 'like Dorothy or evacuees'.

Pym's reflective mood in the summer of 1941 was heightened by the fact that Dor and Links had decided to sell Morda Lodge. The house was large and expensive to maintain, and Hilary was working and living away from home with little sign of returning

to Shropshire. The Pyms found a new house called Blytheswood
and in September Barbara began planning her new bedroom.
Moving away from her childhood home was an important
moment. Sorting out old letters, she found the one that Henry
had written to her which had caused such anguish: 'Respect and
esteem – perhaps the same for me now.'[7]

Wartime privations also heightened Pym's preoccupation with
food. There was tea at Garth Derwen, her aunt's house outside
Oswestry. 'Lovely food – tomato sandwiches, blackberry jam-
scones and bread, swiss roll and chocolate cake.'[8] Comestibles
once taken for granted were now elevated to delicacies of the
rarest kind: a large jar of marmalade seemed more desirable than
a new love affair.

One night when Merseyside and Belfast were badly bombed,
Pym had to stay in the air-raid shelter until 4 a.m. It was a clear
night with a cluster of bright stars. The next morning, she was
back at work at the baby clinic. She was tired and emotional,
thinking of Julian and the last time she saw him standing in
the doorway of his house in Eaton Square. In one year, she had
only been as far as north Wales. 'I was altogether in a restless
and unenviable state today wondering whether I ought not to
be in some job or one of the services for my own sake as well
as patriotic reasons.'[9] But there was always the comfort of writing:
'After supper, I did some more writing, which quells my restless-
ness – *That* is how I must succeed!'[10]

CHAPTER XIV

So Very Secret

Pym had begun notes for a spy novel in January 1940, but she was now ready to begin writing in earnest. She used her experience in the ARP to good effect, but the work is Pym's weakest. Self-confessedly, she was struggling with the plot and it is lacking in her unique sense of humour. But there are vivid details of England in the early years of war and 'the rather ludicrous activities of a country village in wartime'.[1]

The heroine, Cassandra Swan, is busy at the militia camp canteen, poaching eggs, cutting thick sandwiches and distributing tea out of a huge urn to the ever-hungry and thirsty servicemen. The village is so dull that 'even the evacuees left us' – though the local people prefer to think of their village as a small town, with its few shops, hairdresser and cinema. Cassandra is visited by one of her school friends, who now has a glamorous job in the 'higher reaches of the Civil Service'. Cassie is a middle-aged spinster whose once-great love, Adrian, is now a politician. She would have liked to have been his wife, but, she has to admit, he never asked her.

One of the characters, Frau Nussbaum, is a refugee from Vienna whose husband has been incarcerated in Dachau concentration camp: 'Oh, we were silent, pitying and remembering horrors we had read about.'² People confuse her origins and believe that she is a German and therefore suspect. An argument breaks out between the women in the camp when Frau Nussbaum shoves another helper out of the way of the toaster: 'We don't want Germans here . . . to have some fat German woman pushing me away from the toaster.'³

There are discussions about the way the war is going, the threat of invasion and the 'jackboot gangsterism' of the Nazis – though they are conceded to be more 'efficient' than the Allies. The dangers of pro-Nazi sentiments are emphasised: it is a crime that can be reported to the police.

When Cassandra's friend Harriet mysteriously disappears from the local hairdressers, the threat of kidnapping, even rape, hangs in the air: 'It was a relief to know that she wouldn't be likely to suffer the sort of experience about which Miss Moberly rather gloated, with shrewd whispers and goggling eyes.'⁴ The elderly Miss Moberly has appeared before, in *Gervase and Flora*.

Cassie returns to Maida Vale, which has been bombed but still has an air of nobility, as though it is a city of ancient ruins. She meets and befriends a prostitute and worries about what Miss Moberly would say if she knew. Though Cassandra has lived a sheltered life, she has often observed the prostitutes who hang around Piccadilly underground station in their high heels.

The prostitute, Jenny Dale, has a message from Harriet and takes Cassandra back to her flat. Cassandra expects to find a messy room with an unmade bed, but the flat is like a Victorian parlour, tidy and neat. Cassandra cannot help looking at the bed and imagining the scenes that have unfolded there. She puts her curiosity down to a subconscious 'Freudian' feeling linked to her state of spinsterhood. Cassandra has renounced sex and this young woman is selling it.

There are two characters based on Julian Amery: a young Balliol man called Hugh Fordyce, whom Cassandra thinks might one day be Secretary of State for India (the post Leo Amery would hold throughout the war), and the older man, Adrian, the love of her life. In London, she realises that she is being followed by Frau Nussbaum and takes refuge (improbably) in Adrian's Eaton Square house, whose front door just happens to be unlocked. The place smells of incense and Turkish cigarettes. Cassandra finds his library and is tempted to pry through his papers, but when she hears footsteps, she hides in an alcove. She longs for a romantic reunion, but when she is discovered, Adrian does not recognise his old love. Though in the prime of life and still 'outwardly' handsome, despite a greying around the temples, his face is 'blank and wooden'. He has become a pompous politician.[5] Nevertheless, he still has the charm, which he switches on 'like an electric fire'. Cynically, she imagines him comforting pensioners and cuddling babies. He is no longer, as she had once written in a poem for him, the 'Jewel of Balliol and Eaton Square / United in him virtues all too rare'.[6]

Pym's wish fulfilment is self-evident. She is rewriting the scene in the library in Eaton Square, where Julian had once kissed her and then broken off the affair, and imagining a romantic reunion twenty-seven years later. Though she longs to rush into his arms, she knows that he is married to his work and that he barely remembers who she is – he is a handsome, charming MP and she has become a 'dried-up spinster' in a faded dress.

So Very Secret ultimately fails as a novel. The spy novel is not Pym's genre and she is not a master of intricacy of plot. The characters, for once, are flat and lifeless. Nevertheless, it was her first sustained experiment in first-person narrative, which is handled ably. It gave her the idea and structure that she would execute so perfectly in the character of Mildred Lathbury in *Excellent Women*.

And it helped her to find her great theme. Cassandra is frustrated by male incompetence. 'Men are so inefficient – why is it that they take twice as long as we do over the simplest little job?' Part of her enjoys the freedom conveyed by her spinster-hood and she finds the male species often repellent: 'As I am unmarried I have no very great respect for men.'[7] Pym wrote on the flyleaf of the manuscript: 'Is *Spinster* an occupation – very definitely!'

CHAPTER XV

Operation Bullseye

Julian was often on Pym's mind. Though not hearing directly from him, she kept her ear to the ground for news of his movements. On his twenty-second birthday (27 March 1941), she put a vase of daffodils next to his photograph. Two weeks later, she placed a vase of spring flowers for the one 'who may be now in the Balkans and whom I shall always love'.[1] And two weeks after that, she finished a first draft of her story, 'About me, Julian and the ARP'.[2] It was titled, 'Goodbye Balkan Capital'. She had finished it and typed it out in a matter of weeks. Pym had read in the *Telegraph* that Julian had been made captain; she was proud of his achievements. His war career was even more exciting and glamorous than she had anticipated.

Julian Amery was never going to be content with a desk job. Soon after meeting Sandy Glen, he had become involved with the Special Operations Executive (one of his mentors always said he wanted to be a John Buchan character), an organisation formed to conduct espionage, sabotage and reconnaissance in occupied Europe. SOE was sometimes known as 'Churchill's Secret Army', or the 'Ministry of Ungentlemanly Warfare'. Julian was made to sign the Official Secrets Act and given the code name 'AHA'.

Pym had been keeping up to date with developments in the Balkans since the Italian invasion of Greece on 28 October 1940. On 6 April 1941, Germany invaded Yugoslavia. Julian headed to Istanbul, where he embarked on a number of successful secret missions. He would risk his life in many undercover operations during the war, including 'Operation Bullseye' – a daring operation into Nazi-occupied Yugoslavia in which an SOE group was put ashore by submarine.

Pym submitted her short story to the popular literary periodical *Penguin New Writing*. Founded by John Lehmann, a committed anti-fascist, it featured leading writers of the day, including W. H. Auden, Christopher Isherwood and Stephen Spender. As well as being an evocative record of her life as a young woman serving with the ARP, it was another love letter to Julian Amery. Just as Pym would scan the newspapers to see if he had been 'killed in action', so too does her heroine, Laura Arling, who meets 'Crispin' at Oxford:

> She was remembering Crispin at a Commemoration Ball in Oxford . . . they had danced together an improper number of times . . . and at 6 o'clock, when the dance was over, they had gone on the river in a punt and had breakfast. It had been like a dream, walking down the Banbury Road in the early morning sunshine, wearing her white satin ball gown and holding Crispin's hand.[3]

Laura is deeply in love, but when the short-lived affair is over, she remembers Crispin's kisses and the beautiful things he has said and she longs for letters which never come.

When the war begins, Laura borrows a translation of *Mein Kampf* from Boots' lending library. She never worries about Hitler and the Balkans. After the fall of France, she is relieved that Hitler is going in the opposite direction, the *Drang Nach*

Osten – or push to the east. She is horrified when she then realises that Crispin's 'Balkan Capital' is now being invaded.

Laura has found it fairly easy to track Crispin. She consults *Harmsworth's Encyclopaedia* to give her some local colour of his Balkan town:

> The British Legation was in the old part of town near to the famous Botanical Gardens. Laura often thought of Crispin walking there on fine spring mornings, perhaps sitting on a seat reading official documents, with lilacs, azaleas and later scarlet and yellow cannas making a fitting background for his dark good looks.[4]

Like Pym, Laura is worried when the Balkan states sign the Axis agreement on 1 June 1941; all of Albania, Yugoslavia and Greece were under Axis control. Greece was placed in triple occupation and Yugoslavia was dissolved and occupied. Most alarmingly, Germany had gained a significant strategic advantage in having direct access to the Mediterranean.

On the fall of Belgrade, Sandy Glen and the rest of the British legation fled to the coast and were evacuated by sea. Laura imagines Crispin 'in his shirt sleeves, burning the code books, stuffing secret bulky documents into the central heating furnace, a lock of dark hair falling over one eye'. She imagines a hasty exit by 'special diplomatic train', with Crispin, sleeping in a comfortable cabin, 'dark windows shuttered'. Maybe even the luxury of the *Orient Express*. But then Laura is overcome by a strong dose of reality:

> But Europe was never sleeping and now less than ever. Things happened in these hours when human vitality was at its lowest ebb; bombers rained death between one and four in the morning, troops crossed the frontiers at dawn . . . But it was 'Goodbye

Balkan Capital!' and the train was rushing through the darkness to deposit its important passengers, blinking like ruffled owls in the early morning sunshine.[5]

The truth was somewhat more prosaic. Julian Amery was having emergency dental treatment back in London and had missed the evacuation from the Balkans. During the operation to remove his wisdom teeth, a bomb exploded, knocking the anaesthetist to the ground; the operation went wrong and Julian ended up with a broken jaw and a serious infection.[6] He was told to stay in England to recuperate. He was furious at having missed out on the action.

CHAPTER XVI

Miss Pym is offered a Job in the Censorship Department (German) and hears News of Friedbert

Nora Waln was an American journalist and anti-Nazi writer who wrote a best-selling book, *Reaching for the Stars* – a damning exposé of the Third Reich, published in 1938. It was based on her real experiences living in Germany between 1934 and 1938. Waln loved her adopted country and believed that the German people would rise up against the Nazis.

The first manuscript of her book mysteriously vanished from Germany, but after returning to England, Waln rewrote it from memory and sent a copy to Himmler with an insolent description. He retaliated by seizing seven children, friends of Waln's, whose names had been disguised in the book but whom he tracked down. Waln entered Germany secretly and in an interview with Himmler offered to serve as a hostage for the children.

Himmler offered to release them and as many other people as she could list on a large sheet of paper, if she would promise to write nothing further about Germany except romantic historical novels. Waln declined the offer because, she said, 'if you make a bargain like that, God takes away the power to write. If you don't tell the truth you lose your talent.'[1]

In 1941, Waln wrote and took part in a series of radio plays for the BBC, where she met and befriended Hilary Pym. At some point there was a discussion about Barbara and her relationship with an SS officer. It was by this route that Pym heard some news of Friedbert Glück. Nora Waln had told Hilary that he had gone 'Anti-Nazi'.[2] Pym noted the news in her journal, adding a cryptic phrase in German, which seems to translate as: 'Oh Henry, you were right'. (Henry Harvey had never truly believed that Friedbert was a committed Nazi.)

On 13 November 1941, Pym was invited to an interview at the Censorship Department in London. Fearing that her German was rusty, she spent October and early November brushing up, reading Goethe and Rilke. There were also Friedbert's letters, which evoked troubling memories: 'After tea translated a letter from F. one of the last I had and painful to me. One feels one ought to be ashamed of ever having been fond of a German. Where are you now?'[3] Thus prepared, the interview went well: 'feeling excited and pleased and hopeful'.[4] She had a letter from the Censorship Department requiring her to sit two language tests.

That autumn Pym was disappointed to hear that her Balkans short story had been rejected by *Penguin New Writing*. Undeterred, she carried on with her spy novel, which was to be dedicated to Julian Amery, throughout October and November. She was also busy with the family's house move. There was much tidying and sorting to be done. She found an old Victorian frame in which she inserted a photograph of Julian in the Union Club, and added a small picture of Balliol chapel and a pressed orchid. On 7 December she went to hang curtains at the new home, Blytheswood, and enjoyed a supper of ham and chips. The next morning, the day of the house move, came news of the Japanese navy's attack on Pearl Harbor: 'later heard Winston and Roosevelt'. The following day a letter came from the Censorship

Department offering her a job in Bristol. She would be starting within the week.

After accepting the post, Pym wrote in her diary: 'it will be lovely to be with Poopa'. Hilary was living in a communal house in Bristol and arranged for Barbara to join them. Pym left Shropshire on Sunday 14 November and went by train to Bristol. Another amorous adventure lay ahead.

BOOK THE FOURTH

From the Coppice to Naples

CHAPTER I

Miss Pym moves to a 'Select Residential District' of Bristol

The Coppice was a large double-fronted Edwardian house on the outskirts of Bristol, overlooking Clifton Suspension Bridge. It was rented by the BBC when, after the war broke out, they evacuated some of their staff, with families, to Clifton.

When Pym arrived in December 1941, Hilary introduced her to Dick and Mary Palmer and Honor Wyatt. Between them, they had six children. It was a warm, noisy, fun household, with cosy chats in the large back kitchen and happy children running around the huge garden. Honor Wyatt, like Hilary, worked in the BBC Schools Department. She was a scriptwriter for children's programming and a published author. Among her plays and scripts for radio was a series called 'How Things Began', a sequence of short plays about evolution. Hilary arranged music for radio broadcasts, including those of Honor's. They all became close friends.

Honor Wyatt was to become a much-loved mentor to Barbara Pym. A glamorous and bohemian figure, she was separated from her husband, Gordon Glover, who worked in London – though he was often in Bristol visiting the children, Julian and Prudence. Gordon, a writer and broadcaster, was a philanderer and perhaps not temperamentally suited to marriage, but the separation was amicable. Before the war they had lived in Spain where they befriended the poet Robert Graves and his lover, the writer Laura Riding. In 1937, Honor had published a novel, *The Heathen*, with the Seizen Press, which Graves and Riding co-founded and ran together. Both she and Gordon had now moved on to other relationships. She was seeing an industrial psychologist called George Ellidge, who was now serving with the RAF, while Gordon had a girlfriend called Anna Instone, who worked in the Music Department of the BBC.

Honor was a warm, maternal figure, and a fabulous cook. She took Pym under her wing. Prudence recalled her mother's instinct that within one hour of meeting Barbara Pym she knew they would be friends for life. For her part, Pym became devoted to Honor and to the children. It has sometimes been assumed that Pym disliked children and found them difficult. Certainly, she was often exasperated by the young evacuees in her charge, but that was in different circumstances, where the work was exhausting and she rarely had a chance to form bonds before the children were taken away and replaced by others. Now she formed a close bond with golden-haired Prue Glover.[1] She was only two and her brother six, when their mother first moved to Bristol.

The communal arrangement was a happy one. Pym wrote to the Harveys, explaining her new set-up: 'We share with two families, who work with Hilary and there are altogether six children so we know all about communal living, though the house is big enough for us to have our own sitting room and to keep ourselves to ourselves if we want to.'[2] The house had three storeys; Barbara and Hilary shared the first floor with Honor and the children. Honor had a large bed-sitting room, leading to a smaller bedroom shared by Julian and Prudence. 'The Girls' (as Honor called the Pym sisters) shared a bedroom.

They had meals together in a 'cosy little area' remembered well by Prue, with suppers eaten on a round table covered with an oilcloth.

Afterwards, they would sit around the fire, listening to music and chatting whilst they mended clothes. The Girls would discuss at some length their outfits for the following day. Hilary, Prue later recalled, was the 'far prettier' of the two, smaller and more curvaceous. Barbara was tall, slim and elegant and had prominent front teeth, 'a bit like Joyce Grenfell', though at the time, through her little girl's eyes, she did not notice such details, as she loved Barbara so much.

Prue's pen portraits of Pym are striking, as she genuinely captures Barbara's unique personality and sense of humour. Pym teased the little girl for being rather prim. One evening Honor bathed her and dried her by the fire. Prue was shy and did not want Barbara to see her naked, so she grabbed the towel to cover herself. Pym thought this hilarious and quickly adapted a Stevie Smith limerick: 'Oh, Miss Prudence Glover is SO refined. She has no bosom and no behind!' The little girl responded: 'That's not a nice song, is it mummy?', leaving them all howling with laughter.

Barbara also invented a son called Christopher, who was always better behaved than Prue. 'Christopher would never behave like that,' she would say. She told Prudence that Christopher was at boarding school and spent his holidays big game hunting with his father. Prue recalled Hilary and Barbara as the 'aunts I never had', though it is clear that she was closer to Barbara. Julian was less keen, though; as Prudence admits, the Pym sisters were not so good with boys. Prue remembered that Barbara's work was 'top-secret'.

Pym's first day at the Censorship Department was pleasant enough. She did some 'codes etc' and cycled back to the Coppice, where she enjoyed an excellent meal of stew, then rhubarb and cream.[3] After supper, she sat by the fire and chatted to Mary

Palmer. The next morning, she cycled off to work and opened her first batch of letters, one of which looked suspicious. The censors were called 'Examiners' and Pym felt that she was finally making an important contribution to the war effort. In *Excellent Women*, Mildred Lathbury, one of Pym's most memorable heroines, works as a censor during the war: 'no high qualifications appeared to be necessary, apart from patience and a slight tendency towards eccentricity'.[4]

Like London and Liverpool, Bristol was heavily bombed during the Blitz. One of the common types of bomb dropped on the city were canisters, referred to locally as 'Goering's bread baskets', containing a large number of incendiaries. These caused numerous fires and were designed to generate panic amongst the citizens and to stretch the fire services to the limit. On the home front, men and women volunteered as fire-watchers, who would raise the alarm in the event of such fires. Pym volunteered for once-a-week fire-watching duties.

The Coppice continued to be a fun and pleasant household for Pym: later she remembered it as 'Chek[h]ovian', but by then she had met and fallen in love with Gordon Glover.

CHAPTER II

In which we meet a Philandering Gentleman called Gordon Glover

On Christmas Eve, Honor's estranged husband came to stay for the festivities. Gordon Glover was handsome, charismatic and funny. Rather than the classical elegance of Henry Harvey, he had craggy good looks, with dark curly hair tinged with grey, and blue eyes. He had a beautiful speaking voice, inherited by his son, Julian (who would become a highly respected classical actor, working for the Royal Shakespeare Company and subsequently becoming famous for his *Game of Thrones* character and for voicing Aragog the spider in the *Harry Potter* movies).

Pym was immediately mesmerised. There were long discussions about music and literature in the Coppice's warm and cosy back kitchen. Gordon introduced her to classical music and they shared a similar sense of humour. But he was still in a relationship with Anna Instone and, for the moment, they were content with being friends. He reminded Pym of Harvey. She wrote to Henry to tell him about Gordon, 'a great friend made since I came to Bristol'. 'He is a journalist, very amusing, a great philanderer, but very sweet and kind and as I haven't fallen in love with him I see only his best side.' She teased Henry for his attachment to obscure Restoration authors: 'He wouldn't say "Otway is remarkably fine" though.'[1]

Pym would sit and chat for hours with Gordon. There were Sunday morning drinks and 'talks about food and Catholicism', and there was an evening when they discussed the 'Barbellion passage we both like – about the dead haunting the places where they have been happy'. The reference is to *The Journal of a Disappointed Man* by W. N. P. Barbellion, a searingly honest, often sad, sometimes very funny, diary, published just after the First World War, by a young man who had multiple sclerosis and died at the age of thirty. The work was a huge influence on Denton Welch, another writer who would be of enormous importance in the later life of Pym.

Gordon, like Pym, loved ephemera. He introduced her to Logan Pearsall Smith's *All Trivia*, a book of aphorisms on the pleasures of small things, such as 'the busy bees', 'empty shells', 'the rose'. Pearsall Smith was also a stickler for correct English language usage and was a devotee of Jane Austen, referring to himself as a 'Mansfield Parker'. The discovery of a mutual love of both Austen and *All Trivia* was another bonding moment for Pym and Glover, validating her own interest in 'the trivial round, the common task'. Hilary later described Gordon as a delightful companion. He had a 'splendid way with words and quotations that matched Barbara's own and he wore his knowledge of literature and music lightly, as Jock and Henry had done'.[2] Gordon loved the English countryside and was a keen ornithologist.

Hilary had news of Julian Amery. He was now a major in the 'Persian Army': 'How beautiful, how right, how more than mildly amusing,' Pym noted.[3] It was now spring, Barbara's favourite season, and there were almond trees and forsythia blossoms in the streets of Clifton, which reminded her of North Oxford. In the clear evening light she picked daffodils in the garden. But Pym also felt a new maturity; the war was taking its toll on her spirits: 'a little less joyousness and hope in myself – a more sombre, damped down, possibly more suitable frame of mind'.[4] She admitted to feelings of loneliness while firewatching:

> Firewatching. West wind and small rain and I thought all the usual things coasting down through the dark on my bicycle – riding or walking in the dark, especially to firewatching, is surely the most detached and lonely time . . . and now I'm sitting in this uncosy high-roofed room with no sound but the ticking of my common little clock and the click of my companion's knitting needles.[5]

She loved the poetry of Matthew Arnold and found herself reciting lines from his works as she drew the blackout curtains in the fire-watching station:

> The foot less prompt to meet the morning dew,
> The heart less bounding at emotion new,
> And hope, once crush'd, less quick to spring again.[6]

But thoughts of Julian Amery were comforting and improved her mood: 'the heart can still bound a little at the idea of Jay in a fez (dark red, I hope) and the idea that people might one day whisper about me and say – Wasn't there once something about a *Persian Major*?'[7]

There was better news for Britain, allaying fears of imminent invasion. Hitler had turned his focus to the Soviet Union and the Luftwaffe had been reassigned to the eastern front. The sustained bombing of British cities had ended in May the previous year. The last air raid on Liverpool took place on 10 January 1942, destroying several houses on Upper Stanhope

Street. By a curious twist of fate, one of the houses destroyed was number 102 – once the home of Hitler's half-brother Alois, his Irish wife Bridget, and their son, the Führer's nephew, William Patrick Hitler.

CHAPTER III

The Marriage of Miss Hilary Pym and the Birth of a Baby

Later that year, 1942, Pym had a letter from Henry's sister announcing the news that Elsie Harvey had given birth to a baby girl. It had been a long time since Pym had heard news from the Harveys, who were now living in Stockholm. She wrote at once congratulating them: 'You cannot imagine how pleased I am at this news and how happy to know that you are safe. I have thought of you constantly during these last two years and it has been awful having no news.'[1]

Pym explained to the Harveys that she had no time for writing as she was so busy with her war work. She was not permitted to tell them that she was working in the Censorship Department. 'You will have to guess what would be most suitable for me as you remember me,' she joked: 'I find the work very interesting, though the secrecy is rather annoying, as I can't talk about it or share jokes with any except my colleagues.' She said that she couldn't bear to read novels about the war, 'so in bed at night I read Jane Austen and Byron'.[2]

They still had plenty to eat, she continued, 'although we can't get oranges and grapefruit and bananas (Do you remember bananas?), we have excellent lettuces and cabbages and carrots etc straight from our garden and raspberries and blackcurrants too'. Pym informed Henry that Oxford was 'quite untouched', although not her beloved Cologne: 'I did love it so.' She joked about the Harvey baby being a girl: 'Perhaps it's a good thing she isn't a boy – how heartbreaking for some poor girl in the English Reading Room twenty years hence!'[3]

All in all, Pym was thoroughly enjoying her new life. No longer cocooned by Oxford or home, she was working, earning her own salary and feeling very independent. Hilary was to be married in August. Her husband, Sandy Walton, was serving with the RAF. He had read architecture at Cambridge and shared Hilary's love for Greece. Pym told Henry that Sandy reminded her of Jock: 'fair and tallish and very musical – he has set some of John Betjeman's *Continual Dew* to music!' As was conventional in wartime weddings, the bride wore daywear. Clothes were still rationed and only available with coupons, so all but the wealthiest brides required clothes that could be reused. Hilary wore a pale blue crepe dress and coat, while Barbara sported 'a dull pink crepe dress with a lovely romantic black hat with a heart-shaped halo brim', purchased in Bath.

Life at the Coppice continued to be lively and fulfilling. For the first time in years, Pym was surrounded by like-minded people, well informed about art and literature, all of whom had interesting jobs. The household often had breakfast at the Copper Kettle and supper together in the BBC canteen. Sometimes they went to concerts in the city at Colston Hall. In the summer evenings, there were walks to the Rocks and the Commercial and the Club. When Gordon came for the weekend, he and Pym would stroll arm in arm, chatting and flirting, alongside George and Honor.

In his letter, Henry had included a photograph of his baby daughter. It must have been a wistful moment seeing the little girl, but Pym was her usual brave self, calling the child 'a charming baby, so intelligent looking'.[4] Now that Hilary was married and Henry had a baby, Pym was thinking about her own future. She told Henry that it was strange to think that she had a new set of friends and that he had not met any of them.

CHAPTER IV

Mr Gordon Glover makes a Bold Declaration to Miss Pym

On 24 October 1942 Gordon declared his feelings, telling Barbara: 'in a queer kind of way, I'm in love with you'. Pym was flattered and excited. They had their first kiss on a moonlit walk near Clifton Suspension Bridge.

Finding herself 'embarked on a kind of love affair', she confided in Henry that it was 'not of her choosing', and that it had happened 'very unexpectedly'. Although she described it as 'very nice so far', she had few expectations that it would last. 'I don't suppose we shall ever be able to get married, so perhaps Belinda and Harriet will come true after all.'[1] She was rushing ahead of herself in even thinking of the possibility of any kind of long-term commitment from Gordon. Pym knew that he was still technically married to Honor and that he had a girlfriend in London, but she was swept off her feet by this older, sophisticated man. A few weeks later, she shared her feelings with Henry: 'I am very, very happy, but the future is rather dark, as far as my personal affairs are concerned. We just do not know what is going to happen to us – but at present we are happy and that is a lot these days.'[2]

Pym destroyed her regular diary for 1942 – the time covering

the affair with Gordon Glover. The events were too painful
for her to hold onto and it marked another turning point in
her life. She was too afraid to tell her parents that she was
involved with a married man with young children, who was
the husband of her close friend. The secret was also kept from
young Prue, who had no idea that her father was having an
affair with Barbara.

The courtship involved walks around Clifton, movies, 'drinking
in Bristol's nice pubs' and conversations in the Rocks Hotel.
Gordon took her to see *Gone with the Wind*: 'Four hours
wallowing in it, so much so that by the end my eyes were quite
dry even through so many deathbeds.' There were trips to the
medieval village of Abbots Leigh, visits to churches and grave-
yards – where Gordon expressed his dislike of marble chips on
top of gravestones, a detail that delighted Pym and which she
would save up for a novel.

Pym was also feeling the pressure of being single and unat-
tached following Hilary's marriage to Sandy. Honor was deeply
in love with George Ellidge and did not seem to be surprised
or hurt by her estranged husband's love affair with her new best
friend. Nevertheless, it was an odd set-up with Honor and
Gordon's children, Julian and Prue, all living there together.

Despite knowing that Gordon was a womaniser, Pym fell
deeply in love. She wrote love letters to him in her favourite
room in the fire-watching shelter. By Sion Hill, near the Rocks
Hotel and the Portcullis, Gordon gazed into her eyes and called
her his bright and shining Ba.

Christmas was fast approaching and Barbara made herself a
special new dress, blue-green, with a full skirt. She was brim-
ming with love and happiness and longed to show Gordon her
new Christmas outfit. Then, out of the blue, three days after
Christmas, he abruptly called it off. He told her that he thought
it best that they should part so that she could find someone else

to marry; that he would not be able to get a divorce for at least a year and a complete break would be for the best.

She again confided in Henry: 'Did I tell you I was in love and that it was all hopeless?' It was a 'really dramatic Victorian renunciation', she continued, 'the sort of thing I adore in novels, but find extremely painful in real life'. It was a devastating blow, but Pym tried to make light of it, saying that maybe they would be reunited in the future: 'We neither of us wanted any other kind of relationship so a complete break was the only thing.'³ Reading between the lines, Gordon had hoped for just a fling and Pym clearly wanted commitment. He had no intention of marrying her and was trying to extricate himself without giving her too much pain: he was a kind but weak man. The affair was over after just two months. Pym minded, she told Henry, because she and Gordon shared the same ridiculous jokes. She considered it hell being away from him.

Pym destroyed her diary but she filled two notebooks with her feelings about the Gordon affair and its demise. They were headed 'After Christmas I' and 'After Christmas II'. The account was written as a diary, with some of the pages excised: 'I went into the Public Library. It is open till seven and was now full of ruins of humanity, come into the reading room for learning. And on my blotting paper I write "A Testing Time", in Red Pencil to remind me.'

She was having difficulty sleeping but drew comfort from a phrase that she had read in *Trivia*: 'So I never lose a sense of the *whimsical and perilous charm of daily life*, with its meetings and words and accidents.' The phrase would come to inspire her novels: 'there's still the whimsical and perilous charm perhaps. I don't want to lose that.'⁴

CHAPTER V

It's That Man Again

Gordon's rejection cut deep. He was Pym's first older lover and was a father figure, just as Honor fulfilled a maternal role. She loved her own parents, but they were not on the same intellectual level as the Glovers. Gordon's close friendship with Robert Graves and Laura Riding enhanced his literary standing in Pym's eyes. Once, she crept into Honor's room and read something that Gordon had written to Graves in 1936: 'The enthusiast is in a state of perpetual dissatisfaction but tries not to give himself time to feel his dissatisfaction. He hopes secretly for satisfaction, for something that will woo him into certainty.'[1] She began reading Graves's *Wife to Mr Milton*.

It did not help that the name of 'C. Gordon Glover' kept popping up as the byline of articles in the weekly *Radio Times*, but in her usual good common-sense way, Pym tried not to mope. She was always good at poking fun at herself. One night she dreamed of both Julian Amery and Gordon:

Darling Jay, *mein Kleines*, this is half your book. Imagine after my death two old men wrangling over it. One a dried-up politician, the other a burnt-out old ruin, the most waspish member of the Savage Club. Both so unpleasant that it is difficult to imagine how either of them could possibly have been loved by such a delightful person as the present writer obviously is![2]

But in reality, Gordon's rejection induced a depressive phase that Pym likened to entering a 'dark tunnel'. He told her that she would be over him by spring, but she envisaged 'an endless stretch of months to be got through – a long dreary stretch until it doesn't matter any more'. Grief was a bat that hovered around her 'like a squander bug . . . Dusty old creature, to think I've still got you, after ten weeks.'[3]

In terms of literary expression, Pym was experimenting with a more 'stream-of-consciousness' style of writing:

> The other day I thought 'And now it's Spring' and decided that this would be quite a good title for a novel. Why don't you write it? Ah, but *is* it Spring? I know that the air is warm and sunny, birds sing at dawn and twilight and the daffodils are out in the Coppice garden and violets blue and white, sweeter than the lids of Juno's eyes – I know, but what about the dusty heart?[4]

There were constant reminders of Gordon in his children. His son, Julian, who looked so much like his father, rushing out with a box of birthday Liquorice Allsorts to tell her that they were a present from daddy. His daughter, Prue, running away to the suspension bridge before being found safe and well.

Barbara's grief would burst upon her, 'tears in my eyes because I suddenly remembered Gordon with his hair smoothed down sitting opposite me at breakfast in the Coppice kitchen on a Monday morning'.[5] When she cycled down to Sion Hill to see friends, she was flooded with memories: 'And the bridge was lovely in the twilight and horrid people sat in the window of the Rocks and I was filled with horrible nostalgia and love for him.'[6] On a bus ride to Avonmouth there were more tears and then at lunchtime, she positively howled.

She had enough self-awareness, as with her affair with Henry Harvey, to know that she partially enjoyed the misery of heart-break; that it was like undertaking an exercise that would prove useful to fuel her imagination and that the feelings were somehow at a remove, experienced in the third person:

> Well, on Friday, she came back from Avonmouth, loitered a little at the Academy and then, with a sudden wave of inspiration, went and had some tea in the Berkeley. Ludicrous place with palms and mirrors, but no orchestra now. It was the end of the day and she felt rather a ludicrous object sitting there drinking tea, eating bread and butter and smoking a cigarette . . . at 5.35 I left and thought of Gordon just beginning and wondered if he was feeling nervous. Then home, very tired, drained of all emotion.
>
> Firewatching was quite peaceful. There is a curious timeless-ness about it, as if one were *really* in one's marble vault.[7]

She wondered about attending a Tchaikovsky concert, which was a reminder of Gordon. It would leave her torn to pieces. Should she go or stay: 'Reader what *will* she do?' she wrote in her diary, 'See next Friday.'[8] As though, once again, she was writing a picaresque novel.

Spring brought back memories of Julian Amery and their romance, the Parks, the Botanical Gardens and lunch at Balliol. Pasted into her 'After Christmas' diary, was a newspaper cutting about Captain Amery, praising him for having had one of the most adventurous careers of the war. It listed his many achieve-ments and noted that his adventures had begun even as an undergraduate at Balliol. It was a reminder, too, that her affair with a younger man had been tremendously exciting.

Honor was a huge comfort. She had been through it all with Gordon and had come out the other side. Pym and Honor had begun listening to a light entertainment radio programme that they both loved. It was one of the BBC's most popular wartime shows, credited with sustaining public morale and having over twenty million listeners. Even the king and queen were avid fans. It was called *ITMA – It's That Man Again*. Newspaper editor Bert Gunn, father of the poet Thom Gunn, created a memorable *Daily Express* headline, referring to the never-ending news of Hitler in the build-up to the war: 'It's That Man Again'. The BBC borrowed the phrase for the title of its comedy series, which hosted a cast of much-loved characters, recognisable by their catchphrases. The show was a vehicle for the talents of Liverpool comedian Tommy Handley. *ITMA* followed the adventures of Handley as he undertook a series of (fictional) bizarre jobs. The first series began with him working on a private radio station, but he later moved on to work as Minister of Aggravation and Mysteries at the Office of Twerps, the mayor of seedy seaside resort Foaming-at-the-Mouth, and governor of the South Sea island, Tomtopia.

Hattie Jacques played the part of Sophie Tuckshop. The show also featured characters such as Colonel Chinstrap and Mrs Mopp; it generated catchphrases like 'Can I do you now, sir?', 'I don't mind if I do', 'I'll have to ask me dad', 'TTFN' (Ta ta for now), 'd'oh' (anticipating Homer Simpson), and, from a German spy: 'This is Funf speaking'. One of the best lines was Sophie Tuckshop's 'I'll be alright now' after describing a long list of foods that she has consumed. The household at the Coppice were huge fans of *ITMA*. Pym was in need of good cheer and laughter and the wireless again provided a lifeline. But even there, Gordon managed to make his presence felt. He was presenting a radio show about the countryside called

'Introducing This Week'. Pym listened in, of course: 'My own darling raving dilettante, what is a leaf-nosed bat?' she quipped. She had found herself 'a new torture song' called 'I'm Going to See You Today'.

Pym noted that she wrote in her diary 'only when I am depressed, like praying only when one is really in despair'. Honor, knowing that Pym was suffering, did her best to keep her busy. They took the children to the seaside at Weston-super-Mare. She thought it a 'large bright Betjeman place'. For a while, they forgot about the war until they found themselves in the middle of a serious invasion exercise and were twice turned back for unexploded bombs. After that, they walked along the beach to the pier, 'eating sweets and gathering little pink, yellow and white shells'. On the pier they looked at the naughty peepshows and went on the rides: 'What a place to come to when one is lonely and miserable,' she wrote.[9]

The next day was Julian Glover's birthday party and Barbara made sandwiches whilst listening to Mendelssohn on the radio, 'and of course I wept a little over the slow movement, alone in the back kitchen, my hands immersed in the washing-up water, need I say'. After the party ended, she gathered fresh flowers for her room and felt melancholy: 'I am ashamed to say that I am sometimes just plain jealous when I think of other people who can be with Gordon. It is sometimes intolerable to be a woman and have no second bests or spares or anything.'[10]

Hilary had her husband, Sandy, home, which perhaps compounded Pym's feelings of loneliness. Honor was deeply in love with George. Pym felt that she was the only one whose happiness had been snatched away.

I wrote home, went to the post, pumped up my bicycle, put cotton over the peas. And then lay on a mattress with my face close to the ground, thinking about that poem by Robert Graves, the man seeking lost love, who has become so sensitive he can hear wormtalk and moths chumbling cloth.[11]

Later, Honor and Pym 'Baldwinned our legs – she was delighted, never having used a Baldwin [electric shaver] before.'[12]

Pym's feelings of depression continued. She was reading Charlotte Mary Yonge's *The Daisy Chain*, 'so well-written, very Compton-Burnett and very sad'. Back in the office, she felt 'very Rip Van Winkle to find people away and on the point of leaving and the blackout *stuck* halfway across the skylight of our room, casting a gloom, *quite* a gloom as they say, over the place'.[13] She tried to pull herself together. Gordon's rejection continued to hurt, as though she somehow knew that this was her last hope of a conventional relationship consisting of marriage and children. 'Oh darling, how peculiarly insensitive your sex is,' she wrote in her 'After Christmas' journal.[14] She turned again to writing a new story:

> Oh mumbling chumbling moths, talking worms and my own intolerable bird give me one tiny ray of hope for the future and I will keep on wanting to be alive. Yes, you will be alive, it will not be the same, nothing will be quite as good, there will be no intense joy but small compensations, spinsterish delights and as the years go on and they are no longer painful memories.[15]

It was time for a change in her circumstances. She needed to leave the Coppice. Pym went up to London for an interview, staying with her old Oxford friend, Rosemary Topping. 'Last Friday I joined the Wrens [Women's Royal Naval Service]. It is done – I am calm and happy about it and sometimes excited – all settled. Like Going over to Rome. And Cardinal Newman has gone and I'm still reading *The Daisy Chain*.'[16]

Meanwhile at the Censorship Office there was a hum of excitement about a new circular which called up all examiners under the age of forty-one for service. Pym felt smug because she had already decided to apply for the Wrens. She was ready for a new chapter of her life.

CHAPTER VI

Miss Pym has a Medical Examination

On Tuesday, 30 March 1943 Pym was due to attend a medical assessment as part of her application for the Wrens – 'unless I'm having a period, which I will be'.[1] She was about to turn thirty, single and geared up for a new challenge. If she had not volunteered for the Wrens she may well have been called for factory work, for which she would have been ill-suited.

She heard news of Gordon, who was staying with some mutual friends. He was not happy, but his friends 'thought it might be a good thing for him to have to work things out for himself'. The friends did not allow him to 'dramatise himself' as was his wont. Pym, however, felt compassion towards him: 'But oh I hate to think of him being unhappy and me not being able to do anything for him.' Nevertheless, she was determined to move on with her life: 'I've never before felt so conscious of "making a life for myself".'[2]

Pym's medical examination went well, though it took two hours to complete: 'First of all we filled out the medical form – then went upstairs and undressed, except for shoes, knickers and coat – then produced a "specimen" into a kind of enamel potty with a long handle like a saucepan – of which I was quite glad.'[3] She was pleased when she was informed that her case was marked as 'urgent', suggesting that 'they probably had something in mind for me'. Her work at the Censorship Office was helpful to her case. She was by now desperate to become a Wren: 'my heart is set on it'.[4]

It was all a very welcome distraction, but then news of Gordon came and, momentarily, set her back. Pym had been wrestling with feelings of jealousy towards his children and, to some extent, Honor: 'How could I bear not to have as much of him as she has had and still has in the children.' She loved Honor, but she also knew that Honor had a history with Gordon and, with that, she could not compete. Prue, who only learned of the affair in later years, remembered that her mother was angry at the way that Pym had been treated by Gordon and believes that the end of the affair was Pym's reason for wanting to join the Wrens:

I loved my father dearly but he didn't treat women very well. He had had several affairs over the years, which is why my mother left him. They always remained good friends. But, when he dumped Barbara, my mother was furious with him for treating her dear friend so shabbily. Barbara was inconsolable and thought they would marry. It was his behaviour that led her to join the Wrens for the rest of the war, as a sort of escape.[5]

Gordon and Honor's divorce was gaining speed. Honor told Pym that Gordon had 'supplied the evidence' (presumably of his serial infidelities). This threw Pym into turmoil, as Gordon had used the excuse of his married status to call off their affair: 'I couldn't help thinking how joyous I *might* have been at this stage being reached. Whereas now I have no reason to hope – I don't even know if Gordon ever thinks of me and nobody can reassure me on that point.'[6]

Pym felt that she was going round in circles. After her medical, she came home to the Coppice kitchen, usually the hub of life and activity, to find it very tidy and silent. It brought back memories of 28 December, when Gordon had ended their relationship and she had walked through the house crying. She had sat on Honor's bed and tried to explain why she was so upset. Honor, who clearly knew more than she was letting on, tried to comfort Pym by saying that she didn't think Gordon was the right person for her and that Pym was brooding over an idea. Honor more than anyone knew Gordon and his self-absorption. But Pym was still clinging to her fantasy: 'Surely I *didn't* see what wasn't there?'[7] On the suspension bridge she saw a girl ('rather plain') being kissed by a Dough boy (American soldier) and had another pang: 'Lucky pigs I thought.'[8]

There were, however, 'small compensations' and 'spinsterish delights'. She spotted fabrics at Bright's department store: 'red spotted chiffon for a spinsterish nightdress', bought beauty aids at Woolworths and had breakfast at the Copper Kitchen: 'we were served by the usual inefficient waitress, who is like "Can I do you now, Sir?" in *ITMA*.' Hilary was back and made a delicious salad with pilchards and then rhubarb for pudding. They then listened to *ITMA*. Afterwards they had 'a long technical conversation about Tampax!'[9]

April was extremely warm and Pym gardened and gathered vegetables and flowers. She spent her Sunday morning scrubbing potatoes and making salad: 'Surely my spiritual home is in the Coppice back kitchen?' To her surprise, Honor, usually a source of great strength and common sense, was suddenly in tears. Pym brought her tea and they had a long talk about the burden and continual strain of 'being splendid'; how, under unbearable pressure, 'something snaps'. (This would become an important theme in Pym's novels.) Gordon was being difficult about the divorce. Honor showed Pym the divorce petition, 'a horrifying document, but perhaps faintly comic'. She talked about her marriage and Gordon's new play, which was about his breaking off a love affair with another woman. She told Pym a story about Gordon's behaviour that Pym found fascinating. He had taken his lover, Anna, to a concert, telling her that the last time he had been at the venue it was with another woman for whom he no longer cared. To Gordon's bewilderment, Anna burst into tears: he thought she ought to be pleased.

Pym wrote down her feelings about this incident, which had stoked her creative imagination: 'What a haunting scene for a novel – it could have taken place in a churchyard where he has been with someone he once loved. And she, the new one, sees it happening again and again.'[10]

'Gordon', she imagined the long-suffering heroine saying, 'if you ever take any other woman to Abbotsleigh, may you never rest peacefully in your grave with the marble chips on top.'[11]

CHAPTER VII

In which Miss Pym pays a visit to her Old Love, Rupert Gleadow

By the spring of 1943, Pym was one of the lucky ones. Nobody she knew had yet been killed in the war. She had had her share of heartbreak, but she was a resilient young woman, still full of life and hope. Her first love, Rupert Gleadow, had not fared so well.

In December 1937, in Paris, Rupert had married a beautiful French woman called Marguerite Rendu. Less than a year later, Marguerite had died, probably in childbirth, leaving a baby daughter, Sylvie. Rupert was distraught. He wrote to Barbara, saying that she had probably seen the announcement of his wife's death in *The Times*. He told her that he'd been 'terribly weak in health, which is only natural'.[1] He asked her to see him or drop him a line and ended with a poignant reflection:

One learns to love, you know and I began learning in 1932. It seems incredible to realize that in those lovely days none of the tragedies of life had yet happened. But if we had not had those wonderful times together probably I should not have known those sublime heights of love which Marguerite and I together achieved and which will always remain a light to my life.

So you see you have made a difference to my life which I
shall not forget.[2]

Rupert wrote again, a year later, from near Bridport in Devon:
'This last year has been pretty unpleasant for me, but I am now
staying with people who are very nice and are willing to bring
up my daughter with their own children.' He told Pym that he
had been in St Tropez when the war broke out and that the
journey back across France had taken a long time. He said that
he had no intention of doing any war work, at least until forced
to: 'it is a waste of time for an intelligent person. Hitler is
doomed anyway.' He ended his letter: 'I hope there are still 67
pubs in Oswestry and that you are in love with some beautiful
person as usual.'[3] His letter was written in coloured ink, a
reminder of the letters he sent to her as an undergraduate. He
also sent a photograph of his daughter Sylvie and Pym replied
that she had inherited his large black eyes. 'You are quite right
about my daughter having large black eyes,' he responded, 'but
in other ways she takes after the mother, being fair, fearless and
fond of animals.'[4]

Rupert was not the kind of man to be on his own for long.
He told Pym that at the outbreak of war he had seduced a virgin
in St Tropez. He was now living in London with a woman called
Helen, who was a painter: a 'beautiful blonde with blue eyes'.
It was, he told Pym, love at first sight for them both: 'Our days
are as blissful as our nights.'[5]

Helen Cooke had grown up in Oxford, where her father was
Regius Professor of Hebrew at Christ Church. Helen, a gifted
painter, and her sister Betty studied art at the Ruskin School in
Oxford. Betty Cooke married a member of the Pinney family
(slave owners who had once rented a house in Dorset to William
and Dorothy Wordsworth) and moved into their ancestral home,
Bettiscombe Manor, where there was a 'screaming skull' said to

belong to an African slave whose remains were buried there. Helen and Rupert, meanwhile, were now living in another place with interesting associations: Cheyne Walk in Chelsea, looking over the river – a road that had at various times been home to the composers Arthur Sullivan and Ralph Vaughan Williams, the philosopher Bertrand Russell, the poets Dante Gabriel Rossetti and T. S. Eliot, the artists J. M. W. Turner and James Whistler, the actors John Barrymore and Laurence Olivier, the novelists George Eliot, Bram Stoker, Henry James, Somerset Maugham and many other notable figures. First World War memoirist Vera Brittain, now a pacifist, was in residence at the time.

On 10 April 1943, in the midst of her heartbreak over Gordon, Pym rang the bell and Helen opened the door: 'Are you Helen?'

'You must be Barbara?'

I've done this before, Pym thought, 'in the summer of 1938 when I met Elsie for the first time in 86 Banbury Road'.[6]

Barbara liked Helen immensely. She had blonde curly hair and 'very blue eyes' and was 'sweet and vivacious'. The two women had a 'good gossip' before Rupert arrived home on his bicycle, looking 'quite his old self'. They had dinner with cowslip wine and amusing talk. There seemed to be no awkwardness at all. 'I was conscious of feeling happier than I had done for a long time,' wrote Pym. The next day was equally pleasant. Rupert and Helen had a morning engagement, so they left Pym with a breakfast tray and a copy of *Tristram Shandy*. Then at eleven she immersed herself in 'a delicious bright green bath with pine essence and bright pink Spanish geranium soap'. The Gleadows gave her a good lunch of olives and a flan and they opened a tin of apricots. After lunch, all three of them took a stroll in Battersea Park, 'all the flowering trees were out – lilacs nearby, double cherry and magnolia'. When discussing her love life and her broken heart, the Gleadows told Pym that 'her eyes had too much sparkle for one who had been crossed in love'.[7]

There was little contact with Rupert after this visit, though a brief glimpse of Sylvie Gleadow comes in a memoir by Susanna Pinney, Helen Gleadow's niece. According to Susanna, her mother, Betty, held a large house party at Bettiscombe Manor to which Helen and Rupert were invited, along with the writer Sylvia Townsend Warner and her lover, Valentine Ackland. Rupert did a tarot reading for the screaming skull. Susanna noted the presence of a little French girl called Sylvie, 'smooth-haired, well brought up'. She recalled that Sylvie had been brought up in France with her godmother, but spent her summers in Bridport with her father and stepmother, Helen.[8]

Back at the Coppice, Pym was given a warm welcome by Honor. 'I really feel it did me good going away and being with Rupert and Helen, who are so blissfully happy together they hardly seem to be real. Oh, but it *can* be done.'[9]

CHAPTER VIII

Miss Pym passes her Interview

Honor Wyatt was clearly getting a little impatient with Pym's endless moping about Gordon. She advised her, not unreasonably, to have an affair to get him out of her system. 'I quite agree,' said Pym, 'but OH DEAR.' She was finishing a new blue satin nightdress: 'Lucky pig who ever gets to . . . well reader fill in the rest yourself.'[1]

The government, in a bid to keep the people of Britain fit and well, initiated a radio fitness programme 'Up in the Morning Early', named after a poem by Robert Burns. There were ten minutes of exercises for men, then ten for women. Pym and Honor decided it would be a good idea to participate: 'certainly helps to dispel that feeling of lowness with which one usually starts the day. One gets instead an agonising stiffness in the backs of the legs, so that one feels trembling and doddery.'[2] Honor said that Gordon would laugh if he could see them at their exercises.

There was more discussion about the impending divorce: it seemed that Gordon already had a new lover, though he was refusing to divulge any information. Pym swung back and forth; one minute she was convinced that if Gordon wasn't the best and the real thing, which she hoped, then she might find someone else. The next, she remembered that it was six months to the day that 'my poor darling declared his ill-fated love and started me on this chunk of misery'.[3]

Pym and Honor went shopping in Clifton and came back with string bags bulging with tins of treacle, packets of Shredded Wheat, cakes and buns. On the way home they discussed 'the technique of misery'. Pym was still feeling very low and the rain fell on her half-day and Bristol was only 'half-alive' with most of the shops closed, so she returned to the Coppice. The 'bats' were back in her head:

> I came home and did some sewing and gave myself a little concert of Dohnanyi, Brahms and the Classical Symphony. The latter is quite spoilt so I may well count it as a dead loss. The nicest lover I never had and the rest of it and A ring is round but not round enough and The sea's deep but not deep enough and I will fight for what I want and if I can't have it, then I will have nothing, but NOTHING!
>
> The beech trees are out in tender green leaves – the spinster feels like going rushing out into the garden and embracing them, crying Thank you, *thank* you! You at least do what is expected of you and never fail . . . I must have many bats (all with broken wings) flying around in my head.[4]

On 26 May, Gordon's autobiographical play *Farewell Helen* was broadcast. Honor and Pym were 'tense and nervous'. Pym made a cold supper of asparagus, hard-boiled eggs and potato salad.

> I knitted feverishly – the sleeves of my black jumper. The time came. It was exciting and clever and funny and rather embarrassing – Spain and darling, darling, darling and Oh so typically Gordon. None of it really applicable to me. The bit of La Rochefoucauld he once quoted to me in a letter came in.[5]

The play was about a young man who made an agreement with his lover that if one of them felt 'even the tiniest bit tired of one another' then they should be honest and say so. But when the time comes, he loses his nerve and lacks the courage to be honest. Though Pym believed the plot was not applicable to her, she must have been struck by the lack of moral fibre in Gordon's hero, John.

Afterwards, she felt both excited and depressed and decided that she should write a play.

More importantly, she went to London for the selection boards for the Wrens. It was a nerve-racking experience. There were eight girls and she was the last to be interviewed at the end of the day. Three Wren officers sat on a panel, firing questions: 'one grey-haired and soignée, another motherly and wearing a hairnet and the third dark and massive and ominously silent'. At the end of the interview, they said they would be in touch within a couple of days. 'After it was all over, I felt exhausted and depressed and would have given the rest of my life for the comfort of Gordon and a drink with him.'[6]

Pym stayed the night at Kew with Rosemary Topping and she was glad to drink beer and flop in the green sheets, 'wearing my new blue satin nightdress – my body spread-eagled like a corpse'. The night was hot and the war felt very close. At 2 a.m., the sirens went and she heard gunfire in the distance. She lay awake, thinking of Gordon, 'longing hopelessly for him'. She was frightened, too, about the decisions she had made: 'panic came over me at what I had done and the life that was before me'. But her Pym pragmatism kicked in: 'Everything seems gloomy and dark when you're lying awake in the middle of the night. One day, perhaps soon – it will be better.'[7]

There was good news. She heard that she had passed her Wrens interview. First Officer Salmond, 'curly hair and a faint Scots accent', told her that she must serve three months in the ranks and after that she was sure of her commission. 'I was very pleased and happy.'[8]

At Whitsun, Pym went to stay with Hilary and Sandy in their country cottage in the South Downs. They had other friends to visit and ate sausages and potatoes and ham and chicken. She wasn't unhappy but still 'remote and lonely'. She missed having someone special: 'One feels so without a chap especially when *one* has had one. A nice lump of misery which goes everywhere like a dog.'[9]

There was worse to come. Gordon began behaving badly towards Honor and the children. He was being 'sticky' about their allowance and then demanded a large armchair that was in the sitting room at the Coppice. Pym was indignant on the children's behalf and the business of the armchair was a step too far: 'But oh darling – can my love stand this? May it not be the beginning of the end. Could it be because of an armchair that I first began to fall out of love with you! But of course one doesn't fall – it's a slow wrenching away, painful at once, after-wards just sad and dreary.' Like many women in the throes of a broken heart, Pym cut her hair short. She also tried to find humour in the situation – 'I have sunk very low. I emptied tea leaves out of the window' – and poked fun at herself for the unromantic setting of her affair with Gordon: 'Oh Coppice back kitchen full of kisses and jokes and tears – and the blackcurrants are ripening.' It helped that she disliked Gordon's novel, *Cocktails*, which Honor had lent her to read. She could not find any interest in it: 'so brittle and unreal'.[10]

Mercifully, her new life now beckoned. An envelope arrived with a one-way ticket to Rochester in Kent, where she was to complete her Wrens training. There was a list of regulations about clothing and a warning of no alcohol. She would not be allowed even the smallest of double gins. On her last Sunday at the Coppice ('a sweetness and sadness about everything and everybody'), there was tea in the garden and a supper with her health drunk in cider. Later, she looked through Honor's press cuttings and found a wedding picture of 'the two people I love best in the world'.[11]

Pym's work colleagues gave her a present of an expensive box of talcum powder and she gave Prue her wreath of flowers from Salzburg and Honor a scarf with Edelweiss from Dresden. There was a quick dash home to Oswestry and on her return to Bristol a theatre visit with Hilary to *Uncle Vanya* at the Theatre Royal, 'a wonderful play and well acted. So very like the Coppice – except that we don't sit down under our sorrows – no we are drearily splendid and even join the Wrens.'[12] Then it was her very last day in Clifton: 'It's raining, trees – the beech tree swaying in the wind – Julian shouting and Scarlatti on the radio . . . preparations for Prue's birthday party – she looking intolerably sweet in a white smock with my wreath of Austrian flowers in her hair.'[13]

The biggest wrench, however, was leaving Honor. Pym made her dear friend a final cup of tea and then they left for the station. Honor held her hand in the taxi and there were many tears shed. 'As she said she and I were the worst possible people to be left together at the end.' On reaching London, she took the 2.27 to Rochester, 'a bright green train that stopped at every station'. Miss Pym's new adventure was about to begin: 'Got to Rochester just before four and staggered along with my suitcase (helped by two kind Wrens) to the Training Depot.'[14]

CHAPTER IX

Miss Pym experiences Life in Uniform

It was almost like being back in boarding school, though Pym thought that the Nore training depot resembled a North Oxford Victorian Gothic house. Up until now, she had only lived with people of her own class and education, but the Wrens recruited from far and wide. At first, she struggled with the class differences, with many of her fellow trainees not on the 'same wavelength'. Her cabin mate was just nineteen, though 'my own class and quite nice'.[1]

There was a lot to learn about life in the Wrens, such as the naval terminology. The bedrooms were called cabins (hers was Beehive XI); the Tea Boat was where they congregated for tea; 'fo'c'sle' was the recreational room, and 'fatigues' were her duties. At the moment, she was a 'Pro-Wren', not yet given a uniform or proper duties, so there was plenty of time for writing up her journal.

For supper, the first evening, they had toad in the hole and bread and jam; for breakfast scrambled eggs and bacon and cornflakes and tea: 'Good!' It was hinted that Pym might be 'white paper entry', which meant potential officer material, though, 'I can see now that one *must* be in the ranks first!'[2] She was amused to be in the YMCA canteen, on the other side of the counter, so to speak: 'I never thought in the days when I used to serve in the old YM that I should be one of the Troops myself one day.'[3]

In many respects, the culture shock was the biggest challenge. Many of the girls recruited were from working-class backgrounds, with names like Vera Potts and Peggy Wall, rather than Honor, Prudence and Flora. 'I don't think there are really any of our kind of people,' she confessed to her diary. She missed her life in Clifton and shed tears when Honor sent her a newsy letter about the Coppice. 'Honor in her curlers, Flora finding a nest of insects in her desk and Dick (Palmer) joyously examining them under the microscope.'[4] Honor and Gordon had brought culture and sophistication to Pym, taking her beyond the Oswestry days of Jack Payne and his dance hall orchestra. She had been introduced to Berlioz, Brahms, Haydn and Mozart. And she had listened to radio plays with Honor, as they chatted and knitted. But in the fo'c'sle, the radio was tuned to the Forces Programme, blasting out *Happidrome* and *Memories of Musical Comedies*. She would rather have been back at the Coppice with Honor, talking, having a cup of tea and listening to the more highbrow fare of Marlowe's *Edward II* on the Third Programme.

Pym, always happy to have an alter ego (Sandra, Pymska, Miss Pym), coped by concealing her true self. She went for a solitary walk around Rochester, where she found a tea shop and took the opportunity to wander among the tombstones in the cathedral: 'And for about half an hour I was my old gothick self – the self that I've had to put off while I've been here.'[5] At least her roommate was reasonably interesting, with a 'long, melancholy face and I can see her when she is older as an English gentlewoman – one of her names is Mildred'.[6] Pym would use this name when she created her most memorable genteel spinster, Mildred Lathbury.

For all the class differences, she was fascinated by her fellow

Wrens. There was a small, dark-haired girl who used to be a secretary for a literary agent, and a 'plump wanton-looking Wren with gold rings in her ears and dark hair – and pink nails'. However, Pym liked spending her free time alone. She had a copy of *Tristram Shandy* with her, and soon she had purchased apples and cherries and a copy of the *Radio Times*; she spent a happy hour lying in her bunk 'eating and reading a Graham Greene novel'.[7]

Pym liked other women, but she adored male company. '*Too Many Women*', she noted in her diary. She still missed Gordon and ached for Honor and her friends at the Coppice. Honor wrote to say that Gordon had heard the news about her going into the Wrens and said he hoped it would turn out nicely for her. 'My only reaction is – well *(dear)* it had better be! I was a little disappointed, having expected some message a little less dreary,' Pym wrote waspishly in her journal.[8]

Pym was formally enrolled and kitted out in her proper uniform. 'My hat is lovely, every bit as fetching as I'd hoped, but my suit rather large though it's easier to alter that way.'[9] She was also given a mackintosh and greatcoat, three pairs of black hose, gloves, tie, four shirts, nine stiff collars and two pairs of shoes, and drafted to a holding depot at Westcliff-on-Sea, near Southend. Her new roommate was a girl called Beatrice Pizzey. Instead of clocks, the day was divided into watches, first bugle at 6.30 a.m. and the last 'Pipe Down' at 10 p.m. The work was more strenuous: 'Gardened till lunch, then squad drill, then scrubbed a room in Palmerston Court. Quite worn out.' She found Southend depressing: 'definitely a *common* place with no charm as far as I could see . . . cheap stores – pin-tables and amusement halls – cinemas – the whole place smelling of fish and chips'.[10] She felt there was no beauty, no dignity or nostalgia, only decay. Her homesickness for the Coppice overwhelmed her and left her 'howling'.

Wanting Gordon still comes into it. Now that the novelty of
being a Wren is wearing off. WRNS – you aren't giving me
enough. I'm doing my best, trying to see the funny side, looking
out for churches and buildings, writing it up, talking to various
people and trying to take it all as a great chunk of experience
– an extraordinary bit of life – but I want music and intellectual
companionship and affection – to be able to lavish it as I did
at the Coppice.[11]

As ever, she comforted herself with 'the whimsical and perilous
charm' – there were small things to look forward to, letters from
home, cinema visits and cigarettes.

After a week had passed, it was confirmed that Miss Pym was
a 'white paper entry' and she was moved to the regulating office,
where she was given more responsibility and better pay ('had to
march a squad of Pro-Wrens back – managed quite successfully').
But she was also beset by feelings of inadequacy: 'We had
Divisions and I couldn't swing my arms properly so Third Officer
Honey had to move me. Gradually people will begin to discover
what a fake I am – how phoney is my Wrennish facade.'[12]

There were brighter moments: a tug trip with some Irish
Merchant Navy, 'one had a little sacking bag full of cockles
which he offered to us, also cigarettes. The sea was rough and
the spray sometimes drenched us.'[13] Her self-confidence was
growing and being busy was a blessing. She was also learning
the valuable life lesson of how to deal and cope with people
from all sorts of class and background: 'I'm not frightened of
anyone. It has given me confidence – and I feel I can do something I thought I couldn't before.'[14]

CHAPTER X

Introducing 'Wren Pym'

Life at Westcliff was proving to be more congenial. Pym began going to dances with some of the sailors and marines who were stationed there and she attended concerts with her more like-minded fellow Wrens.

For her first weekend of leave, Pym went home to the Coppice. Everyone admired her uniform and she was overwhelmed by the 'luxuriant greenness' of the garden. On Saturday morning, Hilary brought her breakfast in bed: 'toast seems a luxury and a soft bed'. Later Pym walked with Honor and they talked a little about Gordon. Pym acknowledged that it was best to try and forget him.

There were other weekend visits. She went to stay with Rosemary in London. They had a pint in the Star and Garter and then a stroll in Kew Gardens. The two women talked about their lives as they walked and Rosemary was encouraging about Pym's decision to join the Wrens. That October 1943, Pym recalled that it was a year to the day that Gordon declared himself and they had their brief, stormy but heavenly two months.

Pym was immersed at this time in Virginia Woolf's *A Room of One's Own*, which she found both delightful and profound.

Woolf's extended essay, first published in 1929, was based on two lectures she had delivered at Cambridge, which argued for a literal and figurative space for women to write within a literary tradition dominated by men. To put it more simply: a woman needed £500 and a room of her own in order to write fiction. Perhaps, just as importantly for Pym, the narrator identifies herself as a woman who has rejected marriage and children in order to be a writer. She has learned that it is crucial to be true to yourself: 'it is much more important to be oneself more than anything else. So Virginia Woolf. I wonder what she would have made of service life.'[1]

When Pym returned to the Coppice for a weekend, however, there was upsetting news. First, Honor told Pym that her divorce from Gordon was imminent. Pym's initial feeling was of elation – the thought that Gordon would finally be free. But the next day she was crushed when, on asking Honor, she replied that Gordon's intentions had never been honourable; he'd never intended to marry her, even had he been free to do so. Gordon had told Honor that he 'didn't intend to make any more "experiments"'. It was a cruel, wounding term. He had also described to a mutual friend his affair with Pym 'as a pleasant sentimental episode which was now closed'. This was a bitter pill. 'So now what becomes of my illusion that this was a great renunciation and that he had even for a moment wanted the same things as I do?' wrote Pym. In a fit of rage, she tore up his letters. At the same time, she felt that she still loved him and would ache for him: 'sweet, hopeless person, the most delightful companion'.[2]

In the morning, she felt calmer. Pym was glad that she had been courageous enough to press Honor for information about Gordon's true feelings. When she returned to London, via Paddington, she felt that she was the loneliest person there. On the train to Westcliff, she sat at a table with a Canadian soldier, who offered her a cigarette. They began talking and he insisted on paying for her meal. This act of kindness moved her deeply: 'I couldn't say to him – you've brought comfort and friendliness to a rather lonely and miserable person, but that's what he did.'[3]

On Friday 22 October, Pym spent most of the day wondering how Honor was getting on with the divorce. Finally a telegraph arrived: 'Successful and Painless. Love. Honor.' She went to London for a solitary jaunt and found herself in Lyons Corner House having a second breakfast. Then, after a concert, she returned there and sat next to two men. One of them was very dark and good-looking, reminding her of her 'dear Friedbert'.[4] They soon got talking and the dark man told her that one should never feel lonely at Lyons.

But she did feel lonely, and the prospect of another winter made her depressed. She knew that, despite their divorce, Gordon belonged to Honor: 'how completely he is Honor's really'. She remembered him sitting by the fire in Honor's room, telling her 'whatever happens *you* mustn't be made unhappy over this affair'. Pym wrote a rather poignant, funny poem in his honour, starting out from his regular column in the *Radio Times*, in which he 'introduced' a well-known public figure:

Introducing – You in the Radio Times
Successful, Byronic, rather second rate,
Me in the Wrens pretending to be a sailor
Drearily, splendid, bravely accepting my fate

(or romantically celibate?)[5]

She wrote to tell Henry Harvey that she had recovered from the Gordon heartache after a full nine months – 'like having a baby'. She also felt that Gordon had let her down 'pretty badly . . . and it's the loneliness I feel more than any special *need* for him'. She told Henry that she had met up with Gordon and now felt indifferent towards him and that, although charming, he was 'hopelessly unstable'.[6] Which made him sound a little like Henry himself.

Getting her commission was a much-needed boon and in March 1944, Third Officer Pym was posted to a large neo-Palladian house nineteen miles from Southampton, 'with beautiful grounds full of camellias, azaleas and rhododendrons . . . and a view over to the Isle of Wight'. She told Henry that the house once belonged to the Rothschilds and before that the Mitfords: 'Unity's family, you know, lived there.' Unity, almost the same age as Pym, equally entranced by pre-war Nazi Germany, had been left severely brain-damaged by her suicide attempt. On Hitler's special orders, she had been hospitalised in Germany and then transported home to her family, accompanied by her youngest sister Deborah, the future Duchess of Devonshire.

Pym was assigned to the Censorship Division of the Wrens, due to her experience in Bristol. Her new officer's uniform gave her immense pleasure. It was made-to-measure with gold buttons and a tricorn hat, 'with a rather beautiful naval badge, blue and gold and crimson'. Preparations were being made for the invasion of north-west Europe and the south coast of England was an important staging post for the Allied forces as they waited to open up the second front. It was an exciting time, though everyone expected the losses to be severe: 'I am vaguely depressed waiting for things to happen, as we all are now. I wish it could be over and done with – we shall know so many people in it and I suppose a good many of them won't come back.'[7]

Pym wrote to tell Henry that she had had a short-lived romantic entanglement with a petty officer at Westcliff, but broke it off: 'So it looks as though you and Jock may get your way and have me as Miss Pym all my life.'[8] Meanwhile, Mrs

Pym sent a drawing from *The Tatler* of Captain Julian Amery, which made Barbara's heart turn over.

Pym remained in Southampton until September 1944, when she heard the exciting news that she was being posted overseas – to Naples.

CHAPTER XI

Third Officer Pym is posted to Naples, where she meets 'Pay-Bob' Starky

On 17 September 1944, just over three months after D-Day, Pym began a Naples journal. From the ocean liner *Christiaan Huygens*, she recorded her first impressions of Italy: 'layers of orange and pink and biscuit-coloured buildings and in the evening, a mass of twinkling lights'.[1]

The Allies had invaded mainland Italy a year before, with General Montgomery's Eighth Army crossing from Sicily and the Americans landing at Salerno. Within weeks, they had entered Naples and, in conjunction with a popular uprising, freed the city from occupation. The port was now a key centre for maintaining control of the Mediterranean during the final phase of the war. There was still fighting against the retreating Germans in the north, and thousands of troops passed through the naval base in Naples. It was a place of intense but short-lived affairs, bustle and intrigue. There were far more men than women, providing opportunities for an exciting social life.

Barbara had a cold in her first week, and had no sense of smell, but once she recovered she breathed in incense or perfume passing a barber's shop. She noticed a lot of poverty in Naples; the people 'rather ragged and dirty, but some girls nicely dressed and pretty, nearly all wearing shoes with very high wedge heels – many priests'. She preferred Capri, with its lemon groves, royal blue convolvulus, rich puce bougainvillea and hanging bunches of grapes. The warm air and blue sea were a welcome change from grim, grey Southend.[2]

On the voyage over, Pym had snatched kisses with a lieutenant called Michael. Now in Naples and Capri, among romantic baroque villas and churches, the warm-scented air fragrant with citrus and pine, there were ample opportunities for flirtations with handsome officers in their white uniforms.

Initially Pym felt a sense of ennui, 'a faint feeling of dissatisfaction with life here, the dull day's work and empty round and the fear that I shall never, never write that novel'. But in Capri she was entranced by the Villa San Michele, built by the innovative Swedish psychiatrist and author, Axel Munthe. It stood on a plateau 330 metres above the sea, looking across the Bay of Naples and the Sorrentine Peninsula, with a view of Mount Vesuvius in the distance. Munthe had created an extraordinary garden, often described as the most beautiful garden in Italy. He planted camellias, flowering ash, azaleas, wisteria, hydrangeas, roses, agapanthus, busy Lizzie and hundreds of other plants from the Mediterranean and other regions of the world. The indigenous wild flowers included acanthus, myrtle, broom, rock rose. To contrast with the vivid colours, he planted rich green ivies, box, thuja and mosses. There was an avenue of cypress and a colonnade fragrant with wisteria. Munthe built outdoor 'rooms'; shady courtyards, pergolas and arbours for respite in the hot summer months. He added sculptures and antiquities, many of which he had found and dug up in the garden. Pym liked best a 'cool little courtyard' filled with 'Roman pieces'. When she walked in it, 'white-walled and peaceful with trees against the sky', she felt tearful: 'The peace, the beauty, the antiquity, perhaps something of the feeling I have for churchyards came over me.'[3]

Inside the villa, Pym was taken with the beautiful old furniture and the inscribed Roman sculptures: 'Oh the *agony* of not knowing Latin!' Above his desk, in his study, she was entranced by a great stone head of Medusa, which he spotted in the clear water by the old foundations of Tiberius's bath. 'How wonderful to have seen it before anyone else did,' she noted. Looking out over the sea, was a gigantic 3,000-year-old Egyptian Sphinx. Visitors were encouraged to make a wish, so Pym 'wished a simple wish that *could* come true'.[4]

Down in Anacapri, she walked along a pleasant little square which had shops filled with souvenirs, 'corals, straw hats, cameos and the little silver bells which are supposed to be lucky. Of course I bought one, being sentimental and a little superstitious.'[5] She loved Capri so much that she rather dreaded her return to Naples, but she soon grew to enjoy the city and felt the exhilaration of being in a foreign land. There was dancing on the quarterdeck of HMS *Sirius* and a trip back on the motorboat by moonlight, with 'wind and spray and stars – dark shapes of ships and the lights of Naples'.[6]

Pym saw *Rigoletto* at the opera house (luscious, red and gold and baroque), which boasted an elaborately painted ceiling. The admiral invited some of the Wrens to his villa, romantically situated with a terrace overlooking the bay. Another party was held at an Italian apartment which was full of original furnishings – 'a lovely big table of mirror glass – portraits round the walls, with one of which I fell in love – a young man, looking like Jay in 17th century dress'.[7]

There were still moments of boredom ('an exquisite experience to be savoured and analysed like old brandy and sex') and a longing to be with 'her own kind' – Pym finding many of the people from working-class backgrounds 'dreary'. Her prejudices were soon to be challenged when she began a flirtation with a young paybob (supply officer, usually the person responsible for the accounts). Pym initially thought him rather common. However she was attracted to his dark good looks and his height. 'The first person in Naples with whom I've had any conversation. About sex!'[8] His name was Iain, though his nickname was Starky, the same name she had given her kangaroo. He was unlike any other man she had met. He was blunt, sarcastic and very sexy: 'He has a cynical attitude to life and the technique of outrageous rudeness.' He found Pym attractive and, above all, he was taken by her wit and clever conversation: 'He told me I would make a good mistress because I would be able to hold a man's attention by my intelligence.' The evening, she noted, followed its usual course: 'an expertly sensuous kiss leaning against a wall . . . and no word since!'[9]

Pym had never had an affair with a man who was not from her own social class. She found Starky intriguing: 'He is rude and impossible and casual, in themselves quite attractively provoking qualities.' She told herself that she was flattered by his attention. But she also felt that he was the only person that she could talk to about anything, 'though not cultured as far as I know'. She was also surprised to find that she felt 'fiercely protective' towards him, as he seemed to be disliked by the other Wrens. As well as being tall and handsome, he had 'nice short-sighted eyes'. The only trait she disliked was his accent: 'his voice gets on my nerves'.[10]

When she heard that Starky was to return to England, Pym found herself minding. She was desperate to make contact and sent notes for him to the Navy House. She saw him standing on the balcony, gazing across the bay. 'Oh let him be gone and no more hankering for this, second rate as it is.' One of her fellow Wrens, Morag, told Pym that she 'enjoyed wallowing in emotion'. It was a perceptive remark that Pym allowed had some truth in it, but it did not stop her from minding: 'Does one *ever* learn not to mind.'[11]

Plans changed and Starky did not leave for England, so they were soon reunited at a dance. Pym could not help noticing that he lacked social skills: 'he is gauche and rather ineffectual, but so sweet'. She was tired of the 'handsome and conceited Flags [Flag officers]', and helpless in the face of the sexual attraction she felt for Starky. They went to his cabin, 'where we lay in the dark and talked a little and loved a little and there was the same good thing between us as we had the evening of Mac's party'.[12]

There were still class barriers between them. He thought she was in love with him because she called him 'darling' so many times, which she found funny. Starky was clever but unsophisticated: 'Our relationship is physical and intellectual, but not, repeat, *not* cultural.'[13]

Perhaps more importantly, he made her laugh. They took a romantic trip to Mount Vesuvius. The woods were very pretty leading up to the bay. They hired a guide and long sticks and made the climb, plodding through the ash and lava. Starky, she thought, proved himself well and carried her hat and bag. 'We looked down at the crater and then came down hand in hand and hysterical with laughter as I kept falling down.'[14] On the drive home, they were both silent, as he was returning to England and they knew that the affair would not last. They decided on a late last drink and ended up at a party, Starky, drunk and sentimental, ruffling her hair. They said goodbye at 'the Wrennery' (her digs), 'me saying "Thanks for a lovely volcano" and him "excuse me for kissing you goodnight with my glasses on".'[15]

Pym was well aware that the affair had no future: 'It isn't, as we said, that one's cynical, it's that one *knows* from experience that these things peter out.' But she did miss Starky and felt gloomy on the second anniversary of the Gordon declaration: 'Two years ago tonight – if Gordon hadn't said "In a queer kind of way I'm in love with you," I shouldn't be in Naples now.'[16]

She wrote to Jock, telling him about Starky. As ever, his advice was astute and more than a little dry: 'I do not think you would be very long happy with your handsome beast, irresistible as the appeal of handsome beasts is to intelligent and educated people. I hope you will not throw yourself away.' He teased her for *not* becoming entirely a 'bluff salt', telling her that 'I have formed a beautiful picture of you returning, enriched like [Jane Austen's] Captain Wentworth, with prize money and finding happiness with some faithful curate.'[17]

Persuasion was much on Pym's mind. She had taken a copy of the novel to Naples and copied passages into her notebook. Pym was struck by Austen's phrase 'desolate tranquillity' to describe Anne Elliot's mood. She wrote out a famous passage about women's fidelity in the face of their 'confined' lives:

> We certainly do not forget you so soon as you forget us. It is, perhaps, our fate rather than our merit. We cannot help ourselves. We live at home, quiet, confined, and our feelings prey upon us. You are forced on exertion. You have always a profession, pursuits, business of some sort or other, to take you back into the world immediately, and continual occupation and change soon weaken impressions.[18]

Later, in one of her novels, she would put across a very different view: that women's domestic lives are an effective distraction from matters of the heart. That men are more likely to brood than women. She also copied out a more hopeful passage from *Persuasion*: 'when pain is over, the remembrance of it often becomes a pleasure. One does not love a place the less for having suffered in it, unless it has been all suffering, nothing but suffering.' Pym wrote down Austen's beautiful and unforgettable iteration on female constancy: 'All the privilege I claim for my own sex (it is not a very enviable one: you need not covet it), is that of loving longest, when existence or when hope is gone!'[19]

Knowing that she was subject to fits of misery, Pym resolved to stay away from parties: 'Parties and drink are a bad thing when one has a little misery lurking somewhere.' She and Starky began a correspondence, but they both knew it was a 'war-affair' of the 'live-for-the-moment' kind. Trips to the island of Ischia with her colleague Morag helped. She bought a heart-shaped basket for her sewing and they walked around the isle, finding it 'beautifully green. Oranges and orange blossom with shining green leaves, lemons, vines, bougainvillea, mild sunny air.' They chanced upon a delightful ruined castle that offered: 'Sentimental delight in decay.'[20]

Pym had her sense of humour, as ever, to sustain her. One of Starky's friends pleaded with her to go to a party – 'said he was sure Starky would have wanted it – just as if I were Starky's widow!' Soon she was dancing with a sailor in 'Cyclamen chiffon' to the magic of '"Long Ago and Far Away"' – 'oh so cheek-to-cheek'. She was pleased to hear herself described as 'that very blasé Wren officer with a perpetually bored expression'. Her friend Cynthia told her that she was also known as 'the girl with the fascinating eyes'.

Starky had been a pleasant interlude, but not one she cared to repeat. Gordon sent a letter 'so funny and sweet' that it brought a sudden rush of tears to her eyes. The fact remained that Starky would never have suited Pym in the long term and Gordon's letter was a reminder of 'how much my *own* sort of person he was and is . . . please can't there be somebody like that again'.[21]

CHAPTER XII

The End of the War

Pym made the most of her time in Italy. She travelled to Positano, Amalfi and Ravello – which she found romantic at twilight. She saw cypresses, olives, an orange grove and a Byzantine church.

On Christmas Day, she went to a party at the villa of an admiral – 'quite enjoyable but I am never at my ease there, feel Jane Eyre-ish and socially unsuccessful'. In some respects, her affair with Starky had upended her class prejudices. She now found the flag officers fake and insincere: 'Danced with Flags and Astley-Jones, both doing their stuff – charm etc. How artificial it all is. I wonder if they feel it.'[1]

In the spring of 1945, with the end of the war nigh, Pym spent her leave exploring Rome and the countryside outside the city: 'Country lovely – brilliant green grass, yellow-green trees, blossoms, cypresses as one gets further north. Villages on hills, grey with a church spire or cupola – but ruined with sightless windows . . . Little white wooden crosses mark the graves.' The wooden crosses were not the only signs of the cost of the war. In the town of Frosinone she saw: 'horrifying damage. Like the Blitz but more desolate.'[2]

The wide pavements and the light in Rome reminded her of the German capital before the war: 'magic twilight (as I first saw Berlin in 1938)'. Pym had come a long way since the days of Friedbert and singing the 'Horst Wessel Lied'. In St Peter's ('vast and unchurchlike'), she noted the marble in various colours, the white cherubs and holy water basins. It was Palm Sunday and everyone carried little palm crosses and sprigs of myrtle. She peered into the Vatican City, 'in the hopes of seeing carpet slippers slopping up and down the backstairs'.[3]

Although she had not started a new novel, she had written down many ideas in her notebook, ranging from 'The Opera House on an April evening', to 'the dusty plants where we stub out our cigarettes'. Another idea for a story was 'the haunted feeling of places and objects too, in villas and houses now taken over by the military'.[4]

Pym was still in Naples when news came of the German surrender and the end of the war in Europe. Her journal is silent on the subject. There are no descriptions of any of the celebrations that broke out, no mention of the losses suffered.

Jock's brother, Don, who had written to Pym throughout the war and who had offered her such support and encouragement to carry on writing, was one of the casualties of war. His death in Normandy in the summer of 1944 left his elder brother bereft. He would pay tribute to his beloved brother in his North Oxford novel. Jock would never return to live in England. He cherished Pym's bereavement letter. He told her that he could bear no one else's sympathy: 'You can imagine how broken I am.' He told Pym how he had envisaged a future only with his brother:

You know as well as anyone what it means – all my mind and memory are bound up with him and I am rather like the last survivor of a race, talking a dead language all by myself. And other things go with him, the flat, Oxford . . . I don't think it was unduly selfish to hope he would be the survivor . . . he was much stronger in character and better fitted to survive alone.

Please pray for me: I am afraid of the future, more of the consolations than desolation, I think.[5]

Jock wrote from Gaza, thanking Pym for sending lines from
John Betjeman, telling her that he had shed tears from the poem
and that Betjeman was one of the writers belonging to his
brother and him, along with Jane Austen and Henry James. He
closed his letter with deep affection: 'Dear Pym, take care of
yourself in foreign parts – I do need you there for my empty
old age – we old, life-worn people will have so much to say
when we meet.'[6]

And then there were the Amery brothers. Pym had heard
nothing from Julian, other than what she had picked up from
the news, but his family's story would end tragically. Julian had
told Pym something of the trials of his elder brother. From the
outset, John had been a wild and difficult child, whom neither
school nor parents could control. He was constantly in trouble
and asking for financial assistance. John was passionately anti-
communist and had become a pro-Nazi British fascist. During
the war, he had made propaganda broadcasts for Nazi Germany.
In 1945, he was arrested in Milan and sent to prison in London,
where he awaited trial for high treason. If found guilty, his
sentence would be death by hanging. Julian was devastated and
did everything he could to help his brother, even suggesting the
defence that he was not legally capable of being a traitor to
England as he had become a Spanish citizen. He could not
believe that John was a traitor.

In November, John Amery's trial for treason began. Leo
suggested that his son was insane, but the claim was dismissed.
At the last minute, John changed his plea to guilty. On 18
December 1945, he was hanged by the neck and buried in
Wandsworth prison cemetery.

Barbara, too, faced a death in the family that year, though

one far less public. Her mother was diagnosed with cancer and operated upon. A few weeks after VE Day, Pym asked for compassionate leave. She returned to England and was assigned to WRNS headquarters in Queen Anne's Mansions in London, waiting to be demobilised. Barbara and Hilary spent as much time in Oswestry as they could, devotedly nursing Irena through what would be her final illness. On 10 September she died. Family life, like the war, was over. Barbara Pym left Oswestry for good, determined to make a new life in London.

After the war had ended, Friedbert Glück wrote to Pym. She kept a note of the receipt of his letters, but made no comment on their content. It was a part of her past that she thought was best kept locked up in the lumber room.

BOOK THE FIFTH

Miss Pym in Pimlico

CHAPTER I

In which our Heroine and her Sister take up Residence in London

In November 1945, Barbara and Hilary moved into 108 Cambridge Street, Pimlico, on the corner of a garden square. It was 'not a very good district, but perhaps we shall raise the tone', wrote Pym.[1] Her room was on the second floor, with windows on two sides, offering a view of Warwick Square and St Gabriel's church. It was difficult to find digs post-war, as so much of London had been bombed, so the Pym sisters felt grateful to have a light airy flat within walking distance of an Anglo-Catholic church that remained standing (though most of its windows had been blown out).

Following Irena's death, Blytheswood was sold and their father had moved into a hotel in the centre of Oswestry. Hilary and Pym furnished their rooms in Pimlico with pieces from the family home. The house belonged to a Mrs Monckton, whose husband was a colonel, still away in the army. The Pym sisters had to share a bathroom with the occupants of the flat above. Though Barbara liked her spacious room and her independence, she was aware of the 'humiliations' of her position as a single woman, such as not having a bathroom of her own. This was something the upper-middle-class Virginia Woolf never had to worry about.

Pym would use the details of her time in Pimlico to create the world of London 'bedsit-land' in her next novel, *Excellent Women*. Widely regarded as the most successful of her books, its heroine, Mildred Lathbury, is one of those 'splendid women' whom most people take for granted: 'I have to share a bathroom, I had so often murmured, almost with shame, as if I personally had been found unworthy of a bathroom of my own.'[2]

Pym was pleased when Henry wrote on hearing of her mother's death. She told him what a miserable time she had had, but that she felt better now she was away from Oswestry. She explained that her nerves were 'frazzled' after six years of war: 'If I can get a nice little job to earn me a bit of money I shall then settle to writing again and see if I can get a nice novel or something published.' She mentioned that Jock had also written: 'he seems much happier and is enjoying the sinshine – oh dear what an unsuitable mistake to make – of course I mean sunshine'.[3] Henry and Pym were all too aware that homosexual liaisons were more readily available and less likely to lead to criminal prosecution in the Mediterranean than in Britain.

Jock, who had been evacuated from his beloved Greece during the war and was now living in Egypt, had been urging Pym to get back to her writing. She told him that she had taken up the manuscript of *Some Tame Gazelle*: 'Like mine, your writing life is solidly rooted in the past and lives largely on memories.'[4] Jock replied that he was writing his own North Oxford novel, to be called *North Oxford*, or *The Last Enchantments*. He teased her about Pimlico: 'one called it South Belgravia in polite circles'. But she was happy to be in like-minded company with Hilary. Jock, having lost his brother, the closest friend he ever had, reminded her of the comfort Hilary brought to Sandy.

In January 1946, following demobilisation, Pym began looking for a job: 'Heaven knows what I shall get, but I must earn some money.' Post-war London was grim. Food and clothes rationing would continue for several years. Pym, like many others, found rationing far more difficult to cope with after the war than during it: 'now that the war is over one doesn't seem to be able to put up with things so easily'. A job, she thought, would be 'the best way of keeping out that *Angst* from which we all suffer in some degree nowadays'. She duly found one: 'I am turning into an anthropologist as I now have a job at the International Institute of African Languages and Cultures.'[5] Miss Pym had entered the world of anthropology. It would provide superb copy for her ever-fertile imagination.

CHAPTER II

Miss Pym the Anthropologist

By the summer of 1946, less than a year after her mother's death, Pym's family life had altered dramatically. She wrote to Henry to tell him about her change of circumstances: 'I have so much news that I had better just fling it at you in Compton-Burnett style. Hilary and her husband have separated and my father has married again and given us a very nice stepmother of suitable age and a dear brother and sister, whom I have not met.' She felt that her sister was much happier without her husband, who was 'much too cold and intellectual and logical to live with'. It had been a typical war marriage, entered into with an undue degree of haste. The separation forced Pym to consider the right ingredients for a happy union. Many people, she wrote, were not madly in love when they married, but 'turn out very well'. Ever the romantic, she told Henry that she would, personally, prefer to marry for love, 'even if it wore off, as I am told it does'.[1]

However, she now seemed resigned to the fact that she was and would remain a spinster: 'Maybe I shall be able to keep my illusions as it doesn't look like I shall ever get married.'[2] There are several references to her being a poor spinster, to the extent that one wonders whether she is protesting too much. The desire to be a published author took prominence over the desire for marriage and children.

From this time on, Barbara and Hilary Pym would live together in a manner envisaged in the novel Barbara had written when she was twenty-two. The sisters were extremely compatible, shared the same jokes and lived in great harmony together, though each had their own circles of friends. It was a relationship that echoed the life of Pym's literary heroine, Jane Austen, who lived contentedly with her sister, Cassandra.

Furthermore, the unravelling of the private lives of the people to whom she was closest softened the blow of feeling that somehow she had failed in her emotional life. The Harveys' marriage was in trouble and they would soon divorce. Jock was living in Alexandria, but had plans to return to Cairo. Pym reflected on the life they had lived as a trio on the Banbury Road in Oxford all those years ago, writing to Henry: 'It is pleasant to feel that you and Jock will never go quite out of my life now.'[3]

Around this time, Pym stopped writing journals in favour of notebooks, in which she scribbled ideas, thoughts and experiences. There was a new, more subdued tone to her writings and letters. Part of the reason for not keeping a journal was because she was becoming extremely busy with her job at the International African Institute. She had secured the post through a friend whose aunt was secretary there. In another of those strange Pym coincidences, her name was Beatrice Wyatt, the name of Pym's heroine in *The Lumber Room*.

Pym joined the institute on 28 February 1946. It was located in Lower Regent Street on two floors of an office building with an impressive view of the Mall. On the top floor was the library, run under the supervision of a formidable woman named Ruth Jones. Pym's old colleague, Margaret Bryan, from the Censorship Office in Bristol, also worked at the institute.

Pym thought her boss, Daryll Forde – the institute's newly appointed director and Professor of Anthropology at University College London – 'brilliant' with 'great charm but no manners and is altogether the sort of person I ought to work for!' The International African Institute had been founded in 1926 as the International Institute of African Languages and Cultures. Pym helped to edit the institute's seminar papers and monographs and later worked as assistant editor on Forde's quarterly academic journal, *Africa*. It was her first full-time job and she threw herself into it with her usual energy and commitment. It also gave her more good material for her novels. An anthropologist, she felt, was close to a novelist: both were concerned with the study of human behaviour.

Pym attended Forde's lectures to familiarise herself with her new subject. 'On Monday[s] I spend th[e] day at University College and the London School of Economics, attending lectures on anthropology. Would you believe I could sink so low? But it helps me with my work, which is quite interesting though I work for a maddening Professor', she explained to Henry Harvey, before thanking him for bringing her the rare delicacy of a grapefruit and telling him that she had cut her hair, making her resemble a poodle or a sheep.[4]

A handsome man in his forties with a shock of grey hair, Forde was an exacting boss who did not suffer fools gladly (one of his favourite expressions was 'nobody is indispensable'). Though Forde was an indefatigable fundraiser, money at the institute was always short: Pym was paid a modest salary of £5 per week. Forde had spent some of his early years at Berkeley in California, where he carried out ethnographic fieldwork amongst the Yuma tribe of Arizona and the Hopi Native Americans of New Mexico. From 1935 he worked in Nigeria with the Yako people. His work in Africa resulted in several volumes under the title *African Worlds: Studies in the*

Cosmological Ideas and Social Values of African Peoples. Forde would remain director of the International African Institute until 1973; Pym worked alongside him throughout this time. Though utterly brilliant and dedicated, he had a reputation for being insensitive, and would often reduce Pym to tears. He expected the same standards of everyone around him, sometimes finding it bewildering that his fellow workers had lives outside the institute.

The rest of Pym's colleagues were female. Beatrice Wyatt was the only one strong enough to stand up to Forde. She was older than he was and had an equally forceful personality. 'Bea is so domineering,' he would complain, and she would respond: 'Daryll is not a gentleman.'⁵ However, they respected one another and both of them were utterly dedicated to the institute. Pym's first main project was working on Forde's new enterprise, 'The Ethnographic and Linguistic Survey of Africa', an ambitious attempt to map all the tribes and languages in Africa. Each separate volume was written by an expert in the field and Pym's job was to keep in touch with all the authors, edit their work and compile the index for each volume.

Pym heard from Jock, who was delighted that her living arrangement with Hilary looked to be permanent, or at least for the foreseeable future: 'it sets you and Hilary free now from all other ties to spend your old age together . . . It seems an ideal position and ought to inspire you to get on with *Some Tame Gazelle*'.⁶

Jock was arranging a transfer to the University of Cairo. He was a third of the way through his North Oxford novel, telling Pym that he would use the Thomas Hardy appellation 'Christminster' for Oxford. He had disguised certain aspects of his characters, he explained, for fear of being sued by Christine Pakenham, 'in any case she would be ill-advised to do so'. He told Pym that the ending was so sad that he could hardly bear it. The book was to be called *The Last Enchantments*, 'from dear Matthew Arnold. A beautiful title, don't you think.'[7]

Jock's letters were invaluable to Pym and she preserved them carefully (whereas she destroyed most of Henry's). Liddell was an important link to her past, but he was also shining a light on her future. It was he who cajoled, nagged and encouraged, and it was he who persisted in believing in Pym's potential as a published writer. It was something that she clung to as she turned again to the revisions of the novel that Jock loved so much.

CHAPTER III

In which Mr Jock Liddell persists and persuades Miss Pym to revise her Novel

Jock was now living in a garden flat in Cairo with his dog Sappho and the Honourable Edward Gathorne-Hardy. Eddie was a flamboyant homosexual and one of the original 'Bright Young Things'. He was immortalised as Miles Malpractice in Evelyn Waugh's *Vile Bodies*. Jock wrote to Barbara from Cairo, telling her about Eddie and their life together. He described him as 'a tall man of forty-five, in places inclined to corpulence'. Sappho was 'so happy', even though Eddie did not care for dogs.[1]

Knowing Pym's love of delicious food, 'even when [for you] it is only a beautiful memory', he described his luncheon menus in detail: eggs stuffed with mushrooms in a cheese sauce, tomatoes tossed in hot butter and brandy, strawberry mousse; on another occasion, 'cold consommé, fried prawns in anchovy sauce, cold duck and a strawberry cream ice – all in the arbor in the garden'. Jock adored his garden, where he and Eddie grew roses and mint, and plucked young vine leaves to stuff with rice and raisins à la Grecque. Jock signed off his letter with an account of how 'lovely slices of breast of duck now repose on golden aspic jelly, surrounded by slices of orange', while Pym froze in

Pimlico with an electric fire and rationed offal.[2] She sent out an appeal to Henry: 'We have *enough* to eat but it is so deadly dull most of the time. Do bring me a grapefruit or an orange from Sweden if there are any. But at least we have some Camembert cheese at the moment, so life has its little glories.'[3]

In the summer of 1945, Jock had met with his publisher Jonathan Cape, who remembered Pym and her novel. Jock delightedly wrote to Pym of that meeting in Ivy Compton-Burnett style:

'Once you introduced two very attractive young women to me,' said Mr Cape in a lascivious tone.

'That would be the Miss Pyms,' said Robert in the reserved tone of one recollecting Miss Manning's experience.

'One of them wrote a book,' said Mr Cape. 'I did not publish it, but yet it remains in my mind. Why should I remember it?'

'Because it's such a good book,' said Robert in a full salesman tone, 'What other reason could there be? I should not expect you to forget it.'

'Yes, there must be something about it,' said Mr Cape. 'Do you still see the author? What does she do?'

'She will always write,' said Robert. 'I think she is a natural writer.'

'I think I should see that book,' said Mr Cape.

'I will give you Third Officer Pym's address,' said Robert quickly.

'No, no,' said Mr Cape. 'Will you not write to her. Be vague. I do not know that I wish to see the book exactly as it was before.'

'I do not think that Third Officer Pym would let you see it without revision,' said Robert firmly.

'Let her make it more malicious,' said Mr Cape in the tone of desiring to make a book strong enough for the Cape list.

'What was it like?' said Mr Wren Howard.

'It was very funny,' said Robert, 'with much, perhaps too much, apt quotation.'

'Oh, I should not like that,' said Mr Wren Howard.

Is this not interesting news? Let us hope that it is great news.[4]

A week later, Jock urged Pym to consider the advice: 'Don't take Mr Wren Howard too seriously about quotations . . . take Mr Cape's wish for malice quite seriously. Proust, you know, went round all of his characters making them worse. What can you do with the Archdeacon?' Jock offered to read the manuscript thoroughly and suggest an edit. Pym sent it off to Cairo and he went through it chapter by chapter, making sound and judicious suggestions for omissions and clarifications: 'When Belinda's thoughts are confused, do not let them confuse the reader – cf Miss Austen and Miss Bates – who is always more coherent than she means or seems to be.'[5]

Pym followed Jock's guidance but found the revisions difficult and had put the manuscript to one side after starting her job at the institute. Now, in the summer of 1947, the indefatigable Liddell urged her again to revise *Some Tame Gazelle*: 'But why have we yet no work from your pen, Dear Barbara? Did you never nurse the dear gazelle? Mr Cape must be very impatient.'[6] And in December: 'Why don't you finally tame that Gazelle, and send it to dear Mr Cape. Publication would encourage you and then we might hope for more from your pen.'[7] Pym was procrastinating and told Jock that she couldn't get it done. But he was obdurate: 'It's the sort of book that is needed.'[8]

By April 1948, Pym was able to report that she had finally managed to work on the novel. Jock insisted that she should write to Cape to tell him about her progress: 'It will be a great satisfaction to have it by one's bedside.' He said that he'd happily send a covering letter to Cape on her behalf: 'I should be proud to introduce such an author to the dear house in Bedford Square.'⁹ She persevered with her revisions and at last, a year later, she was able to write with the good news that Cape had finally accepted *Some Tame Gazelle* for publication. Jock, with typical generosity, sent his warmest congratulations:

Dearest Barbara,

This is delightful news! Not wonderful, for I do not wonder at it. How very glad I am that you too will be a Cape author – perhaps we may meet at one of those charming functions at Bedford Square . . . Fancy that you will be a novelist of the 'fifties' – did we think of that in days past in the dear house in the Banbury Road? You will forgive me for wishing for people to still be here to enjoy this – Aunt Janie, Don and your mother – you must have felt it too. But Hilary and I must do what we can to rejoice with you – and I do so very much.¹⁰

Jock had shown himself to be a true and devoted friend. It was his constant encouragement and his belief in the talent of his friend that gave her the final push to revise and resend her manuscript. Miss Pym was about to become a published author.

CHAPTER IV

Miss Pym finally tames her Gazelle and it is released to the World

The novel's epigraph explains its curious title: 'Some tame gazelle' is a phrase from a poem about loneliness called 'Something to Love' – which might have been a better title for her novel – by an obscure early nineteenth-century poet and dramatist called Thomas Haynes Bayly:

> Something to love, some tree or flow'r,
> Something to nurse in my lonely bow'r,
> Some dog to follow, where'er I roam,
> Some bird to warble my welcome home,
> Some tame gazelle, or some gentle dove:
> Something to love. Oh, something to love!

Pym encountered the poem in one of her favourite volumes of poetry, a hilarious collection published in 1930 under the inspired title: *The Stuffed Owl: An Anthology of Bad Verse.*[1]

Following Jock's advice, Pym omitted every single Nazi, Russian and Finnish reference and much of the personal Oxford detail. The swastika that Belinda pins onto her dress, which in the original manuscript 'Dear Helmuth' presumes to be a sign

of her sympathy with the National Socialist party, is replaced
with a seed-pearl brooch. The photograph of Hitler is replaced by
a photograph of Dr Nicholas Parnell. The Nazi Relief Fund is
now a collection for the 'poor in Pimlico'. There are no direct
references to Oxford or the Bodleian Library. Nor is the small
country village named. As a result, the novel is given a timeless
air that could place it in any pre-war English village. Extra
characters are added, such as ladies' companion Connie Aspinall
and dressmaker Miss Prior. The curate is no longer Henry's son,
but a young man called Edgar Donne. Pym removed the character of Dr Parnell's musical brother, who had been based on
Don Liddell. And the Archdeacon, now at one remove, became
more rounded and less of a caricature.

Pym's experiences during the war years had given her work
added maturity and depth. Belinda, the heroine, has far more
of an interior life and cuts a more tragic figure than the rather
silly heroine of her first iteration. From the opening lines Pym
is firmly in control of her narrative. The original beginning:
'Tomorrow, thought Belinda, I have to go to the dentist, or is
it the day *after* tomorrow?' is replaced with the much stronger:
'The new curate seemed quite a nice young man, but what a
pity it was that his combinations showed, tucked carelessly into
his socks, when he sat down.'[2]

When Pym first created her heroines, she described them as
spinsters in their middle forties and had great fun imagining
what it would be like to envision her own life as a spinster. Now
that she was no longer a young woman of twenty-one, and with
a firm belief that she would not marry, her portraits became
more finely nuanced and poignant. Men are scarce in her English
village (a reminder that she was, in fact, writing post-war) and
her female characters earn their own crust.

The seamstress, Miss Prior, is a compelling new character,
eking a living by her ability to alter clothing and make soft

furnishings. Though the pre-war setting is retained, so there are no specific references to clothes rationing, it is a given that few of the women have shop-bought dresses. Similarly, the novel is studded with references to distinctly unglamorous food: cauliflower cheese, boiled chicken, Ovaltine, tinned soup (sometimes thinned with potato water), baked beans and rissoles.

Belinda Bede, a rather anxious people-pleaser, worries about feeding her friends and her 'help'. Early on, Pym delivers a pitch-perfect scene between Belinda and Miss Prior, who comes to the Bede cottage expecting a good lunch and is displeased to find that she is given cauliflower cheese rather than the meat that she was expecting. Miss Prior, Pym explains, is not a 'meek little sewing woman', but someone who inspires 'Fear and Pity' in Belinda. The scene is carefully calibrated to reveal the tensions between the two women and their keen sense of social distinctions.

Miss Prior is too grand to sit with housemaid Emily in the kitchen, but not grand enough to eat luncheon with the sisters, so she is presented with food on a tray in the morning room. Belinda feels sympathetically that Miss Prior's whole life is 'just a putting up with second best all the time', and yet she is easily offended: 'She was so touchy, so conscious of her position, so quick to detect the slightest suspicion of patronage. One had to be *very* careful with Miss Prior.' She is described as 'a little dried-up woman of uncertain age, with a brisk, bird-like manner and brown, darting eyes'. Quick to notice and criticise, she asks for the window to be opened and for a duster to polish the room: 'I think we all work better in bright, clean surroundings, don't you?' And when plump, handsome Harriet asks for her new dress to be cut out of the brown velvet she has bought, bird-like Miss Prior regards her critically: 'I wonder if it's going to be big enough on the *hips*? That's where you usually need it, isn't it?'[3]

The battles between Pym's women may be small, but they are significant. The scene builds beautifully. Miss Prior disapproves of the two dead vases of chrysanthemums, their stems 'black and slimy in the yellow water'. Then, much to her consternation, there is no toilet paper in the downstairs lavatory – she is given a copy of the *Church Times* to use for her ablutions.

The final horror comes when Belinda discovers that Miss Prior has not touched her cauliflower cheese, though she has devoured the damson flan:

> 'Oh dear, I'm afraid you haven't enjoyed your lunch, Miss Prior,' said Belinda, who now felt near to tears. 'Don't you like cauliflower cheese?'
>
> 'Oh yes, Miss Bede, I do sometimes,' said Miss Prior in an off-hand tone, not looking up from her work.
>
> Belinda went on standing in the doorway watching Miss Prior negotiating an awkward bit of chair cover. Then she looked again at the tray, wondering what she could say next. Then in a flash, she realised what it was. It was almost a relief to know, to see it there, the long greyish caterpillar. Dead now, of course, but unmistakable. It needed a modern poet to put this into words. Eliot, perhaps.[4]

Belinda knows that if the same thing had happened to her, she would have pretended that she hadn't seen the unwelcome visitor and would have carried on eating, but Miss Prior is using the incident to humiliate.

The moment is unexpectedly saved, however, when Miss Prior switches her criticism to Agatha Hoccleve:

> 'Between ourselves, Miss Bede, Mrs Hoccleve doesn't keep a good table. At least *I* never see any proof of it. An old dried-up scrap of cheese, or a bit of cottage pie, *no* sweet, sometimes. I've

heard the maids say so, too, you know how these things get about . . . You always have such nice meals, Miss Bede and you give me just the same as you have yourselves, I know that. After all, it might just as easily have been you or Miss Harriet that got the unwelcome visitor today,' she concluded with a little giggle.[5]

Small things matter to Pym (the trivial round, the common task), and her heroine is suddenly overcome with emotion:

Belinda's eyes filled with tears and she experienced one of those sudden moments of joy that sometimes come to us in the middle of an ordinary day. Her heart like a singing bird and all because Agatha didn't keep as good a table as she did and Miss Prior had forgiven her for the caterpillar and the afternoon sun streaming in through the window over it all.[6]

The shift in mood and tone is exquisitely rendered, without so much as a bat's squeak of sentimentality. Pym has found her subject matter and a depth of vision and understanding that her twenty-one-year-old self could not have envisaged.

Jonathan Cape had urged Pym to be 'more malicious', and she put his advice to good use in her rendering of the character of Archdeacon Hoccleve, in which she drew heavily on Henry Harvey's traits and peccadillos.

Henry Hoccleve is melodramatic, self-dramatising and lazy; he complains constantly about the amount of work he does, affects an 'eighteenth-century style melancholy' and sports a look of 'malicious amusement' to those he considers inferior. But he is a fabulous and unforgettable creation. Belinda loves him, despite his many faults: selfish and demanding as he is, he only has to smile at her and she melts. Pym retained many of the old in-jokes. Henry Harvey's Venetian red socks make an appearance, his blue hat; his phrases such as 'These yew trees are remarkably fine'; his penchant for Middle English and for quoting the Greater English Poets; his complaints about moths spoiling his clothes; his inability to get up in the morning; his delicate stomach. His habit of reading aloud.

But, as with Pym, time has dulled Belinda's passion for Henry and she is able to observe him with cool detachment. When the Archdeacon visits the sick, she notes: 'There was something about a deathbed that appealed to his sense of the dramatic.' He loves nothing better than the sound of his own voice: 'As he could not sing, he made up for it by making his voice heard as much as possible in other ways.' Belinda observes how he is quick to criticise women: 'I thought women enjoyed missing their meals and making martyrs of themselves.' He calls his wife a 'fool' for not being a better housewife. The mature Belinda is more cynical about him than the doting undergraduate: '[men] just expect meals to appear on the tables and they usually do'. She is thankful that she has escaped marriage to Henry: 'It was obvious that Agatha had a very difficult time with him.'

Nevertheless, there is an erotic scene where Belinda darns the Archdeacon's socks, which leaves her feeling flustered. Knitting and darning become sensual acts. 'If she has knitted him a pair of socks, perhaps she is not entirely lacking in the feminine arts,' Belinda notes of a present given to a young curate. Belinda is a very good knitter and darner; Agatha is not. Belinda longs to knit a sweater for Henry, but she knows that his wife will strongly disapprove: 'Obviously the enterprise was too fraught with dangers to be attempted.' The sock-darning episode is erotic because Henry is still wearing it. He stretches his long leg onto Belinda's little chair, so she can reach the hole in his heel. Belinda is so discombobulated that she inadvertently pricks her needle into his foot. She has found the experience 'upsetting and unnerving', and she worries about what Agatha will say if she discovers the intimate act.

Pym's comic tour de force is Henry's sermon on the theme of Judgement Day, in which he puts the fear of God into his mild and genteel flock of parishioners:

> The Archdeacon paused impressively and peered at his congregation; a harmless enough collection of people – old Mrs Prior and her daughter, Miss Jenner, Miss Beard and Miss Smily . . . the Misses Bede and the guests from the vicarage – Count Bianco – Miss Liversidge and Miss Aspinall – of course they did not realise but he was going to tell them. 'The *Judgement Day*,' he almost shouted, so loudly that Harriet had to take out her handkerchief to stifle her inappropriate amusement and old Mrs Prior let out a kind of moan. 'That day may be soon,' he went on, 'it may even be *tomorrow*.'[7]

The congregation are shocked and stunned by the ferocity of Henry's terrifying sermon: 'Even Belinda thought the Archdeacon was going a little too far when he likened his congregation to such as '*call aloud for ev'ry bauble drivel'd o'er by sense*. Whatever it might mean it certainly sounded abusive.'

Bishop Grote's Lantern Lecture (in this version transposed from Hawaii to Africa, suggesting the influence of the International African Institute on Pym's literary work) is another episode of high comedy. The villagers lapse into uncontrollable giggling as Bishop Grote recites the African alphabet, sings native songs and shows unsuitable images of phallic-like objects – Harriet, who is manning the lantern slides, inserts one image upside down with hilarious effect.

Pym largely follows her original plot line, though she adds an extra thread – that of the Bishop's love for Belinda. The scene of his proposal is yet another comic set piece. When she rejects him (shades of Elizabeth Bennet and Mr Collins) he soon finds solace in the arms of another willing spinster, Miss Aspinall. Belinda spurns the Bishop's offer of 'respect and esteem', as Pym had once spurned Henry's similar offer of friendship. However, Belinda also knows that her fervent passion for Henry has 'mellowed into a comfortable feeling, more like the cosiness of a winter evening by the fire than the uncertain raptures of a spring morning'.

Pym did not necessarily follow her agent, her publisher and Jock's advice to be more malicious in her writing. But she permits a minor key to permeate the mood of her work, which would become one of her leitmotifs: 'I loved you more than Agatha did, thought Belinda, but all I can do now is keep silent. I can't even speak to Florrie about the dusty mantelpiece, because it's nothing to do with me. It never was and it never will be.'[8]

What Belinda fears above all is losing her sister to marriage and facing the prospect of loneliness and old age.

CHAPTER V

In which Miss Pym enters the Age of Dior and the Beveridge Report

One day in the autumn of 1948, Pym was at Waterloo station. Standing in front of her was a man she recognised. It was Julian Amery. They had not set eyes on each other since before the war. She had read about his courageous and daring exploits, and he had somehow survived. She had survived, too. What happened next? Probably exactly what she anticipated: he took her hand and was his charming self. No more than that. Pym always found it hard to let go of her past loves. As she wrote in *Some Tame Gazelle*: 'If only one could clear out one's mind and heart as ruthlessly as one did one's wardrobe.'[1]

A fresh wardrobe was indeed another matter. Clothes rationing ended in 1949 and with it the 'Make-do and Mend' campaign. In 1947, Christian Dior launched his 'New Look', which contrasted strongly with the more severe fashions of the 1940s. After the hardships of the war, people were ready for a change. Fabric was luxurious and voluminous, the silhouette hourglass rather than boxy, shoulders soft rather than squared. Skirts were full and billowing, falling to below the mid-calf and bodices were extremely tight, accentuating the wasp waist. In order to achieve this look, women wore heavy-duty elasticated underwear or boned corsets. Nylon and elastic that had been used for the war effort began to be used for a variety of clothing, especially undergarments. Harriet Bede's roll-on elastic corset is used to comic effect in *Some Tame Gazelle* and her appearance wearing only a Celanese vest and knickers roots her firmly in the post-war synthetic fabric fashion camp.

These new artificial materials became known as 'miracle fabrics', as they could be easily washed and dried. This was important in the post-war world, where domestic help was hard to find. A Hoover advert for the *Daily Mail* in 1950 promoted 'Three Servants for Every Housewife: the Hoover cleaner, the new Hoover washing machine and the Hoover floor polisher'.

Pym was fastidious about her portrayal of clothing in her first novel, where it is often used to denote character. Belinda wears 'marocain' (a kind of hard-wearing, tweedy fabric), Harriet velvet and flowered voile, the curate's combinations are 'Meridian'. Agatha wears a well-cut dress of striped Macclesfield silk. Edith Liversidge wears a shapeless old-fashioned grey dress with unfashionably narrow shoulders. In the forties and fifties, women's outdoor clothing was formal. Hats, gloves and scarves were still worn. With more women at work, the fashion magazines aimed their advice at this new burgeoning market. Hair was shorter and the permanent wave meant fewer trips to the hair salon and less work than during the previous decade of waves, pins and victory rolls.

The government, concerned about the post-war birth rate, was keen to promote marriage, home-making and child-rearing, whilst recognising that women were needed to meet the labour shortage. The 1942 Beveridge Report had emphasised that marriage was a partnership, an economic unit with a division of labour amongst equals, but in practice women still got the short straw: 'The great majority of married women must be regarded as occupied on work which is vital though unpaid, without which their husbands could not do their paid work and without which the nation could not continue.'[2] A survey of 1951 showed that housewives typically worked a fifteen-hour day.[3]

Pym worked long hours at the institute, for her modest wage of £5 a week. Hilary's salary at the BBC was much better and sharing their living expenses helped the finances. Barbara's bank balance in 1949 was £35.12s.1d., the equivalent of little more than £1,000 today.[4] Pym tried to supplement her income by writing short stories for magazines, such as *Harpers* and *Women and Beauty*. Her story 'The Jumble-Sale' was published in 1949 by the latter. She also submitted a radio play to the BBC, *Something to Remember*, which was broadcast in 1950.

The short stories were never hugely successful and they did not find a market. Her genre was the novel. After she delivered *Some Tame Gazelle*, she began writing a new novel in her room. In Pym's short stories, she had been experimenting with first-person narration and this was her first attempt at a full-length novel in a first-person voice. Her desk overlooked St Gabriel's church and she set her new novel in Pimlico.

Pym later wrote about what she came to call the 'Excellent Women Theme' (its earlier iteration was the 'Splendid Women' theme, dating back from her experiences on the home front): 'I'd probably noticed that unmarried women seemed to be expected to do all kinds of things that nobody else was willing to do.'[5] It was something of which she had personal experience and about which she would write beautifully.

By January 1950, she had typed eight and a half pages of her new novel. Although Pym stopped writing a formal diary, she began to keep notebooks for diary-like entries and observations:

Seen from the top of a bus – a woman and clergyman sitting on hard chairs in Green Park and talking with animation.

Pimlico (Warwick Square) heavy with the scent of lime blossoms.

Excellent women enjoying discomfort – one bar of a small electric fire, huddled in coats.

The electricity man comes – has to check among the swinging wet stockings and knickers but the expression of his serious, rather worried blue eyes does not change.

Men should be given the opportunity for self-sacrifice as they are in their natures so much less noble than women.[6]

For many readers, *Excellent Women* is Pym's masterpiece. In her first draft, she described the book as follows: 'In brief it is the story of a woman – a pleasant humorous spinster in the middle thirties – who gets continually embroiled in other people's affairs.'[7] That Pym closely identified with the magnificent Mildred Lathbury is suggested by her notebooks of this period, in which she employs the first-person when she is speaking about her heroine: 'I go out shopping with Dora and we see Allegra and Fr Malory sitting on deckchairs in the park . . . Then Allegra asks me to lunch with her – I wonder why? She eats little and makes me feel inferior . . . what is to be done with Winifrid – can she live with me?'[8]

John Betjeman, one of Pym's favourite contemporary poets, would review *Excellent Women* and give it the highest praise: 'for me it is a perfect book'. He added, poignantly in a world that had been shattered but not broken by the war: '*Excellent Women* is England and, thank goodness, it is full of them.'

CHAPTER VI

In which we read of an Excellent Woman

It was not only the Beveridge Report that gave considerable attention to the status of married women. Newspapers and women's magazines also gave undue emphasis to the home-maker and dutiful wife and mother. Magazines such as *Woman's Own* and *Good Housekeeping* greatly increased their circulation, and middle-market newspapers introduced sections especially aimed at a female readership. Lip service was paid occasionally to single, working women, but the majority of the features were devoted to the housewife: how to dress at home, how to raise children, how to get a man to propose – 'show a bit of leg' suggested Amy Landreth of the *Daily Mail*.

As we have seen, Pym's letters as far back as 1938 contain many references to herself as a spinster, the term itself having seemingly unattractive connotations. She described herself as 'an old brown spinster', a 'bewildered English spinster', 'this dreary spinster', a 'lonely spinster'. By 1950, at the age of thirty-seven, she was (more or less happily) resigned to the fact that she would never marry. 'Spinsters' and the state of being unmarried would continue to occupy her creative output.

In *Some Tame Gazelle*, Belinda is a 'contented spinster'. In her next novel, *Excellent Women*, she would take for her heroine a much younger spinster, Mildred Lathbury, who is in her early thirties. Like Pym, Mildred worked at the Censorship Office during the war, where she 'learned much of the weakness of human nature', and now works part time at the 'Society for the Care of Aged Gentlewomen'. She lives in a London flat with a shared bathroom, overlooking Warwick Square. Mildred worries about who will be there to grieve for her when she is dead. Her underwear is even 'drearier' than her friend Dora's 'fawn locknit knickers'. She feels 'spinsterish and useless' and expects 'very little – nothing, almost'. Her self-loathing is such that a glance at herself 'in a dusty ill-lit mirror was enough to discourage anyone's romantic thoughts'.[1]

Somehow, Mildred manages to become involved in the lives of the people around her, who in turn appear to give very little consideration to her needs or feelings. From the start, Pym slyly references her literary alter ego: 'Let me hasten to add that I am not at all like Jane Eyre, who must have given hope to so many plain women who tell their story in the first-person.' Mildred does not mind very much being single, as she recognises the compensations, but she is constantly being made aware by others that spinsterhood equates to failure. That she is herself a 'splendid' or 'excellent' woman is of no comfort. She knows that she is capable, sensible and rational, but that only seems to be a reason as to why she is exploited. She is far more Anne Elliot than Jane Eyre.

It is the casual, unfeeling neglect from her friends and neighbours that is so deeply shocking. They believe that Mildred has an empty life because she is unmarried, which makes them feel justified in asking her to perform duties and tasks that they simply would not dream of asking anyone else. Nobody in the novel sets out to be unkind, but nobody takes the trouble to discover anything about Mildred's inner life or even to notice her feelings. Mildred is intelligent, funny and kind. She has a keen sense of the ridiculous, and observes the world around her with amusement and compassion: 'The sight of Sister Blatt, splendid on her high old-fashioned bicycle like a ship in full sail, filled me with pleasure.'[2] She does not see herself as other people see her. But everyone takes her for granted.

The plot revolves around two couples, the (unhappily) married, glamorous Napiers (Helena and Rockingham, known as Rocky), and the vicar and his sister, Winifred and Julian Malory – his name clearly a variant on Julian Amery. Mildred is, unwittingly, at the centre of the two plots. The Napiers' marriage is threatened by the presence of renowned anthropologist Everard Bone, while a beautiful, unscrupulous widow, Allegra Gray, disturbs the amity of the Malory siblings.

Pym's world in *Excellent Women* is distinctly post-war London. We are in an era of bombed-out churches, food rationing, bedsits; men coming home from war to find their hasty marriages are defunct; electric fires and nylon stockings, and knickers hanging on a washing line in the kitchen. Though the setting is in London's Pimlico, it has a similar feel to the country village world of *Some Tame Gazelle*.

Pym used much of her own experience to add local colour. St Mary's church is based on St Gabriel's. The self-service cafeteria in the Coventry Street Corner House is where Pym and her colleagues from the institute often used to dine. The ruined church of St Ermin's was based on St Saviour's, Pimlico, and St James's in Piccadilly – where Pym once saw a woman making coffee on a Primus stove. Both churches were badly hit during the Blitz: bombs took out almost all the stained glass on the west side of St Saviour's. The blast damage can still be seen today.[3]

Pym's strong but stealthy proto-feminism rises to the forefront in the character of gentle Mildred Lathbury. From her Oxford journal – when she provocatively suggested that women had more right to philander than men, gradually building from the poor and unsatisfactory way that she had been treated by her lovers – Pym does not hold back from her incipient belief that men are selfish and careless. It is always the splendid women who end up with their hands in the kitchen sink: 'And before long I should be certain to find myself at his sink peeling potatoes and washing up; that would be a nice change when both proof-reading and indexing began to pall. Was any man worth this burden?'[4]

Mildred is imaginative and sensitive. She is resourceful and dripping with dry humour and common sense. Some of Pym's best one-liners are given to her: 'Surely many a romance must have been nipped in the bud by sitting opposite somebody eating spaghetti?' And the unforgettable: 'I was so astonished that I could think of nothing to say, but wondered irrelevantly if I was to be caught with a teapot in my hand on every dramatic occasion.'[5] When she wants to be alone, Mildred retires to the kitchen sink where no men will follow her.

In *Some Tame Gazelle*, Pym had quoted one of her much-loved platitudes, but she had qualified it with a waspish codicil:

> '*The trivial round, the common task* – did it furnish *quite* all we needed to ask? Had Keble *really* understood? Sometimes one almost doubted it. Belinda imagined him writing the lines in a Gothic study, panelled in pitch-pine and well dusted that morning by an efficient servant. Not at all the same thing as standing at the sink with aching back and hands plunged into the washing-up water.[6]

Now, with Mildred Lathbury, she takes her beliefs one step further. Pym had once proclaimed to her journal: 'Oh darling [Gordon], how peculiarly insensitive your sex is!' But in *Excellent Women*, she reveals this sentiment in all its pathetic glory.

It is not only Rocky Napier who disappoints. He is all good looks and charm, flirting with Wrens in the Admiral's villa in Naples (as did the real-life 'flag' Rob Long) and romancing his Italian girlfriend even though he is married to Helena. We almost expect it of him. It is the vicar, Julian Malory, who is deeply dispiriting. He esteems and respects Mildred, but is infatuated by the elegant and fragrant Allegra Gray, who uses her beauty to exploit not only gullible men, but the good nature of women such as Winifred and Mildred. She wants Julian's devoted sister out of the way and expects that sad, lonely Mildred will oblige her by offering Winifred a place to live. Beautiful women in Pym's world are used to getting their own way. But Mildred does not want to live with Winifred. Nor does she want to please Allegra or Julian.

From the opening lines, Pym sets out her theme: "'Ah you ladies! Always on the spot when there's something happening!' The voice belonged to Mr Mallett, one of our churchwardens and its roguish tone made me start guiltily, almost as if I had no right to be discovered outside my own front door.'[7]

Helena Napier is a working woman – an anthropologist – who turns a blind eye to her husband's philandering, but takes revenge by a flirtation with a colleague. The splendidly named Everard Bone is perhaps an allusion to the villain of a remarkable novel called *Vera* by Pym's admired Elizabeth von Arnim. In that novel, Everard 'gaslights' his young wife, and keeps her a virtual prisoner in the marital home.

Helena (whom we are told is not an excellent woman) assumes along with everyone else that unmarried women have empty lives. When she discusses her imperfect, hasty 'war' marriage with Rocky, she speaks dismissively to Mildred: "'Of course you've never been married," she said, putting me in my place among the rows of excellent women.'[8] Mildred's old friend, William Caldicote, a thinly disguised version of Jock

Liddell, does not want her to 'throw herself away' in marriage: 'But my dear Mildred, *you* must not marry . . . Life is disturbing enough without these alarming suggestions. I always think of you being so very balanced and sensible, such an excellent woman. I do hope you're *not* thinking of getting married.'[9]

When Everard Bone finally does notice Mildred, he treats her ungraciously: '"Oh, I expect we shall be going somewhere for dinner," he said vaguely, "You may as well come too."' It is a similar kind of carelessness that makes Helena Napier use Mildred's toilet paper in their shared bathroom. It's a small detail, but, as always in Pym, revealing of character: 'The burden of keeping three people in toilet paper seemed to me rather a heavy one,' Mildred notes, drily.[10]

When Mildred and her friend Dora return to their old boarding school for a ceremony to honour her old headmistress, she feels that she is being judged by her friends: 'For after all, what had *we* done? We had not made particularly brilliant careers for ourselves and, most important of all, we had neither of us married. That was really it. It was the ring on the left hand that people at the Old Girls' Reunion looked for.'[11]

In fact, Mildred enjoys her single life and when she looks around at the married people around her, she does not feel envy. The Napiers' marriage is troubled and Mildred is sickened that she is, unwittingly, dragged into their messy relationship. Helena and Rocky play emotional games with one another, but they need an audience. Mildred becomes inextricably bound up with the disintegrating marriage. She goes along with Rocky to hear Helena and Everard read a jointly written paper at a meeting of the Learned Society of Anthropologists. Afterwards, Rocky begins to ask frivolous questions, chiefly to annoy his wife and Bone, as he suspects they are having an affair:

'What was that about a man being expected to sleep with an unmarried sister-in-law who is visiting his house?' he asked.

'That's called a joking relationship,' said Everard precisely.

'Not exactly what one would call a joke,' said Rocky, 'though it could be fun. It would depend on the sister-in-law, of course, Does he *have* to sleep with her?'

'Oh, Rocky, you don't understand,' said Helena impatiently. It was obvious that she and Everard did not appreciate jokes about their subject.

'I wonder if the study of societies where polygamy is a commonplace encourages immorality . . . Do anthropologists tend to have many wives at the same time?' he went on, 'Have you found that?'

'They would naturally tend to conceal such things,' said Everard with a half-smile, 'and one could hardly ask them.'

'Oh, they are drearily monogamous,' said Helena, 'and very virtuous in other ways too. Much better than many of these so-called good people who go to church.' She turned a half-amused, half-spiteful glance towards me.[12]

Mildred knows that she is being used by the Napiers in their passive-aggressive one-upmanship: 'I have never been good at games; people never chose me at school when it came to picking sides.' Furthermore, Helena twists the knife deeper into Mildred: '"You and Everard seemed to be having an interesting conversation," said Helena at last. "Was he declaring himself or something?" Her tone was rather light and cruel as if it were the most impossible thing in the world.'[13]

Mildred, walking past the parish hall, hears the sound of working-class Teddy Lemon (loosely based on Iain aka 'Starky') and his friends, and 'much prefers his rough honesty' to the superficial charm of the Napiers: 'My heart warmed towards them, so good and simple with their uncomplicated lives. If only I had come home straight after the paper.' The 'undercurrents' between the Napiers and 'their disturbing kind of life' is distasteful to Mildred, leading her to reflect that 'Love was rather a terrible thing.'[14]

It is tempting to suggest that Pym was channelling some of her own distaste for the complicated love life of the Glovers and her own part in it. She recorded in her diary at that time that a pleasant afternoon spent with one of her old female friends made a refreshing change from life at the Coppice. Similarly, Mildred enjoys spending time shopping with a girlfriend: 'I forgot all about the Napiers and the complications of knowing them. I was back in those happier days when the company of women friends had seemed enough.'[15]

Mildred *is* happier in the company of her female friends. She is tired of the gay bitchiness of William Caldicote, the superficial charm of Rocky, and even Father Julian Malory has become a disappointment. He has allowed himself to be 'taken in' by the beautiful but cold widow, Allegra Gray. Julian arrogantly believes that Mildred is in love with him but is too cowardly to tell her of his love for another woman. He ensures that Allegra breaks the news of his engagement. When he subsequently meets Mildred, she is shocked that he seems to *want* her to be upset by his news, merely to inflate his ego:

'Ah, Mildred, you understand. Dear Mildred, it would have been a fine thing if it could have been . . . it's so splendid of you to understand like this. I know it must have been a shock, a blow almost, I might say,' he laboured on, heavy and humourless, not at all like his usual self. Did love always make men like this? I wondered.

  'I was never in love with you, if that's what you meant,' I said, thinking it was time to be blunt. 'I never expected that you would marry *me*.'

'Dear Mildred,' he smiled, 'you are not the kind of person to expect things as your right even though they may be.'[16]

Here, we are worlds away from the gorgeous comic simplicity of *Some Tame Gazelle* and *Crampton Hodnet*. Pym is writing on a whole new level. All of her rage at Gordon Glover and his cowardice in not telling her the real reason for his rejection – that she was merely a pleasant interlude – is contained in this masterly scene. 'I saw that it was no use trying to convince Julian that I was not heartbroken at the news of his engagement.'

Mildred is not jealous of Allegra, for she sees her as she is: a beautiful but hard woman, who is used to having her own way and who will turn Julian's sister out of doors the moment she gets a chance. Love, or infatuation, makes Julian behave badly and cowardly. Similarly, Everard Bone loses his nerve when he discovers that Helena intends to leave her husband for him. He flees to Derbyshire and asks Mildred to break the news that he is breaking off the affair. Mildred, not unreasonably, responds: 'But men ought to be able to manage their own affairs . . . After all most of them don't seem to mind speaking frankly and making people unhappy. I don't see why you should.'[17]

Time and time again, Mildred is used by other people to sort out their mess. Life is made up of 'small unpleasantnesses'. It is as though her feelings never count. The sad truth is that she knows it: 'I pulled myself up and told myself to stop these ridiculous thoughts, wondering if it is that we can never stop trying to analyse the motives of people who have no personal interest in us, in the vain hope that perhaps they may have just a little after all.'

When Winifred Malory is turned out of her house after a quarrel with Allegra, it is Mildred who is left to pick up the

pieces. When Rocky and Helena separate, it is Mildred who is
left to sort out their dirty flat and send on the furniture. It is
Mildred who finally reunites the estranged couple. Why wouldn't
she? She's an excellent woman.

CHAPTER VII

In which Miss Pym
leaves Pimlico for Barnes

Pym's new landlady sounds as if she had sprung from the pages of one of her novels. Her name was Mrs Beltane, and she was 'scented and jingling with bracelets'. Pym and Hilary had decided to move from Pimlico to larger accommodation south of the river, in the suburbs. They had found a spacious two-bedroomed flat with a sitting room, kitchen and bathroom, at 47 Nassau Road in a converted house in leafy Barnes. Mrs Beltane, 'refined and preoccupied by her appearance', lived on the ground floor.[1] She told the Pym sisters that Harrods delivered to Barnes, though it was unlikely that they could afford to shop at Harrods.

Barnes, bounded by the River Thames, Barnes Common and Richmond Park, felt very much like a village. It had literary associations dating back to the time of Henry Fielding, who spent the last few years of his life in a house overlooking the common. It was not on the underground circuit, so Barbara took the number 9 bus to work at the International African Institute. Around the same time, the offices and library of the institute moved to new premises in Fetter Lane, just off Fleet Street.

Barbara shared an office with young Cambridge graduate,

Hazel Holt, who would become a great friend and her first biographer. Holt remembered Pym as 'a tall, quiet, reserved woman'. The pair shared a small rather dingy office with olive-green filing cabinets and 'cigarette-scarred desks' facing one another. They typed on old-fashioned typewriters using two fingers. Holt recalled the map cupboard, which was under Barbara's control. It was waist-high and Pym would spend much of her time crouching on the linoleum floor 'in search of an elusive map'. Behind Pym's desk was a bookcase containing all the file copies of the ethnographic survey *Africa*, jostling next to a motley collection of novels and poetry. More exciting was their version of a 'juju', containing 'magical objects', including a Nigerian wooden bull-roarer, feathers and a lock of Holt's hair (which Pym had snipped off one dull afternoon when she was feeling bored). If the women needed a new reviewer, or if the proofs were late, they would make an offering of a pressed flower or a paperclip to their 'juju' – 'only partly in jest'.[2]

Around this time, Pym wrote another radio play called *Parrot's Eggs*. It referred to a custom attributed to the Yoruba tribe in west Africa, who would apparently send their king a parrot's egg when they wished him to resign by suicide. The play was never performed.

All of this delicious anthropological detail and more would find its way into Pym's stories. In *Excellent Women*, Everard Bone is worried sick that he has been spotted by colleagues in a compromising position with Helena Napier, and Mildred tries to comfort him by saying: 'Anthropologists must see such very odd behaviour in primitive societies that they probably think anything we do here is very tame.' Bone responds drily: 'Don't you believe it.'[3] In one of her notebooks of ideas, Pym wrote: 'The Hadzapi will eat anything that is edible except the hyena.'

Holt was an English graduate and was surprised to learn that Miss Pym had published a novel called *Some Tame Gazelle*. She assumed that it was a book about game-hunting in Africa and did not bother to buy a copy. When a friend lent her a copy, she was 'enchanted' and now looked with 'considerable interest' on this reserved woman 'who had written this perfect book'.[4]

Pym's first book was published in May 1950 and received good reviews, which no doubt bolstered her confidence. Praise from the reviewers focused on Pym's wit, 'so gentle that the reader scarcely notices the claws', and her interest in village life and small things: 'working in *petit point* she makes each stitch with perfect precision'. Unsurprisingly and surely much to her delight, some of the reviewers drew comparisons with Jane Austen: 'There is a touch of Trollope here, of Mrs Gaskell, Jane Austen and Mrs Thirkell, but Miss Pym's sharp fresh fun is all her own,' and: 'This excellent first novel on a theme of English village life is in the direct tradition of Jane Austen.' Happily, most of the reviewers found it funny: 'I may have been in a singularly happy mood when I read it, but I found it quite uproariously funny,' wrote one. Another spoke of its 'rich comedy' and 'its quiet and good-humoured ironies'. The review by the novelist Antonia White in the influential *New Statesman and Nation* was glowing: 'she is a modest and original writer who owes nothing to anyone'. For a first novel, this was excellent coverage and it encouraged Pym to keep writing. White's perceptive review drew attention to the subtext of the humour: 'Her portraits of three clergymen . . . are gentle but relentless, as a conscientious snapshot can be more devastating than the cruellest caricature.'[5] Whether by design or not, Pym's novels would darken in tone as she matured, though she always leavened them with her unique sense of irony.

Her friends wrote to congratulate her. John Barnicot's wife, Elizabeth, told her that she could hardly put it down. Jock was pleased that she hadn't spoiled it, and said that it was still the book they knew and loved, with every tiny blot removed. Pym was no doubt longing to hear from Gordon. He was now remarried (with indecent haste) and wrote that he was intending to buy a copy of 'Some Tame Gazelle – or is it lame gazelle?' A week later he wrote that he found it 'quite, quite delightful – Hoccleve and Mbawawa are beautiful creations'.

Fan letters preserved by Pym praised the character of the Archdeacon. So what of the Archdeacon himself? Pym sent Henry a copy, 'without an inscription so you can give it to somebody as a birthday present. I should never know.' She told him that she hoped it would amuse him: 'Please don't notice all the places where I ought to have put commas.'[6]

Henry did not reply until September. He was now separated from Elsie and was in a new relationship with a German woman called Susi. Susi seemed to be somewhat threatened by his relationship with Pym. Henry quoted from a letter that Susi had written to him about the book. She hadn't enjoyed it at first: 'I suppose I was a little annoyed about the extraordinary claim she has on you, too. But soon she caught me.' Her praise was grudging, but she ended with a generous and honest, if ambivalent, sentiment: 'What a good heart she must have! I don't ever want to meet her. She moved me to tears when I finished it this morning.'[7] It is typically insensitive and 'Archdicanially' of Henry to have added this passage from his insecure new lover.

By February 1951, she had completed *Excellent Women* and was starting a new novel which would draw on her Oxford years and her life working in an office. It would also draw on her failed love affair with Gordon Glover. In her notebook, she made it explicit that her new anti-hero would be based on the man she felt had so badly let her down.

CHAPTER VIII

In which Jock and Henry return (briefly) to the Story

Jock Liddell's friendship with Henry Harvey had always been complicated, but by the 1950s it was almost broken.

Jock's loyal support of Pym during the Henry years was partially governed by his own love/hate attitude towards Harvey. His unkind depiction of Henry in his Oxford novel *The Last Enchantments* had not helped the relationship. Jock, who could be so kind and professed to hate cruelty, was capable of directing lacerating cattiness onto those he loved or had once loved. In the novel, Henry is 'Cyprian' – a womaniser and a breaker of hearts. Pym is one of his victims: she is 'Steeple Crampton', who writes Cyprian 'noble and tear-stained letters'.[1] Cyprian's lovers say that they will always follow his career with interest. Liddell adds nastily, though truthfully, 'they must have found it difficult to follow, for it never came to much and was rather devious'. It would no doubt have hurt Henry to read Liddell's words: 'He was not my friend, for we did not really like each other – but as we lived on the same staircase, habit and laziness caused us to spend a lot of time together at one period in our university careers.' Cyprian is peevish, selfish and self-centred; his worst vice is envy.[2]

If a tone of bitterness had set in, it may be partially explained by the heartbreaks that Jock had endured – the death of his beloved brother and that of his lover, Gamal. The two men had died within months of one another. Back in 1944, and before he had met Eddie, Jock had confided in Pym about his great love affair. Gamal was an Egyptian pilot who crashed his plane in fog over the hills of Cairo. It had been devastating for Jock. The two men had spent every moment together that they could manage. Gamal was, he wrote, 'one of those lovely radiant personalities who make everyone happy where they go'. He was supposed to be on his way to see Jock when the air crash happened. The Englishman was left distraught: 'I thought I should go out of my mind at first.' A bad attack of asthma had distracted him and Gamal's family were loving and supportive – he told Pym that they had shown 'the most touching devotion to me'.[3]

With Gamal's death, he continued, he had lost something 'wonderful and unrepeatable' and a love that he had never deserved. He had suicidal thoughts – 'I want life to stop' – but felt that he must try to go on. When Don died two months later, Jock was broken. He had suffered much and some of the pain and anger he felt was projected onto Henry Harvey. Jock had repeatedly warned Pym that Henry would feel analogous 'rage, pain and jealousy' when she published Some Tame Gazelle. Pym seemingly was still loyal to the memory of Henry and did not rise to the bait. Nor did Henry seem to seethe with rage and jealousy. If her portrayal of gossipy, 'spiteful old-maidish' William Caldicote in Excellent Women was a rebuke to Jock, he did not seem to take the hint or to mind very much.

Jock's parody of Henry – 'Cyprian was a student of Human Nature, he said (he took a very bad degree in History)' – strikes one of the few unkind notes in what is a beautiful and almost unbearably sad novel. It is also a poignant love letter to Oxford and to Liddell's beloved brother. The narrator returns to Christminster (Oxford) after the war and his brother's death. 'I could say something of the heartache with which I walked under the dripping branches of trees, leaning out of the drenched gardens of our residential suburb – oh, beloved city, to which my heart is tied by a thousand nerve-strings and all of them twisted with pain.'[4]

CHAPTER IX

Miss Pym the Novelist takes Tea with the Distinguished Author Elizabeth Bowen in the Company of Several Homosexuals

Jock had joked that Barbara was once again 'Miss Pym', which is how she was referred to at the African Institute. From her notebooks and her new novel, *Jane and Prudence*, one could deduce that she found office life sometimes tedious and dull. There was the inevitable filing, index-compiling, proofreading, broken up by lunch and the welcome sound of the tea trolley. But now Pym had another life. That of a Jonathan Cape published author.

She had always loved her alter egos (Sandra, Pymska and the rest) and she had toyed with the idea of publishing her novels under a pen name such as Crampton Pym.[1] She felt sure that her colleagues, and in particular her boss Daryll Forde, would not read her novels. She might then have been surprised by one of her fan letters, which came from the distinguished Oxford anthropologist C. K. Meek, fellow of the Royal Geographical Society and the Royal Anthropological Institute, who was a frequent visitor to the International African Institute: 'I enjoyed the fun you poke at anthropology, including the two passages which were clearly written under the boredom of having to wade through my "Sudanese Kingdom".'[2]

Such moments of potential embarrassment did not stop Pym from using her working life and her colleagues as copy for her novels. One evening, when the day's work was done, she was invited for a drink in the office with the formidable Mrs Wyatt and Daryll Forde. She wasn't quite sure if she had been invited or had misread the invitation. She thought this misunderstanding would be good in a novel, once again conflating herself with a fictional heroine, who would be a secretary: 'She the secretary (or me) isn't quite sure if he meant *her* to have a drink too.' She decided that in her story, the drink would be with one of 'his' friends and she would feel inferior in 'dress and wit'. The 'he' of her next novel was to be Dr Grampian, based on Daryll Forde: 'D[aryll] should be the model for Gramp. If there is one cigarette in his case, he looks regretfully, even thoughtfully at it, then takes it himself.'[3]

Meanwhile, Pym was enjoying her success as an author. In the previous November, she had gone to a tea given for the author Elizabeth Bowen. She'd been invited by some Oxford contemporaries, Jacqueline Hope-Wallace, a civil servant, and Philip Hope-Wallace, who was drama critic of the *Manchester Guardian* and a music reviewer for *The Gramophone*. Both were gay. They shared a house in St John's Wood with another Oxford contemporary, Veronica Wedgwood (of the famous pottery family). Veronica, later made a dame, wrote many widely read works of seventeenth-century history. She and Jacqueline were faithful partners for nearly seventy years, from their under-graduate days until Dame Veronica's death in 1997 (Jacqueline lived to over a hundred, dying in 2011). Their 'charming' drawing room was on the first floor of the house: 'Coral red curtains and turquoise walls – small Victorian chairs and "objects" . . . a kind of cosy shabbiness.'[4]

Elizabeth Bowen – posh, Anglo-Irish, sophisticated, bisexual – was in black with grey and black pearls and pretty earrings, 'little diamond balls'. Pym thought her stammer was not as bad as she had expected. Pym was a little intimidated: 'the young author in her nervousness talks rather too much about herself.' They spoke about methods of composition. Elizabeth said she was 'better at a typewriter than curled up in an armchair'. She was kind to Pym, the budding author – 'obviously feels she ought to know more about me than she can possibly know'.[5]

The tea party was an important moment for Pym, the older author and the younger together, and, especially given the bohemian quality of the company, no doubt made her feel a million miles away from her office job. One of the guests at the tea party told Pym that two of the editors at Cape, Daniel George (Bowen's editor) and William Plomer, were in agreement over the quality of her book. They both thought it 'very amusing' – apparently such concord between them was a rarity. South African-born Plomer was also gay. He had moved in the Auden– Isherwood circle in the thirties and later wrote libretti for Benjamin Britten. A sharp-eyed editor, who recognised the talent of Ian Fleming (he would be the dedicatee of *Goldfinger*), he wrote poetry under the pseudonym Robert Pagan and included openly homosexual relationships in a number of his novels.

The following January, Pym had tea at Fortnum's with the novelist Elizabeth Taylor, who was a friend of Jock's. Taylor was an almost exact contemporary. Her first novel, *At Mrs Lippincote's*, published in 1945, had been well received and she went on to write a further eleven novels, as well as short stories. Her novels depicting middle- and upper-class life are beautifully observed and psychologically acute. Taylor had greatly admired Jock's *The Last Enchantments* and had written to him to express her emotional response: 'It was love I felt; yes when I have read your books I feel more loving.'[6] They began a deep and intimate correspondence, which lasted until her death. One of her short stories, 'The Letter Writers', was based on her epistolary relationship with Liddell.

Elizabeth Taylor was also a friend of Ivy Compton-Burnett. Jock reported that when Ivy first met Elizabeth she remarked: 'She is a young woman who looks as if she never had to wash her gloves.'⁷ Taylor was extremely beautiful and elegant and it is possible that Pym felt intimidated. By this time, Taylor had published her fifth novel. Jock thought her fourth novel, *A Wreath of Roses*, a masterpiece. He also said that this was the time that Taylor was attacked by envious reviewers. Years later, Pym said that Taylor was socially shy and was sometimes misunderstood as being aloof or bored.

With such exciting literary encounters, as well as publisher's lunches with editor Daniel George, Pym had finally achieved success as an author. *Excellent Women*, published in 1952, would be her most popular and widely acclaimed novel. In the meantime, she was well ahead with plans for a third novel. Once again, Pym was leading a divided life – Miss Pym, personal assistant to Daryll Forde, and Barbara Pym, the author.

Nineteen fifty-two was also the year that Pym would meet a man who would be of great importance in her life. His name was Bob Smith. He was a friend of Jock's and had expressed an interest in meeting the author of *Some Tame Gazelle*. Bob was Pym's type, dark and handsome, with a touch of Julian Amery about him. He was six years younger than her and desperate to get his first novel published. He wondered if she might be able to read his work and give an opinion. Miss Pym was willing to meet him and give it a try.

CHAPTER X

The Celebrated Miss Barbara Pym

Pym's old love, Henry Harvey, remarried in 1952. Earlier that year, Jock had sent Pym a rather extraordinary letter: 'Elsie is divorcing Henry – what a relief it is to write irreverently of Henry and how angry he'd be! Like people making fun of the Devil . . . I'd like [Susi] to make Henry happy and take him RIGHT OUT OF OUR LIVES. This must confirm you in your state of single blessedness.'[1]

But Pym was long past romantic feelings for him. 'We were both young and stupid in those days,' she told Henry. 'You can be quite sure I don't bear you any ill will about anything . . . now we can have the satisfaction of being mean to each other – I by not giving you a copy of my new novel and you by not buying it.'[2] She had, however, been ruminating on her failed relationship with Gordon Glover. She recalled her discussion with Honor about Gordon's treacherous penchant for sharing the same special interests with different girlfriends. Logan Pearsall Smith's *All Trivia*, for example, and visits to churchyards, and theatres.

Her new novel, *Excellent Women*, was published in March that year. The reviews were even more positive (not always the case with a second book) and the title became a 'Book Society

Recommendation'. Marghanita Laski of the *Observer* raved: 'I don't think I've ever before recommended a novel as one that everybody will enjoy', while the *News Chronicle* made that most flattering of all possible comparisons: 'We needn't bring Jane Austen into it, but Miss Pym is writing in a great tradition and knows it.' The review from John Betjeman must have been especially gratifying, given her long-standing admiration of his poetry. He emphasised the splendid humour of the novel, describing it as a 'perfect book' with 'acid powers of description'. Pym's wit, 'quiet restraint', and shrewd powers of observation were noted. Praise from other writers was important to Pym. The author F. Tennyson Jesse wrote a careful and perceptive letter to Jonathan Cape: 'It is very brilliant indeed to write about what most people would think were dull people and make them all absorbingly interesting. That is what she has achieved . . . It is beautifully done.'[3]

The book was a triumph. One of her friends wrote to tell Pym that the *Times* bookshop had sold out of copies and that W. H. Smith had a charming display in their window. Elizabeth Barnicot thought Pym was a better novelist than Jock Liddell. A poignant fan letter came from Winchester: 'For 17 years I was in the category of "excellent women" myself . . . my experience, thoughts and emotions were so exactly like Mildred's that you might have been writing about me.'[4] Strikingly, some of the readers responded to a note of sadness and wistfulness in the portrayal of Mildred. Jock, with his usual acuity, wrote that 'the tone is beautifully and faultlessly managed – one feels Mildred genuinely expects so little for herself that it is almost sad'. The *Irish Times* also drew attention to the novel's undertow, 'under a varnish of superb comedy . . . there lurks a most poignant tragedy'. Another reviewer, David Cox, found it 'entertaining and disturbing', with Pym's portrayal of men almost embarrassingly acute: 'I'm sure every "man" who reads it will ask himself: Am I very dull? Am I very inconsiderate? Do I imagine women are in love with me when they obviously aren't?' Perhaps the only dissenting voice was that of a reader who thought the book spoilt by 'touches of vulgarity', asking priggishly (and unintentionally hilariously) 'who does it please, to talk about Ladies' Rooms and sanitary paper?'[5]

The note of tristesse that some of the reviewers and readers observed may well have irritated Pym. To her mind, Mildred Lathbury was not a figure of pity, though she is pitilessly put upon. Pym's next heroine (also a single woman, who is about to turn thirty) scorns smug married couples who live dull, conventional lives. She enjoys the freedoms of her independent life. Prudence Bates closely resembles Pym and offers a spirited rebuttal of the 'sad spinster' myth.

CHAPTER XI

The Tale of Jane and Prudence

Jane and Prudence opens with an Oxford gaudy held at Prudence's old college. Jane Cleveland, Prudence's former tutor and now friend, is married to a clergyman and has a daughter. Prudence Bates is a good-looking, cigarette-smoking, gin-swilling, beautifully dressed, unmarried working woman with her own flat in London and a string of boyfriends. Of all Pym's heroines, Prudence is the one who represents how Barbara Pym would have liked to see herself – though she never flattered herself into thinking that she was beautiful. It is striking that Prudence was also the name of Gordon Glover's daughter, with whom Pym had continued to enjoy a warm friendship.

Overtones of Jane Austen's *Emma* sound in the relationship between Prudence and Jane, which resembles that between Emma and her former governess Miss Taylor. Pym references *Emma*, too, in her joke about Austen's most famous spinster: 'Prudence disliked being called "Miss Bates"; if she resembled any character in fiction, it was certainly not poor silly Miss Bates.'[1] Pym noted in her journal for February 1952, that she was rereading Jane Austen 'to see how she tied up the loose ends'.[2]

Prudence, who is educated in a women's college similar to

the one Pym attended, had a stream of admirers in her student days: 'Lawrence and Henry and Philip, so many of them . . . all coming up the drive, in a great body'. Jane describes Prudence's love affairs as an 'occupation', and Prudence is now in love with her difficult, married boss, Arthur Grampian, who barely notices her existence.

As Pym observed in her notebook, 'Gramps' was based on Daryll Forde, which rather begs the question: did Pym have a similar crush on her married boss? When Prudence tries to explain her feelings for Dr Grampian, she describes their relationship as '*negative* . . . the complete lack of *rapport* . . . You see underneath all this, I feel that there really is something, something *positive*.' Jane tries to stifle a yawn.[3] Miss Bates works as 'a sort of personal assistant' to Dr Grampian and looks after 'the humdrum side of his work, seeing books through the press and that kind of thing'. She becomes irritated by her friends and relations, with their obsessive desire to see her happily married: 'I often think being married would be rather a nuisance. I've got a nice flat and am so used to living on my own I should hardly know what to do with a husband.'[4]

Pym alternates her narrative between Jane's conventional and rather boring married life in a country parsonage and Prudence's single, more exciting but erratic life in the city. If Prudence is scornful about Jane's life, Jane pities Prudence who had 'got into the way of preferring unsatisfactory love affairs to any others, so that it was almost becoming a bad habit'.[5]

Unknown to her closest friends, Pym had been having an affair with a married man. His name was Thomas Kendrick, and he was the father of her close friend and fellow Wren, Frances. Tom was keeper of British and medieval antiquities at the British Museum, and, in the year that Pym began her affair, was appointed museum director. He was a jovial man, and a collector of bus tickets, which he mounted on the wall of his official residence. He sent Pym a postcard on which he drew a special bus ticket with a red corner, and told her that if she ever found such a ticket she would be 'more than ever welcome'.[6] A surviving letter is suggestively flirtatious: 'I am so glad you liked our matinee idols. You could not believe they would turn into such coy tarts.'[7] Tom was known to be a philanderer. He was not on good terms with his daughter, Frances, and she had no idea that her father and best friend were lovers. The affair began with lunches, and then became more intimate, though it was never serious. Pym made no reference to the relationship in her journals, and it soon fizzled out. Prudence Bates later appears again in Pym's 1958 novel, *A Glass of Blessings*, as the glamorous single woman who has continued to date married men.

In another echo of *Emma*, Jane Cleveland plays 'matchmaker' with Prudence and an attractive widower, Fabian Driver. As we have seen, Pym often based her characters on real-life models. She later wrote in a piece about her compositional methods that many of her male friends claimed they were the model for Rocky Napier. The fact that Rocky was her most conventional romantic hero was perhaps the reason, she joked. She claimed that Rocky was a composite of three men she had known. But there was only one man she based Fabian upon – and that was Gordon Glover. Fabian is a 'Gordonish' type – a philanderer, who is incapable of sexual fidelity and is so heartless that he brings his lovers to meet his wife. After his wife's death, this monster of ego and selfishness places a large photograph of himself atop her grave instead of a headstone.

Pym had contemplated publishing her Gordon journals, 'After Christmas', but seems to have abandoned this idea, perhaps feeling that it would be a step too far. She would have to be content with Fabian. The character bears more than a passing physical resemblance to Gordon Glover: he is handsome, leonine, with curly hair, greying at the temples. He wears a 'carefully casual tweed suit' and 'brogued suede shoes'. He married Constance, a 'gentle, faded-looking' older woman, who brought him 'a comfortable amount of money as well as a great deal of love'. Her death has come as a great shock to him because 'he had almost forgotten her existence'. Now, rather than philandering, he is playing the role of the 'inconsolable widower'. He is described as being fond of 'grand gestures' rather than 'niggling details'.

The person revealing the details about Fabian's character to Jane Cleveland is a spinster, Jessie Morrow. In name, appearance and status, she is the same character from Pym's North Oxford novel, *Crampton Hodnet*, but this reincarnation is colder and more hardened. When Jane first meets Fabian in church it is significant that he is carrying a large, phallic marrow. His first words are also revealing of character:

> 'Of course, a man must have his meat,' pronounced Mrs Mayhew.
> 'Certainly he must,' said a pleasant voice in the porch.[8]

Fabian, conscious of his good looks, has mastered an intense stare that women find irresistible. He is gallant and charming. He tells Jane Cleveland that he lives alone, having to cook and look after himself: '"One manages," said Fabian, "one has to, of course." The third person seemed to add pathos, which was perhaps just what he intended, Jane thought.'[9]

Jane soon discovers that Fabian is looked after by a competent cook, who feeds him 'casseroles of hearts'. She is struck by the symbolism: '"A casserole of hearts," murmured Jane in confusion, thinking of the grave and the infidelities. Did he eat his victims then?' Nevertheless, Jane (perhaps unkindly, certainly unwisely) decides he would 'do for Prudence',[10] and it is not long before they begin a love affair.

According to Pym's first biographer, Jane Cleveland was based on Irena Pym. As with Jessie Morrow and Miss Doggett, a version of Mrs Cleveland appears in *Crampton Hodnet*. Jane has large eyes and short, rough curly hair like Irena's. She dresses untidily, always looking as if she's about to feed the chickens. Jane is clever, fond of quoting lines of verse from the English poets, but there is a quality of vagueness about her which is a source of irritation to her daughter, who is about to go up to Oxford. There is more than a touch of Julian Amery in the character of the smooth-talking MP Edward Lyall, whose 'charming smile . . . seemed to include everybody'.[11]

Prudence loves Jane, but is also irked by her shabbiness of dress and 'her rather loud, bright voice'. She also resents Jane's attempts to marry her off – as Pym resented her own mother's romantic interventions. Jane is another example of a bright, Oxford-educated woman who has not fulfilled her 'early promise', and whose research and career have been curtailed by marriage and motherhood.

Prudence has also not fulfilled her early promise. She works in an office alongside Miss Clothier and Miss Trapnell and two typists (one of whom is the marvellously pretty and giggling Marilyn) who also make the tea. Pym trains her unerring eye on office politics as the female staff quibble and spar with one another in an unedifying game of petty one-upmanship:

'I wonder if we might have one bar of the fire on?' asked Miss Clothier at last.

'Oh, it isn't cold,' said Miss Trapnell. 'Do you find it cold, Miss Bates?' . . .

'No, it doesn't seem cold,' she said.

'Well, of course I have been sitting here since a quarter to ten,' said Miss Clothier. 'So perhaps I have got cold sitting.'

'Ah, yes; you may have got cold sitting,' agreed Miss Trapnell. 'I have only been here since *five* to ten.'[12]

The influence of Ivy Compton-Burnett can be heard in the passive-aggressive conversations between Miss Clothier and Miss Trapnell:

> 'Would you like a biscuit, Miss Clothier?' asked Miss Trapnell . . . 'These are Lincoln cream. My grocer always saves them for me.'
>
> 'Thank you', said Miss Clothier. 'I wonder if Dr Grampian would like one?'
>
> 'I shan't offer them. He gets a good lunch at his club and I expect he had a good breakfast.'
>
> 'Miss Bates might not like it if you were to give him biscuits,' said Miss Clothier obscurely.
>
> 'There would be nothing in it if I did,' said Miss Trapnell.[13]

Though Prudence is irritated by her female colleagues, she believes she is intellectually superior. She rails against men like Dr Grampian, despite her love for him. Whilst he dines on smoked salmon in his 'grand club with noble portals', Prudence eats shepherd's pie or stuffed marrow alone in a small rather grimy self-service cafeteria. What Pym's work colleagues thought of her novels can only be guessed at. She perfectly captures the banality, the monotony and the shabbiness of office life, with the weak cups of tea, occasionally enlivened by cigarettes and tinned Nescafé.

Fabian is too in love with himself to love anyone else. He sits in the pub, 'contemplating his reflection in the looking-glass framed with mahogany and surrounded by bottles'. He lies to Jessie Morrow when he tells her sadly that his late wife was fond of quinces. She sees through his ruse: 'As if Fabian had known or cared what Constance was fond of – why, Miss Doggett had several times offered her quinces and she always refused them.' His 'little romantic affairs' during his marriage are 'to bolster up his self-respect'. He recalls how his wife invited his lovers for the weekend, where they would sit under the walnut tree discussing him, 'or so he had always imagined'[14] – just as Pym and Honor had endlessly discussed Gordon and his foibles. Though Prudence realises that Fabian is a bit of a bore, she thinks they will make a handsome couple.

Prudence's colourful clothes provide clues to her life. She entertains Fabian at her flat in a dark-red velvet housecoat. Jane realises when she sees the garment that Prudence must be his mistress. At the office she wears dark, elegant, printed dresses, which stand out against the other women's cottons and rayon. At the Clevelands' dinner party, Jane wears an indeterminate summer dress, whilst Prudence is dressed in filmy black chiffon. Tensions arise at Fabian's tea party when Jessie Morrow deliberately spills tea over Prudence's well-cut lilac dress. Prudence does not know that Jessie is a rival for Fabian's affections. There is something cold and shocking in Jessie's pursuit of Fabian, knowing as she does what a monster he is and how badly he behaved to his wife. In a masterly touch, she seduces Fabian wearing his dead wife's blue velvet dress that she has purloined.

Shoes are an indicator of class. Constance's are those of a gentlewoman, 'long and narrow and of such good leather'. By contrast, Fabian is imagined as wearing brown and white shoes. Jock Liddell noted that such indicators suggest Constance has married beneath her and that Fabian is 'common'. His vulgarity is also suggested in his taking a country walk without an umbrella.[15] Fabian, of course, cannot bring himself to tell Prudence that their affair is over. He asks Jane to break the news: 'Fabian clasped his hands together in a despairing gesture. "Oh what am I to do," he moaned, pacing about the room. "I haven't the courage to tell her yet."'[16]

Jane's already dim opinion of Fabian is compounded by the knowledge that he gave Prudence the same volume of poetry that his wife had once given him. Worse; he has included the very same verse inscription. This gesture is Pym's *Trivia* moment. The feeling of betrayal when a lover shares the same token or cherished book with another woman: 'Had it been somewhere in the back of his mind for all those years, to be brought out again, as a woman, searching through her piece-bag for a patch, might come upon a scrap of rare velvet or brocade?'[17]

But Pym has the last laugh with Fabian. He has been trapped in a marriage with Jessie, who makes it clear that she will not tolerate infidelity. And then, with a last devastating flick of the switch, Pym consigns Fabian/Gordon to literary posterity with an innocently withering comment from some young undergraduates. 'Do you think this Fabian man attractive?' one called Paul says to his girlfriend, Flora.

To which she replies: 'Yes, I suppose so, in a rather used Byronic sort of way. But he's rather middle-aged really.'[18]

CHAPTER XII

In which Miss Pym meets Robert Smith, is promoted to Assistant Editor of *Africa*, and Marks & Spencer takes Umbrage

Once again, Jock Liddell proved himself to be a good friend when he sent Robert Smith to Pym. Bob was a civil servant who had met Jock in Egypt. He had also worked for the Foreign Office in Poland, which had inspired him to write a novel, *The Winter World*. Bob was six years younger than Pym, but his rather old-fashioned manners and 'deep clerical-sounding voice' made him seem much older. They shared much in common – going on 'church crawls' together and discussing books.[1]

Pym seems to have had her usual crush: 'The agony of wondering if he will send a Christmas card!' According to Hazel Holt and Hilary Pym, the romance quickly settled into a firm and solid friendship. As with Barbara's friendship with Jock, it would last until the end of her life. But why did the initial spark so quickly burn out? Had Pym read the signals wrong? Bob Smith never married; his romantic interests did not lie with women. The poignant Pym theme of an unattainable love was beginning to take a new direction.

In February 1953, Pym sent the manuscript of *Jane and Prudence* to Daniel George, the editor at Cape whom she shared with Elizabeth Bowen. But she wasn't wholly confident in it: 'I had wanted the contrasting lives of Jane and Prudence, in town and country, to stand out more. As it is they are perhaps just two rather tiresome and unsuccessful women.' Pym also expressed concern about chapter 12 in which Jane asks Prudence if she is Fabian's mistress. David replied positively, but with the recommendation that she omit some of the 'Oh dear, Oh, Oh well' exclamations. She also began working on what would become her fourth published novel, which was to be set in the work world of anthropology and home life of London suburbia.

Upon Beatrice Wyatt's retirement, Pym became the assistant editor of *Africa*, seeing the journal through the press from copy-editing to final proofreading, while Hazel Holt was promoted to become her assistant. Holt recalls Pym's sense of pride in her job. One of her new duties was to be in charge of the *Africa* advertisements. Holt remembered that with the more important clients, such as banks and airlines, she would 'assume the faintest hint of Madison Avenue'.[2]

Pym's third novel to reach print, *Jane and Prudence*, was published in September 1953. The reviews were respectful, if not ecstatic. The *Observer* found the structure too 'loose and rambling not to disappoint after *Excellent Women*'. Likewise the *Manchester Guardian* considered it a 'horrid disappointment' after *Excellent Women* – her characters 'miseducated nincompoops'. Nevertheless, Frederick Laws of the *News Chronicle*, who had raved over *Excellent Women*, described *Jane and Prudence* as 'a brilliant and charming novel, which you will not easily forget'. And the redoubtable socialite, author and occasional book reviewer Lady Cynthia Asquith noted the 'deft dialogue . . . almost as delectably dry as Miss Compton-Burnett'.[3]

Friends and acquaintances were supportive. The general feeling was that she was 'getting into her stride', as one friend suggested. Several friends preferred it to *Excellent Women*: 'The characters seem more real – particularly Prudence.'[4] Jock found it witty and kind and sharp. A blow was suddenly struck, however, when a letter arrived from the legal department of Marks and Spencer. The store had taken umbrage at Jane Cleveland's comment about their clothes: 'When we become distressed we shall be glad of an old dress from Marks and Spencer as we've never been used to anything better.'

The letter could almost have come straight from the pages of a Pym novel: 'This reference is clearly derogatory of the Company as both in terms and by implication it suggests that dresses worn by this Company are of inferior quality and unfit for wear by persons of the class who buy their hats from Marshall's or Debenham's.' Cape responded robustly that no harm had been intended and Pym wrote dutifully that she had the greatest respect for the store: 'The ironical thing is that I regularly buy and wear their clothes and think them excellent.'[5]

Finally, Cape agreed to alter the offending passage in future editions, though this does not seem to have happened. The incident was just the kind of 'umbrage taking' that Pym found most amusing. The fact that the legal department took such a strong line suggests Pym's ever-growing popularity as a novelist. The letter from Marks and Spencer actually quoted the fact that Pym had been described as the author of books 'worthy of Jane Austen' as a reason for their threat of legal action.

CHAPTER XIII

Miss Pym enters the New Elizabethan Age

On the cool and drizzly day of 2 June 1953, Queen Elizabeth II was crowned at Westminster Abbey. There was a marathon eight-hour-long live BBC broadcast, a breakthrough for the history of television. For most people it was the first time they had watched an event on TV. An estimated thirty-two million British people tuned in, with a further one million listening on the radio. Barbara Pym noted the date in her diary, as she had recorded the death, lying-in and funeral of the queen's father, George VI. Pym had gone to the lying in on 13 February 1952 – 'very dim and cold, footsteps muffled on a thick carpet . . . the face of one of the yeomen of the guard, carved out of wood'. She noted the glitter of diamonds from the crown and the white flowers on the coffin.[1] And she began to wonder whether these ancient rituals were so very different from the tribal customs studied by the academics who submitted their papers to the institute.

In Pym's next novel, which was set in the world of anthropological research, her young hero observes the television aerials silhouetted against the London skyline, describing them as 'a symbol of the age we live in'. Tom, who is an anthropologist, may think they look 'almost beautiful', but he is saddened by his uncle's addiction, which prevents him from joining in the fun of the village carnival and festival: his uncle has become 'a kind of prisoner, or a sacrifice laid before the altar of the television set'.[2] The wit comes from the anthropological metaphor in which a distinctive but mundane feature of contemporary life is described in similar terms to the tribal practices Pym read about in the learned pages of *Africa*.

It was details such as this that gave Pym's novels a sense of realism and authenticity. One of her admirers wrote a fan letter in which he praised her understanding of 'post-war human beings'. All the pomp and ceremony of the queen's coronation shed some much-needed glamour on post-war Britain, where meat was still rationed at 2 shillings a week.

Pym's anthropological novel, as yet untitled in 1953, shows her at her most grimly realistic. She sets much of the action in London suburbia and in the research institution of a red-brick university. We are a far cry from the glamour and glittering charm of Oxford, where the chestnuts flower and the undergraduates punt on the river. The fabulous high-camp aesthetes of *Crampton Hodnet*, Gabriel and Michael, are superseded by the chippy, working-class students, Mark and Digby. Pym casts a coolly critical eye on the world of post-war London academia.

Her heroine, Catherine Oliphant, writes short stories for women's magazines. She lives in a London flat, on the shabby side of Regent's Park, over a newsagent's shop, with her boyfriend, Tom Mallow. Tom comes from an upper-class family, whose family seat is in Shropshire and, to their dismay, has become an anthropologist doing field work in Africa.

Hazel Holt claimed that neither she nor Pym had much interest in anthropology, but this is not borne out in the novel that would become *Less Than Angels*. Pym, many years later, gave a talk for the wives of Oxford University dons, in which she said that her work at the African Institute was 'indirectly useful' to her life as a writer of fiction: 'The anthropologist goes out into the field to study so-called "primitive" societies and to note their customs. Coming nearer home, this technique can be very well applied to our own society, to the things that go on in our everyday life.'[3]

Pym would use this analogy to good effect in *Less Than Angels*. Jokes of a sexual nature about African customs such as polygamy and the ritual of sleeping with the sister of one's wife abound, as well as insider references to research practices and academic jargon. 'And no expression of disgust, astonishment or amusement must show on the face of the investigator,' says one of the characters, who had read this in an anthropologist's manual, just as Pym had herself.[4] Pym also presents British customs with their own peculiar resonances and idiosyncrasies, especially in post-war England, where the usual hierarchies have become blurred. A 'crisis' occurs in the library of the new centre over whether or not to invite the students to a drinks party, which is taking place in the library for the research staff. A debutante dance in Belgravia is 'as rewarding as any piece of native ceremonial'. Women put on their 'war paint' to 'trap' men.

The impoverished students, Mark and Digby, come to Catherine's when they are hungry, 'like trusting animals, expecting to be fed'. Pym's people have their own strange customs. Catherine likes to do her housework in the evenings, which raises a few eyebrows. Alaric Lydgate likes to wear African masks to conceal his emotions and withdraw from the world. Mrs Skinner beats out her dusty rugs in the evenings, 'like native drums'. The weekly seminar at the research centre is 'a barbarous ceremony, possibly a throwback to the days when the Christians were thrown to the lions'.[5]

A young first-year student called Deirdre Swan falls in love with Tom and they begin a love affair, despite the fact that he is living with Catherine. When Catherine discovers the betrayal, Tom tentatively suggests having a polygamous relationship: 'He began to form a sentence about polygamy and about how primitive societies were really better arranged than our own civilization, but another glance from Catherine stopped him.' Tom is selfish and lazy when it comes to women; his real love is anthropology. He betrays Catherine by taking Deirdre to the very same restaurant to which he has taken her for a romantic meal and then convinces himself that Catherine is to blame for his affair: '*She* had driven *him* away, really when it came to the point.'[6]

A striking scene occurs when Tom's aunt comes to Catherine's flat to remonstrate with her about living with her nephew. Mrs Beddoes of Belgravia is well dressed and good-looking, with a nervous manner. She is a recycling of the thinly disguised version of Julian Amery's mother, whom we first met in Pym's unpublished home front novel. Mrs Beddoes has heard the rumours that her nephew is living in a poor part of London with a woman, but Catherine is not what she expects of a 'mistress'. Catherine puts her straight: 'women who live with men without being married to them aren't necessarily very glamorous . . . they can be faded and worried-looking, their hands can be roughened with housework and stained with peeling vegetables.' Mrs Beddoes scolds Catherine for living with Tom: 'it was very wrong of you'. But the younger woman refuses to be intimidated: 'Yes, of course women do think the worst of each other, perhaps because only they can know what they are capable of. Men are regarded as being not quite responsible for their actions.'[7]

Tom, who studies 'kinship ties' in the field, has been drawn to orphaned Catherine precisely because of her lack of family complications: 'It was better when women were without kinship ties, like Catherine, he thought dispassionately and then they could be rejected at will and without the likelihood of any awkward repercussions.' With this barbaric thought, Tom damns himself in the eyes of the reader. He has turned against his class, his privileged background and his country, and 'thrown it all away' to go to Africa. But when he contemplates the English system of debutante balls, he sees little difference in their customs: 'For really when one came to consider it, what could be more primitive than the rigid ceremonial of launching a debutante on the marriage market?'[8]

When Tom decides that he does not really want to marry anyone (a third woman appears from his past as a potential mate) and wishes to return to Africa, Catherine is coolly unsympathetic: 'How soothing it will be to get away from all this complexity of personal relationships to the simplicity of a primitive tribe, whose only complications are in their kinship structure and rules of land tenure, which you can observe with the anthropologist's calm detachment.'[9] She now has no illusions about Tom's detachment and egotism and yet when he calls to ask her to wash and iron his clothes, she, of course, submits without demur.

Catherine resents the fact that her own creative writing is deemed inferior to dull academic research that nobody reads. 'A thesis *must* be long,' she tells Deirdre. 'The object, you see, is to bore and stupefy the examiners to such an extent that they will *have* to accept it.' Then, in an emotional outburst, she goes one step further in a condemnation of academic writing that seems so raw and heartfelt that it must have reflected Pym's own frustration with the caution and evasions of all the articles she had to edit for *Africa*: 'Oh, what cowards scholars are! When you think of how poets and novelists rush in with *their* analyses of the human heart and mind and soul of which they often have far less knowledge than darling Tom has of his tribe.'[10]

In the background of *Less Than Angels* there lingers another rejected lover. Elaine is, we are informed, the same age as Anne Elliot of Jane Austen's *Persuasion*. Unlike her sisters, she has been left at home following Tom's rejection, which has left her heart-broken:

> She might, if she had come upon them, have copied out Anne Elliot's words . . . 'We certainly do not forget you so soon as you forget us. It is, perhaps, our fate rather than our merit. We cannot help ourselves. We live at home, quiet, confined and our feelings prey upon us. You are forced on exertion. You have always business of some sort or other to take you back into the world immediately and continual occupation and change soon weaken impressions.' But Elaine was not much of a reader; she would have said that she had no time, which was perhaps just as well, even if she had missed the consolation and pain of coming upon her feelings expressed for her in such moving words.[11]

Pym *was* much of a reader and these were the words that she copied out in Naples in 1943, which had given her such 'consolation' and 'pain' when she was getting over her own heartbreak. Comparisons had been made and would continue to be made with Jane Austen and here Pym pays tribute to what she deemed Austen's greatest novel. Pym was fine-tuning her own comic talents and allowing a greater emotional intensity to flow from her prose.

But her world was a more frightening place. 'Two wars, motor-cars and newer and more frightful bombs being invented all the time,' says one of the anthropologist students, wearily. And there was, too, an 'Evelyn Waugh-like' mood in her sense that this new world was perhaps not necessarily a better one. Tom Mallow, though 'detribalised himself', looks sadly at the once-beautiful Georgian houses of Belgravia, now turned into flats or offices: 'If we lamented the decay of the great civilizations of the past, he thought, should we not also regret the dreary levelling down of our own?'[12]

CHAPTER XIV

Miss Pym goes to Portugal

Soon after *Jane and Prudence* was published, Pym was asked a question that seemed, somewhat disingenuously, to cause her some surprise: 'You don't think much of men, do you?' Her response was to say that it wasn't her attitude at all and that some of her best friends were male.[1] It must, however, be admitted that Barbara Pym's male characters are more often than not shifty, feckless, selfish and self-dramatising, relying on excellent women to solve their difficulties. 'Women are very powerful – perhaps they are always triumphant in the end,' says one of her female protagonists.[2]

Perhaps this criticism led her to create a very different kind of unattainable male hero for her fifth published novel. Piers Longridge is a teacher of Portuguese. In the late summer of 1954, Pym went to Portugal with her Wren friend, Frances Atkin. They went by boat, accompanied by 'music and flowers in the first class lounge'. On the bus after disembarking, she noted the 'fluty well-bred English voices . . . rising above the natives – talk even of Harrods'. Everything was 'spotlessly clean'. She was thrilled by the vivid colours and the flowers – 'red and pink geraniums and carnations' – and the hotel that smelt of 'euca-lyptus leaves, carnations and pine furniture polish'. She spotted a parrot and a Siamese cat and noted the abundance of donkeys with panniers. There were heaps of red-gold maize cobs sprawled out in the sun, and pumpkins. She saw old windmills on hills and a nun going down to the beach with a herd of little girls in pink dresses and straw hats.[3]

Later, in the dining room, she observed the Portuguese families and how late in the evening they ate, even with small children, 'rubbing their eyes and yawning'. A beautiful thin Portuguese woman, whom she christened 'La Traviata', was there with her daughter, 'a doll-like little girl in a frilly dress, her hair done in earphones'. Pym was in reflective mood and scribbled notes for a poem or a short story: 'Carrying you like a bracelet on my wrist – not heavy now, but always there. The contrast between the damp and dim freshness of the garden, with the half sun and white brilliance of Lisbon.'[4]

Frances and Barbara travelled around Portugal. Pym noted the women in tartan skirts, with gold crescent-shaped earrings peeping out from the black shawls that covered their heads. The houses in pink, white and biscuit; oxen wearing pretty-sounding bells around their necks; boats painted in bright colours. Along the shore were racks of tiny fish, split open and drying in the sun as men and women pulled in the fishing nets. Some of the colours reminded Pym of her Naples days. Less pretty was a chicken head 'kicked about in the dusty path'. All of her observations were carefully preserved in her notebooks. Four Englishmen, for example, wearing straw hats 'as if fearing the sun'. One was handsome, 'but rather decayed – vicious looking'. Another was bald, spectacled and wearing a Panama with the packing creases still showing.[5]

In the evening the sky was a clear pale blue and the countryside 'pale tan and green'. Frances and Barbara drove through Portuguese villages and visited the castle at Palmela and then Setúbal, 'wide, rather dusty squares, very spacious, planted with

Judas trees'. Then on to Sintra, where Pym wished she had packed a copy of Byron's *Childe Harold*, as it had a famous description of the beautiful hilltop town. Later, they stopped off at a church with votive offerings and wax dolls. She spotted a young priest, very well dressed, talking to another man and smoking with a cigarette holder. Reaching the coast, she found Estoril 'very like Bournemouth . . . on the promenade sits an old man with a stall of second-hand objects. Some of the jewellery, rings, etc must surely have belonged to exiled royalty.' She also wrote a character sketch of herself in Portugal:

> The Englishwoman (about forty) is almost aggressively sunburnt and displays her rather scrappy neck and chest in a low cut cotton dress. She sits in a canvas chair, wearing sunglasses and a scarf on her head, meditatively picking the skin off her nose (or peeling). NB this is me . . . she takes out some bright blue knitting.[6]

Back in London, she returned to reality with a bang, lunching at the senior common room in the university's School of Oriental and African Studies: 'cold meat and salad and no wine'. But she continued her interest in Portugal by signing up for Portuguese lessons at King's College, London.[7] Now in her early forties, she was feeling her age: 'I cannot reach up to pluck the prickly balls off a plane tree. Once it might have looked young, charming and gay, now only middle-aged and eccentric.'[8]

CHAPTER XV

Bill

Jonathan Cape himself had by now read and enjoyed *Less Than Angels* and promised he would try to sell it abroad, though warning that American publishers were 'funny people' who made decisions not on the basis of whether a book was good, but whether it would sell well. He had failed to sell overseas rights on her previous novel. Pym wrote to Bob Smith: 'I had a letter from Jock recently. He liked *Jane and Prudence* very much. But the Americans and Continentals most definitely *don't* and now I am feeling a little bruised!' But she was sanguine: 'So humble yourself, Miss Pym and do not give yourself airs.'[1]

On 17 October 1955, *Less Than Angels* was published. It was favourably received, particularly by Pym's friends and fellow novelists. Elizabeth Barnicot was particularly impressed by Pym's treatment of 'The Young' – 'I especially liked Mark and Digby'. Jock enjoyed the 'tantalising glimpses' of the Anglican Church, but wanted 'stronger incense'. Elizabeth Taylor liked it best of all her novels so far and enjoyed finding out that academics could have 'failings' like other people and be 'just as childish'.

Despite Cape's warning, he did manage to sell *Less Than Angels* in the United States, for which Pym received a $500 advance. Nevertheless, UK sales were relatively poor, mainly due to the

Miss Pym in Germany
with 'dearest Friedbert'

Miss Pym looking chic on her
European tour

Miss Pym sunbathing with German friends – swastikas on flagpoles behind

Hitler arrives in Hamburg on the same day as Miss Pym

CIVIL DEFENCE

WOMEN WANTED FOR EVACUATION SERVICE

OFFER YOUR SERVICES
TO YOUR LOCAL COUNCIL
OR ANY BRANCH OF WOMEN'S VOLUNTARY SERVICES

NATIONAL
SERVICE

The Pym family answered the call and
took in evacuees from Birkenhead

Gordon Glover and
Honor Wyatt's wedding

Off duty at Nine

ARP girl wearing her tin hat,
like Miss Pym, and ready for fun

Gordon Glover of the BBC, who broke her heart (again),
after which she became Wren Pym

Wren Pym sees the world in the last year of the war:
the view from Villa San Michele on Capri

Miss Pym at her desk in the African Institute: editor by day, novelist by night

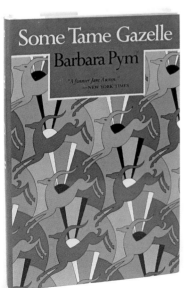

At last, a published author:
'a funnier Jane Austen'

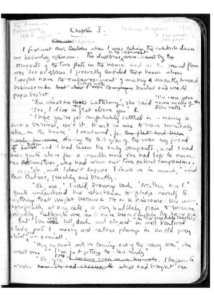

In the act of writing:
manuscript of *Excellent Women*

Beloved cats

Beloved Skipper

Beloved sister (outside
Barn Cottage, Finstock)

Miss Pym with her friend
and loyal fan, Philip Larkin

BARN COTTAGE
FINSTOCK
OXFORD OX7 3BY

16th March 1978

Dear Philip,
    How very kind of you to write so quickly
(beautifully typed letter — 2 long-haired secretary),
and to send me the ~~fiction~~ booklet which I
shall treasure, especially with the inscription.
Its fascinating and when I read your piece in it
I remembered what you had said in the ~~truth~~
though I hadn't realised quite how deeply you
were involved.   But looking at the whispering
scraps of poetry mss in the illustrations it made
me regret that the novelist's remains are so
much messier and more chaotic.
        Yesterday I went into the garage and
delved in the packingcase a tea chest where the
MS remains of Miss Pym are deposited and I
came up with what you see on the attached list!
I suppose 'draft' is more appropriate than 'version'
but the way I wrote, and still do was to work
straight on to a typewriter with a handwritten
draft or a few notes or even nothing. If whole
chapters exist in handwriting it is because I didn't
have a typewriter available at the time, was
away or ill in bed (the first version of Quartet

Letter to Larkin: 'Dear Barbara,
Dear Philip'

'No - it just passes the time.'
'That's right.'

Churchill Ward 7

21 - November.

A cold raw Typical
November day. But we
got there and I've just
eaten a kind of supper-
~~vegetab~~ vegetable soup,
baked beans and
Sausage! After the removal
of 4 pints of fluid!
The luxurious mixed or
unisex ward is surely
Donne.
Difference of sex no more
we knew
Than our guardian
angles do....

Miss Pym's last notebook entry, as she lay dying

closure of the large wholesale booksellers, Simpkin, Marshall, who had ordered substantial copies of her previous novels and been the key to their distribution to bookshops across the country. Suddenly, exciting news came from Twentieth Century Fox, who expressed an interest in buying an option on the novel. A copy was sent to Fox's London agent, Bill O'Hanlon, and he asked to meet with Pym. There appeared to be an attraction between them and they had a further rendezvous, going to a play together at the Polish Candlelight Club in Chepstow Villas. But the relationship floundered with a mishap on a further date.

Pym wrote that it was supposed to have been 'an evening of seduction' in Bill's office over the Rialto cinema. It all went wrong, however, when she needed to use the bathroom and there was a fiasco about the location of the ladies' room and then, finding it locked, having to fetch the key. Then the key got stuck in the lock. Eventually, they went to a pub to find another ladies' loo: 'there was such a strong element of farce that one couldn't help laughing'. But clearly Bill was unimpressed, as they appear not to have met again. Nor was the novel optioned by Fox. Nevertheless, inspired by the interest in her work, she pondered on her next novel. She had an opening line, but as yet no plot.

Pym had been wondering about a theme, writing in her notebook: 'WHAT IS MY NEXT NOVEL TO BE?' In the pub with Bill O'Hanlon, she had noticed the presence of 'happy little queer couples'. She also knew that she wanted to write about the clergy. She had thought of a working title, *The Clergy House*, but as yet she did not know how to develop the plot. At a service at St Mary Aldermary in Watling Street, where a church friend, Canon Freddie Hood was based, she heard the incongruous sound of a telephone ringing through the organ music. It gave her the idea of her opening. 'It can begin with the shrilling of the telephone in Freddie Hood's church.'[2] But what then?

CHAPTER XVI

What a Saga!

One of Pym's favourite writers was the novelist, playwright and journalist Rachel Ferguson. Ferguson was a suffragette, who had been a campaigner for women's rights from the age of sixteen. She worked for *Punch* magazine, writing under the name 'Rachel'. Her first novel, *False Goddesses*, was published in 1922, but it was with her second, written over a decade later, that she became a literary sensation. *The Brontës Went to Woolworths*, as its unforgettable title suggests, is an absurdist novel which centres around the lives of the eccentric Carne sisters.

The fatherless sisters, Deirdre, Katrine and little Sheil, live with their mother in a bohemian household in Bloomsbury. Imaginative and quirky, the Carne girls spin webs of stories around household objects, toys and pets, and public figures whom they have never met. They describe a strange fantasy game, 'the saga', which involves finding out the intricate details of other people's lives. The main target of their saga is a high court judge, Sir Herbert Toddington (Toddy). The details range from his choice of pyjamas, to his favourite tipple, to his relationships with women. Much of the saga is completely invented, though the girls stalk his house and his place of work to add touches of realism to their inventions. The boundaries between fantasy and realism begin to dissolve when, by coincidence, the girls meet the Toddingtons for real.

Though the book was a success, its quirky humour and eccentricity confused some readers. The girls' obsessive-compulsive interest in Lord Toddington (a man they had never met) was seen as just too bizarre. When the girls finally meet Toddy, they have to pretend *not to know* all the real details about his life that they have discovered, leading to hilarious consequences. Sometimes, they forget what they did know and shock him when they reveal details that they definitely should not know. In justifying 'the saga' in one of her personal memoirs, Ferguson agreed that some readers might find her 'certifiable': 'I don't doubt that Freud would have plenty to say about it and all damaging . . . So be it!'[1] The point is that one either gets the joke of the saga or not.

Pym did certainly get the joke. She had, ever since she was a girl, loved finding out about the lives of other people. It was partly what made her such a good novelist of observation. Her habit of 'stalking' Julian Amery, turning up to his family's house in Eaton Square, staring into the windows, was all part of her own saga. Now, when Pym and Hilary were living together in Barnes, they began to play the game in more earnest. They had always enjoyed looking out of the window and inventing lives for people outside. New neighbours appeared, two young men and a dog. Barbara and Hilary began snooping from their drawing-room window, just like sisters Rhoda and Mabel in *Less Than Angels*. In that novel, the sisters draw great satisfaction and enjoyment from observing the goings-on outside their twitching net curtains: 'What was the point of living in a suburb if one couldn't show a healthy curiosity about one's neighbours . . . the sisters had been sitting in Rhoda's bed-sitting room, which commanded an excellent view of the next door back garden. They often did this on the lengthening spring evening.'[2]

The Pym sisters would look out for the men and give them nicknames: the larger one was 'Bear', the smaller, more delicate-looking man they dubbed 'Squirrel' or 'Little Thing'. The dog, which was a poodle, they called 'Tweetie'. They would watch as Bear and Squirrel took Tweetie for a walk beside the river. Once, the sisters followed them on a walk and Hilary tried to pet the dog. 'Squirrel' was unimpressed, saying: 'He wouldn't come to *you*.' Far from feeling insulted, the sisters were delighted that they had finally heard Squirrel's voice.

Hazel Holt, Pym's great friend, became involved in the Bear saga. At work at the institute, the two women invented mini sagas about the home lives of their colleagues. Pym was always much better at the invention than Hazel and sometimes her prophecies came true. There were also Pym sagas about the lives of her three cats, just as Ferguson's Dierdre Carne invents a saga about their terrier dog, Crellie. But, as Hazel Holt suggests, the Bear and Squirrel saga was the most extensive one that Barbara and Hilary invented.

Bear had a grey car (a Hillman Husky) and would drive off on Sundays wearing a cassock, leaving the Pym sisters even more intrigued. Barbara and Hilary had hired a car for a holiday and so were able one Sunday to follow Bear dressed in his cassock. They tracked him all the way to Kilburn, to the church of St Lawrence the Martyr. They sat at the back of the church and were delighted to discover that Bear was the organist. After the service, the women were asked to tea in the church hall, where they were welcomed by the vicar's wife, who was holding a jar of sugar and a pink plastic apostle spoon.

Pym's 1956 literary notebook contains an exhaustive log of the comings and goings of the two men: 'Little Thing seen on escalator at Piccadilly Circus'; 'B[ear] at St L[awrences] pm.' Even if there was no sighting, she would write down: 'Nothing'.[3] Pym noted everything from cleaning the Husky car to Squirrel's orange pullover – a detail she would use in *A Glass of Blessings*.

The strange household became even more exciting when another young man joined Bear and Little Thing. They called him Paul. Then Squirrel left, Paul moved out and Little Thing moved back in with another man they called Tony. It was all very confusing and very intriguing:

Well – Little Thing is definitely here, but what an elusive little creature we are, like a moth coming out only at night. Hilary and I saw him coming from the bus stop about 10.30 last night . . . When he made to cross the road to his house he (knowing that someone was behind him) flung out his arms in a ballet-like gesture and ran across the road. The 'friend' *might* have been Bear, for Bear was definitely there on Sunday. We saw him emerge about 5 o'clock wearing a rather nice brown tweedy suit (milk chocolate bar, solid all through) . . . but no Paul. Is there being a sort of rapprochement? Tony is still in residence with masses of peculiar-looking friends.[4]

Then, to her great excitement, Hilary spotted Tony going into the staff entrance at Heal's department store: 'STOP PRESS! . . . what about going there for our office lampshades?' Pym asked Hazel.

Pym encouraged Hazel and Bob Smith to become involved in the saga, meticulously plotting sightings and 'stalking', most often to St Lawrence's church, though also to a cemetery and a florists in Shepherd's Bush. Once even to a private hotel in the West Country. 'It was a lovely saga,' recalled Holt, 'after a while, we knew a great deal about the main characters.'[5]

Except that the young homosexual men, who surely valued their privacy, had no idea that they were being followed in this bizarre way. And by two single middle-aged women. After all, homosexuality was still illegal. This was the period when figures such as the actor John Gielgud, the baronet and captain of industry Sir David Milne-Watson, and the MP William J. Field all found themselves arrested for importuning ('cottaging') in public toilets.

The point about the Carne sisters, and their saga, is that they are in search of a father figure. Toddy is a surrogate for their own dead daddy, and much of Deirdre's fantastic and clever invention is to console and amuse her fragile and anxious little sister. Pym's motives are perhaps less easy to understand. Initially, the men were fictitious 'characters' rather than real people, but then, as with Rachel Ferguson's heroines, Barbara would meet and befriend Bear and his circle. She was becoming ever more interested in homosexual men.

The Bear saga would provide rich pickings for the next novel, which was germinating in Pym's mind. And then there was Denton.

CHAPTER XVII

Darling Denton and Orvil Pym

Pym had always been drawn to unattainable men. Henry had not reciprocated her love, Gordon was married with children, Jock was homosexual, and it now seemed that Bob shared the same 'proclivities'. His letters mentioned special friendships with men, usually met abroad. Pym's latest obsession was the ultimate in unfeasibility: a homosexual author who was deceased.

She had long been fascinated by homosexual relationships, probably dating from her time at Oxford. In her journals, Pym had expressed a wish to write a great homosexual novel, but so far it had eluded her. Then, on holiday in Portugal, she had read a book that she had found utterly compelling. Entitled *Maiden Voyage*, it was by Denton Welch. She became, in her own words, 'besotted' with the author. She collected and read everything that he had written.

Welch was a painter and a writer, born in 1915. A 'weakling', he was mercilessly bullied at his posh boarding school, Repton, by, among others, a boy called Roald Dahl, who would also become an author (he had been bullied himself – the usual cycle). Welch ran away from boarding school at the age of sixteen and relocated to China; this is the story that is told in *Maiden Voyage*. He returned home to study art at Goldsmiths College in London. At the age of twenty he was knocked from his bicycle by a car, leaving him with a fractured spine – an echo of the tragic accident that Pym and Irena were directly involved in back in 1935. Though Denton recovered, he spent the remainder of his life in pain and enduring various operations and procedures, which eventually led to his early death. Writing and painting were ways to distract himself from his physical disability. He suffered from bladder and kidney infections and from partial sexual impotence.

Denton was openly homosexual. His autobiographical novel, *In Youth is Pleasure*, is a shocking and beautifully written account of his early life. It begins with the hero in a hospital bed encountering his first sexual experience with a nurse who is washing between his legs. Welch wrote in stylish, candid prose that still feels entirely fresh. He died in 1948 at the age of thirty-three.

Pym was entranced. She was drawn to Denton's wacky, outrageous sense of humour and his interest in the trivial, the mundane, which he transcends into something magical and ethereal. A jewel box, peach melba, a picture on a biscuit tin, a scent bottle. His narrators are often discovered visiting antique shops, where they find lovely objects in other people's junk.

During his illness, Denton restored an eighteenth-century doll's house.[1] For a miniaturist writer interested in the culture of objects and small things it was a labour of love, and he described the process in precise detail. Denton had long cherished the dream of living in a Georgian house and he poured out his longing into the doll's house. He restored the delicate stair rail ('I feel sure that it is a Chinese Chippendale fret') and, scraping back a piece of wallpaper, was delighted to discover its original date of 1783. Pym read and reread every precious word.

Denton's prose is shot through with a painter's palette of colours. Fruit is 'violent pink'; treading in a cow pat and breaking through the crust reveals 'darkest richest green . . . like velvet or jade or creamed spinach'; mushrooms, 'with their flattened damaged gills radiating from a centre', look like 'shrunken scalps of coarse Oriental hair'. Pym relished such sentences as 'Nothing could be gayer than a red lacquer coffin' – 'Oh darling Denton,' she wrote, as if he were a lover.[2]

Welch's works are full of sex, though he is never vulgar. On one occasion, the hero steals a ruby red lipstick and paints his face and his nipples a rosy red, before embarking on a sensuous dance. He masturbates in long, luscious green grass. Later, he scourges himself in front of a mirror with a leather strap. Another schoolboy is turned on by a reading of *Jane Eyre*.

Denton Welch's novels lack incident and plot, but are characterised by evocative and highly original language and expression. One can see why Pym was drawn to them. She pored over the journals and hunted down a copy of *In Youth is Pleasure*. How delighted she must have felt to discover the name that Denton chose for the self-styled narrator: Orvil Pym.

CHAPTER XVIII

Tracking down Orvil Pym

Once again, Pym involved her friends in her latest obsession. Hazel, to whom she was becoming increasingly close, shared her enthusiasm for Denton, especially the journals, 'frustratingly edited by Jocelyn Brooke'.[1] Brooke was himself a homosexual and a neurotic novelist (his *Orchid Trilogy* was sometimes praised as a small-scale English equivalent of Marcel Proust's *In Search of Lost Time*). He expurgated homosexual references, potential libels and material that he considered repetitive or irrelevant. Pym was frustrated because she wanted to know every detail of Denton's brief life. Hazel Holt recalls that she and Pym knew the journals almost by heart. They would set each other quizzes to test their knowledge. But reading every word was not enough and Pym set out to discover more about her idol. She went to Somerset House to obtain a copy of his will and decided that she would go on a pilgrimage to Greenwich and find 34 Crooms Hill, where Denton once lived. There, she sat down on the low stone wall opposite, in the rain, under her umbrella and took in every detail of his house: 'Three floors, white painted windows, dull red brick, net half curtains.' She gazed for a few moments, but saw nothing.[2]

Another time, Pym went with Bob Smith to Lord Burlington's

Chiswick House, west of London. In 1942, Denton Welch had wandered around the landscaped gardens, with its lakes and grottoes, furious that the villa and its grounds had been left neglected and fallen into disrepair: 'I thought that this lovely romantic patch could be made into the most beautiful garden in all England.'[3] Pym noted: 'Denton would be glad to know they are restoring the villa.'[4] A year later, she made another Denton pilgrimage to his final house, Middle Orchard, in the village of Crouch in Kent. She took her friend, Ailsa Currie, who lived nearby. Denton was a lover of picnics, so in his honour they picnicked on cheese, Ryvita, hard-boiled eggs, chocolate, and coffee in a flask. They tracked down his house, which was a white clapboard with a balcony on the side.

Holt recalls that Denton was as if alive to Pym in a way that few actually living authors ever were. She was especially interested in his homosexual relationship with Eric Oliver, who posthumously published Denton's letters and his third novel. They were a tempestuous couple. Having been introduced by a mutual friend in 1943, Denton was immediately captivated by Eric's dark good looks and intelligence. Openly homosexual, he had long been attracted to men of a lower class than himself. Eric Oliver, an itinerant agricultural labourer, claimed to be bisexual and although he was drawn irresistibly to Denton, he was not sexually drawn to him. Denton had to sleep on a plastic sheet for incontinence and his partial impotence was problematic for Eric.[5]

Nevertheless, there was a physical relationship of sorts. In one letter, Denton apologises for constantly pestering Eric and he is often found bewailing the fact that he had not met Eric before his accident, when he was younger and still virile. They shared a bed together when Eric came to stay for the weekend at Pitt's Folly Cottage in Tonbridge, where Denton was living in the early 1940s. Their relationship, troubled by Denton's neediness, adoration and moodiness, was further complicated by Eric's dependence on alcohol. Denton would beg Eric to stop drinking so heavily, but then, following a quarrel, would lure him back to Pitt's Folly with the promise of more drink.

They were an odd couple: Denton, small of stature, with a limp, tiny feet and pointed aristocratic features; Eric, strong, muscular and masculine – but he was also sensitive and kind and deeply insecure. Denton wanted to take care of Eric every bit as much as Eric took care of invalid Denton. After his house was destroyed by a German V2 rocket in 1944, Eric moved in with Denton, first at Pitt's Folly and then at Middle Orchard. The latter was rented to the men by Denton's closest female friend, the artist Noël Adeney, who seems to have fallen in love with Denton, even though she was married and knew that Denton was homosexual. She later wrote a novel about her relationship with him, entitled *No Coward Soul*.

The theme of a married woman falling in love with a sensitive, troubled homosexual man began to ferment in Pym's mind. In a journal entry of 1956, she remarked on the 'terrifying' modern-day woman, with exposed bosom and permed hair: 'no wonder men turn to other men sometimes'.[6] Her obsession with Bear and Little Thing also fired her imagination. She now had her theme in place and it would lead to one of her most brilliant (and certainly most underrated) novels.

CHAPTER XIX

We drink a Glass of Blessings

John Bayley was a young fellow in English at New College, Oxford. As an undergraduate, he had been tutored by Lord David Cecil, Goldsmiths' Professor of English. Later Cecil and Bayley became colleagues and great friends. Bayley, soon to be married to the novelist Iris Murdoch, would become one of Pym's ardent admirers.

During the long summer vacation, Bayley visited the local library in the English village where his parents lived. He was looking for something light and entertaining to offset daily struggles with *Beowulf* and *Paradise Lost*. He found a copy of Pym's *A Glass of Blessings* and was enchanted. When he arrived back at Oxford, David Cecil asked him if he had read any good books over the 'long vac'. Bayley told Cecil about Pym's novel: 'Good title' was Cecil's response and he promised to look out for her books. Bayley was not at all sure that Cecil would remember. But he did. Not only did Lord Cecil read her latest novel, he read all of her works and wrote to Pym to congratulate her on her success.

Pym needed encouragement of this kind; *A Glass of Blessings* did not receive the success of her earlier works. She had hoped that it would be published in time for Christmas sales, but the novel was delayed until April 1958. Reviews were lukewarm and she wrote, despondently: 'Only three reviews up to 29 April, none wholly good. They say my humour deserts me when dealing with romance, that I am tone-deaf to dialogue, that I am *moderately* amusing.'[1] This last barb clearly stung.

David Cecil's 'fan letter' was a blessing: 'Forgive a total stranger writing to tell you how very much he enjoys your books,' he wrote. 'You have so much sense of reality and sense of comedy and the people in your books are living and credible and likeable. I find this rare in modern fiction.'[2] Pym was surely delighted by this fulsome praise from an Oxford don renowned for his readings of Jane Austen. Later on, John Bayley and David Cecil would agree that *A Glass of Blessings* was her finest novel, contrary to the consensus of the newspaper critics.

This, Pym's fifth published novel, was a departure in theme and tone. A melancholic note is sounded in the heroine Wilmet Forsyth's hopeless infatuation with a homosexual man. She is rich, elegant and attractive; in her early thirties, she has been married for ten years, though childless, and has suddenly discovered that her husband is a bore.

The reviewers disliked Wilmet, believing her to be self-absorbed and spoilt. The critics focused on the 'clergy house element' and Pym herself worried that it was 'too churchy'. Several critics wrote about the High Anglican theme: 'An Anglo-Catholic frolic garnished with a froth of Kensington conversation and a flurry of Fathers.' One of the few positive reviews, from the *Daily Telegraph*, saw beneath the High Anglican frolics of kleptomaniac Mr Bason, common Father Bode, and fasting, incense-burning Father Thames. Peter Green was the only reviewer to notice the homosexual element: 'her naive heroine, all unawares, falls in love with an obvious homosexual'.[3]

Piers Longridge is one of Pym's most memorable and vivid characters. He is good-looking, cultivated and intelligent. He teaches Portuguese at night school and works as a proofreader. He is charming to Wilmet, flatters her with sincerity and, before she knows it, she has fallen in love. Piers seems to return her affection. But he has a secret. Wilmet believes that she has discovered his secret when she catches him in a deliberate lie. When he tells Wilmet that he is going back to work (following a lunchtime mass), she sees him hurrying into a London wine lodge.

A sensitive reader will pick up the clues from the outset, such as when Wilmet's mother-in-law, the marvellous Sybil, discusses the new applicants for assistant priests. She refers, darkly, to those clergymen interested in 'youth work', noting: 'we know the kind of thing that sometimes happens: the lurid headlines in the gutter press or the small sad paragraph in the better papers'.⁴ Though her son throws her a warning glance, Sybil continues to speak about 'those fallen ones' who get defrocked or go to rehabilitation. Here, Pym was drawing on a real-life case at her church, St Michael's, where the vicar was discovered to be a paedophile preying on choirboys.

Wilmet is, however, infatuated by Piers and cannot see what the reader sees. It requires a writer of great skill and tact to manage the narrative in this way. Wilmet is correct that Piers has a problematic relationship with alcohol (similar to that of Denton Welch's lover, Eric Oliver), but she does not, cannot, perceive the reasons *why* Piers is a dipsomaniac. Piers is, admittedly, flirtatious with Wilmet, inviting her to clandestine lunches and walks in the park and by the Thames in Barnes, where they see the Harrods Furniture Depository, a detail Pym remembered from her riverside walks with Bob Smith. In a charged moment, Piers asks Wilmet if her husband is the jealous type. When she replies in the negative, Piers responds: 'I should be if you were mine.' For a moment, we also miss the signs and wonder if Piers *is* in love with Wilmet.

Piers's drink problem gets worse and he disappears for a stretch of time, only to re-emerge sober and smartly dressed for a party. When Wilmet is given a secret Christmas present, an inscribed antique trinket box, she immediately assumes it is from Piers. There is more than a hint of Jane Austen's Emma Woodhouse in her misunderstanding of people and events. Despite the mystery surrounding troubled, charming Piers, Wilmet still cherishes hope for a secret love affair. When she telephones him, on an impulse, she is surprised and more than bemused to hear a 'slightly common' male voice, which she assumes to be his 'colleague'. No, she cannot speak to Piers, he says, in his flat, northern vowels. Still, Wilmet does not guess the truth.

As she hurtles towards the final denouement, with 'the delicious, walking-on-air feeling' of being in love on a balmy May day, going to meet Piers for tea, there can only be one outcome. Piers rebukes Wilmet for 'talking like one of the cheaper women's magazines'. But it is not until he is walking her to his flat, near Shepherd's Bush, that the terrible truth dawns.

That it occurs in a grocer's shop is a typical Pym touch. On the way home, Piers stops by the shop where his 'colleague' can be found. Peering into some biscuit tins, like a character in a Denton Welch novel, is Keith: small, dark and good-looking. Pym uses animal imagery to describe the man who Wilmet now realises is her rival. Keith's short, cropped hair glistens 'like the wet fur of an animal . . . like a hedgehog or porcupine'. It is only when he speaks in his 'flat, rather common little voice' that she is finally awakened. It is a painful, awkward moment and an embarrassed silence ensues, broken by a discussion of streaky bacon:

> 'What do you think, Wilmet?' asked Piers. 'Which is the best kind of bacon?'
> 'I don't know,' I said, unable to give my attention to bacon. 'It depends what you like.'[5]

Wilmet's first feeling is sadness, 'as if something had come to an end', before shame and indignation set in. Too late to back down, she is forced to confront the fact of Piers and Keith's living arrangements and to endure the tea that Keith has prepared so painstakingly, with his pink and white morsels of gateau on plastic doilies. It is only when Piers walks her to her taxi that she vents:

> 'So that is the person with whom you live.'
>
> 'Yes. He's obviously taken a great fancy to you,' Piers smiled, 'do you like him?'
>
> 'He seems a nice boy,' I said, 'but rather unexpected.'
>
> 'In what way unexpected?'
>
> 'You said you lived with a colleague from the press. I suppose I'd imagined a different sort of person.'
>
> '*You* always said that I lived with a colleague. But aren't we all colleagues, in a sense, in this grim business of getting through life as best we can?'
>
> I said nothing, so he went on. 'My dear girl, what's the matter? Do you think I've been deceiving you, or something absurd like that?'
>
> 'No, of course I don't,' I said indignantly. But of course in a way, he had deceived me.[6]

Piers tells Wilmet that he *enjoys* coming home to a person who is not intellectual, echoing a sentiment that Pym recalled in her notebook of 1956: 'on occasions of unhappiness too one might unburden oneself to one's hairdresser and enjoy the cosiness of non-intellectual conversation'. It is striking that Wilmet is not at all shocked by Piers's homosexuality, only by his deception.

The next surprise, in a novel that keeps surprising, is Wilmet's discovery of how much she likes Keith. He comes to tea and she sees how he has saved Piers from his alcoholism and his self-hatred. Keith, a catalogue model from Leicester, is kind and good. A compelling composite of 'Little Thing' (black jeans and tangerine shirt) and Denton's lover, Eric Oliver, he is hard-working, fastidious and deeply caring. He has standards of taste: he fingers Wilmet's curtains to ensure that they are fully lined.

Wilmet learns from her snobbish attitudes, in the manner of Emma Woodhouse. Piers's rebuke to her cuts deep: 'After all I didn't really mean to imply that you're to blame for who you are. Some people are less capable of loving their fellow human beings than others.' But Piers is wrong. Wilmet learns to love and accept Keith. She is also confronted with her husband's 'brief encounter' with another woman, Prudence Bates. Wilmet is so sure of Rodney's fidelity and his predictable dullness, that she fails to see him as a desirable human being with his own needs and desires: 'I had always regarded Rodney as the kind of man who would never look at another woman. The fact that he could – and had indeed done so – ought to teach me something about myself, even if I was not quite sure what it was.'[7]

Wilmet finally discovers that there is no reason why her own life should not be 'a glass of blessings too. Perhaps it always had been without my realizing it.'[8]

CHAPTER XX

In which Miss Pym goes to Swanwick

In August 1957, Pym attended a writers' conference in Swanwick, near the picturesque Peak District of Derbyshire. There were talks given by publishers and writers on tips for getting published. Phyllis Bayley from *Vanity Fair* gave a talk on the magazine story and there was a panel in which delegates were invited to ask questions, some of which Pym found tedious: 'It really makes one despair when someone gets up and asks if publishers like chapters to be all the same length.'[1] More fun was to be had visiting Haddon Hall and Chatsworth House, the seat of the Duke and Duchess of Devonshire. The duchess was Deborah 'Debo' Mitford, sister of Unity the Nazi. One wonders if Pym reflected on the different paths the sisters had taken.

The writers' conference gave her the opening for her new novel. Dulcie, the heroine, who has been jilted, attends a conference in Derbyshire to help mend her broken heart and for the opportunity to meet new people, 'and to amuse herself by observing the lives of others, even if for only a weekend and under somewhat unusual circumstances'. Dulcie, thought by Pym's friends to be the heroine most like the author herself, spends a large proportion of her life 'prying'. She works part-time as a researcher, usually proofreading and compiling indices for editors, and wonders if one day 'the time will come when one may be permitted to do research into the lives of ordinary people'.[2]

In contrast to the treatment of previous snooping heroines, Dulcie's hobby is portrayed in uneasy terms. Pym's stalking of Bear (there can be no other word) had resulted in a trip to a private hotel in the West Country, where Bear's mother was the proprietress. There, she had also visited the graveyard to discover the death date of Bear's father. She copied out the inscription on his tombstone and drew a picture in her notebook. Her churchyard visit and the West Country hotel were recreated in *No Fond Return of Love*, when Dulcie goes to 'Eagle House' to discover more about Aylwin Forbes. Tall, rugged and handsome, he is the editor of a journal. He is a philanderer whose long-suffering wife finally departs when he is found kissing pretty Viola Dace, who is compiling his index. Dulcie convinces Viola to accompany her on the 'research trip' to Devon, where they stake out the hotel and then finally meet Forbes's mother and brother, Neville.

In her 'Bear log', Pym had written: 'Isn't it time this log stopped?' Then, in dark ink, she has underlined the word 'Yes'. She continued the record of her sightings, nonetheless. Her uneasiness about her stalking of Bear and his lovers is the engine that drives *No Fond Return of Love*. Dulcie begins her search on Forbes by looking in the telephone directory for his address. Once she finds it, it is easy to contrive an 'accidental meeting'. The discovery that Forbes has a clergyman brother leads her to investigations in the local public library and even the Public Record Office:

For this was really the kind of research Dulcie enjoyed most of all – investigation – some might have said prying – into the lives of other people, the kind of work that involved poring over reference books and street and telephone directories. It was most satisfactory if the objects of her research were not too well known, either to herself or to the world in general.[3]

The clerical directory *Crockford's* leads to the discovery that Neville Forbes is a vicar in north-west London. Later, at a jumble sale, she meets Aylwin's estranged wife and discovers that Neville has been involved in some unpleasantness with a young woman. Dulcie knows that her snooping is 'strange and rather deceitful', but she is unable to stop herself.

Later on, Dulcie makes a point of going to his church in order to uncover more details about the 'trouble' he is in. Viola Dace (who has rented a room from Dulcie) is surprised by Dulcie's curiosity about the Forbes brothers. Dulcie, again, tries to explain her interest: 'It's like a kind of game. It seemed – though she did not say this to Viola – so much safer and more comfortable to live in the lives of other people – to observe their joys and sorrows with detachment as if one were watching a film or a play.'[4] Her love of 'finding out about people', she knows, is 'a sort of compensation for the dreariness of everyday life'.[5] Living in the lives of other people is about as good a definition of the novelist's art as one could imagine.

When Dulcie invites Aylwin to a dinner party, she forgets what she should *not* reveal about her knowledge of his life. She feels that her intense curiosity could potentially land her into trouble. When she persuades Viola to accompany her to the Eagle Hotel, she again feels a stab of shame: 'One goes on with one's research, avidly and without shame. Then suddenly a curious feeling of delicacy comes over one. One sees one's subjects – or perhaps victims is a better word – as being somehow degraded by one's probings.'[6] Pym, of course, had the excuse of being a novelist. Her own 'intense curiosity' about the lives of others was what made her such an observant writer. Dulcie, who admits she is neither a novelist nor a detective, does not have the same excuse for prying and hence there is a degree of self-loathing that is new to the Pym heroine.

In her private journals, Pym was toying with the feeling that 'one wasn't a particularly nice person. (Selfish, unsociable, uncharitable, malicious even).'[7] She had been plagued with this sense since her wartime days and had confided feelings of self-loathing to her diary in a distressing incident when she made a complaint about a washbasin in a ladies' cloakroom. All these years later, the incident is recreated in *No Fond Return of Love*.

> 'What a nuisance,' she said, as a tall woman came into the cloakroom, 'somebody's cluttered up the basin with flowers and I wanted to wash my hands.'
>
> 'I'm very sorry,' said the woman rather stiffly. 'I'm afraid the flowers are mine. There wasn't anywhere else to put them.'
>
> 'Oh, I didn't realise,' said Dulcie apologetically. 'Of course one must put flowers in water to keep them fresh.'
>
> 'I'm taking them to an *invalid* . . .'
>
> 'An *invalid*,' Dulcie repeated, 'I *am* sorry. If only I'd realised.'[8]

When Maurice, the man who jilted her, returns, suggesting that they should reunite, Dulcie refuses his charmless proposal. There is no *Persuasion*-like Anne Elliot and Captain Wentworth happy ending. Nevertheless, Dulcie's quietly cynical attitude towards men and marriage does not prevent her from seeking love, even if that love is merely 'cosiness' or the gratification of being needed: 'Those are the people from whom one asks no return of love, if you see what I mean. Just to be allowed to love them is enough.'[9]

It is the ending of *Mansfield Park* that Pym invokes at the close of the novel, though there is an element of ambiguity in Dulcie's happy ending. When *No Fond Return of Love* was published, Pym sent a copy to Bob Smith: 'You are one of the few who know how *truly* B. Pym it is – but really Dulcie had an easy time of it compared with us searching for Bear's church, didn't she?' Bob replied, astutely: 'It's not, I think, your easiest book, but somehow the most purely Barbara Pym, her art at its quintessence.'[10]

CHAPTER XXI

In which Miss Pym goes over to Rome

On a cold day in late October 1959, Pym viewed a semi-detached house at 40 Brooksville Avenue across the road from Queen's Park and close to St Lawrence's church, where Bear played the organ. Not then gentrified, it was surrounded by council estates and blocks of flats in Kilburn and Kensal Rise. However, the park was pleasant, with a Victorian bandstand, the street was quiet and tree-lined and the houses pretty, with small walled front gardens.

She and Bob Smith loved their 'church crawls', and had visited numerous London churches, attending high mass at All Saints' in Notting Hill and a less incense-laden service at All Saints', Margaret Street, Fitzrovia. Both churches were Victorian Gothic Revival in architecture and Anglo-Catholic in allegiance. As we have seen, a spontaneous visit to a lunchtime service at St Mary Aldermary in the City had inspired the opening of *A Glass of Blessings*. Father Twisaday from All Saints' Notting Hill ('an elderly dried up celibate, irritable and tetchy') had provided rich material for Father Thames.

Pym's pursuit of Bear had led her to St Lawrence's in Queen's Park and this was the church where she decided that she wanted to worship. The move to a less salubrious part of north-west

London was partly to be closer to the church and partly as a result of the 1957 Rent Act, which pushed up rents and gave increasing rights to the landlord rather than the tenant. The sisters, having rented for many years, wanted a house of their own. Hilary, who had more money and financial security thanks to her job at the BBC, bought the property, which had a garden suitable for their tabby cat, Tatiana, but a cold winter and burst pipes delayed the house move.

Finally the sisters were able to move in, deciding that the drawing room should be on the first floor, where there was better light and a view. The sisters would sit in the window, looking out on their neighbours, just like the sisters in *Some Tame Gazelle*. Many of the details of the house and its environment would find their way into the pages of Pym's new novel, *An Unsuitable Attachment*.

Pym told Bob that Brooksville Avenue now felt like a proper home. They borrowed a modern red sofa and chairs from one of Hilary's friends, hung magnolia cream curtains and brought in Bear (Maurice) to decorate the sitting room in yellow and grey striped wallpaper. They bought an 'all-over' grey carpet on hire purchase. Best of all, there was a small garden with hyacinths, daffodils and forsythia in full bloom, perfect for feline adventures.

Bob had kindly offered to lend the Pyms some of his furniture that was currently in storage. When the sisters went along to the facility, she learned that another woman had been there, too. Pym had not known about Bob's other female friend and the incident was stored up to be used as a plot point. Pym liked to relate bits of church gossip to Bob: 'Terrible goings-on at the Church of Ascension . . . much too strong for a novel. Vicar accused by Sunday School teacher of having intercourse (sexual) with her 75 or 80 times.'[1]

In the spring of 1961, Pym went on a work trip to Rome, for an anthropology conference. She flew in to Leonardo da Vinci airport, where she saw nuns 'waving handkerchiefs and with bunches of flowers to welcome back a Mother Superior'. At the opening gathering of the conference, she noted that most of the delegates were carrying or wearing raincoats. She 'felt like Prudence, overdressed in cream Courtelle'. Later, at the Ritz Hotel – 'walls covered with pleated silk, gold plush sofas and chairs, pictures of Roman emperors' – they had drinks and canapés.[2]

Ever observant, Pym noted the thin stray cats of Rome, 'mostly grey tabby or tortoiseshell, which are said to be fed by elderly ladies', and the Spanish Steps, 'massed with red, pink and white azaleas'. There was a lengthy excursion to Amalfi and Ravello: 'Acres of lemon groves . . . also for oranges with stalks and leaves still on them and the little bunches of dried lemon leaves which you unwrap to reveal a few delicious lemon-flavoured raisins in the middle.' Ravello cathedral had a pulpit supported by marble lions. In the garden of the Villa Ridolfo, there was a marble lion licking its cub.[3] Much of this detail would also be used in *An Unsuitable Attachment*. The trip to Italy also evoked memories of Naples. Pym's new novel would feature a working-class man, loosely based on Starky, who would fall in love with an elegant and aloof older woman, Ianthe.

CHAPTER XXII

A Sketch of Philip Larkin

Pym was feeling good. She was delighted to receive a fan letter from the poet Philip Larkin, who had written to say that he wished to write a review essay about her career to date. In the event, he had been too late for the publication he had in mind, but Pym wrote back to express her thanks: 'Perhaps, if you still like doing it, I could let you know when my next is ready . . . it will be my seventh novel which seems a significant number.'[1]

With Larkin's encouragement, she continued to work hard on her new book, which was going slowly. She told Larkin how much she had enjoyed his novel, *A Girl In Winter*, wondering whether he might write a second, or would he be sticking to poetry? Larkin penned a generous write up of Pym in the *Guardian* and continued on his long review essay.

Not yet forty, Philip Larkin was a tall, shy, balding man, who wore thick spectacles and still retained traces of a childhood stammer. He was the senior librarian at the University of Hull and the author of two novels and two volumes of poetry. Larkin's somewhat unprepossessing appearance and his 'librarian' persona belied an outrageous, scatological sense of humour and a sharp wit.

There were similarities between Larkin and Pym. Both hailed

from middle-class families; both had gone to Oxford, where they had been transported into new worlds and experiences that were formative. Both of them found lifelong friends from higher class backgrounds, which in many respects alienated them from their families and left them permanently displaced. Whilst at Oxford, like Pym before him, Larkin created an alter ego. His was a writer called Brunette Coleman, who wrote bawdy lesbian stories. *Trouble at Willow Gables* is set at a girls' boarding school, parodying the 'jolly hockey sticks' style of Angela Brazil. Its (incomplete) sequel, *Michaelmas Term at St Bride's*, is set in an Oxford women's college. In part, Larkin wrote his stories to amuse his Oxford friends, in particular Kingsley Amis. 'I am spending my time doing an obscene Lesbian novel in the form of a school story,' he told another Oxford friend.[2]

For all of their lives, Larkin and Amis wrote filthy letters to one another, trying to outdo one another in explicit, outrageous language, often signing off their letters with obscenities: 'Don't forget my book you fuckpot', 'I often tear pages out of books of that kind to clean my arse-hole with after I have shat'.[3] Another habit was to add the word 'bum' to people or places. 'Margaret Thatcher bum', '*Penguin Book of Contemporary British Poetry* bum', 'Handel bum', 'handsome bum Philip'. As Larkin's biographer Andrew Motion suggests, this was part schoolboy humour, part experimenting with a mockery of pomposity and middle-class respectability: 'the discrepancies between what can be said or shown in public and what in private' would become a feature of their mature writing.[4]

Larkin and Amis both got firsts at Oxford. Amis named his firstborn son after Philip: 'My little son has a face like that of an ageing railway porter who is beginning to realise his untidiness means he'll never get that ticket-collector's job he's been after for 28 years.'[5] In later years, their friendship was largely based on their correspondence. Larkin, at heart deeply shy and socially awkward, often preferred friendships that were epistolary.

Despite the schoolboy frolics and heavy drinking at Oxford, Larkin completed his first grown-up novel by the age of twenty-one. Set in wartime Oxford, *Jill* is a beautifully written, poignant story about a lonely, lower-middle-class undergraduate who finds it difficult to adjust to university life. The hapless hero, John Kemp, invents a sister (Jill) to assuage his sense of worthlessness and inferiority and to impress his odious, thuggish contemporaries, who bully and manipulate him. This was not at all Larkin's own experience of Oxford, but many of Kemp's insecurities, deep feelings of loneliness and escapes into a world of fantasy were Larkin's own.

Like Barbara Pym, Larkin took a job to supplement his writing career. Indeed, many hours of library time were spent writing and redrafting his literary output or scribbling letters to his friends. His correspondence with Pym lasted until her death. His letters to her are, as his literary executor Andrew Motion puts it, some of the 'funniest and most charming' he ever wrote.[6]

Their epistolary relationship began in a formal fashion – 'Miss Pym' and 'Mr Larkin' – but soon developed into a tone of genuine friendship and intimacy. Larkin, who had been introduced to Pym by his sister Kitty ('the only clever thing to do with books she did in her life'), deeply admired Pym's novels.[7] Larkin had a complicated personal life and both his lovers, Monica Jones and Maeve Brennan, were Pym fans.

The correspondence began just after the publication of *No Fond Return of Love*. Larkin told Pym that he had given away his first copy and lent out his second. He sent Pym his impressions on a second reading: 'I thought all the Devon part was splendid and it was nice to meet Wilmet and Keith again. There is something very special about these two: they are memorable not only in themselves but in their relation, as if Wilmet's reward for her *sins* is this ridiculous unwanted incubus, or do I mean familiar.'[8] He particularly admired Wilmet and Keith's unlikely friendship, despite – or because of – their love for the same man. In fleshing out Keith's character, Pym had scribbled an entry in her notebook, which shows the extent of her profound understanding of the nature of human relationships – in this instance seeing the perspective of a homosexual man: 'When I meet Keith I am surprised that he does not seem to be jealous, until it occurs to me that he does not need to be.'[9]

Pym replied to Larkin: 'poor Wilmet and Keith. I think incubus or familiar describes him very well.'[10] Hilary had been tidying her desk and found an old photograph album that reminded Barbara of a 'lovely poem of Larkin's. His "Lines on a Young Lady's Photograph Album".'[11] The poem, based on a true event in his life, shows the narrator wistfully looking through a photograph album that belongs to his lover. The images choke him with emotion, bringing back to life a girl in pigtails, clutching her cat, then a once 'sweet girl-graduate', and then her past lovers. The narrator is reminded of a past that he can't be part of: 'We cry, Not only at exclusion, but because/ It leaves us free to cry.'[12]

Few writers have captured this profound sense of exclusion, of separation and loss, better than Larkin in his poems and Pym in her novels.

CHAPTER XXIII

No fond Return to Print

With the new move to Queen's Park, things were looking up. Pym's work was beginning to reflect the changing times. Laurel, in *No Fond Return of Love*, sports a beehive hairstyle, wears mini-skirts and listens to rock'n'roll. Penelope in *An Unsuitable Attachment* is boho-chic, with quirky clothes. She too sports a beehive.

The relationship between a working-class man and a middle-class woman also reflected the new age. In 1960, Princess Margaret married commoner Antony Armstrong-Jones. The service at Westminster Abbey was the first royal wedding to be televised. By 1960, 79 per cent of households, including the Pym sisters, owned a television set.[1] Pym wrote vividly, too, about bedsit land and the sadness and loneliness of town-dwelling far from supportive communities, whether they be church or village. She felt that she was adapting to what Prime Minister Harold Macmillan called the 'Wind of Change' that was sweeping across the time.[2]

Philip Larkin would describe Pym's new novel, *An Unsuitable Attachment*, as 'the most solidly churchy' of her books in terms of subject matter, but still typical of the 'undiminished high spirits' which characterised her early works. There is a melancholy undertow to it, however, which reflects the isolation of people and the disintegration of community life in post-war London.

The novel is set around a north London parish. Sophia Ainger is a vicar's wife, who has married 'beneath her'. Mark and Sophia Ainger are childless, and she dotes on a beautiful but spoiled tortoiseshell cat called Faustina. Like Pym's cat, Minerva, she has a golden streak down her nose, giving the effect of a beak. Faustina is given full rein at the vicarage, allowed to eat from their plates and to jump on the beds and furniture, scattering cat hairs wherever she lands. The vicar is first discovered buying plaice for all three of them in a fish and chip shop on the less salubrious outskirts of his north London parish, incurring the disapproval of an indomitable spinster, Sister Dew, a retired nurse:

'Good evening vicar – been getting fish for pussy?'

When he turned round, rather startled, the voice went on, 'Oh, *I* know what you've got in the bag – you can't hide anything from me!' . . .

'How you do love pussy,' Sister Dew went on. 'Only the other day I was at the vicarage, seeing Mrs Angier about my stall at the bazaar . . . and there was pussy bold as brass, if you please, walking into the lounge as if she owned it.'

But she does, Mark thought, though he said nothing.[3]

Sophia is a matchmaker and wishes to marry off her sister, Penelope, to an eligible young social anthropologist, Rupert Stonebird, who has moved into the parish. Penelope is a child of the sixties, with her beehive hairdo, false eyelashes and tartan trousers. But Sophia's plans appear to be thwarted by the appearance of another new neighbour, a librarian called Ianthe Broome, who, as a canon's daughter, seems to be a rival for Rupert's affections. Ianthe is tall and elegant and identifies herself as 'an

Elizabeth Bowen heroine – for one did not openly identify oneself with Jane Austen's heroines'.[4]

The chief librarian, Mervyn Cantrell, is a fussy, disappointed middle-aged bachelor who once aspired to a job in a university library, and lives with his disagreeable old mother. He appoints a new assistant, John Challow, a handsome young man with an intense gaze, who has previously worked as a film extra. Ianthe, a social snob, is attracted to John but suspicious of his pointed shoes, which are 'not quite what men one knew wore'. She is surprised when she finds him reading a volume of Tennyson's poems.

Most of the characters in *An Unsuitable Attachment* are deeply lonely. Mark Ainger feels displaced by his wife's obsessive love for her cat. Rupert Stonebird is married to his work: his research is 'extra marital relations in the Ngumu', but he has little feeling for real human emotion. He would like a wife, but more as an adornment to his house. He knows that cool, elegant Ianthe is more suitable wife material, but he is sexually attracted to Penelope, whom he thinks of as a 'pre-Raphaelite beatnik'.

Once more, Pym uses the world of anthropology to depict the machinations of 'civilised people'. Rupert as an eligible bachelor is an object of curiosity for the parish of St Basil's, and he is observed as closely and as warily 'as wild animals hidden in long grass'. At a dinner party, we meet again the egregious Everard Bone, now married to Mildred Lathbury. The guests discuss the life of the writer who writes the same novel over and over again and the anthropologist who reuses the same material, 'like a housewife faced with the remains of yesterday's stew and wondering whether it can possibly be eked out for another meal'. Everard tries to explain his philosophy: 'Haven't the novelist and anthropologist more in common than people think? . . . After all, both study life in communities.'[5]

At Christmas time, the single people without children feel at their most lonely. Ianthe and Rupert return home from work to cold and empty houses. When Sophia dresses her Christmas cake, her only decoration is a rather sad, solitary figurine of Santa Claus. Her husband describes him as looking like 'King Lear in the snow deserted by his daughters'.[6] Pym's world is still peopled with splendid women, such as Sister Dew, who keeps herself busy with church life, and Daisy Pettigrew, who keeps a cattery in her basement. But there is also Miss Grimes, who lives in a single room in a house at the mercy of a nosy social worker who advises her to spend her pension on vegetables rather than the comforting Spanish wine she craves in the evening.

It is not only at Christmas time that lonely people feel at their worst, but also when they are poorly with nobody to attend to their needs. When Ianthe is ill, she is visited by the vicar's wife, and her neighbour, Rupert Stonebird, who fills her hot-water bottle. However, when John Challow falls sick, he has nobody, and Ianthe decides that she must pay him a visit. Pym's attention to detail is immaculate. Ianthe visits John's bedsit, bringing flowers and barley water, and sees that he is in bed. She is shocked by his squalid flat: the narrow bed with its cheap eiderdown, the dirty patterned rug, the chocolate brown linoleum.

> In one corner there was a sink and a gas ring, partly hidden by a screen, a pile of unwashed crockery on a small table and a red plastic bucket filled with empty tins, tea leaves and broken egg shells. Indignation surged up within her – that he should have to live like this.[7]

In homage to Elizabeth von Arnim's *The Enchanted April*, the action moves from cold, grim London to Italy. In Arnim's novel, Italy is a magical place where cold marriages are rejuvenated, and love affairs are kindled. Likewise, Mark and Sophia drew closer together; not only in the heat of the sun, and the glories of Rome, but because, for once, Mark is not sharing his wife with Faustina. In an Italian garden, Rupert kisses Penelope. Ianthe and Sophia take a trip to Ravello to visit Sophia's aunt. Ianthe is bewitched by the setting: "'It's lovely," she said. "It reminds me of *The Enchanted April* – wisteria and the roses".'[8]

In Italy, Ianthe is hit by the realisation that she loves John Challow. When she is probed by Sophia, she confesses her feelings. Sophia, knowing that John is both younger and socially inferior, is shocked by the unsuitable attachment (forgetting that she herself has married 'down'), telling Ianthe that John 'isn't the sort of person one would *marry*'. She (lamely) tells Ianthe that 'you're one of those women who shouldn't marry' – that she should be a 'splendid spinster'.[9] Later, Sophia thinks of Ianthe when, at the end of the evening meal, she unties a little bundle of lemon leaves, 'leaf after leaf until the fragrant raisins were revealed at the centre'. The lemon leaves seem to be a suitable metaphor: 'This process surely had something in common with uncovering the secrets of the heart, as Ianthe, aided by Sophia's probings had uncovered hers.'[10]

Sophia is convinced that marriage based on different social backgrounds can never be a success. But the world has changed. Social conventions have changed. Ianthe, despite the age gap, despite the class boundaries, and to the horror of most of her friends and family, does marry John Challow. Pym was again moving with the times. *An Unsuitable Attachment* ends happily, but a darkness reverberates in her depiction of loneliness, especially for the women who so often seem to draw the short straw. There's a flash of the old Pym wit in the remark from vicar, Basil Branche, as he views the married couple: "'Imparadised in one another's arms," as Milton put it . . . "Or encasseroled".'[11]

Pym was satisfied with her work. She sent it off to Jonathan Cape, her long-standing publisher.

Nothing could have prepared her for the blow of the rejection. When the letter arrived, cold and informal, with its clear indication that she was not going to be published in the near future, she was left devastated and humiliated. It evoked all of the rejection that she had endured in her life, from Henry Harvey to Gordon Glover and those in-between: 'To receive a bitter blow on an early Spring evening (such as that Cape don't want to publish *An Unsuitable Attachment* – but it might be that someone doesn't love you anymore) – is it worse than on an Autumn or Winter evening?'[12]

She had been, in her own words, 'offloaded'. And the men responsible had not bothered to give her the courtesy of a face-to-face meeting or a telephone call. It was the most cowardly and cruellest of rejections and it affected her for a long, long time.

Barbara Pym now entered what she would call her wilderness years.

BOOK THE SIXTH

The wilderness years

CHAPTER I

Miss Pym's Annus Horribilis

Nineteen sixty-three was the coldest winter on record for over two hundred years. The 'Big Freeze' began in December and ended in March. Bitter winds from the Arctic dipped temperatures far below zero, and in some parts of Britain the snow was over five feet deep. Roads and railways were blocked, villages cut off for days. Telephones and power lines were brought down, leaving people without electricity. It was so cold for so long that the sea started to freeze around coastal areas and icebergs were spotted in the Thames.

The house at 40 Brooksville Avenue was freezing and sparsely furnished. There was no central heating. The Pym sisters had electric fires, coal fires in the bedrooms and a couple of paraffin stoves. Pym told Philip Larkin that she seemed to be endlessly crouched on her knees, filling the stoves. Even the toilets at St Lawrence's church had frozen over. In February, the power lines had failed: 'no heat from electric fires and no TV picture till 10.30 p.m. Luckily we have coal and paraffin too, though, and we managed to avoid frozen pipes and bursts which is a great blessing.'[1] The sisters had received a terrible shock with the news that their father was bankrupt and they had helped him out financially. Money was tight. Pym's salary was meagre and now her writing career appeared to be over.

Unsurprisingly, Pym's outlook was bleak in this time. The bitter cold ('frigid hostile air') made her life a misery. Nineteen sixty-three was swiftly becoming her annus horribilis. In February, the month when Sylvia Plath took her own life just three miles away, the house at Brooksville Avenue was burgled twice in quick succession. First time around, the thieves took jewellery and Hilary's camera. When they returned the following week, they stole Pym's typewriter, an electric fire and some silver.

In the same month that Cape dropped Pym, the Beatles released *Please Please Me*. The four working-class lads from Liverpool were a breath of fresh air, defying the old-fashioned elite with their irreverent razor-sharp wit, mop-top hairstyles and catchy pop songs. Beatlemania had begun, and with it a cult of youth and working-class rebellion in which Pym's world suddenly looked unfashionably middle aged and middle class – though she herself liked their records. Philip Larkin's tongue-in-cheek poem 'Annus Mirabilis' cited 1963 as the year of the invention of sex in the UK. In December 1961, the Minister of Health, Enoch Powell, announced that the oral contraceptive pill, Conovid, would become available by prescription through the National Health Service at the subsidised price of two shillings per month. Sexual intercourse without fear of pregnancy had begun, but rather too late for Barbara Pym.

Meanwhile, as Larkin also noted in his poem, unexpurgated copies of D. H. Lawrence's *Lady Chatterley's Lover* were circulating freely as a result of the verdict in the infamous obscenity trial of 1960 ('Is it a book that you would have lying around in your own house? Is it a book that you would even wish your wife or your servants to read?' prosecuting counsel Mervyn Griffith-Jones had asked the jury in his opening statement). As publishers and readers felt newly licensed to take on sexually explicit material, the novels of Miss Pym suddenly looked prim. In America, the Kinsey Report, *Sexual Behaviour in the Human Female*, had led the way in suggesting that the bedroom could be a place where fun happens, rather than one's duty. Now Britain was following along: 1963 saw the publication of UK editions of Helen Gurley Brown's celebration of *Sex and the Single Girl* and Betty Friedan's book that launched the second wave of feminism, *The Feminine Mystique*. Helen Gurley Brown's manual, which stayed on the bestseller list for over a year, made her position clear:

> *Should a Man Think You Are a Virgin?*
> I can't imagine why, if you aren't. Is he?
> Is there anything particularly attractive about a thirty-four
>   year old virgin?[2]

This is an attitude that chimed with Pym's liberal attitude to sex in her personal life. She was one of the most liberated, independent women of her time. Ever since Oxford, she had been sexually active and unashamed of being so. One of her friends explained: 'You see, Barbara liked sex.'[3] Nor did she feel the need to settle down to a conventional married life, despite several offers. The trouble was, her novels of quiet female independence did not exactly brim with sex, drugs and rock and roll.

And then there was the Profumo affair, a story combining sex and politics that had been bubbling away since 1961, but which in the summer of 1963 would dominate the headlines of every newspaper, as the nation slavered over the 'call girl' Christine Keeler and watched the trial and suicide of Dr Stephen Ward with lurid fascination.

Pym, smarting from her rejection by Jonathan Cape, was further discouraged by the lack of interest from other publishers in novels that seemed tame and outdated. She wrote to Philip Larkin:

Many thanks for your kind letter of astonishment and indignation . . . the more one looks at the books now being published, not to mention the stirring events of this year, the less likely it seems that anyone, except a very select few, would want to read a novel by me. I could almost offer my services to Dr Stephen Ward as a ghost writer, for he is a Canon's son.[4]

CHAPTER II

Miss Pym takes Umbrage

Pym was angry. She wrote a furious letter to her sometime publisher, saying that she felt that she had been badly treated. Wren Howard of Cape was obdurate, telling her that her books had not brought any profit and with the closure of Smith's circulating libraries and the reduction of Boots' libraries, novels were harder and harder to sell.

Her friends rallied. Philip Larkin wrote again to say that he was bewildered that Cape were taking this line. Jock wrote that a new editor, Tom Maschler, was probably responsible. Seeing the way the wind was blowing, Jock had defected to another smaller publisher the year before. According to Pym, Maschler had 'off-loaded' other loyal authors in favour of only publishing bestsellers 'like Ian Fleming'. She was reduced to the humiliating task of touting the manuscript of *An Unsuitable Attachment* to other publishing houses, meeting again and again with rejection:

23 April Posted *Unsuitable Attachment* to Heath . . .

3 May Heath returned *Unsuitable Attachment* . . .

30th May Sent *Unsuitable Attachment* to Ivor Guest at Longmans . . .

6 June Had *Unsuitable Attachment* back from Longmans.[1]

It was ill luck that the novel's central thesis – that a cross-class relationship was widely regarded as 'unsuitable' – seemed horribly out of kilter with the times. The publishers who rejected the book missed her irony, rather as generations of 'Janeites' have imagined Austen to be a romantic novelist: far from endorsing the notion that such liaisons were 'unsuitable', she was fully prescient of the allure in the idea of 'posh girls' dumbing down. Princess Margaret's romance with Tony Armstrong-Jones was only the most high-profile example. The photographer David Bailey pursued middle- and upper-class girls: 'all us working-class lads love a posh girl', he famously remarked.

Novels such as John Braine's *Room at the Top* (1957) had glamorised the working-class hero. The problem for Pym was that her working-class hero, John Challow, wasn't sufficiently well drawn. Part of her knew this and she would have been happy to revise the novel if Cape had given her the chance. As she wrote to Philip Larkin: 'I fear the attachment is not so unsuitable as some of the public (reading) might wish.'[2]

It felt especially hard to be considered behind the times when she was in so many ways ahead of them. The Wolfenden Report of 1957 had recommended the legalisation of homosexuality, and then only for men over the age of twenty-one, but decriminalisation did not come for another full decade. Pym's novels, in which homosexual men (from different social classes) lived happily together, older women had love affairs with younger men, and free-spirited young women such as Prudence Bates dated married men and conducted love affairs outside of marriage, were anything but prim. If only Cape had had the wit to see beyond the genteel facade of her social comedies and find the grit below.

Pym was now working on another story about a woman's love for a homosexual man, though this time with a new twist. Pym's 'annus horribilis' had been brightened by one silver lining. The previous summer, Bob Smith had introduced her to a friend he had met on holiday in Greece. He was an extremely good-looking, charming and much younger man. His name was Richard Campbell Roberts, though he was known to his friends as Skipper. Pym fell catastrophically in love.

CHAPTER III

Hullo Skipper

Pym was now approaching fifty. She was feeling her age in a world she was increasingly finding uncongenial and alien. The sixties era, with its emphasis on youth culture, seemed to be so very different to her own and yet, she too had experienced much in her lifetime. She wrote to Bob Smith expressing her feelings as she approached middle age: 'I thought, surging through Smith's in Fleet Street today, I'm just a tired-looking middle aged woman to all these (mostly young) people: yet I have had quite a life and written (or rather published) six novels which have been praised in the highest circles.'[1]

Despite believing herself to be 'tired-looking', she was still attractive, with her charming 'lop-sided smile'. Her friends and acquaintances remember her as tall and well-dressed but a little remote and reserved. Hilary was the more lively sister. Life had bruised Pym. The giggling Oxford undergraduate in her outlandish 'Sandra' clothes had given way to a more sober, reflective and careworn woman. But she was still open to love and being loved.

And then, in the summer of 1962, she met Skipper. He was virile-looking, rugged and handsome, with a gorgeous wide smile. He was eighteen years Pym's junior and hailed from the

Bahamas, where his family had been amongst the first white settlers. The Roberts were prosperous and lived in a large, ocean-front colonial-style mansion called 'Lucky Hill', perched on the crest of a promontory overlooking Montague Bay in Nassau. Richard's father, Sir George Roberts, was a lumber merchant who subsidised and standardised the transformation of mail-boats. Three of his vessels were named after his three sons, Richard, Gary and Noël.

Sir George Roberts also played a leading role in the political life of the Bahamas. He was a leader of Government House from 1949–54 and then president of the legislative council. He married Freda Genevieve Sawyer in 1929 and Richard, their eldest son, was born the same year. Pym was just a few years younger than Richard's mother, with whom he had a complicated relationship. He told Pym stories about her grand life in the Bahamas, her magnificent jewels and her black butler. She owned peacocks. Pym was fascinated. His life in this exotic location seemed to her full of rich material for fiction, but she feared it was beyond her range.

Skipper was exciting and glamorous, but he also possessed a 'little-boy-lost' appeal. He had never had a proper job and seemed aimless and lacking in purpose. Every winter he returned home to Nassau. In the summer, in England, he dabbled in antiques and art. Skipper made and lost friends. He was sometimes unreliable. He was also hiding a secret from his family. Skipper was homosexual.

It appears that Pym knew about Skipper's sexual orientation from the start, but it did not prevent her from falling deeply in love with him. He seemed to enjoy her affection and attention. He was impressed by the fact that Pym had published many novels and was highly regarded by his friend, Bob Smith. Their relationship grew slowly, with dinner invitations and the exchange of books.

Skipper's London flat was located in the glamorous district of Lancaster Gate, a stone's throw from Hyde Park. It was an elegant two-bedroomed apartment in a white stucco building, a far cry from Brooksville Avenue. He shared his flat with an actor called Maurice Quick. Pym wrote several letters to Skipper, which he found 'almost as charming as your novels with [their] shafts of irony'. It was not long before 'Dear Barbara' became 'Dearest' and then 'Darling Barbara'.[2]

CHAPTER IV

Miss Pym visits Keats's House
in Hampstead

For the eleven years that Pym lived in Brooksville Avenue, she did not publish a single novel. But she did not stop writing. As with many writers, it was a compulsion. Her notebooks reveal several different plot lines.

One idea, inspired by her work at the African Institute, was on that favourite theme of anthropologists, polygamy: 'An old woman living in a village with her two husbands (a modern instance of polyandry), one divorced – but, poor thing, unable to cope on his own.' The first husband would live in a shed in the bottom of the garden, where hot dinners are sent down. The second husband, Hilary, wouldn't mind sharing the house with the first husband, but is worried about what the villagers might think of the arrangement: 'few of these good people are familiar with what one might call polyandry'. Another was a story about a middle-aged woman with an Italian lover: 'His hatred of Naples and Neapolitans. Love of Guinness. He eats too quickly whereas she likes to linger over her food. He is preoccupied with death.'[1]

Skipper was beginning to join Pym's social circle, meeting Jock Liddell in Athens during a summer break. Jock wrote to

Pym to say that he had enjoyed talking to Skipper and his friend 'Michael from Bangkok'. Back in England, dining with the Pym sisters, Skipper told the sisters all about the 'literati' who flocked to see Jock. He had invited Skipper and Michael from Bangkok to an event with the novelist Elizabeth Taylor. Skipper thought Taylor very bored, but Pym assured him that boredom was her usual manner, which concealed her shyness.

Skipper invited the Pym sisters to a cosy dinner in his flat. He then returned to Nassau to spend Christmas with his parents and sent what Barbara described as a very pagan Christmas card. She prepared for winter, cleaning her paraffin stove, filling the coal shed and turning a small dining room into a winter sitting room.

After her rejection from Cape, Pym had put *An Unsuitable Attachment* aside and started to write a new novel, which she called *Spring*. In her notebook of 1962, she noted down that she had bought a little Italian bowl, with a lemon and leaves painted inside. It was chipped, but still gave her immense pleasure: 'I begin to wonder if I'm getting to the stage when objects could please more than people or (specifically) men.' Objects and antiques also reminded her of Denton Welch and the use he made of them in his novels. But meeting Skipper and sharing his love of antiques had given her a plot point for the new novel she was writing: 'A man, dealer in antiques, goes to a parish jumble sale in search of Victoriana and there gets involved in things he would rather not have experienced.'[2]

In August, on a soggy day, Pym made a pilgrimage to John Keats's house in Hampstead. The outlook was disappointing, with a view of ugly modern houses. Inside it was 'austere and simple', and she noted the red stone engagement ring that Keats had given to Fanny Brawne: 'almandine: a garnet of violet tin . . . set in gold'. The curator had filled the conservatory with flowers, begonias, pelargoniums, geraniums and bunches of grapes hanging from a vine. 'We try to keep it a thing of beauty,' said the curator, quoting Keats.[3] Pym would use the visit for the setting of an important scene in her new novel.

She also went to the new Henry Moore–Francis Bacon exhibition in the underground gallery at Bond Street. She was alone and noted other solitary visitors. In a grand antique shop in Bond Street, she observed a young man sitting alone, waiting for customers. Thinking of herself and Skipper, it occurred to her that a woman admirer might be a great nuisance always going in to see him.

Pym still cherished hopes of publishing *An Unsuitable Attachment*. Skipper had also suggested a new title, 'Run Away Love'. But she replied firmly: 'This is not a B Pym title.' She toyed with several new titles: *Wrapped in Lemon Leaves*; *A Plate of Lemon*; *The Lemon Leaves*; *A Lemon Spring*; *Hidden in Lemon Leaves* . . .

10th July Sent *Wrapped in Lemon Leaves* to Macmillan

1 August *Wrapped in Lemon Leaves* came back from Macmillan.[4]

Another rejection. A note of sourness crept into her journal as she gave vent to her feelings towards Cape and their insistence on 'contemporary novels': 'men and Americans' seemed to be all the rage. The final straw, she told Larkin, came when she heard that Cape were about to publish a book by 'one of the Beatles: John Lennon? I think?'[5]

Skipper invited the Pym sisters to an opening of an exhibition of Thai paintings. She went along, pleased to see that the champagne was flowing and the exhibition splendid: 'but all the pictures are much too expensive for us'. Skipper was attentive, 'very sweet and wearing a becoming summer suit of some dark silky material'.[6]

Pym told Bob Smith that Hilary was now secretary of the parish council at St Lawrence's. Still smarting over Cape's rejection, she told Bob: 'Who wants to read mild novels by Barbara Pym?' Pym usually met with Bob when he came back to the UK for an annual visit and they often dined in Soho, enjoying *osso buco* – Italian braised veal and vegetables. Pym promised she would write a scene in which their favourite dish was eaten. Bob had a new companion, 'a wicked friend from Lagos'.

Life at the institute, though busy, was not fulfilling. She told Bob: 'I am writing this in the office on a Friday afternoon, surrounded by the raw material for the April *Africa*, the proofs of various books and a shopping bag containing tins of cat food, frozen fish cakes, packet soups etc.'[7] Daryll Forde arranged for a performance of an adaptation of Amos Tutuola's controversial Nigerian novel *The Palm-Wine Drinkard* (1952). Based on Yoruba folktales, this was the first African novel to be published in England. Pym was unimpressed: 'That would be one entertainment Miss Pym would *not* like to attend.'[8]

Much of Pym's leisure time was now taken up with St Lawrence's. She told Bob that many of the congregation were Nigerians and that many of the adults were being baptised. A pretty girl called Florence asked Pym to stand as godmother. After the ceremony there was a party with Coca-Cola, British wine, tea, cake, biscuits 'and delicious Nigerian rice and fish with hot peppery sauce'.[9]

There had been another burglary at Brooksville Avenue and so the sisters installed a metal frame over the kitchen window, where the intruders were getting in. Skipper, meanwhile, was opening an antique shop in Sloane Street. It was called L'Atelier and he was planning to decorate it with indigo walls and a purple carpet. He donated some antiques to the St Lawrence's Christmas bazaar and asked Pym to go to the theatre with him. She had given him copies of *A Glass of Blessings* and *Excellent*

Women. He told her that he found the latter witty, but 'terribly sad'. She wrote to Bob: 'Why is it that *men* find my books so sad? Women don't particularly. Perhaps they have a slight guilt feeling that this is what they do to us and yet really it isn't as bad as all that.'[10]

It is interesting that Skipper made no comment on *A Glass of Blessings*, in which the heroine falls in love with a homosexual man, eventually accepting and befriending his lover. Pym's friends joked that she made events happen in real life by first writing about them. Her fleeting attraction to Bob Smith and her admiration for Denton Welch may have given her the plot point of a woman falling for a homosexual man, but her relationship with Skipper proved just how painful it could be. In her novels, homosexual men were often drawn in the Denton Welch versus Eric Oliver mould, playing off the sensitive, effete, fragile one (Denton) against his hunky, unintellectual foil (Eric). The problem with Skipper was that he was the perfect composite: he was extremely masculine and macho, with his broad shoulders and strong physique, but he was also sensitive, artistic and intelligent, with a love of antiques and objets d'art.

Skipper would break Pym's heart, but the relationship inspired her greatest novel, which she would call *The Sweet Dove Died*.

CHAPTER V

Of Wistfulness and Whitsun Weddings

Philip Larkin was one of the first people Pym contacted when faced with her humiliating rejection from Cape. His support was instantaneous and his resentment fierce. For the rest of her life, he never stopped fighting for her rehabilitation. As in the early days Jock had encouraged and supported Pym's writing, helped her to find a publisher and an agent, now Larkin took on that role. He and Pym shared a similar sense of humour, a love of the commonplace and trivial, and a dislike of publicity. Larkin guarded his private life and was happy living in the relative obscurity of Hull. Pym wrote: 'Yes, I have a shrinking from publicity too, which is just as well as I seem to be doomed to failure and to sink down into obscurity.'[1]

But it would be a mistake to suggest that the relationship was one-sided. Pym was just as encouraging, probing Larkin as to why he didn't write more novels (she suggested, accurately, that first and foremost he wanted to be a novelist rather than a poet) and frequently, though gently, pressing for another volume of poetry. They shared memories of Oxford. Pym had not read *Jill*, which was to be shortly reissued by Larkin's new publisher, Faber and Faber. Larkin planned to write a new introduction: 'an anti-twenties piece – no ortolans or Diaghilev or Harold Acton or Sebastian Flyte, just grammar school boys clumping about in OTC uniform and one bottle of wine a term (the ration)'.[2] Pym responded with her own 'thirties' version of Oxford:

> I suppose when you were at Oxford *nobody* came into The George wearing a silver lamé shirt or went around with a lizard on their shoulders or carried a toy kangaroo – and that was the early thirties when I was up. But surely there must have been *girls*, even in the austere one-bottle-of-wine a term forties (shoulder-length pageboy hair, square shoulders and short skirts).[3]

By the end of the year, Miss Pym and Mr Larkin were now 'Philip and Barbara'. Larkin told her that his girlfriend, Monica, was a Pym addict and her favourite character was Catherine Oliphant in *Less Than Angels*; 'curiously enough my least favoured', he added. Pym responded: 'Catherine used to be quite a favourite heroine of mine but she now seems less real to me than Wilmet and Prudence (my own favourites).'[4] Larkin, knowing her deep disappointment and the blow to her confidence, was keeping her characters alive. He went to a librarians' conference, joking that nobody fainted, as a character in *A Glass of Blessings* does in a similar setting.

One silver lining in an otherwise dull and cold Christmas was a letter from Skipper, who was back in the Bahamas. He revealed his 'inferiority complexes' and his troubled relationship with his mother. He had had a 'fearful row' with her and confessed to Pym that, although he knew his mother loved him, she 'disliked him intensely as a person'.[5] He hated the 'rich proles' and 'tax dodgers' who flocked to the Bahamas in search of winter sun and told her that he avoided town, only going in to buy a copy of *The Times*: 'The latter I find is as necessary to me as tea is to you.'

He added: 'We must try to do some of the things in 64 that

were impossible last year for a great number of reasons, like repeat visits to the Kardomah.'⁶ The Kardomah, which makes several appearances in Pym's novels, was one of her favourite cafes. It originated as a coffee shop in Liverpool, close to the Cavern Club, and became a haunt for the Beatles. Pym frequented the London Kardomah, on Piccadilly, which boasted a bright wall mural of peacocks. She liked the cosy basement and spent many an hour there with Skipper.

Pym told Bob Smith that her new novel 'was beginning to flow . . . and ideas come crowding into BP's bounding heart and teeming brain'. She did not tell Bob that Skipper was the inspiration. But her frequent mentions of him in her letters reveal her growing infatuation. She had visited his antique shop just before Christmas: 'He comes to see us quite often, his car now knowing the way down Carlton Vale.'⁷

By now, Pym had discovered the identity of the mystery woman mentioned at the furniture storage unit, which had given a plot line for A Glass of Blessings. She was called Joan Wales and was a friend of both Skipper and Bob. Pym had now met Joan and she told Bob how much she liked her and hoped the feeling was mutual. Bob had asked Pym to give Joan a turn of having the furniture she had borrowed from him. He told Pym that he would give it back to her in his will. Pym thought that the whole saga was like something out of a Henry James novel. 'Even I dried-up, cynical and disillusioned as I am, haven't yet got to the stage when I would prefer a few nice pieces of furniture to a dear friend,' she joked.⁸

The sad truth was that Barbara did have to be careful with her finances. With only her poor pay at the institute, she was missing the extra income from her novels. She did not want to become over-reliant on her sister. The year before, they had renovated their kitchen and put in a lovely yellow and white sink, but it meant that their annual holiday had to be postponed.

They were now planning an early summer holiday in May. Hilary had been saving for an extended trip to Greece and Barbara planned to join her for part of it and see Jock in Athens.

Skipper invited her to dinner, often with his actor flatmate Maurice Quick. One time, Joan Wales was there. Pym felt jealous:

> bit much to have to listen to Maurice Quick praising Joan and saying 'what a lovely sense of humour' she has when I sit there dumb and uninteresting. How often do women have to listen to praise of other women and (if they are nice) just sit there agreeing. And yet men don't do it maliciously, just in their simplicity.[9]

On Easter Sunday, Pym went to supper with Skipper: 'We eat cosily in almost total darkness (one candle).' On the mantelpiece she noticed many Easter cards and a telegram – testaments to his popularity. But it somehow made her feel sad: 'One couldn't really give him anything that he hadn't already got. It gives one a hopeless sort of feeling.' His bedroom was flamboyant: 'Roman Emperors . . . on the wall facing the bed which is large and covered in orange candlewick.'[10]

On May Day, she and Skipper went to the opera at Covent Garden. They sat in the Crush Bar, 'the great oil paintings, the flowers (real)' – Skipper crunching ice as they drank orangeade. Already, Pym was turning her own latest crush into a fictional scenario. Her heroine – a beautiful, elegant widow – falls in love with a homosexual/bisexual man, but they embark on an intense affair: 'If "they" went to Covent Garden Leonora would like to feel the touch of his sleeve against her bare arm . . . Close, intimate red and gold semi-darkness.' The figure based on Skipper was initially called Quinton (later changed to James). 'Quinton plays his part with rather self-conscious enjoyment.'

Pym, with her capacity for self-knowledge, knew that the fiction-alised Skipper was based on fantasy: 'Here he is mine she thinks, the young admirer she has created for herself.'[11]

In February, Philip Larkin sent her a copy of his new poetry collection, *The Whitsun Weddings*. She was delighted: 'I wondered if I'd ever *told* you how much I liked your poems.'[12] One of her favourites, she said, was 'Faith Healing'. It depicts a (Billy Graham-like) male American faith-healer, who is administering hope to a line of unloved, unfulfilled women. The women are in need of kindness and redemption. They are given their 'twenty seconds' of the faith-healer's benediction, before being moved on:

> In everyone there sleeps
> A sense of life lived according to love.
> To some it means the difference they could make
> By loving others, but across most it sweeps
> As all they might have done had they been loved.
> That nothing cures.[13]

Larkin's collection sold 4,000 copies within two months of publication and established him as perhaps England's most popular poet. Like Betjeman's poetry, it spoke to the common wo(man) in the post-war age, but with an absence of nostalgia or sentimentality. He wrote about the everyday world that people knew and in language they understood, somehow transforming the mundane into something magnificent. His theme, like Pym's, was provincial England, spiritual despair and the thwarted lives of such figures as 'Mr Bleaney', deceased previous occupant of a rented bedsitting room, bleakly furnished with, 'Bed, upright chair, sixty-watt bulb, no hook/ Behind the door, no room for books or bags'. The narrator is forced to confront his own life choices: 'That how we live measures our own nature.'[14] And yet, in the collection there are moments of great beauty and affirmation in poems such as 'An Arundel Tomb', 'The Whitsun Weddings', and 'Love Songs in Age'. Larkin told Pym that he had ordered the poems in *The Whitsun Weddings* to create a variety of moods so that if the reader wasn't enjoying one, then at least the next one would be different.

In July, Larkin reread all of Pym's novels, 'in one fell swoop'. He told her that *Some Tame Gazelle* was her *Pride and Prejudice*, 'rich and untroubled and confident and very funny'. *Excellent Women* was even better than he remembered, 'full of a harsh kind of suffering . . . it's the study of the pain of being single, the unconscious hurt the world regards as this state's natural clothing'. Mildred, he felt (much in the vein of Jock Liddell), 'is suffering but nobody can see why she shouldn't suffer, like a Victorian cab horse'. Larkin's analysis and close reading were exact and he cut to the heart of Pym's genius in his observation of her ability to capture mood: 'Once again I have marvelled at the richness of detail and variety of mood and setting.' John Betjeman had visited Larkin and they 'rejoiced' together over her work.[15]

Philip's kind encouragement helped Pym to begin writing again. She had written almost eight chapters of her new novel about an older woman falling in love with a homosexual man. She was also revising *An Unsuitable Attachment*. Jock had promised to edit it and offer suggestions for improvement, so she took the manuscript with her when she visited him.

In May, Barbara and Hilary set off for Greece. Pym enjoyed Athens, finding Jock much the same as ever, only fatter with white hair. She also saw Henry Harvey and his second wife. She took a boat tour around some of the Greek islands and had a happy time, but she was still feeling insecure and vulnerable. Jock threw a party, inviting his other novelist friends, Elizabeth Taylor and Mary Renault. The latter had graduated from Oxford a few years before Pym, met a fellow nurse called Julie Mullard while training at the Radcliffe Infirmary (they remained a couple all their lives), nursed Dunkirk evacuees, won a massive $150,000 prize from MGM studios for her first post-war novel, and had now embarked on the writing of a string of best-selling historical novels set in an ancient Greece unapologetically brimming with homosexuality. She arrived resplendent in gold lamé. Barbara berated herself as: 'Miss Pym (a failure) in her simple black.' At a local taverna, Pym noticed the displays of food and lurking black cats. In the beautiful Zappeion gardens, oranges dripped from trees and the garden shrubs smelled deliciously fragrant. Her imagination was let loose: 'here a middle-aged English or American lady might be picked up by a young Greek adventurer'.[16]

She was back home in London at the beginning of June, leaving Hilary to stay in Greece for several more weeks. In her sister's absence, Pym's friendship with Skipper took on a new intensity. She planned to celebrate her fifty-first birthday with him. Just the two of them.

CHAPTER VI

Darling Richard

At his new flat in Sussex Gardens near Paddington railway station, Skipper poured champagne and gave Pym a lovely present – a Victorian china cup and saucer with a frieze of a lady and her cat. This was generous, since Skipper disliked cats and had taken a particular objection to Pym's beloved Minerva, and teased Pym for the way she spoiled her.

Pym's friends worried that she would feel lonely without Hilary, but she took the opportunity to visit her father in Oswestry, noting that Dor, although eighty-five, was still alert and pottering about the house. And Skipper was an attentive and amusing companion; Pym enjoyed being escorted around London in the company of this handsome, energetic much younger man. Without the vigilant and beady eye of Hilary, who had taken on the role of Pym's protector, Skipper was free to flirt and have fun. But there was also a darker side to his ebullient personality, which Pym was soon to discover.

The pair spent much of the summer of 1964 together: 'Oh what a month August was too!' By now he was 'Darling Richard'. They walked in Hampstead, went to the Huguenot Cemetery – 'all beautiful in the dark, warm evening'. In a little Roman Catholic church, Skipper lit a candle. Pym decided not to light one herself and was reduced to silence: 'It is a bit too much like something in a BP novel.' There were romantic walks to Windmill Hill, Admiral's House and the home of the novelist John Galsworthy. They played a game of peeping into people's uncurtained windows and even letterboxes. Skipper's letters suggest the intensity of the relationship: 'My Darling Barbara, How marvellous last night was – it smoothed over the rough patches of the last week with great gentleness. Thank you. Thank you. Thank you.'[1]

Their time together was interrupted when Skipper's father died suddenly. He turned to Pym for comfort: 'The warmth of your affection has done so much for me that words really fail to express my gratitude.' And then dashed back to Nassau to comfort his mother and sort out the complex legal problems around his father's death. His mother refused to wear widow's black, arousing the ire of the local community and Skipper was horrified that his mother expected him to make his permanent home with her; a wish he had no intention of fulfilling. He wrote evocatively of the beautiful weather in the Bahamas: 'Each morning brings the *dawn blessing* – a gentle sweet rain that makes the garden a Paradise by breakfast time – I know how much you would love it.'[2] But there was no invitation to his island Eden; no doubt he was anxious about how his mother would feel about his relationship with a woman close to her own age.

Pym asked him to read *An Unsuitable Attachment* and make suggestions. Despite his appearance as charming but flighty, he read it with great attention. He thought it 'excellent' but flawed, and offered wise and constructive advice for improving the narrative. He told her to cut some of the extraneous details, and focus more on the central relationship between Ianthe and John Challow. Above all, he saw that the main problem was Pym's depiction of a working-class hero. He told her that Challow needed more work: might he be Irish? He said she should base him upon the working-class naval officer she met in Naples; to reveal his charm, his being touched by the 'Blarney stone' – perhaps show him flirting with another woman, arousing Ianthe's jealousy. Skipper felt that the scene where Ianthe visits Challow's bedsit should be more erotically developed: 'She must respond to his physical attractions, say hairs on bare arms (as he sleeps in an old shirt which would also explain him not getting out of bed) and longs to touch him. Pity, tenderness, lust, love.' Pym read his suggestions carefully, noting 'does a gentlewoman know it as lust? Well, what do you think?'[3]

Skipper advised more chapters revealing John's inner thoughts about Ianthe, his desire to be a gentleman, the way he looks up to her but also 'lusts' after her – that word again. He was correct to see that Pym had not sufficiently drawn out the sexual chemistry between her central characters. His frankness about the revelation of female desire also hit a nerve with Pym, given her increasing sexual attraction to him. In her notebook, she expressed some of her feelings about falling in love with a homosexual man, as usual conflating the heroine (Leonora) with herself: 'She thinks perhaps this is the kind of love I've always wanted because absolutely *nothing* can be done about it.'[4]

Perhaps in order to please Skipper, and missing him in the Bahamas, Pym began visiting antique shops in London. Bourdon House was a superior shop, where she fancied a nice pair of mirrors, but balked at the prices – even the smallest malachite egg would have set her back seven guineas, which she did not have. She stored up all the details of her 'antiquing' for use in the new novel. In her letters to 'Darling Richard', meanwhile, Pym hinted at her loneliness. When she arrived back at her house, after being away for the weekend, she found it looking sad and neglected: 'dusty and full of dead flowers – perhaps a not inappropriate setting for a not-very-well-with-it novelist . . .

how full of fictional situations life is! I am now making fuller use of all this and have gone back to writing a novel that I started some months ago.'⁵

In August there was a quarrel. Pym had written a love letter to Skipper, which she then regretted and asked to be returned. When he sent it back (without a covering note), she felt ashamed and foolish about her 'silly and capricious' behaviour. Then, somehow making it all worse, she wrote again, apologising for her behaviour and then repeating her sentiments: 'Anyway, this little note will contain all the fondness of the other letter, in a concentrated form like a cube of chicken stock or oxo.' She told Skipper that she was 'alone so much', and ended her letter wishing that he were 'very well and reasonably happy – no more of those sad looks that cut me to the heart, Skipper dear'.⁶

The relationship seemed to be following the usual course, with Pym making most of the running and pulling back the power, using her status of novelist as her strongest suit. Then, when he got back to London, Skipper telephoned Pym and asked if she would leave him all her literary notebooks. 'No. No', she reacted – but then suggested to herself that 'he should certainly have' notebook number XX, and 'Perhaps this one too.'⁷ She had told Skipper that he was inspiring scenes in her latest novel, though she did not share the extent to which he was shaping the narrative.

To Philip Larkin, however, she was less positive and more realistic about her literary prospects: 'But every now and then I feel gloomy about it all and wonder if anybody will ever want to publish anything of mine again.'⁸ She confessed to Bob Smith her feeling that her life was full of things 'that didn't quite happen'. Skipper had introduced her to one of his boyfriends, John Clark, and they had all gone for a walk in Kew Gardens. Pym found Clark amusing, but tiring. Skipper told Pym 'he is nothing, now'. Confused, she wrote to Bob asking for confirmation ('Is this true?') and telling him of her moments of 'gloom and pessimism, when it seems as if nobody could ever like my style of writing again'.[9]

Pym was feeling rejection both public and private. She had a foot injury, and was working from home and considering going part-time from the institute, though she could not afford to do so: 'The trouble is I rather lack confidence in myself at the moment and in my ability to earn enough *money*.' Even church life seemed to be in a decline: the size of the congregation at St Lawrence's dwindled Sunday to Sunday, due to a combination of, *'Rome, Death and Umbrage*. A good title for a novel, don't you think?'

She confided in Bob, sharing her financial woes, her gloom about the church and her worries about Skipper, who was becoming increasingly cranky and ill-tempered. She blamed it on the antique business: 'I only wish I could do something to help him.' She joked that if she were famous, he could sell her letters to Sotheby's. She thought it best to leave him to go his way. She also realised that, deep down, Skipper was unhappy: 'I wish he could be happier, but I don't think it's in his nature. I love Bob, I love Richard, I love Rice Krispies . . . perhaps it is better in the end just to love Rice Krispies.'[10]

CHAPTER VII

The Tale of the Sweet Bahamian and the Goddess of Brooksville

'Are you going to fry them?' He asked anxiously.

'Yes – why not?' Immediately she was on the defensive and saw the kitchen as it must appear to his half-American eyes – the washing up from lunchtime, the litter of things not thrown away and the paw-marks on the table.

In silence they watched the sausages lying in the frying-pan. After a while the fat began to splutter.

'They're bursting,' she said unhappily.

'I always prick them with a fork,' he said in a kind tone.

'Well, yes, I *did* prick them.'

'With your fingernail?' He smiled.

'No, with a knife, I *think* . . .'

Afterwards when he had gone, it was that part of the evening she remembered – her appalling domestic efficiency and the meagre meal she had given him when he must have been rather hungry. What was it about him that brought out this curious inadequacy?[1]

Pym sent this novelistic scene (and more) to Skipper in the form of a letter. Its purpose was twofold. Just as she had done with

Henry Harvey, she was flattering Skipper by using him as her muse for her fiction. But she was also desperately trying to explain her own frustrated and complex emotions about their relationship. She went on to apologise for an incident about luncheon meat: 'Who she wondered were the people who ate it for "luncheon"?' Somehow there had been a row. 'Perhaps it had been a desperate attempt to break down the awkwardness and loss of *rapport* she had felt between them.'

Pym used her joke novel-letter to try to process and explain the insurmountable barriers between then:

> In church she prayed for them both and resolved to ask him for a proper meal (with cheese) very soon. It gave her a curious kind of pleasure to think of him preparing his luncheon, arranging his table in the elegant way he always did, in the cool clean Sunday morning ambience of Sussex Gardens, in that bright sparkling air, free from the cats' hairs which caused him so much distress in Queen's Park. Any hairs *there* would be Siamese, as he had pointed out.[2]

Of course it was not the cat hair, but all the unspoken things that neither could fully express. Pym knew this: 'So you see, my dear, how with a little polishing life could become literature, or at least fiction! I hope you get its poor little message, or that it at least entertains you for a moment.'[3]

The letter did the trick and a burglary at Sussex Gardens sent him rushing back: 'now the lovely square gold watch and the platinum and diamond one (in the style of the 1920s) left him by his father has gone'. Pym, with her hair still in curlers, comforted him and gave him tea. They went to an election rally in Hammersmith to hear Alec Douglas-Home: an old school Tory, eldest son of the 12th Earl of Home, he had become prime minister following Harold Macmillan's resignation due to illness in the wake of the Profumo affair. A year on, he was fighting for his political life. The week after they heard him speak, Harold Wilson's Labour Party came to power with a narrow majority.

Later, when Skipper invited Pym back to Sussex Gardens, she felt something had shifted. He still looked as gorgeous as ever, in his scarlet pullover and long navy coat: 'Very sweet, but not, perhaps, Skipper again.'[4] There was then a three-week break, when he was in the Bahamas, with no contact. The following month, they met again for lunch and one evening Pym helped him collect some pictures for L'Atelier. He talked about his mother's peacocks and how they had to be shut up in the greenhouse at night. At a party, everyone told Pym that she was 'blooming'. She mused on the reason for this: 'is that joy at seeing R [Skipper] again or what over three weeks *away* from him has done?' At the Lyons restaurant, she sat alone, watching a man coming to a table whilst his companion, a middle-aged woman, went to fetch his food. It reminded her depressingly of her own relationship: 'fetching food for *him* as I have fetched it for my darling R. on more than one occasion'.[5] There were more apologies, this time from Skipper: 'Do forgive, or better still overlook my behaviour of late. I really am beset by difficulties.'[6]

November was always a difficult month for Pym. December, she told Larkin, was even worse 'because that has Christmas too'. That year, Skipper went home to the Bahamas for Christmas. Pym wrote to him, telling him that she was working on a new novel: 'I hate writing "tender love scenes" and am no good at it – why I wonder? Too inhibited and *behaviour*-ridden no doubt.'[7] He replied that he was lonely, she was in his thoughts, and her prayers for him meant a great deal. She had asked for a photograph and he promised to send her a glamorous one.

At the end of January, in the middle of a Sunday afternoon,

Skipper returned unexpectedly from the Bahamian sunshine to the suburban gloom of Brooksville Avenue. 'Are you still brown she asks idly? He pulled out his shirt and revealed a square of golden brown skin on his belly.' It was, for Pym, an erotic moment: 'She found herself thinking "All thy quaint Honour turned to dust/And into Ashes all my lust".' Except, she noted wryly, 'he probably doesn't have any quaint honour'. At least Skipper wrote her a kind letter, desperate to restore Pym's confidence in her novel: 'You know if you want practical assistance I will do all I can. Winter *will* pass after the long delay, of that I am sure.'[8] And he gamely sent a charming Valentine card.

She wrote him a poem:

O, Sweet Bahamian, cruel Fate
Has sent you to me much too late
Tormenting me with many a Scene
Of Happiness that might have been . . .

Yet I must love you, Dearest Boy –
My Jewel, my Treasure and my Joy –
For though you never can be mine,
At least you'll be MY VALENTINE![9]

A week later, however, there was more upset. She rang Skipper, only to have him say that he 'felt guilty (which I hate)'. She invited him to tea, but he was not at his best: 'in his spoilt little Bahamian mood, full of euphoria, money and sex talk, teasing me and being unkind to Minerva. I get irritated with him.'[10] On one occasion he gave Minerva a whack, which deeply upset her. He wrote a poem to 'The Goddess of Brooksville' (Minerva the cat that is, not Barbara), begging forgiveness:

(With apologies to All Good Poets from Catullus to Sandy Wilson).

Who is Minerva, what is she?
Purring gently on Ianthe's knee.
Goddess of Brooksville, quean of cats,
Pampered Neuter, fantastic fat;
Delighting my mistress with feline graces,
All thoughts of me away she chases.

And when I come on bended knee
Ianthe's making pussy's tea.
Matchless Minnie, cunning cat,
Remember well we had a spat,
And I thee whacked with spiteful glee
To show you could not vanquish me.

But now you jealous wicked kitty
I must pretend to show you pity,
Else I fear Ianthe's rage
Will turn upon me page by page.

So, sluttish 'Nerva peace I offer,
Bowing, scraping, humbly proffer:
Now hide thy claws, come out from Telly
And let me tickle thy vast round belly.
Then once again will Ianthe smile,
Prettily deceived by all this guile.

Oh perfumed pussy, betray me not
Or doomed I be to a sad, sad, lot.[11]

Skipper's fear that Pym's rage would avenge itself on the page would prove to be prescient. In May, she decided that she must end the relationship, but she was in too deep. Hilary, who had recently been ill and hospitalised, was sympathetic, but also told her sister to 'be her age'.[12]

Pym was more angry and upset than she suggested to others. In her journal, she expressed her deepest feelings, which she was somehow managing to suppress: 'Fortunately all the fury and bitterness I sometimes feel has stayed hidden inside me and R. doesn't – perhaps never will – know.' She was determined to 'end it all – but how? And why?' But when Skipper wrote a letter inviting her to dinner for her birthday, she softened her resolve: 'I phoned him and we talked. I must learn not to take "things" so much to heart and try to understand – don't stop loving (can't), just be there if and when needed.'[13]

A huge part of the problem was that Pym did not have enough to do. Larkin's encouragement was, as ever, vital. She told him that she was revising and polishing *An Unsuitable Attachment*, as well as working on *The Sweet Dove Died*, but she was struggling with it: 'Over the coldest Easter for 80 years I tried to beat the first two chapters into a better shape now that the characters are becoming clearer.' And she couldn't help but feel that it was all a waste of time: 'I really still wonder if my books will *ever* be acceptable again when I read the reviews in the Sundays.' Nevertheless, she still wanted fame: 'I think it might be nice to be famous and sought after when one is rather old and ga-ga.'[14]

One of Larkin's most well-known works was a funny and bitter poem about the burden of work. It was called 'Toads', using the metaphor to depict the ghastliness and boredom of everyday life. Work is a toad that squats on us, poisoning six days a week just for the sake of 'paying a few bills'.[15] Pym knew that Larkin would understand this aspect of her unhappiness:

'Today, being surrounded by galley proofs, I feel a bit like your poem about the Toad "work".'16 What she couldn't and wouldn't share was the complications of her personal life. The reticence was mutual – though Larkin did tell her that his 'friend' (Monica Jones) thought Pym should have a character who went over to Rome. She rather approved of the suggestion.

When Larkin proposed that she send the revised version of *An Unsuitable Attachment* to Faber, citing his name, she was grateful. Whilst the book sat with Faber, Pym agreed to go to Christie's auction house to bid for books for Skipper in his absence. He was about to travel to Venice, Greece and Istanbul. Before leaving, he took Pym to lunch at the Kardomah. They ate salmon sandwiches, drank coffee, talked about the process of bidding on his behalf, then walked in the rain to W. H. Smith to buy him some holiday reading matter. 'What a change to be happy for a moment,' she confided to her journal.17

Yet with Skipper away, Pym experienced feelings of 'wonderful peace'. Her bid at Christie's was successful: 'Sharpe's 2 vols of *Birds of Paradise* for 1,000 pounds! It was rather nerve-wracking but rewarding and afterwards lunch at Fortnums.'18 She had enjoyed the atmosphere of the sale room. When Skipper returned from his travels, he was so pleased about Pym's acquisition of *Birds of Paradise* that he took her to dinner and gave her a present of a glass bird from Venice. She was delighted; the little bird ornament would feature in a pivotal moment in *The Sweet Dove Died*.

Her spirits were still high when she received bad news from Faber. Larkin's editor, Charles Monteith, sent Pym a kind rejection letter, but it was another blow to her esteem. 'Now I feel as if I shall never write again . . . rather a relief to feel that I don't have to flog myself to finish the present one since probably nothing I write could be acceptable now.'19 She lost no time in reporting the bad news back to Larkin. She thanked him for all his help, but admitted that she had rather given up hope. Larkin was, understandably, mortified. He was trying his utmost to find Pym a new publisher and had sent Monteith a copy of *Excellent Women* back in February ('They aren't all *like this* but a certain plangent autumnal tone is common to them, which I like very much').[20] Pym replied that she was not surprised by the rejection: *An Unsuitable Attachment* was 'not the kind of book to impress a new publisher'. At least she was busy at work and had a new office carpet, 'speckled black and white that won't show the ash'.[21]

Her problematic relationship with Skipper was still gnawing at her. She wrote a message to herself in her journal:

Rainer Maria Rilke 1873–1936

Princess Marie von Thurn und Taxis 1855–1934

(18 years between them, but *he* was a man of genius).[22]

CHAPTER VIII

In which Mr Philip Larkin is disgruntled (when was he not?)

Al Alvarez was one of the few critics of *The Whitsun Weddings* to give Larkin a hostile review. The collection had established Larkin as one of England's foremost poets, but he was rendered furious by one word. Alvarez described Larkin's world as 'commonplace'. Larkin fumed to Monica: 'I'd like to know what dragon-infested world these lads live in that makes them so free with the word "commonplace".'[1] Later he would tell the critic John Haffenden, 'I don't want to transcend the commonplace. I love the commonplace. Everyday things are lovely to me.'[2] Indeed, one of the reasons Larkin loved Barbara Pym's novels so much was her sensitivity to the commonplace, 'the trivial round, the common task'. In his letters to Pym, he made sure to include ephemera that he knew she would enjoy. His carpet, back from the cleaners, feeling like an unmown lawn; a local party with hot punch, Beatles records, and people dancing the twist; his purchase of a Panama hat with a black ribbon.

Larkin could be bitingly sarcastic about other writers. He described Dylan Thomas as 'an incredibly small and tousled, grubby Welshman. His face is round with a comical snubby nose, fat cheeks, incipient double chin and two flabby lips.' E.

M. Forster was a 'toothy little aged Billy Bunter'. Ted Hughes was 'embarrassing'. To his mother, he ranted: 'Honestly, all writers are utterly awful when you meet them.' Even his beloved Hull received the full force of his vitriol, when he was in the mood. He described the city's Market Place as: 'A horrible chip-infested place with swarms of depressing cut-price, kid-dragging people, caricatures of every vapid vulgarity.'³ By contrast, he always treated Pym with the utmost reverence and kindness.

Now that he had learned about her rejection from Faber, Larkin was indignant. Even before he wrote back to Pym, he fired off a letter to Charles Monteith. This was unusual conduct for Larkin, who feared confrontation. He had spent a lovely day with his editor, during which they had discussed the reissue of his collection *The North Ship*. But now he was quietly furious:

> The only feature of the day I am sorry about is your decision about Barbara Pym. I am not very good at expressing my thoughts on the spur of the moment, but in retrospect what I feel is this: by all means turn it down if you think it's a bad book of its kind, but please don't turn it down because it's the kind of book it is . . . Personally, too, I feel it is a great shame if ordinary sane novels about ordinary sane people doing ordinary sane things can't find a publisher these days. This is in the tradition of Jane Austen & Trollope and I refuse to believe that no one wants its successors today.⁴

Larkin was writing his own manifesto: 'I like to read about people who have done nothing spectacular, who aren't beautiful or lucky.' He wanted to read about people who can see 'in little autumnal moments of vision, that the so called *big* experiences of life are going to miss them'. That such things 'are presented not with self-pity or despair or romanticism, but with realistic firmness & even humour'. Larkin, now excessively riled, went out on a limb, saying that this was the 'kind of writing a responsible publisher ought to support (that's you, Charles!)'. He ended by saying that he would willingly write an introduction to Pym's novel, if 'saying so would help you to review your verdict on the book'. He requested no fee: 'I'd gladly provide it for nothing. In fact I'd be honoured.' He finished with a non-apology: 'Forgive this Sunday morning harangue! But I feel I must stand up for a writer I find unique & irreplaceable.'[5]

Had Pym ever had such a loyal and fervent advocate? The only sadness is that she never fully knew the full extent of Larkin's support. He wrote again to her to express his sympathy, encouraging her to try other houses: 'much of my sorrow is quite selfishly due to the fact that I shan't be able to keep the [new] book on my shelves. Do try a few more people with it!'[6] Nor did Larkin let it rest with Monteith, who had written a long, conciliatory letter explaining his decision to reject Pym. But Larkin was eloquent in her defence: 'In all her writing I find a continual perceptive attentiveness to detail, which is a joy and a steady background of rueful yet courageous acceptance of things which I think more relevant to life as most of us have to live it.' Monteith had suggested that Pym had not sufficiently developed as a writer, but Larkin was having none of it: 'I think *development* is a bit of a myth; lots of writers don't develop, such as Thomas Hardy, or P. G. Wodehouse, nor do we want them to. That is how I feel about Miss Pym.'[7]

Mentioning Pym in the same breath as his beloved Hardy and Wodehouse was testimony to Larkin's admiration. But Monteith was wrong to suggest that she had not developed as a writer. And despite the fact that she feared she was no longer publishable, she would continue to develop.

CHAPTER IX

In which Miss Pym takes Skipper as her Guest to the FANY Club Lunch and he receives a Love Token from Another Man, in the form of a Drying-up Cloth patterned with Dachshunds

The Skipper affair dragged on throughout the summer of 1965. Pym invited him to be her guest at a luncheon of the First Aid Nursing Yeomanry (FANY) Club, of which she was a member. An all-female corps, the yeomanry was established in 1907 to provide assistance to civil and military authorities in times of emergency. Originally founded as a group of women who could provide first aid on the battlefield, it had grown exponentially during the two world wars.

Skipper appeared to be particularly charmed by the women: 'He seems quite at home among them and his eyes shine when one pays him a compliment.'[1] Once again, Pym was pleased to have such a good-looking young man, who was entirely comfortable in the company of women, as her companion. After lunch they went to Peter Jones to choose curtain fabric and then on to L'Atelier, where they sat in the window and people-watched.

In September, Pym had a holiday in Malvern, near the

Welsh border, where she visited Sir Edward Elgar's grave. She carried a copy of Thomas Hardy's poems and went to tea in the Abbey tearooms. In the Priory Gardens, the smell of heliotrope reminded her of Skipper's aftershave lotion, L'Heure Bleue.

She returned to London to good news. BBC radio's *Woman's Hour* was broadcasting an adaptation of *No Fond Return of Love*, which encouraged Pym to approach new publishing houses again. Her friend Hazel Holt even suggested that she should think about publishing her novels privately for her loyal following of readers.

In other news, Pym's old haunt the Kardomah had been renovated. She bewailed the loss of the mosaic peacocks, which had made an appearance in her novels, and felt that the restaurant was losing its unique character. The company were 'improving' the ground floor, but were closing the basement, where Pym had spent many an hour in the company of Skipper: 'Where now will we be able to read and write and brood? First the mosaic peacocks went, now this! What emotions are trapped in that basement.'[2]

She wrote to Bob Smith to tell him that she had been at Sotheby's on Skipper's behalf: 'Miss Pym is still frequenting the sale rooms.' Although she had fun bidding and winning a book about the Bahamas, she told Bob that she was far happier at Hodgson's book auctioneers in Chancery Lane, where 'the prices were more realistic'.[3] Skipper was away and Pym found some solace in comfort-eating a creamy walnut cake: 'Now Skipperless, one begins to understand "compensatory eating". Better surely now to write the kind of novel that tells of one day in the life of such a woman.'[4]

That Christmas, the Pym sisters entertained their friends and there was a party at the institute. Skipper went home to Lucky Hill and then on to Mexico for a holiday with his mother. He sent Pym a long affectionate letter, enclosing a nude photograph of himself swimming in the shallows of the sea. In Mexico, he wrote another letter mentioning that, coincidentally, at a Mexican church he had met an 'acolyte' called Richard Pym. It is impossible to know how physical the relationship between Pym and Skipper ever became, but there is no doubting the intensity of the friendship. It is not common for people who are just friends to send Valentine's cards or nude photographs. But it was also a volatile friendship, with many angry quarrels and letters begging for forgiveness. Skipper's feelings were confused not only by his homosexuality, but also because Pym was almost the same age as his formidable mother. Barbara, as Pym freely confessed, had a sharp tongue and would sometimes scold him.

The new year got off to a bad start when Brooksville Avenue was burgled for the fourth time. On this occasion, the man came through the front window, but was spotted by a neighbour and fled the scene. Pym remarked, rather sadly, that there really wasn't very much left to steal. Though she was sanguine about it, it left her feeling vulnerable.[5]

Matters worsened when Skipper returned. On Valentine's Day, he had sent her a card with the message: 'I send you my heart.' But then Pym learned that he had a new boyfriend, Gordon, who worked at the BBC. Skipper invited the sisters out to dinner to meet him:

Hilary and I dined with Richard and Gordon at a Greek restaurant in Notting Hill Gate. Drinks first at 231. Gordon fortyish but dressed and coiffed in Beatle style. Has brought Richard a present of a drying cloth patterned with dachshunds. All the time they are, as it were, flirting with each other, a thing I hadn't observed before.

It was agony to be a witness to this burgeoning romance:

> I can only cling onto small details – Richard using the little
> Worcester sugar bowl I gave him to hold the olives and other
> times when he wears the scarf and gloves I gave him . . . In my
> bedroom, lonely at the weekend, I can look around and see the
> Victorian cup and saucer, the little glass bird, the plates he gave
> me and sniff the pomander on my bedside table.[6]

Some months later, Pym mused in her notebook on what Skipper
might be thinking about her, beginning by imagining his voice,
then switching to her own:

> 'Barbara is looking very strained – she'll be going on holiday
> soon. Abroad, thank goodness – only postcards needed and the
> weather and complete change will do her good – perhaps she'll
> fall in love with somebody (and out of love with me).' But is
> that what he really wants? R was put on this earth to be loved
> – a great responsibility. He is evasive about Gordon. It occurred
> to me that he may want to protect him from my sharp tongue
> and 'sending up'.[7]

CHAPTER X

Miss Pym is Off-loaded, again

On a warm June day in Athens, Barbara Pym found herself sitting in the back seat of a car with her old love, Henry Harvey. A driver, 'who looked like a younger, benevolent Stalin', drove them on a winding route into the mountains, through the passage of Thermopylae and towards the ancient city of Lamia: 'It seemed strange after more than 30 years to be driving with him again.' Much had passed between them, but they had always managed to hold onto their friendship. Pym noted that she had heard a cuckoo as they travelled through Delphi. Sightseeing in Lamia, she noticed plastic doves being sold in the square, and 'on the back corner of the Hotel Achillia there is a stork's or pelican's nest with young'.[1] Was she wondering, subconsciously, about an alternative life in which a stork had brought her and Henry a baby?

Pym, who had once loved Henry so passionately, said little of her feelings on seeing him again – she was still consumed by Skipper. She was reading Anthony Powell's *The Soldier's Art*, the eighth volume of his epic *A Dance to the Music of Time*. Its theme of separation and unexpected loss suited Pym's mood. She told Bob Smith that it was a great comfort and that she found it a beautiful book. What she didn't know was that Powell was a great admirer of her novels and would discuss them in detail with John Bayley.

Pym's friend, Ailsa, went to the Bahamas and met Richard's mother at Lucky Hill. This only emphasised the fact that Pym had never been invited to meet his family. Ailsa told Pym that Lucky Hill was fabulous: 'It gave me a pang to think of her seeing all this.'[2] Once back in London, Skipper sent a letter asking if they could meet on her birthday, but she was no longer 'Darling':

> My dearest Barbara, A letter is always safer at times like these. I do pray all our clouds have rolled away and that we can meet on your birthday as planned. What would you like – a party or just dinner for two somewhere or perhaps something more imaginative? Do let me know. With much love, Skipper.[3]

Pym dreamt about him. In one dream he was driving, and she realised that he was too drunk to be at the wheel: 'You shouldn't have let him get like this. Then I pick R up in my arms and he turns into a cat.'[4]

Skipper sent a dozen pink Constance Spry roses and a tender note, then left for Spain. In August, after a wet, depressing day, Pym reconciled herself to another period of absence followed by 'a possible approach in September (to get jumble)'. Meanwhile, she was shaken by another local church sex scandal involving a vicar and choirboys. She made a joke about it to Bob: '"Choirboys in the Study" might well be the title for something, maybe a musical . . . I suppose it was hushed up and he was given another chance. What was his *wife* like?'[5]

That month Pym attended a dinner in Malvern given by the Writers' Circle. She was struck by the women in long glittering brocades and fellow novelist Margaret Drabble 'in a beautiful short flowered dress with long sleeves'. Again, she felt dowdy, as she had done in her black dress at the Athens dinner with Elizabeth Taylor. As so often, she chastised herself for being out of sync: 'All with neat little "evening bags" – only B.P. with her black leather day handbag.'[6]

In September, she wrote to Bob, referring to his leave in England that summer: 'I hope your lunch with Richard was a success and that you didn't have to drink weak white wine. I have had no word from him so I suppose I must make an approach myself if I want to get all that rich assortment of jumble.'[7] Perhaps, Pym suggested, she would be on better terms with Skipper in her old age. When he duly turned up with jumble for the church sale, they were 'friendly, of course, but no longer *en rapport*'. She told Bob that she would send him a birthday card, 'but if he doesn't want to see me, that's that'. Then she quoted Keats: 'If it comes not as easily as the leaves to a tree, it had better not come at all.' And she hinted at the real source of her frustration: 'And how *does* he manage all these people in his life, poor boy.'[8]

However, she did go to Skipper's birthday party on 26 October, after which she noted in her diary:

The birthday party – when all these people come bringing gifts and tributes, some presented to him, others lying discreetly in the hall. Books, paté, liqueur chocolates, drink, objects, things to wear like scarves and gloves and pyjamas. Bulbs in a bowl . . . It was a great gathering together of his friends and lovers, past, present and future. Interesting to speculate which had been which.[9]

She was going to have to be content reverting to her role as the observer of love, not the participant.

A few weeks before Christmas, Skipper telephoned and asked her to lunch. Although the meal went well, she suspected that it was a farewell meeting and that she would see very little of him in the new year. He had moved into a new flat, in Rutland Gate, which she thought was much less nice than Sussex Gardens. Hilary – who, after the way he had treated Barbara, had developed an intense dislike of Skipper – was scornful when her sister told her about seeing his new flat – 'Rutland Gate!'

By the end of the year, Skipper had disappeared. Bob Smith assured Pym that he would be back before long, but she knew it was over:

> As for news of R, I fear it is all over now – he did get in touch once but I think it was only because he wanted to get rid of some jumble . . . Life has its farcical moments and perhaps my sense of humour is greater than his. Perhaps my sardonic tongue has sent him away or he has just lost interest, the latter probably.[10]

She concluded, using the same term she had applied to her rejection by Cape, that: 'It would now seem that he has definitely off-loaded me, which I think he has been trying to do ever since he came back from Mexico earlier this year.'[11]

'All I want now,' she told Bob, 'is peace to write my unpublishable novels.'[12]

CHAPTER XI

Mr Larkin to the Rescue

Philip Larkin had confided in Pym that he was experiencing writer's block: 'Poetry has deserted me.' Once again, he was reading all her novels in succession, '& once more found them heartening & entertaining – you know there is never a dull page . . . really, they are entirely original'.[1]

Pym would distil her feelings of rejection into *The Sweet Dove Died*. The endless waiting for the telephone to ring; the feelings that one has been thrown over. By the end of the year, she had finished her first draft. She told Larkin it was a book about an older woman in love with a younger man and that she had left out 'boring cosiness' in favour of 'the darker side'. A friend had described it as 'almost a sinister and unpleasant book'.[2]

Larkin offered to read the manuscript. She posted it a month later: 'I am sending *The Sweet Dove Died* (a thriller about the American Presidential Election?) for you to read and hope it may give you *some* amusement.'[3] He paid her the best compliment of all by reading the manuscript carefully, making valuable edits and suggestions, as Jock Liddell had done all those years ago with *Some Tame Gazelle*. Larkin told her that he found the novel a 'curious mixture of successful and unsuccessful'. The characters were strong, he felt, but their destinies were not clear:

'they move briefly and jerkily, & without any sense of inevitability'. He advised her to omit all the minor characters and focus on the main ones. He also expressed his sense that this novel had more 'feeling', but 'it *is* only potential'. His comments were accurate and acute: 'I think it could be a strong, sad book, with fewer characters and slower movements.'[4]

It is a mark of Pym's good sense and gratitude that she took Larkin's advice on board. Even though she had had several rejections for the book, she felt that nobody had told her 'what was really *wrong* with the book and I felt there must be something'. She explained to Larkin that the novel had begun as one thing and become another. Her busy life at the institute meant that she had had to stop and start and she felt that this lack of continuity had affected the writing. Her feelings had changed towards her central character: 'I started not at all in sympathy with Leonora, who began by being a minor character, but as the book progressed I got more interested in her and really enjoyed writing about her the best in the end.' She had 'lost confidence' and felt 'uncertain of herself'. She also admitted that she was so tired from her day job that she often slumped in front of the television in the evenings: 'What a mixed blessing that great invention is.'[5]

Two of her novels, *Some Tame Gazelle* and *Excellent Women*, were being republished for a Library Association reprint by Chivers of Bath. This was some compensation for the fact that one of the main reasons for Pym's many rejections was the closure of the commercial circulating libraries, where for a small fee readers could rent out books at a time when buying books was still costly. This had been the key not only to Pym's own voracious consumption of fiction as a young woman, but also to her wide readership back in the fifties. She concurred with the sentiments of John Betjeman in his 1940 poem 'In Westminster Abbey', where Boots' lending library is placed first in a list of British national emblems, ahead of 'country lanes,/ Free speech, free passes, class distinction,/ Democracy and proper drains'.[6]

Pym had, since school days, subscribed to Boots, but in 1966 the library closed following the passage of the Public Libraries and Museums Act of 1964, which required councils to provide free public libraries. Many publishers believed that Pym's novels would not sell in the new market and without the support of the subscription libraries. Larkin had warned Pym of the changing climate: 'I'm told that the *economic figure* for novels is 4,000 – and has risen a lot recently. The circulating libraries are diminishing, too – Smith's gone, Boots going.'[7] Now she hoped that the Library Association reprints might suggest that her star was rising again. It would be another nine years, however, before she could find a publisher willing to take her on.

Pym was mildly resentful that Jock Liddell was still getting published. His latest novel, *An Object for a Walk,* featured versions of herself and Henry: 'Naturally, I could detect bits of myself in Flora . . . Poor Henry, what an inspiration he has been.'[8] She seemed to take a dusty view, telling Bob that the book had 'meagre reviews' and been met with a 'lack of enthusiasm'. She was extremely busy with work at the institute, for which she was glad: 'All the same it has helped me overcome the depression that occasionally threatens when I think of nobody wanting to publish my novels and my total failure . . . with Richard.'[9]

Skipper continued to send postcards and a birthday card in June, but he had made it clear that he did not want to see her again. There were times when she was tempted to pick up the telephone, but managed to resist. She stalked his house, seeing if his car was parked outside. She debated whether they could ever be friends again: 'Yet I feel like a cat that's been offered a dish of plain Kit-e-Kat and wonders if it really wants *that*.'[10]

A trip to Oxford with Bob Smith went horribly wrong when

she 'let fly about Richard which rather spoiled things'. Thinking of Skipper caused her acute 'nervous indigestion pain'.[11] She told Bob that it was: 'So *unflattering* to feel that a person really doesn't ever want to see you again – I don't think it's ever happened to me before *quite* like this! Now, alas, I am too old to change myself.' She resolved to herself to be more cautious in future: 'not allowing myself to get fond of anybody'.[12]

Perhaps, she might have added, not allowing herself to fall in love with a much younger homosexual man, who was incapable of returning her love, even had he wanted to do so. In private, she felt humiliated by the failure of the relationship: 'Trying to understand people and leaving them alone and being "unselfish" and all *that* jazz has only the bleakest of rewards – precisely nothing!'[13]

Nevertheless, encouraged by Larkin, she went back to *The Sweet Dove Died* and made all the changes he suggested. Pym poured out all her frustration, her embarrassment, and her humiliation at the hands of selfish Skipper. And, in her novel, she did not shy away from his sexual orientation. In a masterful stroke, she would increase the heroine's despair by making the (anti-)hero bisexual and the subject of three people's desire: an older woman, a young girl and a homosexual young man. Who would win?

CHAPTER XII

In which we read Miss Pym's plangent Masterpiece, *The Sweet Dove Died*

In response to a note asking her to write the jacket blurb for *The Sweet Dove Died*, Pym wrote: 'What is it about? The struggle of two women, unknown to each other, to get a young man who doesn't want either of them.'[1] What the young man wants is another young man.

The heroine is a middle-aged, attractive, elegant spinster called Leonora Eyre. She is in the autumn of her life and wears beautiful clothes in autumnal hues of aubergine and green. During an auction at a Bond Street sale room she faints and is rescued by an antique dealer (Humphrey Boyce) and his much younger nephew (James). Humphrey, a widower, is attracted to the 'exquisite' Leonora, but she is drawn to 'strikingly handsome' and much younger James. He in turn is drawn to her, despite the age gap: 'Her wide-brimmed hat which cast fascinating shadows on a face that was probably beginning to need such flattery. He was attracted to her in the way that a young man may sometimes be to a woman old enough to be his mother.'[2] But James is also attracted to a young woman, Phoebe, whom he has met at a party. Taking her out to dinner, he learns that she is editing the literary work of a girl who has died, Anthea Wedge. James later visits Phoebe in her cottage in the country and they fall into bed, almost to his surprise.

When James leaves to go abroad, he offers Phoebe a loan of some of his furniture, which is stored in a repository. When she goes along, she discovers that another woman, Leonora Eyre, has also been there to take some pieces (just as had happened with Pym and Joan Wales). Phoebe is intrigued by Miss Eyre. In the meantime, Humphrey tells Leonora that James has a mistress in the country. Though she is shocked, she remains calm and swiftly plans to dispose of her rival, Phoebe.

In the meantime, Leonora attends a dinner party given by a work friend, Meg. She has become obsessed by a camp young man (Colin), who has a series of disastrous relationships with different men, always returning to Meg with his tail between his legs. Leonora, cool, controlled, aloof, despises Meg, who devotes herself to Colin and his hapless lovers. She does not yet know that she will suffer in the same way.

Leonora ruthlessly evicts her tenant, an old lady who lives in her attic, so that she can move James in. She also goes to Phoebe's cottage and takes back the furniture items she has borrowed. But all is not what it seems. James has met a man called Ned. Then one day, a young man appears at the door of Leonora's beautiful house, where James is now installed as lodger in the attic. It is Ned. Leonora invites him in to tea. She realises that Ned is a far greater threat than Phoebe: 'however charming he might appear this young man wanted to take James away from her and she was not going to let him'.[3] Ned and Leonora perceive that there can be only one winner in their battle for handsome James.

Pym handles the narrative with great mastery. Though she allows the reader to guess that James is attracted by and to both men and women, the novel is seen through the eyes of Leonora, who is blinded by her own self-absorption and vanity. When she is finally forced to accept the truth of James's sexual orientation, she accepts the battle and sets to it. Though James is bisexual, his primary attraction is to men. Leonora comes to the bitter realisation that she can only lose. She is 'off-loaded' by James. By the time Ned tires of James and sends him back, the relationship is severely broken – like a Sèvres vase that cannot be repaired.

The plot is intricately and delicately managed, but the true genius of the novel is in the writing, which is rich with what Larkin called Pym's 'plangent quality'. She was taking a risk with Leonora, who is not a particularly likeable heroine and whose disposal of Phoebe is ruthless: she deserves the treatment she gets from Ned and yet when it happens, it feels tragic. Ned is perhaps Pym's most sinister character. In a shocking scene, worthy of Henry James in its handling of tone and sinister undercurrents, Ned warns Leonora that she is up against a master. He picks up an alabaster dove – a present from James – and quotes from Keats: 'I had a dove and the sweet dove died;/ And I have thought it died of grieving.'[4] Leonora remembers: 'Ah, yes, of course, that sad little poem.' She is 'relieved that it was something so simple and harmless'. But she has forgotten the end of the poem and this is where Ned proves himself to be heartless:

Ned passed his cup and went on with the verse, his voice lingering
over the words and giving them a curious emphasis.
    'O, what could it *grieve* for? Its feet were *tied*
    With a single thread of my *own hand's* weaving.'[5]

Leonora's 'agitation' is profound and she trembles. Later, in an ugly parody of the Wilmet/Keith/Piers triangle, Leonora visits Keats's house with Ned and James and is rendered miserable by the way she is heartlessly treated. She is taken back to Ned's 'pad'

and her humiliation is complete when she is shown the excep-
tionally wide bed covered in mauve velvet. When she finally
leaves, Ned congratulates James on having 'shook off' Leonora
and describes her as a wounded animal 'crawling away to die'.
He 'laughed in a light cruel way'. Then he tells James: 'Life is
cruel and we do *terrible* things to each other.'[6] It is a warning to
James that he might be dispatched with the same ruthlessness.
Ned is a game-player: 'It had been amusing to see if he could
get James away from Leonora . . . but now that he had succeeded
what was he going to *do* about him.'[7] James is beautiful but
weak, allowing himself to be used by the unscrupulous Ned, who
finally tires of him and sends him back to Leonora. In a wish-
fulfilment plot point, James does come crawling back to Leonora,
but is rejected. Skipper, of course, did not come crawling back.

When Ned visits Leonora to give James back to her, his cruelty
reaches new levels. He almost reduces her to tears, which is his
intention because 'he was good at comforting weeping women'.
If we are in any doubt that Pym was paying homage to Henry
James, we are given a reminder:

'You must *forgive* him,' [Ned] went on. That was what women
should do and even did, in his experience; they overlooked
things, they took people back, above all they forgave.

'But James hasn't asked me to forgive him.'

'He hasn't? Really, Jimmie might have made things a little
easier for him. I expect he will, though and you mustn't be too
hard on him. If he came to you on his bended knees, surely
you'd forgive him?'

Leonora said nothing.

'You mean he could come to the door and you wouldn't open
it – you'd let him go away? Like that scene at the end of
Washington Square? Leonora, I'm sure you read Henry James,
he's so very much *your* kind of novelist.'[8]

But Leonora, almost to her own surprise, manages to rise above Ned's cruelty with a new level of self-knowledge and dignity: 'she supposed she had acquitted herself quite well, perhaps she had won a kind of victory, but it hardly seemed to matter now'.[9]

Pym vented her rage and frustration at Skipper's betrayal and her own fallibility in falling for a young homosexual man who could never return her love. Leonora, with her sharp tongue, makes jibes at James's 'effeminacy'. She cooks him tarragon chicken, as Pym did for Skipper, and he reads aloud from a Sotheby's catalogue, describing the beautiful objects. Leonora even wears Skipper's cologne, L'Heure Bleue.

Humphrey's antique shop, like Skipper's, is near Sloane Square. Beautiful objects in this novel are revealed to be flawed, with a chip here or there. Leonora borrows James's antique fruitwood mirror: she loves it because it hides her lines and only reflects back her beauty. She buys James an expensive brace of porcelain vases as a bribe, just as she imprisons him in her attic, behind bars. She tells him that the bars are a relic of the days when the attic was once the nursery, but it is clear that James has also become a substitute child. When she gives him the precious vases, he feels like a child who has been stuffed full with too many cream cakes.

We have seen before how Pym identified so strongly with her heroines that in her journals she often elides the first-person pronoun with the third. This slippage is even more pronounced in her journals for *The Sweet Dove Died* where paragraphs in Leonora's chilly voice sit uneasily alongside Pym's emotionally chaotic voice: 'Bruised and sore'; 'Only remember that you love Sk[ipper] that is all that matters'; 'Today is so *painful*, I feel raw all over'; 'no word yet since Saturday'; 'All miserable again and determined to end it all . . . but how? And why?'; 'I just sit tight and endure'.[10]

Soon after she redrafted the final version of the novel, Pym made her pilgrimage to Jane Austen's cottage in Chawton, Hampshire: 'I put my hand down on Jane's desk and bring it up covered in dust. Oh that some of her genius might rub off on me.'[11] She need not have feared. The novel she had finished was her true masterpiece, written at the height of her powers. That she did so when she had been cast asunder by both her publisher and her beloved is remarkable. If, as Philip Larkin had suggested, *Some Tame Gazelle* was her *Pride and Prejudice*, then surely *The Sweet Dove Died* was her *Persuasion*. Without the happy ending. It was dedicated to 'R'.

CHAPTER XIII

Miss Pym feels her Age

Jane Austen, the writer to whom Pym was most often compared, had her own years in the wilderness. Her first novel was accepted in 1803, but it gathered dust on a publisher's shelf. It took another eight years for her to get into print. How frustrating it is that if only she had been published in 1803, we would have had many more Jane Austen novels. The same parallel could be made with Barbara Pym. If only *The Sweet Dove Died* had been accepted in 1969, then we would have had several more Pym novels. Like Austen, she kept writing, kept trying to get published, did not fully give up hope.

In August, she sent *The Sweet Dove Died* to Longmans. They sent it back: 'well written' but not for them. 'What's the use of that?' she wrote in her notebook.[1] She explained to Larkin that she had substantially rewritten the book, cut out the minor characters as he had suggested, made it less 'cosy', and composed some difficult final chapters which, to her mind, were her very best writing. Delighted, Larkin promised to speak to James Wright, the fiction editor at Macmillan. Pym took the manuscript along to Macmillan in person, 'avoiding the expense and frustration of the Christmas post'.[2]

Pym had watched a TV programme about the dire state of

fiction publishing. It depressed her and she felt that her chances were not good. 'If only somebody would have the courage to be unfashionable,' she lamented to Larkin.[3] James Wright at Macmillan sent her a long letter, rejecting the novel, but praising its 'perfection of taste'. Pym told Bob Smith that she had never had such a flattering letter about her work, but, yet again, it was the fear of it being a 'risky commercial venture' in the present climate that prevented publishers taking on the book. Pym determined that she would keep sending it round. She thanked Larkin for his kind intervention and sent him a beautifully bound copy of *A Glass of Blessings* as a thank-you present. Wright's letter had at least partially restored her confidence in her own talent.

In April 1970, the publisher MacDonald rejected the novel. Pym decided she would send it out again under the pen name Tom Crampton, with the new title *Leonora*. That autumn, she submitted the novel to Peter Davies, a subsidiary of Heinemann, 'completely out of the blue with no indication that I had written anything else'. One of its directors, a talented editor called Mark Barty-King, wrote back a long letter, quoting five readers' reports, 'some of which were very flattering'. One of the readers had described it as a 'tour de force', another 'very accomplished', but the consensus was that it was not powerful enough to appeal to a sufficiently wide public. On the other hand, one of the less kind reviewers thought the novel 'clever-clever and decadent'. Pym was delighted by this backhanded compliment: '*that* made me feel thirty years younger!'[4]

Philip Larkin offered his usual support, which Pym had come to rely upon. He wrote to say that he read all of her novels, every eighteen months: 'How good they are!' he told her. 'How much what one wants after a hard, even a soft day's work! How vivacious and funny and observant! And feeling of course. It seems fearful that you should be trying not to be "cosy" . . . if I could help by writing a *foreword* – an *appreciation* – of course I'd love to help.'[5]

Bob Smith reiterated the belief that Pym should not try too hard to avoid cosiness. He was now teaching in Nigeria and working on a full review essay of Pym's works, which he planned to pitch to *Ariel* magazine. He sent her an early version, which she found 'most gratifying and soothing to my wounded ego', but she found fault in some of his criticisms.[6]

Pym was feeling her age. Her old publisher, Wren Howard, had recently died and she attended his memorial service. In Dublin, on holiday, she observed a 'lone American lady drinking *creme de menthe* on the rocks to match her emerald ring and the other ladies so old and preserved enjoying exotic cocktails'.[7] She was beginning to see herself as one of them. Even John Lennon, whose music she had so enjoyed when he was just a loveable mop-top, was now 'so repellent-looking-now – like a very plain middle-aged Victorian female novelist . . . I still like their songs, if I don't have to look at them'.[8]

Daryll Forde was retiring from University College London and Pym went along to his Festschrift presentation. She noticed the academic women who had made no effort with their clothes: 'an enviable detachment and when will one ever reach it?'[9] Everywhere there was the sense of an ending. St Lawrence's was in financial trouble and church members fewer and fewer. There was even talk of 'meeting in people's houses rather than going to church'.[10] She began to wonder if she should merely treat her novels as an older woman's hobby, like knitting.

Larkin sent her a copy of his latest book, *All What Jazz*, a collection of his music reviews. It left her in a reflective mood:

The introduction set me thinking back into my own girlhood – and that winding up of the portable gramophone – and the records – ours were mainly of the bands of the day – Jack Hylton and Jack Payne, . . . and my own favourite of Noël Coward and Gertrude Lawrence doing that scene from *Private Lives*.[11]

Larkin was on his way to Oxford (All Souls College, no less) for a six-month visiting fellowship, which also made Pym nostalgic: 'I wonder if Elliston's is now full of well-dressed ladies having coffee mid-morning? I think the warm green-muffled Cumnor Hills were never as Arnold saw them. But Bagley Wood – ah I think it belongs to St John's doesn't it and will have been preserved, bluebells and all.'[12]

Pym's beloved restaurant, the Kardomah, closed for good on 3 July 1970, as she carefully noted down. She visited the library at the London School of Economics. The sight of the students added to her feelings of impending old age: 'Waiting down below at the enquiry desk – the rough students with long hair and strange one-sex clothes make me feel old and vulnerable.'[13]

One of the most poignant themes of *The Sweet Dove Died* is the portrayal of a once beautiful woman growing old. The antique fruitwood mirror lent to Leonora by James is one of her favourite objects because its old glass reflects a kinder image than that seen in modern glass. It is cruel when James takes the mirror back and Ned comments how tired Leonora is looking and treats her like an infirm old woman. Pym was feeling this, too. In her notebook, she wrote of her string bag filled with books and ready-packaged food for one.

In several of her novels, Pym makes a cameo appearance as herself, rather in the manner of Alfred Hitchcock's brief appearances in his own movies. In *The Sweet Dove Died*, she makes two. One is the dreadful 'Ba' (Glover's pet name for Pym), 'toothy' and 'ruddy-faced', who appears at a party and suggests that Leonora do voluntary work to fill her time. But the second cameo is heartbreaking. Pym drew on her own solitary pilgrimage to Keats's house in Hampstead, on that soggy day when she had been so moved by Fanny Brawne's engagement ring:

All the same, the overcast skies and dripping rain spread a pall of sadness over the little house, with its simple bare rooms. There was nobody else looking over it except for a middle-aged woman wearing a mackintosh pixie hood and transparent rainboots over her shoes. She was carrying a shopping bag full of books, on top of which lay the brightly coloured packet of a frozen 'dinner for one'.[14]

Leonora at first looks with contempt at the unnamed woman, 'for anyone who could live this way'. But then, given her own recent unhappiness, she feels a sudden stab of compassion: 'She saw the woman going home to a cosy solitude, but her dinner heated up in twenty-five minutes with no bother of preparation, books to read while she ate it and the memory of a visit to Keats's house to cherish.' And then Leonora 'caught a glimpse of her face, plain but radiant, as she looked up from one of the glass cases that held the touching relics. There were tears on her cheeks.'[15]

The woman is, of course, Pym.

CHAPTER XIV

In trying Circumstances, Miss Pym compares herself to an Amazon

At the close of 1970, Pym was still feeling low. There were some bright spots, such as a poetry event at the National Portrait Gallery, where she heard some of her favourite poems by Andrew Marvell. Also, news from Cape that Chivers of Bath wanted two further reprints, this time of *Jane and Prudence* and *Less Than Angels*. But there were moments of bleakness too, of 'feeling old and vulnerable'.

The new year began uneventfully. Pym was learning to drive, work was busy. Bob Smith told her that his review essay in the magazine *Ariel* would be published later in the year under the title 'How pleasant to know Miss Pym'. In it he described her novels as 'good books for bad days' and played the Jane Austen card:

> Her works are miniatures, exquisitely, nearly perfectly done. But, beyond this, it is her wit and her sense of the ridiculous which make her books both delicious and distinguished. Above all, they must be ranked as comic novels, but the comedy is realistic and demonstrates again and again the happiness and merriment which can be found in the trivia of the daily round – that

'purchase of a sponge-cake' about which Jane Austen felt it proper to write to Cassandra.[1]

Pym was grateful for the piece, but in her notebook her deep frustration was felt: 'What is wrong with being obsessed with trivia? Some have criticised *The Sweet Dove Died* for this. What are the minds of my critics filled with? What *nobler* and more worthwhile things?'[2]

Other things began to fill her mind when she found a small lump on her left breast. Hilary was out of contact, away travelling in Greece again, but Pym was calm and pragmatic. Her doctor sent her straight to hospital, where the lump was found to be malignant: 'Morning at St Mary's Hospital Paddington. O little lump – almost a subject for a metaphysical poem.'[3] Afterwards, she took herself to a pub for a stiff drink.

The hospital acted quickly and the following day they operated and removed her left breast. She wrote to Bob:

Dearest Bob, I don't know how to prevent this letter being a shock to you, as it has been to me . . . everyone has been *marvellous* and all those clichés about one's true friends are proven right. Hazel a tower of strength, Mrs P. C. coming round with grapes, my friends at the Institute rallying round. You will guess it was cancer and that was why they took away the left bosom. I can't make out whether the other ladies here are breastless (like Amazons?) or have other things the matter with them. Everyone is so kind – the black hands and white hands, so cool and firm and comforting.[4]

Just a couple of weeks later, she was convalescing in the garden 'in a rare burst of sunshine'. She wrote to Larkin that she had rather enjoyed the experience: 'To have a lovely rest, to have flowers and grapes and books brought to you and to be a centre of interest is not at all unpleasant! I didn't even mind the students looking at me.' She told him that the lump was small and had been caught early, so she had hopes that there would be no recurrence, 'though I suppose one mustn't be over-optimistic'. Pym was in good spirits. She had liked speaking to the other patients: 'I discovered all you need to do is to make some enquiry and you will get the whole life story.' She was reading long novels again, those of one of her favourites, the prolific High Church Victorian chronicler of domestic life, Charlotte M. Yonge: 'what a wonderful length books were allowed in those days before the telly and all that'.[5]

Another admired author, E. M. Forster, had died the previous year, having failed to produce a novel for the last forty-six years of his life. He had felt unable to write overtly about his homosexuality and considered it would be hypocritical to go on publishing heterosexual love stories. His sexuality only became general public knowledge in the year after his death, when the novel, *Maurice*, written shortly before the First World War, finally saw the light of day. Pym read extracts from it that were serialised in the *Sunday Times*. To Larkin, she wondered what could possibly be regarded as too daring to publish nowadays. Prior to the decriminalisation of homosexuality in 1967, it had been easier for her, as a heterosexual woman, to create overtly homosexual male characters than it had been for Forster as a gay man.

Pym's brush with cancer had made her more reflective and thankful. She was enjoying being away from the institute and told Larkin that she gave thanks for her recovery, in hospital, at home and in church. She acquired a false breast, considering it 'a very fine shape indeed'. She felt that one of the compensations for growing old was not caring so much about 'one's physical beauty and of course [the prosthetic] doesn't show at all when one is dressed'.[6]

Another change came in September, when St Lawrence's church closed down. Pym began worshipping at St Mary Magdalene in Paddington. She liked the music and the amusing vicar who dragged on a cigarette. Meanwhile, she had used her convalescence to finish another novel. It was about 'a provincial university'. Larkin was delighted at the thought of her turning her gaze on 'redbrick academic life'.[7] She told Bob Smith that two of the characters – a mother and son – were exiles from the Caribbean, based on Skipper and his mother. She had few hopes of seeing it published, but wrote it for her circle of friends. 'Prospects of publication seem to get bleaker,' she told Larkin, noting that a woman had set up the Orlando Press – 'erotic books written by women for women? What can they possibly be like? (I shall look out for them with interest).'[8]

Though she and Larkin had not yet met, their friendship was deepening. He was upset about her cancer: 'A good thing you nobbled it quickly.'[9] He was going prematurely deaf and had invested in a hearing aid, which was prone to breaking. Always melancholic, he confided in Pym that he was depressed: 'Has anyone ever done any work on why memories are always so unhappy?'[10] Larkin knew that he was certain of a kind and compassionate response from Pym. But on this occasion she did not agree with him: 'When I'm unhappy or depressed I do find myself remembering *better times*.' She was feeling hopeful and looking forward to the future: 'I want to pass my driving test and I want to publish another novel . . . I am lucky.'[11]

CHAPTER XV

In which Holborn's Renowned Department Store, Gamages, is demolished

Larkin had been rereading *Excellent Women*. He was yet again struck by its brilliance: 'What a marvellous set of characters it contains.' His own private life was, as ever, complicated. He was still torn between Maeve Brennan and Monica Jones – 'the woman I want to marry and the woman I ought to marry'. He told Pym: '*I* never see any Rockys, but almost every young academic wife (I'm a shit) has something of Helena.'[1] Perhaps the portrayal of the weak, philandering Rocky Napier, who can't seem to make up his mind between what he wants to do and what he ought to do, was just too close to the bone.

Larkin had enjoyed Bob Smith's review essay, with its 'sober and sensible praise', but he felt that the essay 'not quite good enough, not as good as you deserve'. Smith 'wallowed' on too much about Jane Austen. Larkin memorably responded: 'I must say I'd sooner read a new BP than a new JA!' Larkin, usually so private and shy, now opened up to Pym about his dependence on alcohol, his constant weight battles and his problems with his mother ('86 in January and soon after seemed to keel over').[2] He shared details of life in a 'provincial University' that he hoped would encourage Pym to carry on with her own campus novel. She worked it through two drafts and then put it aside. It was published posthumously, stitched together from the drafts by her friend Hazel Holt, who gave it the title *An Academic Question*.

In many respects, it was a return to form, with some of the exuberance of *Crampton Hodnet* and *Some Tame Gazelle*. There are the dry one-liners such as: 'Evidently a life spent with card indexes did not make for generosity of spirit.'[3] And there is a strong dose of gossip at the social gatherings of provincial academics. Someone suggests that Coco, the character based on Skipper, is mixed-race, due to his dark colouring and curly hair. Like Skipper in the Bahamas, Coco's family have lived on a Caribbean island for centuries. Unlike Skipper, he has a degree from an obscure American university and a research fellowship in Caribbean Studies.

Caro Grimstone, the young heroine, is married to a university lecturer. She has abbreviated her name from Caroline to Caro in honour of Lady Caroline Lamb, Lord Byron's besotted stalker. She reads the *Guardian* and lives in a new-build neo-Georgian house with modern furniture. When a student turns up at her door, she expects she wants advice about contraception or abortion and is deeply shocked when the student asks to borrow her sewing machine. When Caro volunteers to read at an old people's home, her husband asks her to spy on an old blind anthropologist, who has been a missionary in Africa and now keeps all his unpublished research in a large trunk in his room.

The university has a 'new clean functional Senior Common Room' and a refectory. There are lecturers in sociology and anthropology. All this reflects the expansion of higher education in Britain following the Robbins Report of 1963. In some ways, the university, in a West Country town, feels like a fresh start away from 'the old intrigues and petty academic irritations'. In many ways it is a million miles away from Oxford, with its spires and crusty dons teaching Anglo-Saxon. But the academic rivalry is just as strong. Caro's husband feels like a card in a game of patience, his moves blocked by cards of a higher suit.

Pym's own frustrations with the academic life she witnessed via the African Institute and London University are revealed: the pettiness of the intrigues, the bullying and intimidation, the one-upmanship embodied in a lecturer called Dr Iris Horniblow – who bears more than a passing resemblance to Iris Murdoch, with her striking looks and thick square-cut short hair. Pym had met Iris and her husband John Bayley, who was such a huge admirer of the novels. Murdoch did not care for the novels, though she very much liked Barbara. Larkin had recently met Iris Murdoch at a party and told Pym that she asked him lots of probing questions. Iris Horniblow shocks Caro by asking her whether she believes in sex education.

The novel captures the foibles of academic bullshitters who are forever 'preparing for publication', arguing over footnotes, stealing each other's research and complaining about their 'crushing teaching load'. The head of department, Professor Maynard, two years off retirement, is clearly based on Daryll Forde. He shares Pym's boss's trait of asking of any young academic: '*Is he able?*'

Pym could not rid herself, however, of the nagging doubt that her love for quirky detail was out of kilter with the times. Publishers wanted either fast-paced bestsellers, such as Frederick Forsyth's *The Day of the Jackal*, or demanding intellectual pyrotechnics of the kind displayed in Gabriel García Márquez's *One Hundred Years of Solitude*. In the library of the institute one day, Pym noticed a 'Mr C' eating a sandwich with a knife and fork, the sort of detail she would save for a novel: 'Oh *why* can't I write about things like that any more – why is this kind of thing no longer acceptable?'[4]

Being told by Sir Walter Scott's venerable publisher Constable that a novel like *The Sweet Dove Died* was 'virtually impossible' to be published was another blow. 'What is the future for my kind of writing?' Pym wrote in her notebook. Again and again, she felt like giving up. Perhaps life would be easier if she did: 'Perhaps in retirement and even in the year before, a quieter, narrower kind of life can be worked out and adopted. Bounded by English literature and the Anglican Church and small pleasures like sewing and choosing dress material for this uncertain summer.'[5]

The appearance of two sisters in *An Academic Question* is another of Pym's Hitchcockian cameos: 'Two women who had just retired from jobs in London', come to lunch when Caro is at her mother's. 'They were rather nice, spinster sisters.' One is in her late fifties, the other just sixty. 'Their lives were busy in an admirable way': they speak of making alterations to the garden and plans for a motoring holiday in Shropshire. One of them, Caro feels sure, must once have been beautiful. 'They must have loved in their time, perhaps loved and lost and come through it unscathed.'[6] Hilary had indeed retired from the BBC and Pym had just a year to go before she retired at the statutory age of sixty. The sisters were beginning to think about moving out of London to the country.

The prospect of being 'buried in the country' made Pym appreciate London, but she also felt that so much had changed. The Kardomah had gone, 'so much is being pulled down, especially between Fleet St and Aldwych (By King's College)', and the African Institute was moving to High Holborn. The final straw was the demolition of Gamages department store: 'Oh unimaginable horror!' Pym went to the closing-down sale: 'A dreadful scene with empty counters and tumbled merchandise and people walking about like zombies. This is the year of change and decay, though presumably shoe-box buildings will spring up on the site of decay.' A 'whole period of civilisation' was going before her eyes.[7]

On warm days, Pym spent time convalescing in the garden, dozing on a deckchair. When she finally returned to work, it was in the institute's cramped new premises in Bloomsbury, near the British Museum: 'Now I wander around Bloomsbury, scene of so many and distant past glories. Who can ever live here now?' The move gave her an idea for a new novel: 'all old, crabby characters, petty and obsessive, bad tempered – how easily one of them could have a false breast'.[8]

She was to turn fifty-nine in the summer and once again was feeling her age, especially when she compared herself with the gorgeous young black women in the new office building. Although she put on a brave face to her friends and sister about the false breast, her surgery was inevitably life-altering. Every night, when she undressed for bed, she was forced to confront a different body to the one that she had known all her life. Pym was a woman who enjoyed sex. Ever since her Oxford days, she had been a sexually liberated woman – ahead of her time in her guilt-free, life-enhancing enjoyment of her body. Her private notebooks suggest that the mastectomy cut far deeper emotionally and psychologically than she dared admit:

The ageing white woman in the office. Besides the mysterious depths of the black girls, she has nothing, no depths, no mystery, certainly no sexuality. She is all dried up by the mild British sun, in which she may sit in a deck chair, eyes closed against its ravages.[9]

CHAPTER XVI

Miss Pym moves to Finstock

All those years ago, Pym had written a perfect comic novel about two middle-aged sisters living happily together in a cottage in the country. The sisters, Harriet and Belinda, were thinly disguised versions of Hilary and Barbara Pym. Now the prospect was coming true, much to the delight of their friends. The sisters had been searching in Oxfordshire and had finally settled on Finstock, fourteen miles north-west of the city of dreaming spires. Finstock was a typical Cotswold hamlet with honey-coloured stone houses and a village green. It lay close to the Wychwood Forest and not too far from Woodstock and the magnificent Blenheim Palace.

On a cold, windy and cloudy day, wrapped up warm, with a cat crouching on her desk, Pym wrote to Philip Larkin: 'At least I shan't be tempted to go and sit in the garden and sleep in a deckchair.'[1] She told Larkin that her plan was to live in London during the week and then go to Finstock at weekends and holidays. She planned to retire at the age of sixty, so had one more year working at the institute. Pym, a smoker since her university days, told him that she had finally given up cigarettes.

Barn Cottage was, as its name implied, a recently converted

barn. It dated from the seventeenth century and was in the old part of the village, close to the green and the pub. There were old beams in every room, two bedrooms and a tiny spare room. It had an open-plan kitchen and sitting room, a downstairs bathroom and, much to Pym's delight, a double garage: 'Excellent for storing all those odds and ends we still haven't been able to fit in.' She told Larkin that she thought the new house much better than Brooksville Avenue. Tom the cat made quite a dramatic first appearance at a party for local ladies, when he appeared through the window, with a 'not quite dead mouse in his mouth'.[2]

The village church, Holy Trinity, was famous for being the place where T. S. Eliot was received into the Anglican Church in 1927. 'The church is not very High,' Pym wrote to Larkin, 'but there is quite an enthusiastic congregation of people who have come fairly recently to the neighbourhood. Hilary and I are a bit jaded and cynical about things like bazaars but try not to show it.' The vicar had three churches to cope with: '*not* like the old palmy days of which I write in *Some Tame Gazelle* when every village had its own vicar or rector'.[3]

During the week, Pym rented a room, 'with use of kitchen', in Balcombe Street, near Marylebone station. On Fridays, she would leave the office early and take a train to Charlbury, where she would be picked up by Hilary. Thoughts of impending retirement gave her more inspiration for her new novel about office life and old people:

The death of a younger colleague – that could be part of my novel about old people . . . Love between a middle-aged man and woman (i.e. Jane and Nicholas in *Jane and Prudence*) has softened into mild kindly looks and spectacles. Now consider how it might be in the unmarried middle-aged women in the office. Both have had affairs of some kind but now can express

love only through a tenderness and solicitude towards each other.
'Let me make you a cup of tea.'[4]

Pym's relationship with Daryll Forde had mellowed and he took
her out for lunch to celebrate her twenty-five years with the African
Institute. She told Bob Smith that she felt as if she and her boss
were 'two old people cleaving together' in an alien new world. It
came as a great shock to her soon after this when he had a heart
attack at work one day and was 'dead that same evening'.[5]

Thereafter the institute became a 'rudderless ship'. It would
never be the same without difficult, demanding, charismatic,
Daryll Forde. More than ever, Pym longed for retirement, so
that she could live quietly and write her novels. She had given
up sending out her manuscripts ('21 publishers is enough'). She
would write for her own pleasure. Her notebooks were now
filled with observations of country life: 'the dead (dying) baby
bat in the gutter with its chocolate brown fur . . . the dead bird,
the dried-up hedgehog body, the mangled rabbit'.[6] She occasionally had thoughts of Skipper, especially when she wrote to their
mutual friend Bob. She asked if there was any news of him,
then stopped to remark how lightly she could write that now,
as befitted a woman on the threshold of sixty. Being sixty had
its compensations, she told Larkin, as she lay quietly in bed,
writing her novel about 'four people in their sixties working in
the same office'.[7]

Forde's unexpected death delayed Pym's retirement, but
London was no longer interesting: 'All shops are now Travel or
Photocopying or Employment Agencies, with the occasional
Sandwich Bar.' Not only was Gamages demolished, but also the
old offices in Fetter Lane, where she had worked for twenty
years: 'The emotion that place saw will never be experienced in
210 High Holborn. Now flat – nothing but rubble and a deep
wide hole in the ground.'[8]

Fetter Lane held memories of Skipper, who would be her last great love. Friendships, particularly with Bob Smith and Philip Larkin, were a lifeline for the literary part of herself. She had always had many female friends and now she had made new ones in Finstock: 'Life is very full and the village is in many ways like *Some Tame Gazelle*.'[9]

Then in the spring of 1974, she suffered a minor stroke.

CHAPTER XVII

A Luncheon at the Randolph

Pym was in Oxford's Radcliffe Infirmary for the month of April 1974, recovering from her stroke, which the doctors confirmed was due to excess calcium in her blood and high blood pressure. One of the troubling side effects was a partial dyslexia, which affected her spelling – disastrous for a writer. She worked hard to regain her writing skills.

Philip Larkin, before he knew about her illness, sent her an inscribed copy of his latest collection, *High Windows*. The title was an allusion to his first-floor flat in Hull which looked out onto the park – something which Pym could appreciate, given her own first-floor drawing room in Queen's Park and her Finstock bedroom, which opened out onto the flat garage roof with glorious views of the village beyond. Pym told Larkin that she didn't mind at all being in hospital. She had met some interesting people there and, looking at the very old and infirm, she had thought to herself that perhaps it was best to die in one's sixties. She could not bear to be incapacitated or disabled: it wouldn't be possible to be a '*splendid*' woman in such a condition, she wrote.

Though she was recuperating well, Pym was clearly still struggling to fully recover her writing and spelling capacity. Larkin was deeply concerned about her stroke, but glad that she had the benefit of 'all the medical brains of Oxford to look after you'. He had bought 'an ugly little house, fearfully dear, in a bourgeois area near the University'. He sent her the new address and added his usual words of encouragement: 'I'm sure when you come home you'll set to work on more brilliant novels, in which the unhappy months of this year will be caught up and transmuted.'[1]

Hilary drove Pym to Balcombe Street to collect her things and her unfinished manuscript of the 'older people' novel. By now, Pym felt that she would never be published. Even an article that she had written about the subject and sent to *The Author* magazine had been rejected, which seemed to be 'the final accolade of failure'. But she carried on writing every day, feeling guilty if she had read instead of written in the morning: 'They say Graham Greene writes only 250 words a day, so I should be able to manage that.'[2]

Her health slowly improved and she returned to London for her retirement party on doctor's orders to take it easy and not become 'too emotionally excited'. She was given a lunchtime party with wine and food and a present of the Oxford English Dictionary (which she had requested) and a cheque. She bought herself a large gold topaz ring, worthy, she thought, of Edith Sitwell.

Pym was enjoying her retirement. The institute now seemed such an alien place, with unfamiliar staff and a new, younger director. She had agreed to be a judge for the Romantic Novelists Association and now had the leisure time to read the novels on the list: 'They are extremely varied in type – some historical, others more purely *romantic* in a modern sense. The one thing they lack is humour or irony – and of course one does miss that.'[3] Christmas in Finstock was mild and windy, but there was entertainment with neighbours: 'ginger wine and duck'. And she relished her proximity to Oxford. In the early new year, she revisited her old haunts: 'a walk in the churchyard in Banbury Road, all almonds and prunus in the early sun'.[4]

But even Pym's beloved Oxford had changed. Where she once had tea in Fuller's or Elliston's, she now had 'beef burger, baked beans and chips' in Selfridges. There was 'no smoking' in the Radcliffe Camera. The Randolph Hotel was still the same, and it was there that she arranged to meet up with Philip Larkin. It would be their first ever face-to-face encounter, after a long correspondence of nearly fifteen years. They would have lunch. Pym told Larkin to look out for a woman who was 'tallish with short dark hair . . . I shall be wearing a beige tweed suit or a Welsh tweed cape, if colder. I shall be looking rather anxious, I expect.'[5] Larkin responded with his usual dry wit: 'I am tall & bald & heavily spectacled & deaf, but I can't predict what I shall have on.'[6]

In the event, it was a sunny day and the lunch went very well. Larkin gave many compliments, though Pym was her usual humble self and was reluctant to talk about her work. Their meeting was ambushed by a jovial 'red-faced' stranger who attached himself to the couple and chatted to them for what seemed like hours. In response to Larkin's urgings that she should continue to write, she said that she would try and get on with something.

Larkin told a friend that he had finally met B. Pym. 'It was quite successful (what an odd word "quite" is – "he is quite dead", "this is quite good") but she didn't want to talk about work – hers – much.' Though both Pym and Larkin were at heart rather shy people, the meeting served to further strengthen their bond. He did, however, find her an almost comical figure: 'She was a kind of J[oyce] Grenfell person, if one can say that in a friendly way.'[7]

CHAPTER XVIII

The Kissinger Syndrome and the Return of Henry Harvey

On a winter's evening in Finstock, two elderly ladies in full evening dress made their way to a neighbouring cottage where they had been invited to supper by a young man who worked for Oxford University Press. His name was Paul Binding. He was a budding writer and a former student of Professor Lord David Cecil, who had encouraged him to read Pym's novels. When he discovered that Pym was a neighbour he invited her to supper, but he was shocked to see the sisters so finely dressed on his muddy front doorstep.

He found Pym 'socially awkward and badly dressed', clever and well informed, though he preferred the more lively Hilary. Barbara, he recalled, 'made me feel that strong dividing line between men and women'.[1] He remembered her anger over Cape's rejection. He also detected a suppressed depressive side. Nevertheless, they became friends and in due course Paul Binding would be the one to break the exciting news of the appearance of her name in the seventy-fifth anniversary issue of the *Times Literary Supplement*.

Larkin's encouragement inspired Pym to carry on with her 'retirement' book. It would, she thought, be 'austere and plain'.[2]

The twenty-eighth of July, her mother's birthday, was a time for reflection: 'She would have been 88. Oh the mystery of it all – life, death and the passing of time.'[3] Pym was troubled by a moment of aphasia (memory loss) at a party, when she failed to remember the name of 'Dr Kissinger'. She was embarrassed and worried about how disconcerting it was for the other guests. Later, she felt 'pins and needles' in her right hand and a temporary loss of eyesight. She started calling these moments the 'Kissinger Syndrome' and worried that it was affecting her writing: 'Is this why I am now incapable of finishing this novel that is so near its end?' Her medication (a beta-blocker) was increased: 'In the Library I read the effects it might have – so if you have nausea, diarrhoea, insomnia and generally feel a bit odd, it's just the Propranalol!'[4]

In the meantime, there was news from Jock, who had been recovering from an eye operation. He was very upset that his dear friend, the novelist Elizabeth Taylor, had died. Pym was disheartened to hear that the press took very little notice of Taylor's death: 'After all, she was a friend of Kingsley Amis and Elizabeth Jane Howard who are well in with the *media*.' It made Pym think of her own posterity: 'Still what does it matter, really, such writers are caviar to the general, are they not and fame is dust and ashes anyhow.' Pym told Bob Smith that she was trying to finish the novel, 'but that will be it, positively *no more*'.[5]

That year brought more deaths. Gordon Glover passed away and then Rupert Gleadow. Pym wrote to Bob: 'Two of my contemporaries have died – both men. I should have been a widow twice over by now if I had married either.'[6] She built a bonfire and destroyed her 'Gordon Glover' diary of 1942: 'The person who inspired the main reason for it is now dead.'[7]

The death of Glover hit her hard. Over lunch in a neighbouring village, she thought back upon his web of amorous affairs. Meanwhile, her greatest love, Henry Harvey, came back into her life. Now twice divorced, he had moved back to England, living at Willersey in Gloucestershire not far from Pym. He came to tea, 'with a bad cold and bringing crumpet'.[8] One late evening, Henry returned to Finstock uninvited, tapping on the window. This gave a fright to the Pym sisters, who had recently heard of a burglary and murder of an elderly lady in a neighbouring village. Pym wrote to Henry to explain about the murder and their fear of opening doors to strangers at night. It was a reminder of how vulnerable they felt, especially at night when the village was so dark and quiet. She told him that she planned a holiday to Greece with Hilary and that she still took great pleasure in novel writing, 'even if nothing comes of it in worldly terms'.[9]

There was more distress to come with the death of their beloved cat, Tom: 'He just quietly expired on a copy of *The Times* one Saturday morning. When he died, the fleas left his body.'[10] But they still had Minerva, the brindled tortoiseshell.

Larkin came to Barn Cottage for tea and they walked to the church to see the T. S. Eliot memorial. 'So two great poets and one minor novelist came for a brief moment (as it were) together. Philip took photos of us all with two cats outside the cottage.'[11] Though the relationship between Pym and Larkin was not at all romantic, they were in many ways kindred spirits. Philip was wonderful company – funny and droll and always encouraging. He told her about the mutual Pym fans he had met at parties and literary events. He was a restorative to her spirits and she deeply appreciated his friendship.

In the previous year, she had confided in Larkin her feelings of failure: 'Here I am sixty-one (it looks much worse spelled out in words) and only six novels published – no husband, no children.'[12] Larkin replied with his usual support and good sense: 'Didn't J Austen write six novels and not have a husband or children?'[13] At least Pym had managed to finish her novel, which she gave the working title 'Four Point Turn'. She sent it to the publisher Hamish Hamilton and got the expected response. 'The embarrassment of being an unpublished novelist knows no bounds,' she wrote.[14] Rather pathetically, the only literary consolation of the year 1976 was the publication of a large-print edition of *Some Tame Gazelle*, aimed at the public library market for older readers with failing eyesight.

Pym had endured breast cancer and the mutilation of her body; had a stroke, which caused the temporary loss of the writing facility that meant the world to her; had suffered the death of lovers and friends and a beloved pet. And her literary career seemed irrevocably over. But her life was about to change in the most unexpected of ways.

BOOK THE SEVENTH

In which the fortunes of Miss Pym are reversed

CHAPTER I

A Real Pym Year

Early in the new year of 1977, Pym read the letters of Sylvia Plath. She was surprised to discover how likeable she was: 'All these years I seem to have misjudged her – the kind of person she seems to have been – dates with Amhurst boys and at Cambridge . . . And liking clothes and hair-dos.' Pym was also moved by Plath's feelings of despair and isolation: 'alone in that bitter Winter of 1962–3 in a house in Fitzroy Rd – where Yeats lived – with two young children, starting to write at 4 or 5 o'clock in the morning – deserted by Ted Hughes – that was how it was'. Pym asked Larkin if he knew Ted, saying that his desertion of Plath 'put her against' Hughes. Her feelings of gloom persisted. At church there was only a tiny congregation 'and ought not the Christmas decorations to have been taken down? A lapsed Catholic is no good to man or beast.'[1]

Nevertheless, she continued to work at *Four Point Turn*, adding two extra chapters. She had shown the novel to Larkin in manuscript. He had advised her to make it longer and to rename it: 'I think the title *Four Point Turn* a little smart for so moving a book; it needs something sadder, more compassionate.'[2] Bob Smith also had advice. He wanted more of 'Norman', one of the four main characters, so Pym added some 'bits' about Christmas. But she felt in her heart that she would not be published again. She was part of the old world, not the new. 'Life in 1977,' she wrote to Bob: 'Concorde, costing I don't know how many millions, flies over our heads, clearly visible from our cottage windows, while the road outside is as full of potholes as in the 16th century.'[3]

Then, on 21 January, her life changed almost overnight. In celebration of its seventy-fifth anniversary, the *Times Literary Supplement* asked a wide array of writers to name the most underrated and most overrated authors or books of the past seventy-five years. Barbara Pym was the only writer to be named twice.

Philip Larkin wrote in the *TLS* (immediately above a curious recommendation by Vladimir Nabokov of a minor novel by H. G. Wells): 'The six novels of Barbara Pym published between 1950 and 1961, which give an unrivalled picture of a small section of middle-class post-war England. She has a unique eye and ear for the small poignancies and comedies of everyday life.' And, even more flatteringly (placed between the recommendations of the maverick psychoanalyst R. D. Laing and the avant-garde German composer Karlheinz Stockhausen), Oxford University Goldsmith's Professor of English Literature, Lord David Cecil, nominated: 'Barbara Pym, whose unpretentious, subtle, accomplished novels, especially *Excellent Women* and *A Glass of Blessings*, are for me the finest examples of high comedy to have appeared in England during the past seventy-five years.'[4]

Paul Binding read these accolades as he sat at his desk at the Oxford University Press. After work, driving home through January rain, it occurred to him that the Pym sisters might not be subscribers to the *TLS*. He phoned Barbara when he got back to Finstock. No, she did not take the *TLS*. 'There is something of great import for you,' he told her.[5] Later, Larkin assured

Pym that there had been no prior collusion between him and Lord David.

A story ran on the front page of *The Times* the very next morning. Headlined: 'How are the mighty fallen – according to the critics', it began with the famous names cited among the 'most overrated of the last seventy-five years': E. M. Forster and the historian Arnold Toynbee were the clear winners in this ignominious category, closely followed by Virginia Woolf and Sigmund Freud. But:

> There was a much wider spread of opinion on the most under-rated authors of the century. The only name to emerge twice was that of Barbara Pym, whose six novels published between 1950 and 1961, and now available only in public libraries, were considered under-appreciated by Philip Larkin and Lord David Cecil. Jonathan Cape said last night they might consider a reprint.[6]

It was the first time that Miss Pym's name had appeared in the pages of the national 'newspaper of record' since June 1958, nearly twenty years before, when Jonathan Cape had included *A Glass of Blessings* in a block advertisement for their latest titles (just above the highlight of their list: Ian Fleming's latest James Bond novel, *Dr No*). David Cecil sent a characteristically modest note: 'I learnt to my horror that your books are out of print and that some are unpublished. I do hope that my words and Philip Larkin's will do something to remedy this lapse . . . May I say again, how much I admire your books, with what pleasure I read and re-read them.'[7]

All of a sudden, Pym was hot news. Radio Oxford came for an interview; letters poured in from friends, and the telephone rang constantly. Pym noted that, despite the quotation forced out of them by *The Times*, there was no word from Jonathan

Cape. 'Having just rejected my last novel what could they say, indeed?' It must have been a delicious moment. Eventually they wrote to say that 'they might consider' some reprints. 'That'll be the Frosty Friday,' she remarked, drily.[8]

Best of all was the news that came from Macmillan. The new novel was now renamed *Quartet in Autumn*. This time, there was no dusty rejection letter saying she was out of date and unpublishable. Senior fiction editor Alan Maclean, whose authors included Rebecca West and Muriel Spark, telephoned Pym saying that 'they would *love* to publish the novel'.[9] He told her that he would confirm by post. She wrote to Larkin:

> Dear Philip,
> I haven't *dared* to write to anyone until I actually saw it in print
> . . . but now I have the letter before me and it seems from this
> that you know (perhaps?), so this is just to express my inadequate
> thanks . . . If it hadn't been for you and sending it to Pamela
> HJ [the novelist Pamela Hansford Johnson, who was well
> connected at Macmillan] . . . not to mention, all those *years* of
> encouragement. What can I say that would be at all appropriate?[10]

Larkin was ecstatic. He cracked open a bottle with Monica and wrote a congratulatory letter by return of post: 'Super news! I am drinking (or, come to think of it, have drunk) a half-bottle of champagne in honour of your success. Monica and I are really deeply happy about it: we look forward to publication day as if it were our own . . . Oh I am so pleased: I want a real Pym Year.'[11]

Larkin was to get his wish. It was indeed a 'real Pym Year'. BBC Radio 4 planned to read *Excellent Women* on *Story Time*. Larkin wrote a piece about the novels for the *TLS* entitled 'Something to Love'. This article helped to establish Pym as an important novelist, with hidden depths behind the perfect comedy. Cape, with their tails between their legs, wrote to say they would like to republish all of her novels. Pym was particularly pleased that the senior editor, Tom Maschler, who had been her chief 'blocker', wrote to her personally. Naturally, he wanted to publish her latest novel. 'It was,' she told a journalist ('with evident and rather sharp relish, reminiscent of Pym women'), 'very sweet to me' to tell Maschler that Cape had previously rejected it, so she had decided to publish with Macmillan.[12]

Pym and Hilary celebrated with sherry and whisky. They chatted about the upcoming festivities for the queen's silver jubilee. The Finstock residents gathered to discuss their plans. Pym imagined that similar meetings had been taking place all over the country in dark village and parish halls, with the same jumble of ideas. She had always loved spring, and her notebooks were suddenly full of new life and opportunity, as bulbs sprouted in the garden. The season evoked her happiest memories, such as her time with Julian Amery in Oxford.

CHAPTER II

Tea with Miss Pym

Pym's delight in her new status was infectious. She was taken out to lunch with Alan Maclean and James Wright from Macmillan. She found them 'sympathetic and congenial'. They wanted to publish *The Sweet Dove Died* as well as *Quartet in Autumn*. Pym was being given what she had longed for all those years: attention and kindness. Her sense of humour had returned. She told Larkin that she and her sister had exacted their own particular revenge on Cape: 'Hilary and I invented a Maschler pudding – a kind of milk jelly.'[1]

Pym was deeply grateful to Philip and invited him to a splendid lunch of kipper pâté, followed by veal with peppers and tomatoes, pommes Anna, and celery and cheese. They drank sherry and burgundy. Pym found Larkin 'shy but very responsive and jokey'. They had their photograph taken together before he left in his pale tobacco-brown Rover. Jock Liddell was equally delighted by her success: 'Now someone can write a thesis on "Barbara Pym – the silent years". Ultimately I think our kind of books date the least – and the once "up-to-date" is speedily "out-of-date".'[2]

In May, Pym visited another of her champions, Lord David Cecil. They met at his home in Dorset for tea. She found Cecil and his wife easy to talk to, the time flying by. In a comfortable, agreeable room with green walls and fine family portraits, they sipped Lapsang Souchong and ate brown toast with redcurrant jelly and ginger cake. Cecil was full of praise and told Pym that her novels, along with Anthony Powell's, were the only ones he would buy without reading first. She learnt that Powell was Cecil's fag at Eton. They both agreed that comedy was out of fashion in novels.

More good news was to follow. That year, 1977, Larkin was chair of the judges for the Booker Prize for the best novel of the year. 'So at *least* I can get you read by the panel,' he wrote.[3] He also enclosed a fan letter about her that he had received from John Bayley. The BBC's Will Wyatt came to Finstock to make a short film about Pym for *The Book Programme*.

Pym was especially pleased that *The Sweet Dove Died* was finally going to be published: 'I feel it is one of the best I have ever done.'[4] The BBC film would be called *Tea with Miss Pym,* and feature Lord David Cecil. The filming went well: footage in the churchyard and then tea in the garden with Cecil, who had driven over for the occasion. Minerva the cat provided comic relief, trying to put her paw into the jug of milk. 'Lord D and I chatted and we agreed that the whole thing might easily have lapsed into farce, rather like the Mad Hatter's tea party.' Pym enjoyed the experience immensely. Her only worry was when it was suggested that her treatment of men implied she had a low opinion of the sex. 'My instinctive reply sprang to my lips, "Oh, but I *love* men," but luckily I realised how it would sound, so said something feeble.'[5] Then, in August, it was off to the BBC in Bristol to do a feature for *Woman's Hour*.

Pym's world was enlarging in a way she had never expected. Advance copies of *Quartet in Autumn* arrived at the same time as a large box of copies of reissues from Cape, 'in beautiful brilliant colours with my name in enormous letters!'[6] Then the

Guardian called for a piece and even fashionable *Harpers &*
Queen.

In September, *The Times* published a full-page feature under
the headline 'How Barbara Pym was rediscovered after 16 years
out in the cold'. It reported that, at the time of the *TLS* article,
'Her publisher, Jonathan Cape, was at first even doubtful
whether she was still alive.'[7] The journalist Caroline Moorehead
had been to see Pym at the cottage in Finstock and heard of
how, in the 1960s, she had been turned down by twenty
publishers. Moorehead asked her what she would do if she
made a lot of money from her newfound fame: to the interviewer's astonishment, Pym replied, with her old spirit of
adventure, that she and her sister would go by Concorde to
Latin America.

She was also becoming the object of academic study: an Italian
student writing her thesis on Pym's novels arrived at Finstock
for an interview, 'wearing mauve-tinted' glasses. On publication
day in the autumn, Pym received a telegram from James Wright
and an enormous card from Larkin with a sketch of a dragon
labelled 'Maschler', its heart pierced with a spear. Happiness
beams from her letters. She thought the *Guardian* article better
than the *Times* interview: 'and surely those photographs show
that slightly mad jolly fun face (that I don't much like)'. What
she really wanted was to cultivate a 'dark brooding expression,
but don't think I ever could'.[8]

David Cecil wrote to say that he had seen their television
programme, *Tea with Miss Pym*, advertised in the *Radio Times*
for broadcast on Friday 21 October at 11.25 p.m., adding: 'I had
always thought this was the hour reserved for the late-night
Horror Films.' They had talked of Jane Austen and he said: 'I
think I am rather glad that Jane Austen died when she did. For
me, she is the last fine flower of 18th century civilisation.'[9] Larkin
wrote, following the transmission: 'How pretty and luxuriant

the garden looked. I thought you were jolly good – unflappable and *cool*.'[10]

The garden did, indeed, look luxuriant with white roses and foxgloves. David Cecil, in a light summer suit, described Pym as a novelist who wrote about quiet people in comedies that were devoid of sentimentality. Pym, dressed in a printed blue and white dress, stroked Minerva and spoke fluently and concisely, though she comes across as modest and shy. She wrote in her notebook: 'Quite pleasing and not too embarrassing. Finstock looked better than it really does in various shots.'[11]

Pym had sent Larkin copies of the Cape reprints, with a grateful inscription in each volume. Larkin had endorsed the novels with a quotation. She joked that he should be asking her for a rake of the royalties. Larkin responded: 'It really is a deep joy to me to contemplate them – not *unmixed* joy, because I want to set my teeth in the necks of various publishers and shake them like rats – but a great pleasure nevertheless. I take a selfish pleasure in seeing my name on them.' He was still angry about her years of neglect, 'but nice to think that good writing wins through in the end'.[12]

Now Pym awaited the reviews of *Quartet in Autumn*, and to hear whether, as Larkin had hinted, she might be nominated for the Booker Prize.

CHAPTER III

Miss Pym plays a Quartet in Autumn

The first draft of what would become *Quartet in Autumn* had been written in 1971, whilst Pym was recovering in hospital: 'Obviously one falls a little for one's surgeon. How easily might some lonely, slightly deranged spinster carry this passion to unnatural and embarrassing lengths, going to his home, sending him presents etc. The surgeon would, of course be used to women falling for him.'[1] Once again, she was using her own experience. Pym's novels (published and unpublished) are a candid reflection of her life and times from her Oxford days in the thirties; her time spent in Nazi Germany; working on the home front during the war; her service with the Wrens; her post-war working-woman years in London; the swinging sixties; and now the experience of hospitalisation in the National Health Service in the 1970s.

Pym's interest in trivia, ephemera, the life of ordinary things, roots her novels into specific times and yet they somehow transcend the quotidian and take on a timeless quality. As with Jane Austen, her realism is what enables her readers to inhabit her world, her characters, her sense of place and mood. She was often praised for her 'miniaturist' style, the perfection of her small canvas, though she was frustrated by this reductive view

– the small things *are* the important things she said, over and over again. Yet few critics perceived how bold and innovative she was. Her hilarious portrait of aesthetes Michael and Gabriel in *Crampton Hodnet* ('we like to express ourselves through movement') seem as modern now as when she was breathing life into them in the 1930s. Her sexually liberated women, such as Prudence Bates, were well ahead of their time, way before the advent of the sixties and the contraceptive pill. In *A Glass of Blessings*, Pym depicts a woman's hopeless love for a homosexual man; in *The Sweet Dove Died*, an older woman's obsession for a much younger bisexual man. There is nothing old-fashioned or 'cosy' about her themes.

Now in the seventies, Pym wrote about loneliness of old age and about the welfare state. She wrote about post-war immigration. She wrote about a woman in her sixties, enduring a mastectomy and dying alone, having starved herself to death, despite being under the care of a social worker.

In *Quartet in Autumn*, Pym was innovative in taking four people, bound together only by working in the same office; they are unskilled, inarticulate, poorly educated – not her usual world at all – and depicting them in old age, on the brink of retirement. Two of her characters live in bleak bedsitting rooms. The four characters, Norman, Edwin, Letty and Marcia do not have children or spouses and little in the way of extended families. They need one another, though there is no natural empathy or kinship between them. They live on the margins of society, often overlooked, *making do*.

The public library (no longer Boots' circulating library) is a place where the four characters gather, but do not meet. They go alone at lunchtime. It has become their church. Their preoccupations are solitary. Edwin goes to consult *Crockford's Clerical Dictionary* (as Pym once did) to 'find out' about a new clergyman who has been appointed to one of the churches he frequents;

Norman and Marcia come to the library because it is warm and a 'free' place to sit. Only Letty (loosely based on Pym) comes to the library to read books: sometimes novels, but more often biographies.

Tea is no longer a ritual, a ceremony of teapots and the choice between China or Indian, but a source of companionship and comfort to be mutually enjoyed by friends. The office workers plug in an electric kettle and use teabags. Coffee is instant from an oversized tin, shared to save money. The conversation is stilted, uninspiring; the only thing they have in common, says Norman, is the likelihood of dying of hypothermia.

Pym poured many of her feelings about her breast cancer into the character of Marcia. Though Pym joked about her false breast, some of her deeper feelings are expressed in Marcia's grief about her disfigurement: 'She was not a whole woman; some vital part of her had been taken away.'[2] As Pym did, Marcia has a crush on her consultant surgeon, 'the man who had cut her up'. She discovers where he lives and stalks his home.

Edwin, obsessed with Anglo-Catholicism, longs for the old world of 'cloak and biretta' but now the priests have long hair, wear jeans and play guitars. He is doubtful about the 'Kiss of Peace'. Letty longs for love and companionship, but somehow always fails to 'connect'. In the underground station, a woman is slumped on a seat (is she drunk? drugged?) and Letty is again immobilised by her detachment. A student is the only person brave enough to help the woman, only to be rewarded by a coarse expletive: 'Fuck Off!' Norman is a racist, troubled by the sexy energy of the young beautiful black women who work in his office. He likes to bite off the heads of the black 'jelly babies' he keeps in a bag in the office, telling himself that he's not a racist, he just likes the liquorice flavour.

Marcia is one of the lonely people who 'fall through the net' of the welfare state. Without a community of family and close friends, and with a stubborn desire to be left alone, she is vulnerable. Pym's notebook contains references to those who 'fall through the net . . . Hair net . . .'. Pym was a fan of the Beatles and one cannot help but think here of Eleanor Rigby, 'wearing the face that she keeps in a jar by the door' and the haunting refrain: 'All the lonely people'. But there is also the unmistakable influence of Philip Larkin and his 'Mr Bleaney'. Pym explicitly acknowledged Larkin in a reference to his bleak poem 'Ambulances' towards the chilling finale of her book, when Marcia, now an emaciated, anorectic old woman, is taken to hospital to die alone. There is a glimmer of hope at the end of the novel, but it is merely a glimmer. Letty, glancing at the London pigeons picking insects off other pigeons, reflects: 'Perhaps this is all we as human beings can do for each other.'[3]

CHAPTER IV

Miss Pym attends the Booker Prize

Pym was amused that several readers wrote to her to say that they were delighted to discover that she was not dead. The reviews of *Quartet in Autumn* were enthusiastic. Paul Bailey of the *Observer* remarked on the return (after sixteen years) of 'a considerable stylist, whose quietly accomplished work has been shamefully neglected . . . small in scale, *Quartet in Autumn* is on its own terms an exquisite, even magnificent work of art'. Some of the reviewers observed the sad, darker undertones of the novel in comparison with Pym's other work, 'an unmistakable touch of frost where earlier there had been sunshine'. Most believed it to be among her finest, most sophisticated work. Jilly Cooper, an ardent fan of the early novels (she described them as Jane Austen let loose in Cranford), noted: 'The comedy is bleaker . . . but the compassion for human vanities and the gift for the unexpected are still undiminished.' Fellow novelist Beryl Bainbridge described the book as: 'A beautifully sparse account of four elderly people . . . funny and sad.'[1]

Privately, Bob Smith also focused on its darker tone: 'The effect is rather frightening, despite the relief provided by acute observation of amusing trivia . . . I think that in one sense – perhaps the most important one – it is your best book and yet

I don't look forward to rereading it, whereas I reread your others all the time.'² Jock Liddell agreed that it was her greatest book to date. *Quartet in Autumn* also brought her to the attention of America. *Publisher's Weekly* raved that American critics and readers would find Pym 'pure gold', going on to say, 'though the harmony is in a minor key, the melody is one of beauty, dignity and spirit as these voices, unnoticed by the world, sing on'. *The Chicago Tribune* described the book as 'a small master-piece'.³

Daryll Forde's widow wrote to Pym saying that the novel brought tears to her eyes. She was a doctor and was deeply moved by the portrayal of Marcia and Dr Strong: 'so accurate and sympathetic'. She was only sorry that her husband was not alive to see her success. Peggy Makins, agony aunt for *Woman* magazine and a perceptive critic of Pym, found the book unbearably sad: 'I have the greatest respect for it. It is remarkable and chilling and horribly true . . . I doubt if it could ever be *likeable* . . . it has grim humour, but the loneliness, the withdrawing into one's self, the acute sense of despair – these were an aspect of your insight, which made me, at 62, feel the cold of death.'⁴ Pym also received a letter from the editor of the *Church Times*, which said that although he did not usually review novels, he would make an exception as Pym had given many free commercials for the newspaper.

Pym duly noted the comments about the 'darker' aspects, but remained cheerful about her own declining years, 'being blessed with an optimistic temperament and realising that there is nothing you can do about it'. She was already thinking ahead to the publication of *The Sweet Dove Died*: 'It is totally different from *Quartet* and there are no clergy in it, so goodness knows what people will think of it. Yet it is a chunk of my life, in a sense!'⁵

There was more fun in October, Pym meeting up with Iris Murdoch and John Bayley at Paul Binding's cottage. Iris was charming: 'nice face and pleasant to talk to'. Bayley, 'knowing what he feels about my books made him even nicer to talk to'. He dropped his wine glass, 'which seemed to go off with a loud explosion and there we were all scrabbling on the floor picking up bits of glass'. Then she went to lunch with Henry Harvey at his cottage in Willersey: 'Beautiful day and drive.'[6]

The next day, Pym was telephoned by James Wright, who told her the wonderful news that she had been shortlisted for the Booker Prize. She certainly did not expect to win, but she told Larkin that she was delighted to be attending 'a once-in-a-lifetime opportunity to mingle in the Literary World, perhaps even to catch a glimpse of Maschler!'[7]

On 23 November, Pym was driven with her editors to Claridge's ballroom, finding it 'very spacious inside, white and gold and a roaring coal fire in a sort of hall'. She described her appearance as: 'BP in her 65th year. Tall, short hair, long black pleated skirt, black blouse, Indian with painted flowers (C&A £4.90) and green beads.' She sipped a gin and tonic, whilst being introduced to a group of people, including none other than Tom Maschler. Philip Larkin gave a speech in which he announced that the judges were looking for three aspects: 'Could I read it? Did I believe it? Did it move me?'[8] He then announced that there were two near-misses, Caroline Blackwood and Barbara Pym. Paul Scott was the winner, for his elegiac post-Raj novel *Staying On*, though he was ill and unable to attend the ceremony. Each of the nominees were given a special leather-bound copy of their book.

Pym did not express disappointment for not winning, she had had a 'marvellous evening'. She told Larkin that she was 'so happy just to be in print again that nothing else matters'. And, as always, she gave thanks to the man who had done so much to restore her name and reputation: 'thanks . . . from the most overestimated novelist of 1977'.[9]

The Booker shortlisting led to accolades from all quarters. Foreign rights were snapped up not only in America, where she was beginning to build a loyal following, but also in Sweden: 'I think it might appeal to the Scandinavians.' The press couldn't get enough of Pym and her 'out of the wilderness to success' story. She was invited to do a BBC radio talk for *Finding a Voice* and *The Times* asked her to write an article on anything she liked (she chose the subject of 'a Defence of the Novel'). One satisfying result of her fame was that Tom Maschler was finally treating her with the utmost respect. Not one to hold a grudge, they began writing to one another. She told Philip Larkin that they were now 'Dear Tom, Dear Barbara'.[10]

An American university wanted to buy Pym's papers. Larkin strongly disapproved of selling them abroad and advised her to try for the Bodleian in her beloved Oxford. Pym told him that she valued her notebooks above all, which she had kept since 1948: 'a kind of diary, not only of events and emotions but also of bits and ideas for novels. These I could not let go, while still alive.'[11]

BBC's *Woman's Hour* was adapting *Quartet*: 'Rather unsuitable, I would have thought, but a lot depends on the adaptation.' In the meantime, she began writing a new novel, set in a country village. She told Larkin that money did not motivate her at all and she had decided not to sell her manuscripts to America: 'But the main thing is to feel that I am now regarded as a novelist, a good feeling after all those years of "This is well written, *but* . . ."'[12]

Then, the very next day after the Booker evening at Claridge's, she had a 'nasty turn' and collapsed on the way to lunch with Hilary. She was rushed to hospital, where there were fears she had suffered another stroke, or a heart attack. Later, she was told that she could have a pacemaker fitted, noting that her doctor advised that it 'must be removed at death as it is liable to explode in the crematorium'.[13] He said that she could use this information in a book.

Her symptoms seemed to subside, just in time for the publication of *The Sweet Dove Died*. 'Marvellous press', she noted with delight; '*Times, Guardian, Telegraph, Financial Times*'.[14] It was, perhaps, her most highly acclaimed novel. On the night of publication she and Hilary drank cava. Then came another great accolade: she was invited to appear on BBC Radio 4's flagship programme *Desert Island Discs*.

CHAPTER V

In which Miss Pym is invited as a Castaway on a famous Desert Island

Pym sent Richard Roberts a copy of *The Sweet Dove Died*. After all, he had inspired the novel and he was the last great love of her life. He sent a note from Indonesia, acknowledging receipt. When his fuller response came, he 'wisely didn't make much comment except to say how much he enjoyed it'. When *Quartet in Autumn* had been published, he wrote to tell her that he thought it was her masterpiece. He was too guilt-ridden to admit the brilliance of *The Sweet Dove Died*. Pym was now philosophical about her relationship with Skipper: 'It was all such a long time ago anyway . . . Little did I think that anything as profitable as this novel would come out of it.'[1]

Larkin thought that the final version of *The Sweet Dove Died* constituted 'another sad book and notable addition to your gallery of male monsters, though James is really too feeble to be called a monster'. He noted Pym's cleverness in bringing the reader round to Leonora, who begins as an unsympathetic character: 'the antiques make admirable symbols for a world of delicate and perhaps old-fashioned emotions'.[2] Pym replied that the extremely favourable reception of *The Sweet Dove Died* was 'enough balm to soothe and heal all those wounds when only you and a few kind friends thought anything of my work'.[3] It shot to number 3 in the *Sunday Times* bestsellers list. Critics described it as 'faultless', 'as scrupulous as it is deadly'.[4] Bob Smith rejoiced: 'People do seem to be getting your message these days. Perhaps this is what will distinguish the 1970s from . . . the brutal 1960s.'[5]

In July 1978, Pym went down to London to record her *Desert Island Discs*.[6] She had lunch with the presenter and creator of the programme, Roy Plomley: 'cold salmon' at the Lansdowne Club and then on to Broadcasting House for the recording of the programme. She told Plomley that she was very fond of 'pop songs', but she hadn't chosen any for her interview as she knew she could sing them herself on the island. Her choices were romantic: a waltz from Richard Strauss's *Der Rosenkavalier* ('something invigorating . . . to make me feel happy and cheerful'); Maria Callas singing 'Vissi d'arte' from Puccini's *Tosca*, which gave her the opportunity to talk about her war experiences in Naples, where she had her first experience of opera; a religious piece by Messiaen; and for lightness some *Fledermaus*, and a song accompanied by bouzouki to remind her of her times in Greece.

Barbara sketched an outline of her career: how she didn't write at Oxford because she was too busy enjoying life, but then began her first serious novel at home in Shropshire; her time in the Wrens; her life combining writing with her work at the African Institute. Plomley asked her about the rejection of her seventh novel. 'They lost me,' she says of Cape. He also asked about *The Sweet Dove Died*, which was about to be published: yes, it was 'a more contemporary subject' – she was interested in the idea of a relationship between an older woman and a younger man, which she thought no one had written about before. She did not note that the great drama on this theme was one of her operatic choices, *Der Rosenkavalier*, nor that this was a major theme in at least two of the novels of her admired Elizabeth von Arnim.[7]

Probed about her writing habits, Pym said that she liked to write every morning and thought that 800 words per day was a good result. She told of the notebooks in which she kept quotations, little details of events and everyday occurrences; things remembered from the past, material for 'emotion recollected in tranquillity', as Wordsworth called the writing process. Asked which disc she would select if allowed just one, she chose the Christmas carol 'In the Bleak Midwinter', sung by the choir of King's College, Cambridge: it offered poetry, music and Christian faith all in one.

Her chosen luxury was a case of white wine – 'German, I think' (in memory of Friedbert, who naturally remained unmentioned). Her book – apart from 'the Bible and Shakespeare which are already on the island' – was Henry James's complex, emotionally wrought, late novel of marriage and adultery, *The Golden Bowl*, a further sign of the newly Jamesian reach to which she aspired in *The Sweet Dove Died*.

Among Pym's other choices was Philip Larkin reading his beautiful poem 'An Arundel Tomb'. He wrote to her after the broadcast: 'I taped it (no doubt illegally) so that I shall always have it. I thought you spoke very sensibly and amusingly and though your music was a little "foreign" for me I very much warmed to "In the Bleak Midwinter" . . . though I could hardly bear my tedious voice slogging on.' With his letter, he enclosed a newspaper cutting announcing an engagement between a certain Richard George Larkin and one Elizabeth Ann Pym of Derbyshire. Pym was highly amused and wrote back: 'Do you think we'll get an invitation to the wedding?'[8]

More honours came Pym's way towards the end of the year, when she was made a fellow of the Royal Society of Literature. She was invited to a feast at University College in Oxford and one at St John's ('You will soon have had more college feasts than I've hot dinners,' Larkin teased) and she turned the experience into a short story for *The New Yorker*. Titled 'Across a Crowded Room', it centred upon a college feast in which an elderly woman sees a man across the other side of the room and then is aware that he does not recognise who she is. The *Church Times* also invited Pym to write a short story for their Christmas issue. 'The Christmas Visit' recycled Mark and Sophia Ainger and their cat Faustina, now in a country parish.

It had been a remarkable year and the only blight was Pym's health. She was not able to enjoy eating or drinking alcohol and yet her weight was ballooning. After Christmas was over, she resolved to speak to her doctor.

CHAPTER VI

In which Miss Pym works
on her Last Novel

Towards the end of the *Desert Island Discs* interview, Roy Plomley asked Pym if she was working on a new novel. She replied that she was about a third of the way through one, but that it would require considerable revision before reaching any kind of final form. It was clearly inspired by the return of Henry Harvey, who was being a good friend. He had taken her away for a winter break in Ross-on-Wye the previous December. They planned another winter break to Derbyshire. Pym joked about Belinda and the Archdeacon spending their old age together. It was certainly a curious twist of fate that she and Henry were drawing closer again, now that they were in their sixties. In August, Pym stayed with Henry in his cottage in Willersley. His ex-wife Elsie was also visiting: 'Strange situation dating back over forty years.'[1]

They went on a country walk and along a narrow path: 'Three elderly people walking – not together but in a long line separately, Elsie stopping to pick flowers.' So much had happened in the years since Hilary had to break the news of Henry's marriage to her heartbroken sister. Pym had loved other men – Julian Amery, Gordon Glover, Richard Roberts – but Henry had been her first serious love. He had always rejoiced in her success and though he had published a novel, he was happy to be in her literary shadow. In many respects, things had come full circle. Pym a published, acclaimed novelist and her first love back in her life.

Her new novel was called *A Few Green Leaves*. She finished a draft of it, which she sent to Macmillan, asking them to see it through the press, though her instinct was that it needed more work. The setting was a return to the setting of her first – the English country village. Pym joked: 'When I wrote *Some Tame Gazelle*, I didn't know nearly so much about village life as I do now.'[2] She based her village on Finstock and the local great house on Cornbury, a seventeenth-century royal hunting lodge in west Oxfordshire. One of the customs of Cornbury was that on Palm Sunday the local people were permitted to collect wood from the Wychwood Forest. Pym opens her novel with a similar theme: 'The villagers still have the right to collect firewood – "faggots", as the ancient edict has it – but they're less enthusiastic about that now,' says the rector.[3]

However, the villagers no longer need firewood. They have central heating or electric fires. The world of the English village has moved on. Another change is the transfer of allegiance of the villagers from vicar to doctor. The surgery is a stark new building next to the village hall, and the parishioners no longer feel the need to talk to the vicar, when they have the 'advice and consolation' of the doctor: 'There was nothing in church-going to equal that triumphant moment when you came out of the surgery clutching the ritual scrap of paper.'[4] Even the rector's sister, Daphne, who keeps house for him, insists that the doctor is the most important person in the village. Matters of the body are more important than matters of the soul.

The novel's heroine is Emma Howick, who is an anthropologist, staying with her mother in the village. The mother, who teaches English literature, has named her in honour of Jane Austen's Emma Woodhouse, 'perhaps with the hope that some of the qualities possessed by the heroine of the novel might be perpetuated'. But the daughter is reminded more of Emma Gifford, Thomas Hardy's wife, 'a person with something unsatisfactory about her'.[5]

Emma's old lover, Graham Pettifer, returns to the village. They had been students together, and when she sees him on television she writes to him, and he asks to visit. Unsure of whether he is still married, she sets the table for three, and is surprised when he turns up alone: 'She had never before experienced the curious awkwardness of meeting somebody you had once loved and now no longer thought about.'[6] As with Henry Harvey, Graham reveals that he has returned from teaching abroad, is divorced and living alone. He tucks into the hearty meal that Emma has provided, and tries to kiss her when he leaves. Now that the years have passed, Graham seems to be less tall than she remembered: 'had it always been like that or had he shrunk, diminished in some way?'[7]

Emma decides on a new topic: 'Some Observations of the Social Patterns of a West Oxfordshire Village'. She takes notes on the vicar, the two doctors, the food inspector and former Church of England clergyman, two young academics (often in the pub), a writer, and a church organist. Most of the original inhabitants can no longer afford to live in the heart of the village and have been forced out to the council estate on the outskirts. Emma notes that she has seen nothing of the gentry, in particular Sir Miles of the big house.

The old people still remember the war: Chamberlain's speech on the wireless; evacuee children; smoking cigarettes – a pack of ten in blue packets (but the young people now do not smoke). The task of tidying up the village mausoleum and planting pelargoniums in the graveyard has been outsourced to a young florist, Terry Skate, who has long blond hair and pink rubber gloves. The times are changing.

When Graham comes to live in the village, he imagines Emma will help him settle in; she buys Heinz tins and milk. He still expects her to look after his needs and home comforts, and complains about the tinned food, expecting fresh country produce. She now finds him 'almost comic': 'Did I once love this man?' she asks herself. 'Time has transfigured them into/ Untruth', as Larkin once wrote.[8]

CHAPTER VII

In which Miss Pym makes
her Final Journey

On 8 January 1979, Pym went to consult her doctor about her 'increasing bulk'. He performed various tests and told her what he thought it might be. 'Naturally I seized on the most gloomy (if it would be gloomy to die at 66 or 67?)'[1] She was referred to a consultant surgeon in Oxford, who arranged for her to be admitted to the Churchill Hospital.

In hospital ('purple jelly with a dab of synthetic cream' and 'All right, dear?') Pym was told that there was malignant cancer in her abdomen. It could be treated by radiotherapy or an operation. She accepted the diagnosis bravely, thinking about how cancer affected people in the past: 'If I'd been born in 1613 I would have died in 1671 (of breast cancer).' They decided to treat the tumour with radiation: 'it is a poison and may make me feel sick', she noted. Her own doctor – 'Very kind and practical' – asked Pym where she wanted to end her life, at home or in hospital or a nursing home. She hoped, however, that the radiation would give her some extra months, possibly years. She hoped to finish her final novel: 'May I be spared to retype and revise it, loading every rift with ore!' As usual, she drew deep within for courage and fortitude: 'All humanity is in the Out Patients, those whom we as Christians must love.'[2]

Pym told Bob Smith that she hoped for a few more years of 'good life' and she planned another winter break with Henry, to pursue the historic literary associations of the Midlands. She told Philip Larkin that so far she had experienced no ill effects of the drugs and that she was coping well with the news: 'After all, I have lived eight years since my breast cancer operation in 1971, so I suppose you could say that I *have* survived.' She had no desire to live to be very old, she said, and joked about how to tell people about her terminal illness: 'What, you *still* here?' There was good news about her books. Penguin were going to reissue *Excellent Women* and *A Glass of Blessings* in paperback: 'This is an enormous pleasure to me.'[3]

Larkin found the news about Pym's illness 'most distressing', though he was delighted about Penguin: 'you're really in the big time. All the others will follow . . . no one can read you without wanting more.'[4] He joked that he would buy the whole lot and send them to Cape on All Fools' Day. He also promised to visit.

The draining of the fluid in her stomach made Pym feel more comfortable and the hospital appointments gave her 'amusement and material' for her work. In America, she was being lauded; John Updike wrote a fulsome review for the *New Yorker*. Her beloved cat, Minerva, had to be put down, 'but a new tabby has adopted us and *she* is pregnant, so new life is springing up'. Snowdrops were appearing, as her favourite season began. At the end of March, Pym went to Derbyshire with Henry. They drank Orvieto wine and visited the lovely village of Bakewell, close to Chatsworth. Then they swung into Nottinghamshire, to try to find Byron's home, Newstead Abbey, and had lunch in D. H. Lawrence's Eastwood. On the way home, they stopped for tea at a motorway service station: 'A whole new civilisation.'[5]

Later that month, Pym was invited to Hatchards' Authors of

the Year party. She was amused to find *Less Than Angels* next to an autobiography of Diana Dors. As they were about to leave, she was accosted by the best-selling author of country life bonkbusters, Jilly Cooper, who told Pym that she was a great fan of her work. Then there was a Romantic Novelists' lunch at the Park Lane Hotel, Piccadilly.

The cold weather had given way to a warm spring: 'A fine Easter, sunshine and things burgeoning. I live still!'[6] Four kittens were born in April and the sisters kept a little black one, finding good homes for the others. Pym enjoyed the fact that the birth of the kittens brought a stream of visitors, including children: 'I thought of a splendid title for a novel, *Blind Mouths at the Nipple*.' Larkin came to see her and she was able to show him her favourable American reviews. Pym wrote to thank him for the visit and to tell him that Cape were reprinting *Jane and Prudence* and *No Fond Return of Love*: 'So I wish all neglected novelists could have the good friends and luck that I've had.'[7]

In May, she heard the cuckoo for the first time in the year and was glad to have survived until summer: 'Summer at last (what one has stayed alive for).'[8] She was well enough to continue polishing and redrafting her novel. At a (Catholic) church service in June, she noted the charming Irish vicar: 'At the service I felt I could enrich my novel by giving more about Tom's church, which was probably like this one.' She also began to plan a new novel about two women, starting with their college life: one from a privileged background and one from a more ordinary one. She wanted to bring the war into the novel and perhaps plot a triangular relationship: 'when she comes to stay with her friend she hopes to "get to know her husband better" – with unexpected results'.[9]

Pym turned sixty-six in June and wondered if she'd make it to the age of seventy. In July, she attended a lunch at her old college, St Hilda's, 'and had the usual consolation of not looking as old (or as fat) as some of my contemporaries'.[10]

But by August, she was feeling ill and in a 'poor physical state. Very blown out and feeling disinclined to eat and rather sick.' Thoughts of death continued, though she was facing her end with her usual courage and vim: 'Perhaps what one feels about dying won't be the actual moment – one hopes – but what you have to go through beforehand – in my case this uncomfortable swollen body and feeling sick and no interest in food and drink.' After having some more of the fluid in her abdomen drained, she felt better. She was given new medication to try, but her once healthy appetite had completely gone and she was constantly nauseous: 'A few nips of brandy, Lucozade, weak tea, toast – hardly enough to sustain me.' Later, a doctor called and said he could give her some drugs to help combat the nausea: 'Also he says that champagne is better than Lucozade.'[11] Hazel Holt's son, Tom, had gone up to Oxford that term, which made Pym pensive: 'So he is embarking on what should be the happiest days of his life.'[12] Her Oxford days had been the happiest days of her life. She told Larkin that she was enjoying the sunshine and being very well cared for by Hilary; he asked if he could telephone Hilary to enquire about her health, as he didn't want to exhaust her with conversation.

Hazel Holt was a regular visitor and found her friend 'cheerful and prosaic about her condition and always with some splendid Pym anecdote or "happening"'.[13] Pym's hair had thinned with the radiotherapy and she now wore a kerchief knotted around her head. Tom would sometimes visit, bringing news about Oxford student life. She gave him the plot of a love story, which he wrote for her.

One of her final acts was to send Philip Larkin two finished copies of *Jane and Prudence* and *No Fond Return of Love*. 'The whole six of them look quite handsome in their bright jackets,' she told him, 'and looking at them perhaps I can quote St Hilda's motto: *Non frusta vixi* – though I still wonder if any of this would have happened if it hadn't been for you and Lord D. and the dear *TLS*.' He was, she told him, 'such a good friend'.[14]

Pym made it to Christmas, but in January was moved to Sobell House Hospice in Oxford as she did not want to be a burden to Hilary, who had nursed her with such love and devotion. In her wheelchair, scoping out Sobell House, she observed a wealth of rich 'material' for a future novel she knew she would never write. One of her last visitors was her old love, Henry Harvey. She joked about having to wear a wig. He found her wit and her courage undiminished. By now, she was very weak and fading fast. Selfish old Henry had proved himself, after all, to be a devoted and loving friend. In *Some Tame Gazelle*, Belinda/ Barbara had imagined the Archdeacon being one of her last visitors. She had been granted the wish made when she was a young woman of twenty-one.

She had also achieved her greatest wish of becoming a highly regarded author. Pym left the world with a canon of works that continue to enthral and entertain. She had faced life and its challenges with the utmost spirit and good humour, and now she confronted death with steadfast courage and dignity. She died after breakfast on the morning of 11 January 1980.

EPILOGUE

In which Mr Larkin attends the Funeral of his Much-Loved Correspondent Miss Barbara Pym

Barbara Pym's funeral was well attended. It took place in the Finstock parish church, where T. S. Eliot had been baptised in 1927. One of the attendees was Philip Larkin. He noted that there were family, friends and a representative of Macmillan, her publisher. Larkin sat in a pew directly underneath the plaque commemorating Eliot's baptism. He told Anthony Thwaite (his poet friend and later the editor of his letters) that he regretted Pym's death very much: 'Even at her funeral I found myself looking forward to getting a letter from her describing it all.'[1]

Prudence Glover, who had seen much of Barbara during the years in Pimlico and Barnes, and who had once lived with the sisters when she went to college in London, was devastated by the loss: 'Although I was married with children by then, I couldn't and wouldn't believe she was old enough to die. I remember her with deep affection and know she always loved me.'[2]

In a talk describing her life as a writer, Barbara Pym once said that 'the greatest source of material for character drawing is probably the author's own self. Even when a novel isn't obviously autobiographical one can learn a great deal about a novelist from his works, for he can hardly avoid putting something of himself into his creations.'³ She was the most autobiographical of writers, and, although she never married or had her own children, she knew love, and she wrote about it, in all its manifestations.

Persuasion was Pym's favourite Jane Austen novel, and she could not bring herself to believe that the author of such a beautiful and satisfying depiction of love could not have experienced it herself: 'I don't suppose anybody nowadays would be likely to think of Jane Austen as a quiet spinster who had never known love but only imagined it.'⁴

In a memorandum written after her death, Jock Liddell wrote movingly about his relationship with Barbara Pym. He described himself as greatly fortunate that the young Pym found herself sitting in the Bodleian Library opposite Henry Harvey. Because of that moment, Pym and Liddell would become the greatest of friends. Liddell recalled that Barbara was the first to write to him following the death of his beloved brother; also that in 1945, when he left Oxford for good, it was she who helped him to disband his flat. In 1976, she visited Jock in Greece for the last time. He remembered her as entirely carefree. Liddell admired Pym's courage for continuing to write following the rejection from Cape. She was a 'good, brave, religious woman . . . with equal courage she fought cancer when it came': 'Her work was particularly satisfying to her emotionally, one felt she had no other needs. And she had the very great good fortune of having a devoted sister with whom to share her life, and to be her first and best reading public. She realised all the more what it had been to me to lose mine.'⁵

The sibling relationship, so important to Jock and Donald Liddell (and to his literary heroine Jane Austen and her sister Cassandra) was, as Jock knew, sacred and profound. Hilary's loss was great (she would live for another twenty-five years). The life

Pym had envisaged for herself and her sister, at the age of twenty-one, living in a country cottage in perfect amity, with jokes and laughter and companionship, had come true. Only Jock could fully feel the depth of Hilary's pain on losing such a sister. Never one to cast praise carelessly or to exaggerate the beneficence of human nature, which he often found wanting, Liddell wrote of his lifelong friend: 'I think I have never known anyone else who was so good all through.'[6]

The Larkin poem that Pym loved best was not typical of his usual bleakness and dry wit. It is not about bedsits or 'the toad work' or ambulances or old people in nursing homes. It is a love poem, uplifting and sonorous, about time and timelessness, fidelity and truth. This was the one that Pym chose for *Desert Island Discs*: her friend the author himself reading 'An Arundel Tomb'. The poem tells of a stone effigy of an earl and his countess, lying together in their tomb, their hands clasped together, 'faithfulness in effigy'. It ends with a simple and beautiful sentiment: 'What will survive of us is love.'[7] Barbara Pym was a passionate, deeply loving woman, who loved and was loved. And what survives of her is her readers' love of her novels.

Afterword

Barbara Pym lived through extraordinary times. She went up to Oxford in the 1930s in a traditional world still populated largely by male undergraduates, where women were subject to strict rules of conduct. She spent time in Nazi Germany, befriending a man who was close to Hitler. During the war, she worked on the home front, then as a censor and finally served in the Wrens. In the fifties, she lived and worked as a single, independent woman in London's bedsit land. In the sixties, she witnessed the sexual revolution. Throughout all of this social and political upheaval, she kept a detailed record. Her novels reflect these changes.

And yet, as with Jane Austen, also a 'spinster' writer who lived in a cottage with her sister, Pym's life has been largely assumed to be quiet and uneventful. As we have seen, the first essay review of her novels was written by her friend, Bob Smith. Its title 'A pleasure to know Miss Pym', originated the myth of her as a respectable but constrained 'excellent woman' writer who created a comforting world of English villages, academic communities and suburban parishes. For many readers, 'Miss Pym' offers a cross between P. G. Wodehouse and Anthony Trollope's Barchester. As in their novels, her characters are instantly recognisable: we feel we know a Sister Blatt, a Mildred Lathbury, a Father Thames, a Piers Longbridge.

Hers is a peculiarly British humour. Barbara Pym was an

extremely funny woman. She possessed a talent for comic delivery of a single word which friends, and their children, found irresistibly funny. A friend's son remembered vividly the amusing way she said words such as 'scones'. This 'Lady Bracknell' delivery ('a handbag') is given to Leonora Eyre: 'A *bucket*? . . . Really, did one look the sort of person who would have a bucket?'¹

The humour in her novels is sometimes redolent of British seaside postcard comedy: an overweight spinster suddenly appears in her Celanese vest and knickers whilst the curate is on his way to supper, his own 'woollen combinations' showing through his cassock. That same spinster leaves out old copies of the *Church Times* to use as toilet paper for dressmaker Miss Prior. English gentlewomen abroad are at risk from Italians with 'wandering hands': 'Pinch your bottom they would before you could say knife.' 'Men only want one thing,' says Miss Doggett, but she has forgotten what it is. Her typical subjects are decayed gentlewomen who wear 'good tweeds', always have their knitting needles to hand, and insist on the ceremonial aspects of afternoon tea.

Then there are the lazy clergymen who rely on the splendid women of their parish to do their laundry and invite them to supper. Vicarage gardens are transformed into fairgrounds with coconut shies, bran tubs, jumble sales and vegetable competitions. Excellent women are the kind who hang their dish cloths on a nail by the side of the cooker. The men wear bowler hats and carry briefcases. Soggy afternoons in North Oxford are rendered bearable by undergraduate tea parties, presided over by dowagers. Somewhere in an inner city office, a secretary is bursting into tears after being scolded by her boss for a typing error. An errant caterpillar appears unwanted in a badly washed salad. A curate is nipping into the Crownwheel and Pinion for a sneaky morning drink.

Pym was a lover of small things, and her world abounds with

them: paper spills in a fancy case, an embroidered *Radio Times* cover, a beaded milk jug cover, an antique box, small soap animals. 'Unimportant trifles'. But they bring 'unexpected moments of joy'. Bunches of mimosa in a wheelbarrow, English pears, chrysanthemums and Michaelmas daisies; daffodil buds that look like hard-boiled eggs. Mrs Cleveland of *Crampton Hodnet* misses her estranged husband; when she remembers him coming into the house with a bowl of gooseberries, his affair with a student is temporarily forgotten.

In all this, Barbara Pym's world is the epitome of George Orwell's England of 'old maids biking to Holy Communion through the mists of the autumn morning'.[2] It is an England that in many respects does not exist anymore; perhaps it never did, except in literature and the realm of the imagination. The 'small unpleasantnesses' that make life unhappy do seem to belong to a more gentle age. For this reason, Pym's literary reputation has suffered: it is generally assumed that her novels are entirely whimsical, nostalgic, 'safe'. Yet she always avoided the dangers of flippancy and whimsy. And many aspects of her characters' lives remain all too familiar: it is still the case that the burden of housework falls predominantly on women, and that marriage for women too often begins in romance and ends at the kitchen sink. For many reasons, one senses that she would have understood the #MeToo movement.

Unlike the world of P. G. Wodehouse, Pym's is not a static society. Her themes of loneliness, secret lives and unrequited love are evergreen, but the world of her novels changes perceptibly through the decades of her writing life. The fabric of her society is delicately knitted together and the slightest ruction has consequences. But there are darker undertones, too, and they must be confronted in order to do full justice to her life and work.

I came to Barbara Pym in middle age, finding her on the

shelves of a marvellous, now defunct, independent bookshop in Oxford, run by a brilliant and grumpy man who was a Pym fan. Indeed, he might have walked straight out of one of her novels. I was drawn to the covers of the posthumous paperback reprints published by the women's press, Virago. In bold, primary colours, they portrayed women dressed in 1950s clothes, holding a teacup or a kitten or a glass of wine. I read the first paragraph of *Excellent Women* and laughed out loud in the shop. I was immediately drawn to the extraordinary voice: so Jane Austen-like, but entirely its own. I read one, and then another, devouring each novel greedily.

Because I lived in Oxford, I decided to explore the Barbara Pym archive at the Bodleian Library. I discovered that she kept a diary from her schoolgirl years until her death. She also wrote down thoughts and feelings and ideas for novels in a series of notebooks. She kept almost every scrap of paper: letters, note-books, newspaper cuttings, household lists, postcards. Sometimes ideas for novels are scribbled on tiny pads of the sort that are given to passengers on aeroplanes, or on the back of menus or page proofs. Writing was a compulsion. Even when she was 'off-loaded' by Cape, she continued to craft more novels.

Then I read the first biography of her, by her friend Hazel Holt, with its apologetic title *A Lot to Ask*. I discovered that the story it tells of Pym's life was heavily edited and omitted many of the most important events and details that shaped her novels. It is natural that her friend, who worked closely with her sister, was keen to protect her legacy and her reputation, but much of the richness of her experience and the brilliance of the writing is lost. I turned to the 'autobiography' stitched together from letters and diary extracts under the title *A Very Private Eye*: it proved to be an invaluable resource, reflecting a more sensitive, romantic side to Pym, but it, too, was heavily edited and expur-gated. So I decided to write a new biography, reflecting the full range of the archive. Pym, unlike her great friend Robert Liddell, wanted her life to be told, and her archive to be held at one of the greatest libraries in the world: the Bodleian. In her journals, she makes interventions to the 'Gentle Reader of the Bodleian' who might be writing her life. That she cut out pages of her journals and destroyed sensitive materials also suggest that she desired literary posterity, but was also afraid of some of the darker aspects of her history being revealed.

Some of the evidence that I have uncovered might shock and upset her devoted followers. In mining her archive, I had no wish to 'dig dirt'; the information sheds new light on Pym, both the woman and the writer. Like many young people who lived through the 1930s, she flirted with Nazism. Pym was something of an obsessive personality, especially as a young woman. She learnt to speak German, read a good deal of German poetry and literature, and fell in love with the beautiful countryside. She, like many others, witnessed a humiliated country get back on its feet, and, without the benefit of hindsight, did not perceive (or chose not to see) the true nature of the Third Reich. Nor was she aware at the time how high the stakes would become: as we have seen, the brother of her beloved Julian Amery was hanged for high treason because of his support for Nazi Germany and fascist Italy, and buried in Wandsworth Prison. Later, of course, Pym recanted and was deeply ashamed of her past, editing the Nazi references out of her work. She must have destroyed her letters from Friedbert, but diary entries reveal the extent of their relationship. The story of her affair with Germany remains as a valuable warning from history.

Pym's personal life was always complicated. Most of her love affairs were unsatisfactory or unrequited, but she used her experiences and built them into her novels. Her sexual encounters, from the incident that we might now call her date-rape by Rupert Gleadow, to her affairs with married men, to the pleasure she took in the company of gay men, shaped key aspects of her life and her work. Few women novelists among her contemporaries were so open and unjudgmental about homosexuality in the days when it was still illegal. In two of her mature novels, she shows vulnerable women falling in love with homosexual men, and is highly sensitive to the agonies suffered on both sides. James Boyce, who is bisexual, is seen hovering outside a door hearing himself being discussed by a homophobic neighbour: 'But, darling, one would hardly wish to be a mother to someone like *that*.'[3] By directing her irony against such prejudice, Pym revealed her own pride in her friendships with gay men.

We have also seen that, after the war, when she worked for a distinguished anthropologist, completing her novels in her spare time, she drew comparisons between anthropology and her own life as a novelist. Both professions are concerned with society and human behaviour. Since her death, the discipline of anthropology, especially as practised in Britain during her time, has come under much criticism for either fetishising or patronising 'primitive' tribes encountered during the age of empire. By the same account, some of her jokes about African relics and slide shows of indigenous people belong to a world view that is now obsolete. And yet her underlying point is that she sees little difference between the rituals of these tribal lives and those of English society. Her white middle-class 'savages' are ruthless and predatory. A debutante dance in Belgravia is perceived as a hunting ground: 'what could be more primitive than the rigid ceremonial of launching a debutante on the marriage market?' In Pym's 'civilised' world, the woman gives her man food and shelter; the man gives what he considers to be the 'priceless gift of himself'.

Pym is one of the great writers of the human heart. Her novels came from her own heart: we have seen how highly autobiographical they are. As she grew older and wiser, so too did her novels. Over and over again, she made use of scraps of her experience. Friends, family and colleagues knew that they might find themselves woven into her stories; most of them took it well. Nor did she shy away from unflinching self-portraits, which reveal the extent of her discernment and self-knowledge. Characters she based on herself are rarely flattering, but nor are they self-pitying. Her romantic entanglements often brought her great suffering; she was a sensitive and emotional woman, and, as she grew older, she learnt to conceal her sadness behind a facade that sometimes made her appear aloof. She could be sharp-tongued, as she freely admitted. Yet, those who remembered meeting her as young children recalled her kindness and funniness. She never talked down to children, but treated them as adults.

Pym was a courageous writer and a brave woman. Women are at the heart of her stories. They are not all 'excellent women', but they are flesh and blood. She portrays young women struggling with heartbreak in their private lives and narrow opportunities outside the home. She is the great novelist of the plight of single women in middle age, in the era when the war had killed many potential husbands and the discharge of men from the armed forces had closed many of the employment opportunities that the war had brought. And she writes with great tenderness about the old. Her most acclaimed novel, *Quartet in Autumn*, was pioneering in depicting the lives of four lonely city people on the brink of retirement.

All lives are remarkable, even those that seem to be trivial or commonplace. One of Pym's favourite quotations, much used in her work, derives from John Keble's beautiful hymn, 'New Every Morning is the Love': 'The trivial round, the common task, will furnish all we need to ask.' I have quoted copiously from Pym's diaries and letters because their observations of seemingly trivial things – food, clothes, listening to the wireless

– are so full of wit, warmth and precision that all her manuscripts become little works of art, even as they provide a fascinating social history of the transformation of middle-class women's lives across the twentieth century.

Pym is that true writer whose fiction makes the ordinary extraordinary. Her reputation is secure, but only among a minority of readers. There is a thriving Pym Society, which alternates its meetings between Pym's beloved Oxford, England, and Boston, Massachusetts. North American scholars have written academic studies devoted to her work.[4] Her novels are all back in print. But she remains a cult author rather than a widely recognised name. I have sought to introduce a wider audience to her life, world and work. She deserves to be recognised as the Jane Austen of the mid-twentieth century.

What the young exuberant Barbara Pym most wanted was not love, marriage or a conventional life. She wanted to be different: 'still an original, shining like a comet, mingling no water with her wine'.[5]

Acknowledgements

I am deeply grateful to Tom Holt, son of Barbara Pym's devoted literary executor Hazel Holt, for permission to quote from the manuscripts. The staff of the Bodleian Library in Oxford, notably Gillian Humphreys, Victoria Joynes and Nicola O'Toole, offered incomparable service, without which this book could not have been written. My thanks to Bodley's librarian, Richard Ovenden, for his support for the project. Because I left Oxford in the course of my research, I relied on my research assistant, Felicity Brown, to photograph thousands of pages of manuscript in the archive: she was a wonder, to whom I will be eternally grateful.

It was a great pleasure to get to know the loyal members of the Barbara Pym Society (https://barbara-pym.org/). The impeccable research of Yvonne Cocking, gathered in her *Barbara in the Bodleian: Revelations from the Pym Archives* (published by the Pym Society in 2013), was invaluable. Triona Adams was very kind in first reaching out to me. Yvonne invited us to a delicious lunch ('through all its proper stages'), and we had such fun discussing our love for Pym.

Linda McDougall was extraordinarily generous in not only sharing with me her filmed interviews with people who knew Pym, such as Julian Glover and 'Skipper', but also allowing me to reproduce photographs from her collection. Thanks to Deb Fisher, Jutta Schiller and Kathy Ackley for their support. I don't think we will ever forget our Zoom chat and interview, brilliantly conducted by Kathy. Linda was also involved in editing our interview for the 'virtual' Pym conference that took place in September 2020.

Thank you, as always, to my agents Sarah Chalfant and Andrew Wylie, and to the team at William Collins: this is my ninth book for Arabella Pike, who has become the most loyal friend as well as an exemplary editor. This being by far my longest book, I am grateful to Jo Thompson for making some cuts and especially to Kate Johnson for the arduous copy edit; also to Marigold Atkey for seeing the book through the press.

Thanks to Harry Mount, for directing me to the wonderful article on Pym written by Prudence Glover for the *Oldie* Magazine. Also thanks to Dennis Harrison, owner of the much-missed Albion Beatnik Bookshop, who first introduced me to Pym. Sally Bayley gave her time and expertise, and we shared many a Pym joke over the years; tea and jumble sales often peppered our conversations. Julie Sutherland read the Afterword and gave very helpful advice. A conversation with A. N. Wilson gave me a fresh perspective. Jonathan Bate, always my first reader, read the manuscript, and suggested cuts and changes. Thank you, always, for your loyalty and care. The Bate children, Tom, Ellie and Harry, have been supportive and loving – 'Are you Pyming today, mum?' a constant refrain.

Stephen Pickles and I walked for miles in Oxford, and the surrounding countryside, in search of Pym. We talked and talked on Shotover Hill, where Pym once gathered flowers as 'blue as Geoffrey's eyes', and we found her charming cottage in Finstock one fine sunny English morning. Pickles, one of the most brilliant minds, and one of the most discerning readers of Pym, gave generously of his time and his talent. This book is for him.

Notes

This book is based primarily on the Archive of Barbara Mary Crampton Pym (1913–80), novelist, in the Bodleian Library, Oxford, MSS. Pym 1–178. For the sake of chronological clarity, letters, notebooks and diary entries are cited by date, not manuscript number, but a manuscript number is given for the first citation of each source. Specific page numbers within draft novels are not given. To avoid cluttering the text with reference note markers, only one note is given in passages where there are several quotations from the same source. A detailed listing of the contents of the archive is online at https://archives.bodleian.ox.ac.uk/repositories/2/resources/3235/collection_organization.

The following abbreviations are used in the Notes:

The novels of Barbara Pym:

AGB – *A Glass of Blessings* (1958)

AQ – *An Academic Question* (written 1970–72; published posthumously, 1986)

CH – *Crampton Hodnet* (completed 1940; published posthumously, 1985)

CS – *Civil to Strangers and Other Writings*, short stories and extracts from unpublished novels, edited posthumously by Hazel Holt (1987)

EW – *Excellent Women* (1952)

FGL – *A Few Green Leaves* (1980)

JAP – *Jane and Prudence* (1953)

LTA – *Less Than Angels* (1955)

NFRL – *No Fond Return of Love* (1961)

QIA – *Quartet in Autumn* (1977)

SDD – *The Sweet Dove Died* (1978)

STG – *Some Tame Gazelle* (1950)
UA – *An Unsuitable Attachment* (rejected 1963; published posthumously, 1982)

Where possible, quotations give page references to the readily accessible Virago Modern Classics paperback editions.

Other abbreviations:
ALTA – Hazel Holt, *A Lot To Ask: A Life of Barbara Pym* (1990)
AVPE – Barbara Pym, *A Very Private Eye: An Autobiography in Diaries and Letters*, posthumously selected and edited from her papers by Hazel Holt and Hilary Pym (1984)
BP – Barbara Pym
EH – Elsie Harvey
HH – Henry Harvey
JA – Julian Amery
PL – Philip Larkin
RG – Rupert Gleadow
RL – Robert 'Jock' Liddell
RR – Richard Roberts ('Skipper')
RS – Robert Smith ('Bob')

PROLOGUE
1. Literary Notebook XXVIII (MS. Pym 67, Bodleian Library, Oxford), 11 August 1969.
2. BP to PL, 10 December 1969 (Letters from Barbara Pym to Philip Larkin, Bodleian Library, Oxford, MSS. Eng. lett. c. 859–60).
3. 'Gervase and Flora' (MS. Pym 7), chapter 10.

BOOK THE FIRST:
A SHROPSHIRE LASS

CHAPTER I
1. Letter from BP to RL and HH and EH, Oswestry, early 1938 (MS. Pym 153).
2. Diary (MS. Pym 104), 11 March 1938.

3. Diary, 11 March 1938.
4. BP to RL, 12 April 1938.
5. *ALTA*, p. 12.
6. *AVPE*, p. 4.

CHAPTER II
1. *ALTA*, p. 2.

CHAPTER III
1. Ruth Johnson, *The Story of Our Chapel* (1927).
2. *ALTA*, p. 14.
3. *ALTA*, p. 14.
4. Barbara Pym, *Finding a Voice*, recorded 8 February 1978, broadcast BBC Radio 3, 4 April 1978 (MS. Pym 96).
5. Pym, *Finding a Voice*.

CHAPTER IV
1. 'Young Men in Fancy Dress'.
2. 'Young Men in Fancy Dress'.
3. 'Young Men in Fancy Dress'.

CHAPTER V
1. Letter of recommendation from Pym's Headmistress, Miss Gertrude Anthony, MS. Pym 98.
2. 'Young Men in Fancy Dress', p. 45.
3. *ALTA*, p. 22.
4. *CS*, p. 183.
5. L. W. B. Brockliss, *The University of Oxford: A History* (2016), p. 465.
6. See Brockliss, *University of Oxford*, p. 462.
7. Brockliss, *University of Oxford*, p. 465.
8. Brockliss, *University of Oxford*, pp. 462–3.
9. Evelyn Waugh, *A Little Learning* (1964), p. 171.

CHAPTER VI
1. Holt, *ALTA*, p. 21.
2. *AVPE*, p. 13.
3. *JAP*, p. 84.

CHAPTER VII
1. Diary (MS. Pym 101), 1 January 1932.
2. Diary, 1 January 1932. Blackgate was a central street in Oswestry, where Pym went shopping.
3. 'Beatrice Wyatt' (MS. Pym 6/1), p. 30.
4. 'Beatrice Wyatt', p. 31.
5. Diary (MS. Pym 101), 14 January 1932.

CHAPTER VIII
1. Diary, 15 January 1932.
2. Diary, 16 January 1932.
3. Diary, 17 January 1932.
4. Diary, 20 January 1932.
5. Diary, 20 January 1932.
6. Diary, 22 January 1932.
7. Diary, 23 January 1932.
8. Diary, 25 January 1932.
9. Diary, 27 January 1932.
10. Diary, 28 January 1932.
11. Diary, 2 February 1932.
12. Diary, 7 February 1932.

CHAPTER IX
1. Diary, 24 April 1932.
2. Diary, 26 May 1932. *AVPE* misdates the entry a month before on 26 April.
3. Her letters from RG constitute MS. Pym 149.
4. RG to BP, 18 May 1932.
5. Diary, 27 May 1932.
6. RG to BP, 28 May 1932.
7. RG to BP, no date.

8. Diary, 29 May 1932.
9. Diary, 31 May 1932.
10. RG to BP, 1 June 1932.
11. Diary, 5 June 1932.

CHAPTER X
1. Diary, 8 June 1932.
2. Diary, 15 June 1932.
3. Diary, 18 June 1932.
4. Diary, 20 June 1932.
5. Diary, 20 June 1932.
6. Diary, 23 June 1932.
7. Diary, 24 June 1932.
8. Diary, 24 June 1932, added comment 26 July 1933.

CHAPTER XI
1. RG to BP, 23 June 1932.
2. RG to BP, 26 June 1932.
3. RG to BP, 26 June 1932.
4. RG to BP, 26 June 1932.
5. RG to BP, 7 July 1932.
6. RG to BP, 17 July 1932.
7. RG to BP, 22 August 1932.
8. Diary, 15 and 16 September 1932.
9. Diary, 21 September 1932.
10. Diary, 22 September 1932.
11. RG to BP, 25 September 1932.
12. RG to BP, 25 September 1932.
13. RG to BP, 3 October 1932.
14. RG to BP, 3 October 1932.
15. RG to BP, 3 October 1932.

CHAPTER XII
1. Philip Larkin, *Jill* (1946), p. 21.
2. RG to BP, 12 October 1932.
3. Diary, 15 October 1932.

4. RG to BP, 17 October 1932.
5. RG to BP, 17 October 1932.
6. Diary, October to November 1932.
7. RG to BP, 3 November 1932.
8. RG to BP, 2 November 1932.

CHAPTER XIII
1. RG to BP, 12 November 1932.
2. RG to BP, 1 December 1932.
3. RG to BP, 29 December 1932.
4. Diary, 17 January 1933.
5. RG to BP, 22 March 1933.
6. RG to BP, 29 March 1933.
7. RG to BP, 10 October 1934.
8. RG to BP, 10 October 1934.
9. RG to BP, 3 August 1935. My italics.

CHAPTER XIV
1. Diary, 18 January 1933.
2. Diary, 18 January 1933.
3. Diary, 25 January 1933.
4. Diary, 26 January 1933.
5. Diary, 26 January 1933.
6. Diary, 26 January 1933.

CHAPTER XV
1. Diary, 12 February 1933.
2. Diary, 13 February 1933.
3. BP to HH, 10 March 1933. Pym's letters to Harvey are in a separate Bodleian file: 'Letters of Barbara Pym to Henry Harvey, with cartoons' (MS. 9827).
4. Diary, 1 March 1933.
5. Diary, 27 April 1933.
6. Diary, 29 April 1933.
7. Diary, 29 April 1933.
8. Diary, 30 April 1933.

CHAPTER XVI

1. Diary, 10 May 1933, with note that the entry was composed in July.
2. Diary, 10 May 1933, composed in July.
3. Diary, 10 May 1933, composed in July.
4. Other biographers have assumed that he was bitten by mosquitoes, but a later entry in the diary makes it clear that Pym was the one doing the biting.
5. Diary, 17 September 1933.
6. Diary, 17 September 1933.
7. Diary, 17 September 1933.
8. Diary, 14 May 1933.
9. Diary, 27 May 1933.

CHAPTER XVII

1. Diary, 2 June 1933.
2. Interviewed by Holt, *ALTA*, p. 43.
3. Diary (MS. Pym 102 commences in October 1933), 11 November 1933.
4. Diary (MS. Pym 102), 9 November 1933.
5. Robert Liddell, 'Reflections concerning Barbara Pym', MS. Pym 153, fols. 198–202.
6. BP to HH, 7 June 1933.
7. Diary, 9 June 1933.
8. Diary, 13 June 1933.
9. Diary, 14 June 1933.
10. Diary, 31 July 1933.

CHAPTER XVIII

1. Martin Pugh, *We Danced All Night: A Social History of Britain Between the Wars* (2008), p. 233.
2. Diary, 23 June 1933.
3. Diary, 23 June 1933.
4. Diary, 29 June 1933.
5. Diary, 15 July 1933.
6. Diary, 15 July 1933.

7.   Diary, 22 July 1933.
8.   Diary, 31 July 1933.

CHAPTER XIX

1.   Diary, 31 July 1933.
2.   Diary, 31 July 1933.
3.   Diary, 31 July 1933.
4.   Diary, 1 August 1933.
5.   Diary, 4 August 1933.
6.   Diary, 1 September 1933.
7.   Diary, 4 September 1933.
8.   Diary, 15 September 1933.
9.   Diary, 17 September 1933.
10. Diary, 30 September 1933.

CHAPTER XX

1.   Diary (MS. Pym 102), 4 October 1933.
2.   Diary, 4 October 1933.
3.   Diary, 4 October 1933.
4.   Holt, *ALTA*, p. 40.
5.   Diary, 4 October 1933.
6.   Diary, 4 October 1933.

CHAPTER XXI

1.   Diary, 18 October 1933.
2.   Diary, 18 October 1933.
3.   Diary, 23 October 1933.
4.   Diary, 7 November 1933.
5.   Diary, 9 November 1933.
6.   Diary, 17 November 1933.
7.   Diary, 9 December 1933.

CHAPTER XXII

1.   Diary, 14 December 1933.
2.   Diary, 14 December 1933.

3.   Diary, 19 December 1933.
4.   Diary, 5 November 1933.
5.   Diary, 3 November 1933.
6.   Diary, 2 January 1934.
7.   Diary, 9 January 1934.
8.   Diary, 4 January 1934.
9.   Diary, 7 January 1934.
10. Diary, 9 January 1934.

CHAPTER XXIII
1.   Diary, 13 January 1934.
2.   Diary, 17 January 1934.
3.   Diary, 18 January 1934.
4.   Diary, 18 January 1934.
5.   Diary, 26 January 1934.

CHAPTER XXIV
1.   Diary, above entry for 12 February 1934.
2.   Diary, 19 February 1934.
3.   Diary, 21 February 1934.
4.   Diary, 13 February 1934.
5.   Diary, 23 February 1934.
6.   Diary, 26 February 1934.
7.   Diary, 3 March 1934.
8.   Diary, 2 March 1934.
9.   Diary, 8 March 1934.
10. Diary, 8 March 1934.
11. Diary, 9 March 1934.
12. Diary, 9 March 1944.
13. Diary, 9 March 1944.
14. Diary, 9 March 1944.

CHAPTER XXV
1.   RL to BP, 15 March 1934.
2.   RL to BP, 15 March 1934.
3.   RL to BP, 15 March 1934.

4. RL to BP, 21 March 1934.
5. RL to BP, 21 March 1934.
6. Diary, 23 March 1934.
7. Diary, 20 March 1934.

BOOK THE SECOND:
GERMANY

CHAPTER I

1. Mary S. Lovell, *The Sisters: The Saga of the Mitford Family* (2003), p. 169.
2. See Julia Boyd, *Travellers in the Third Reich: The Rise of Fascism through the Eyes of Everyday People* (2017), p. 219.
3. Diary, 29 March 1934.
4. Diary, 31 March 1934.
5. Diary, 31 March 1934.
6. Diary, 31 March 1934.
7. Boyd, *Travellers in the Third Reich*, p. 301.

CHAPTER II

1. Diary, 1 April 1934.
2. Diary, 1 April 1934.
3. Diary, 2 April 1934.
4. Diary, 2 April 1934.
5. Diary, 2 April 1934.
6. Diary, 2 April 1934.
7. Diary, 3 April 1934.
8. Diary, 4 April 1934.

CHAPTER III

1. Diary, 5 April 1934.
2. Diary, 6–10 April 1934.
3. Diary, 14 April 1934.
4. Diary, 18 April 1934.
5. Diary, 19 April 1934.
6. Diary, 4 April 1934.

7. Diary, 27 April 1934.
8. Diary, 28 April 1934.
9. Diary, 4 May 1934.

CHAPTER IV

1. Diary, 9 May 1934.
2. Diary, 6 May 1934.
3. Diary, 12 May 1934.
4. Diary, 13 May 1934.
5. Diary, 15 May 1934.
6. Diary, 24 May 1934.
7. Diary, 25 May 1934.
8. Diary, 28 May 1934.
9. Diary, 2 June 1934.
10. Diary, 17 June 1934.
11. Diary, 17 June 1934.

CHAPTER V

1. Diary (MS. Pym 103 commences late June 1934), 7 July 1934.
2. *The Times*, 7 July 1934.
3. Unity Mitford to her sister Diana, 1 July 1934, in *The Mitfords: Letters between Six Sisters*, ed. Charlotte Mosley (2007), p. 48.
4. Diary, 10 July 1934.
5. Diary, 16 July 1934.
6. Diary, 16 July 1934.
7. Diary, 18 July 1934.

CHAPTER VI

1. Typescript fair copy of early draft of *STG*, MS. Pym 2/1 and 2/2 (bound in two volumes by BP).
2. Diary, 1 September 1934.
3. Diary, 1 September 1934.
4. *STG* early draft.
5. Boyd, *Travellers in the Third Reich*, p. 169.
6. Boyd, *Travellers in the Third Reich*, p. 169.
7. RG to BP, 20 October 1934.

CHAPTER VII

1. Diary (MS. Pym 103), 1 September 1934.
2. Diary, 1 September 1934.
3. Diary, 1 September 1934.
4. *STG* early draft.
5. RL to BP, 30 July 1934.
6. RL to BP, 4 September 1934.
7. RL to BP, 4 September 1934.

CHAPTER VIII

1. RL to BP, 19 September 1934.
2. RL to BP, 2 October 1934.
3. RL to BP, 2 October 1934.
4. Diary, 4 September 1934.
5. Diary, 7 October 1934.
6. Diary, 4 October 1934.
7. *STG* early draft.
8. *STG* early draft.
9. *STG* early draft.
10. RL to BP, 31 October 1934.
11. *STG* early draft.

CHAPTER IX

1. Diary, 16 November 1934.
2. Diary, 11 December 1934.
3. Diary, 3 January 1935.
4. RL to BP, dated 'Eve of St Mark' (i.e. 24 April), 1935.

CHAPTER X

1. Nancy Mitford, *Wigs on the Green* (1935), pp. 7–8.
2. Diary, 20 April 1935.
3. Diary, 20 April 1935.
4. Diary, May 1935 (no specific date).
5. Lion Feuchtwanger, *The Oppermanns* (1934) p. 261.
6. Feuchtwanger, *Oppermanns*, p. 383.
7. Feuchtwanger, *Oppermanns*, p. 339.

8. Lovell, *The Sisters*, p. 188.

CHAPTER XI

1. Diary, 22 May 1935.
2. Diary, 22 May 1935.
3. Diary, 22 May 1935.
4. Diary, 22 May 1935.
5. Diary, May 1935 (no specific date).
6. Diary, May 1935 (no specific date).
7. Diary, 30 May 1935.
8. Diary, 1 June 1935.
9. Diary, May 1935 (no specific date).

CHAPTER XII

1. RG to BP, 3 August 1935.
2. Diary, 25 August 1935.
3. Diary, 16 November 1935.
4. Diary, 3 November 1935.
5. Diary, 15 November 1935.
6. Diary, 11 November 1935.

CHAPTER XIII

1. Boyd, *Travellers in the Third Reich*, pp. 279–80.
2. Boyd, *Travellers in the Third Reich*, p. 280.
3. Boyd, *Travellers in the Third Reich*, p. 312.
4. RL to BP, 19 January 1936.
5. *STG* early draft (MS. Pym 2, bound in two volumes). Subsequent quotations also from this typescript.

CHAPTER XIV

1. All evidence suggests it was probably the Cowley Road Hospital, which was formerly a workhouse.
2. Diary, 2 December 1935.
3. Diary, 2 December 1935.
4. Diary, 20 December 1935.
5. Diary, 7 December 1935.

CHAPTER XV
1. BP to RL, 17 January 1936.
2. RL to BP, 19 January 1936.
3. RL to BP, 5 January 1936.
4. RL to BP, 10 November 1936.
5. BP to HH, 8 January 1936.
6. BP to RL, 27 January 1936.
7. BP to RL, 27 January 1936.
8. BP to RL, 31 January 1936.
9. RL to BP, 29 January 1936.
10. BP to RL, 19 February 1936.
11. BP to RL, 19 February 1936.

CHAPTER XVI
1. RL to BP, 12 February 1936.
2. RL to BP, 19 March 1936.
3. BP to RL, 13 March 1936.
4. BP to RL, 30 March 1936.

CHAPTER XVII
1. BP to RL, 10 May 1936.
2. RL to BP, 19 March 1936.
3. BP to RL, 10 May 1936.
4. BP to RL, 30 March 1936.
5. BP to RL, 10 May 1936.
6. BP to RL, 30 March 1936.
7. BP to HH, 15 May 1936.
8. BP to HH, 15 May 1936.

CHAPTER XVIII
1. John Middleton Murry, quoted in Karen Usborne, *Elizabeth: The Author of Elizabeth and Her German Garden* (1986), p. 231.
2. BP to RL, 10 May 1936.
3. BP to RL, 11 July 1936.
4. BP to RL, 11 July 1936.
5. Diary, 12 July 1936.

6. Paulina Kewes, 'Langbaine, Gerard (1656–1692), dramatic cataloguer and writer', *Oxford Dictionary of National Biography* (2004), https://doi.org/10.1093/ref:odnb/16007.
7. Diary, 14 July 1936.
8. Diary, 7 June 1936.
9. Diary, 8 June 1936.
10. Holt, *ALTA*, p. 65.
11. Diary, 16 July 1936.

CHAPTER XIX

1. Diary, 15 July 1936.
2. BP to HH, 20 August 1936.
3. Diary, 7 September 1936.
4. Elizabeth von Arnim, *The Enchanted April* (1922; repr. 2015), p. 1.
5. Chapter 13 in *Civil to Strangers*, the revised version of 'Adam and Cassandra', published posthumously (1987), p. 89.
6. BP to HH, 20 August 1936.
7. 'Adam and Cassandra' (MS. Pym 5), fols. 339–40.
8. *Finding a Voice*, BBC Radio 3, 4 April 1978.

CHAPTER XX

1. RL to BP, 24 September 1936.
2. HH to RL, 20 September 1936.
3. RL to BP, 11 October 1936.
4. BP to RL, 14 July 1937.
5. RL to BP, 22 July 1937.
6. BP to RL, 22 July 1937.

CHAPTER XXI

1. Robert Liddell, *Elizabeth and Ivy* (1986), p. 19.
2. Ivy Compton-Burnett, *Manservant and Maidservant* (1947; repr. 2001), p. 34.
3. Henry Harvey, at PEN Club meeting in celebration of Barbara Pym (1985).
4. Ivy Compton-Burnett, *More Women Than Men* (1933; repr. 1983), p. 26.

5. Liddell, *Elizabeth and Ivy*, p. 24.
6. 'Gervase and Flora' (MS. Pym 7), chapter 10.
7. *CS*, p. 379.

CHAPTER XXII

1. BP to RL, 22 July 1937.
2. RL to BP, May 1937.
3. Part of 'Gervase and Flora', including these passages, was published posthumously in *CS*, pp. 171–212.
4. Part of 'Gervase and Flora', including these passages, was published posthumously in *CS*, pp. 171–212.
5. *CS*, p. 184.
6. 'Gervase and Flora', chapter 10.
7. 'Gervase and Flora', chapter 13.
8. 'Gervase and Flora', chapter 15.
9. 'Gervase and Flora', chapter 19.
10. RL to BP, 10 November 1936.
11. RL to Hilary Pym, 6 December 1937.

CHAPTER XXIII

1. Diary, 3 December 1937.
2. Diary, 3 December 1937.
3. Diary, 3 December 1937.
4. Julian Amery in conversation with Naim Attallah, *More of A Certain Age* (1993), pp. 3–4.
5. David Faber, *Speaking for England: Leo, Julian and John Amery – the Tragedy of a Political Family* (2005; repr. 2007), p. 308.
6. JA to BP, December 1937 (MS. Pym 147).
7. Diary, 12 December 1937.

CHAPTER XXIV

1. RL to BP, 11 December 1937.
2. RL to BP, 11 December 1937.
3. Diary, 12 January 1938.
4. JA to BP, no date.
5. Diary, 26 February 1938.

CHAPTER XXV

1. Faber, *Speaking for England*, p. 311.
2. Diary, 26 February 1938.
3. Diary, 28 February 1938.
4. Diary, 3 March 1938.
5. Diary, 4 March 1938.
6. Diary, 5 March 1938.
7. Faber, *Speaking for England*, p. 131.
8. Faber, *Speaking for England*, p. 293.
9. Faber, *Speaking for England*, p. 193.
10. Faber, *Speaking for England*, p. 293.
11. Faber, *Speaking for England*, p. 300.
12. Diary, 5 March 1938.
13. Diary, 5 March 1938.
14. Diary, 8 March 1938.
15. Diary, 11 March 1938.

CHAPTER XXVI

1. JA to BP 19(?) March 1938 (MS. Pym 147).
2. JA to BP 19(?) March 1938.
3. Diary, 29 March 1938.
4. Diary, undated entry made in Oswestry, 1938.
5. 'Reflections by Barbara Pym concerning herself and Julian Amery' (MS. Pym 146).
6. *Finding a Voice* (MS. Pym 96).
7. 'Slough', in John Betjeman, *Continual Dew* (1937).
8. Stevie Smith, *Novel on Yellow Paper* (1936; repr. 1994), p. 123.
9. Diary, undated entry made in Oswestry, early 1938.
10. Personal communication to Hazel Holt, *ALTA*, p. 89.
11. RL to BP, summer 1937.
12. BP to RL, 12 April 1938.
13. BP to RL, HH and EH, 5 April 1938.
14. BP to RL, HH and EH, 5 April 1938.
15. Smith, *Novel on Yellow Paper*, pp. 103–4.
16. BP to RL, HH and EH, early 1938.
17. Diary, April 1938, no specific date.
18. Diary, April 1938, no specific date.

CHAPTER XXVII

1. BP to RL, no date, from Oswestry, early 1938.
2. 'Gervase and Flora' draft, chapter 14.
3. https://en.stsg.de/cms/names-jewish-victims-dresden-1933-1945.
4. Diary (MS. Pym 104), 10 May 1938.
5. Diary, 23 May 1938.
6. BP to RL, 23 May 1938.
7. BP to RL, 23 May 1938.
8. Diary, 26 May 1938.
9. See https://en.wikipedia.org/wiki/Sonnenstein_Euthanasia_
    Centre.

CHAPTER XXVIII

1. Diary, 27 May 1938.
2. Diary, 30 May 1938.
3. Diary, 1 June 1938.
4. JA to BP, 1 June 1938.
5. Diary, 25 August 1938.
6. Diary, 20 July 1938.
7. Diary, 29 August 1938.
8. Diary, 4 September 1938.
9. Diary, 10 September 1938.

CHAPTER XXIV

1. Diary, 30 September 1938.
2. Diary, 30 September 1938.
3. https://www.nationalchurchillmuseum.org/disaster-of-the-first-
    magnitude.html.
4. BP to EH, 31 October 1938.

CHAPTER XXX

1. 'Gervase and Flora' draft, chapter 19.
2. Diary, undated Oswestry entry, early 1938.
3. Unpublished draft novel provisionally titled 'The Lumber Room'
    or 'Beatrice Wyatt' (MS. Pym 6/1–3).
4. 'The Lumber Room' manuscript draft.

5. 'The Lumber Room' manuscript draft.
6. 'The Lumber Room' manuscript draft.
7. 'The Lumber Room' manuscript draft.
8. BP to EH, 31 October 1938.
9. Hazel Holt has misdated *Crampton Hodnet*. She says it was begun in November 1939 and completed two months later in January 1940. But in a letter to Robert Liddell dated 1 January 1940, Pym says that her North Oxford novel was ready to be sent to Cape and that she had been working on it for much of the previous year.
10. BP to EH, 31 October 1938.

CHAPTER XXXI
1. *CH*, p. 56.
2. *CH*, p. 43.
3. *CH*, p. 73.
4. Jane Austen, *Northanger Abbey* (1818), chapter 24.
5. *CH*, p. 4.
6. *CH*, p. 7.
7. *CH*, pp. 102–3.
8. *CH*, p. 114.
9. *CH*, p. 241.
10. *CH*, p. 39.
11. Diary (MS. Pym 105), 11 May 1939.

CHAPTER XXXII
1. *CH*, pp. 46–7.
2. *CH*, pp. 47–8.
3. *CH*, p. 48.
4. *CH*, p. 145.
5. *CH*, p. 35.
6. *CH*, pp. 117–18.
7. 'Reflections by Barbara Pym concerning herself and Julian Amery' (MS. Pym 146), Friday–Sunday 19–21 April 1940.
8. *CH*, p. 120.
9. BP to EH, 21 February 1939.

10. BP to EH, 21 February 1939.
11. BP to EH, 11 May 1939.
12. BP to EH, 11 May 1939.
13. 'Reflections concerning Julian Amery', 12 May 1949.
14. 'Reflections concerning Julian Amery', 12 May 1949.
15. *CH*, p. 217.
16. JA to BP, 2 June 1939.
17. 'Reflections concerning Julian Amery', undated.
18. 'Reflections concerning Julian Amery', undated.

CHAPTER XXXIII
1. Diary, 11 July 1939.
2. Diary, 1 September 1939.
3. Diary, 3 September 1939.
4. 'Reflections concerning Julian Amery', undated.

BOOK THE THIRD:
WAR

CHAPTER I
1. 'Home Front Novel' (MSS. Pym 8–9), p. 68; *CS*, p. 340.
2. *CS*, p. 340.
3. Home Front Novel, p. 68; *CS,* p. 233.
4. Diary, 1 September 1939.
5. Home Front Novel, p. 73.
6. Home Front Novel, p. 74.
7. Home Front Novel, pp. 76–7; *CS*, p. 222.
8. Home Front Novel, pp. 76–7; *CS*, p. 222.
9. Recruitment posters also urged women to join munitions factories: 'Women of Britain: Come into the Factories', 'Fighting Fit in the Factories'; 'On Her Their Lives Depend: Women Munition Workers: Enrol at Once'.

CHAPTER II
1. Diary, 7 September 1939.
2. Home Front Novel, pp. 78–9; *CS*, p. 236.

3.   Diary, 7–8 September 1939.
4.   Diary, 7–8 September 1939.
5.   Diary, 18 October 1939.
6.   *CS*, p. 230.
7.   Home Front Novel, Prologue.
8.   Home Front Novel, pp. 150–3; *CS*, pp. 256–7.
9.   *CS*, p. 257.

CHAPTER III
1.   Diary, 13 October 1939.
2.   *ALTA*, p. 95.
3.   Diary, 30 September 1939.
4.   *Papers Concerning the Treatment of German Nationals in Germany,
     1938–1939* (Foreign Office, Command Paper 6120, 1939), p. 3.

CHAPTER IV
1.   Home Front Novel, p. 8.
2.   'Thy Kingdom Come, O God', a Victorian hymn by Lewis
     Hensley.
3.   Home Front Novel, p. 136.
4.   Home Front Novel, p. 136.

CHAPTER V
1.   Home Front Novel, p. 13.
2.   Home Front Novel, p. 13.
3.   Home Front Novel, p. 14.
4.   Home Front Novel, p. 49.
5.   Home Front Novel, p. 53.
6.   Home Front Novel, p. 57.

CHAPTER VI
1.   Faber, *Speaking for England*, p. 398.
2.   Home Front Novel, p. 16.
3.   Diary, 15 December 1939.
4.   Diary, 31 December 1939; BP to RL, 31 December 1939.

CHAPTER VII

1. Diary (MS. Pym 106), 2 January 1940.
2. BP to RL, 4 January 1940.
3. BP to RL, 12 January 1940.
4. Diary, 31 January 1940.
5. 'Reflections concerning Julian Amery', March 1940, no specific date.
6. 'Reflections concerning Julian Amery', March 1940, no specific date.
7. 'Reflections concerning Julian Amery', 3 April 1940.
8. Diary, 7 April 1940.
9. 'Reflections concerning Julian Amery', 7 April 1940.

CHAPTER VIII

1. 'Reflections concerning Julian Amery', 19–21 April 1940.
2. 'Reflections concerning Julian Amery', 19–21 April 1940.
3. 'Conduct of the War', *Hansard*, 7 May 1940.
4. Diary, 10 May 1940.
5. Diary, 10 May 1940.
6. 'Reflections concerning Julian Amery', 10 May 1940.

CHAPTER IX

1. Diary, 26 May 1940.
2. RL to BP, 17 May 1940.
3. Diary, 16 June 1940.
4. RL to BP, 24 June 1940.
5. Diary, 20 June 1940.
6. Diary, 19 June 1940.
7. 'Goodbye Balkan Capital', MS. Pym 92, fols. 245–61, published in *CS*, p. 344.
8. *CS*, pp. 344–5.
9. *CS*, p. 345. 'Tears, idle tears' is the opening of a famous lyric poem from Tennyson's *The Princess* (1847).
10. *CS*, p. 346.
11. *CS*, p. 347.

CHAPTER X

1.   Diary, 11 July 1940.
2.   Diary, 9 September 1940.
3.   Diary, 7 July 1940.
4.   Diary, 3 October 1940.
5.   Diary, 17 October 1940.
6.   Diary, 21 October 1940.
7.   Diary, 20 November 1940.
8.   Diary, 28 November 1940.
9.   *CS*, p. 347.
10. *CS*, p. 349.
11. *CS*, p. 249.
12. Diary, 31 December 1940.

CHAPTER XI

1.   Robert Liddell, *Elizabeth and Ivy* (1986).
2.   RL to BP, 10 April 1941.
3.   RL to BP, 10 April 1941.
4.   RL to BP, 10 April 1941.
5.   Diary (MS. Pym 107), 8 January 1941.
6.   Diary, 6 January 1941.
7.   Diary, 12 January 1941.
8.   Diary, 9 February 1941.
9.   Diary, 4 February 1941.

CHAPTER XII

1.   Diary, 15 March 1941.
2.   Diary, 13 February 1941.
3.   *The Man I Married*, directed by Irving Pichel (1940).
4.   Diary, 27 May 1941.
5.   Diary, 31 July 1941.

CHAPTER XIII

1.   'Reflections concerning Julian Amery' (MS. Pym 146), 20 February 1941.
2.   'Reflections concerning Julian Amery', 20 February 1941.

3. 'Reflections concerning Julian Amery', 4 July 1941, referencing Edmund Waller's lyric poem, 'Song: Go Lovely Rose'.
4. 'Reflections concerning Julian Amery', 20 July 1941.
5. Diary, 4 July 1941.
6. 'Reflections concerning Julian Amery', 12 August 1941.
7. 'Reflections concerning Julian Amery', 7 September 1941.
8. Diary, 18 September 1941.
9. 'Reflections concerning Julian Amery', 15 April 1941.
10. 'Reflections concerning Julian Amery', 17 September 1941.

CHAPTER XIV
1. 'So Very Secret' (MS. Pym 13/1), p. 2. The version published in *Civil to Strangers* is truncated, with anything deemed to be controversial or distasteful omitted, such as the Nazi references and the encounter with Jenny Dale, the prostitute.
2. 'So Very Secret', p. 19.
3. 'So Very Secret', p. 22.
4. 'So Very Secret', p. 32.
5. 'So Very Secret', p. 125.
6. MS. Pym 97, fol. 71 (written 3 December 1938).
7. 'So Very Secret', p. 20.

CHAPTER XV
1. Diary, 10 April 1941.
2. Diary, 23 April 1941.
3. *CS*, p. 341.
4. *CS*, p. 343.
5. *CS*, p. 348.
6. *CS*, p. 348.

CHAPTER XVI
1. https://www.nytimes.com/1964/09/28/archives/nora-waln-dies-a-journalist-70-correspondent-also-wrote-books-about.html.
2. Diary, 13 December 1941.
3. Diary, 18 November 1941.
4. Diary, 19 November 1941.

BOOK THE FOURTH:
FROM THE COPPICE TO NAPLES

CHAPTER I

1. Quotations and other details supplied here are from Prue Anderton, 'Barbara Pym', *The Oldie*, 1 January 2020.
2. BP to HH, 2 July 1942.
3. Diary, 16 December 1941.
4. *EW*, p. 7.

CHAPTER II

1. BP to HH, 22 October 1942.
2. *ALTA*, p. 107.
3. 'Reflections concerning Julian Amery', 7 April 1942.
4. 'Reflections concerning Julian Amery', 7 April 1942.
5. Diary, 23 March 1943.
6. Arnold, 'Thyrsis' (1861, published 1866), the elegy on his young Oxford friend A. H. Clough, which includes the famous image of the city's 'dreaming spires'.
7. 'Reflections concerning Julian Amery', 7 April 1942.

CHAPTER III

1. BP to HH, 2 July 1942.
2. BP to HH, 2 July 1942.
3. BP to HH, 2 July 1942.
4. BP to HH, 22 October 1942.

CHAPTER IV

1. BP to HH, 22 October 1942.
2. BP to HH, 17 December 1942.
3. BP to HH, 13 May 1943.
4. My italics. Notebook (January–May 1943), 'After Christmas I' (MS. Pym 108), 21 January 1943.

CHAPTER V

1. After Christmas I, 1–2 February 1943.
2. After Christmas I, 22 January 1943.
3. After Christmas I, 27 January 1943.
4. After Christmas I, 23 March 1943.
5. After Christmas I, 10 March 1943.
6. After Christmas I, 27 May 1943.
7. After Christmas I, 14 March 1943.
8. After Christmas I, 14 March 1943.
9. After Christmas I, 11 March 1943.
10. After Christmas I, 12 March 1943.
11. After Christmas I, 28 March 1943.
12. After Christmas I, 28 March 1943.
13. After Christmas I, 10 March 1943.
14. After Christmas I, 18 April 1943.
15. After Christmas I, 29 March 1943.
16. After Christmas I, 10 March 1943.

CHAPTER VI

1. After Christmas I, 30 March 1943.
2. After Christmas I, 30 March 1943.
3. After Christmas I, 8 April 1943.
4. After Christmas I, 8 April 1943.
5. Anderton, 'Barbara Pym', *The Oldie*, 1 January 2020.
6. After Christmas I, 7 April 1943.
7. After Christmas I, 8 April 1943.
8. After Christmas I, 14 April 1943.
9. After Christmas I, 15 April 1943.
10. After Christmas I, 2 May 1943.
11. After Christmas I, 2 May 1943.

CHAPTER VII

1. RG to BP, 5 December 1938.
2. RG to BP, 5 December 1938.
3. RG to BP, 28 November 1939.
4. RG to BP, 20 January 1940.

5. RG to BP, 20 January 1940.
6. After Christmas I, 10 April 1943.
7. After Christmas I, 10–11 April 1943.
8. 'Sylvia, a Memoir', *Journal of the Sylvia Townsend Warner Society*, 18 (2018), https://www.researchgate.net/publication/328542136_Sylvia_a_Memoir.
9. After Christmas I, 11 April 1943.

CHAPTER VIII
1. After Christmas I, 3 May 1943.
2. After Christmas I, 22 April 1943.
3. After Christmas I, 24 April 1943.
4. After Christmas I, 27 April 1943.
5. After Christmas I, 26 May 1943.
6. After Christmas I, 31 May 1943.
7. After Christmas I, 31 May 1943.
8. After Christmas II (MS. Pym 109), 8 June 1943.
9. After Christmas II, 12–14 June 1943.
10. After Christmas II, 20 June 1943.
11. After Christmas II, 27 June 1943.
12. After Christmas II, 5 July 1943.
13. After Christmas II, 6 July 1943.
14. After Christmas II, 7 July 1943.

CHAPTER IX
1. After Christmas II, 7 July 1943.
2. After Christmas II, 8 July 1943.
3. After Christmas II, 9 July 1943.
4. After Christmas II, 12 July 1943.
5. After Christmas II, 9 July 1943.
6. After Christmas II, 7 July 1943.
7. After Christmas II, 13 July 1943; 16 July 1943.
8. After Christmas II, 19 July 1943.
9. After Christmas II, 20 July 1943.
10. After Christmas II, 23 July 1943.
11. After Christmas II, 25 July 1943.

12. After Christmas II, 1 August 1943.
13. After Christmas II, 2 August 1943.
14. After Christmas II, 26 August 1943.

CHAPTER X
1. After Christmas II, October 1943 (no specific day given).
2. After Christmas II, 16 October 1943.
3. After Christmas II, 18 October 1943.
4. After Christmas II, 24 October 1943.
5. After Christmas II, 18 November 1943.
6. BP to HH, 26 May 1944.
7. BP to HH, 26 May 1944.
8. BP to HH, 26 May 1944.

CHAPTER XI
1. Naples Diary (MS. Pym 110), 17 September 1944.
2. Naples Diary (MS. Pym 110), 17 September 1944.
3. Naples Diary, 17 September 1944.
4. Naples Diary, 17 September 1944.
5. Naples Diary, 17 September 1944.
6. Naples Diary, 18 September 1944.
7. Naples Diary, 26 September 1944.
8. Naples Diary, 26 September 1944.
9. Naples Diary, 26 September 1944.
10. Naples Diary, 3 October 1944.
11. Naples Diary, 3 October 1944.
12. Naples Diary, 14 October 1944.
13. Naples Diary, 17 October 1944.
14. Naples Diary, 18 October 1944.
15. Naples Diary, 18 October 1944.
16. Naples Diary, 24 October 1944.
17. RL to BP, 16 November 1944.
18. Jane Austen, *Persuasion* (1818), volume 2, chapter 11, copied into Naples Diary.
19. *Persuasion*, volume 2, chapter 11, copied into Naples Diary.
20. Naples Diary, 26 October–3 November 1944.

21. Naples Diary, 16–21 November 1944.

CHAPTER XII
1. Naples Diary, 25 December 1944.
2. Naples Diary, 24–25 March 1945.
3. Naples Diary, 24–25 March 1945.
4. Naples Diary, 1945, no specific date.
5. RL to BP, 8 August, 1944.
6. RL to BP, 8 August, 1944.

BOOK THE FIFTH:
MISS PYM IN PIMLICO

CHAPTER I
1. BP to HH, 7 November 1945.
2. *EW*, p. 2.
3. BP to HH, 7 November 1945.
4. BP to RL, 24 August 1945.
5. BP to HH, 5 June 1946.

CHAPTER II
1. BP to HH, 5 June 1946.
2. BP to HH, 5 June 1946.
3. BP to HH, 20 February 1946.
4. BP to HH, 17 October 1946.
5. *ALTA*, p. 141.
6. RL to BP, 20 May 1946.
7. RL to BP, 20 May 1946.

CHAPTER III
1. RL to BP, 17 April 1947.
2. RL to BP, 17 April 1947.
3. BP to HH (Bodleian MS. 9827), 5 June 1946.
4. RL to BP, 2 August 1945.
5. RL to BP, 7 August 1945.

6. RL to BP, 13 June 1947.
7. RL to BP, 17 December 1947.
8. RL to BP, 15 February 1948.
9. RL to BP, 26 April 1948.
10. RL to BP, 'Tuesday in Passion week', 1949.

CHAPTER IV
1. She reveals her close knowledge of it in the journal 'After Christmas II', 25 July 1943.
2. *STG*, p. 1.
3. *STG* (published text), chapter 4. To avoid cluttering the text, henceforth page references will only be given for longer quotations from the novels.
4. *STG*, pp. 45–6.
5. *STG*, p. 46.
6. *STG*, p. 46.
7. *STG*, p. 106.
8. *STG*, p. 150.

CHAPTER V
1. *STG*, p. 221.
2. Beveridge Report, 1942, para. 108.
3. Janet H. Howarth, *Women in Britain: Voices and Perspectives from Twentieth Century History* (2019), p. 141.
4. *ALTA*, p. 145; my comparison via Bank of England inflation calculator.
5. MS. Pym 170. Draft letter to *TLS*, undated.
6. Notebook containing manuscript notes and drafts for *EW* (MS. Pym 13).
7. *EW* Notebook.
8. *EW* Notebook.

CHAPTER VI
1. *EW*, p. 128.
2. *EW*, p. 60.
3. With grateful thanks to the Reverend Father Matthew Catterick of St Saviour's church, Pimlico.

4. *EW*, p. 287.
5. *EW*, p. 229.
6. *STG*, p. 229.
7. *EW*, p. 1.
8. *EW*, p. 27.
9. *EW*, p. 61.
10. *EW*, p. 7.
11. *EW*, p. 124.
12. *EW*, pp. 107–8.
13. *EW*, pp. 109–10.
14. *EW*, p. 111.
15. *EW*, p. 113.
16. *EW*, p. 149.
17. *EW*, p. 163.

CHAPTER VII
1. *ALTA*, p. 156.
2. *ALTA*, p. 158.
3. *EW*, pp. 161–2.
4. *ALTA*, p. 157.
5. Newspaper clippings of reviews of *STG* (MS. Pym 163/1). The Antonia White review appeared in the *New Statesman*, 1 July 1950. See further, Yvonne Cocking, *Barbara in the Bodleian: Revelations from the Pym Archives* (2013), chapter 5, '*Some Tame Gazelle:* Some Views and Reviews'.
6. BP to HH, 1 May 1950.
7. Quoted, HH to BP, September 1950.

CHAPTER VIII
1. Robert Liddell, *The Last Enchantments* (1991) p. 17.
2. Liddell, *Last Enchantments*, p. 17.
3. RL to BP, 20 June 1944.
4. Liddell, *Last Enchantments*, p. 220.

CHAPTER IX
1. RL to BP, Tuesday of Passion Week, 1947.

2. See *Barbara in the Bodleian*, p. 84.
3. Literary Notebook III (MS. Pym 42), 17 June 1951.
4. Literary Notebook I (MS. Pym 40), 27 November 1949.
5. Literary Notebook I, 27 November 1949.
6. Robert Liddell, *Elizabeth and Ivy* (1986), p. 17.
7. Liddell, *Elizabeth and Ivy*, p. 11.

CHAPTER X
1. RL to BP, early 1952.
2. BP to HH, 27 March 1952.
3. Newspaper clippings of reviews, and readers' correspondence forwarded by publisher (MS. Pym 163/1).
4. Newspaper clippings of reviews, and readers' correspondence.
5. MS. Pym 163/1.

CHAPTER XI
1. *JAP*, p. 33.
2. Literary Notebook III, 1 February 1952.
3. *JAP*, p. 9.
4. *JAP*, p. 5.
5. *JAP*, p. 5.
6. Thomas Kendrick to BP, 25 January 1951.
7. TK to BP, 2 February 1950.
8. *JAP*, p. 27.
9. *JAP*, p. 29.
10. *JAP*, p. 30.
11. *JAP*, p. 90.
12. *JAP*, p. 33.
13. *JAP*, p. 36.
14. *JAP*, p. 55.
15. Robert Liddell, *A Mind at Ease: Barbara Pym and her Novels* (1989), p. 51.
16. *JAP*, p. 204.
17. *JAP*, p. 178.
18. *JAP*, pp. 206–7.

CHAPTER XII

1. *ALTA*, p. 162.
2. *ALTA*, p. 160.
3. Newspaper clippings of reviews, and readers' correspondence forwarded by publisher (MS. Pym 163/1).
4. Newspaper clippings of reviews, and readers' correspondence.
5. Marks and Spencer Ltd. Correspondence with Jonathan Cape relating to *Jane and Prudence*, 1953 (MS. Pym 163/2), fols. 234–8.

CHAPTER XIII

1. Literary Notebook IV (MS. Pym 43), 13 February 1952.
2. *LTA*, p. 184.
3. 'Ups and Downs of a Writer's Life' (MS. Pym, 98 fols. 79–83), talk for the Senior Wives Fellowship at the United Reform Church, Headington, Oxford.
4. *LTA*, p. 122.
5. *LTA*, p. 42.
6. *LTA*, p. 112.
7. *LTA*, pp. 133–4.
8. *LTA*, p. 167.
9. *LTA*, p. 190.
10. *LTA*, p. 169.
11. *LTA*, p. 189.
12. *LTA*, p. 166.

CHAPTER XIV

1. Interview in *Times Literary Supplement*, 1 January 1978 (MS. Pym 98, fol. 32).
2. *EW*, p. 116.
3. Literary Notebook VI, 1954 (MS. Pym 45).
4. Literary Notebook VI, 1954.
5. Literary Notebook VI, 1954.
6. Literary Notebook VI, 1954.
7. On 7 October 1955 she attended her first class of Portuguese lessons at King's College, London. She continued classes up to at least March 1958.

8.   Literary Notebook VI, 1954.

CHAPTER XV

1.   BP to RS (MS. Pym 162), 22 April 1954.
2.   Literary Notebook VII (MS. Pym 46), 15 May 1955.

CHAPTER XVI

1.   Rachel Ferguson, *We were Amused* (1958), quoted, *ALTA*, p. 175.
2.   *LTA*, p. 28.
3.   Literary Notebook IX, 1956 (MS. Pym 48).
4.   BP to Hazel Holt, quoted, *ALTA*, p. 178. Following quotation from same letter.
5.   Holt, *ALTA*, pp. 177–9.

CHAPTER XVII

1.   Now in the V&A: https://www.vam.ac.uk/moc/collections/the-denton-welch-dolls-house/.
2.   Denton Welch phrases from *In Youth is Pleasure* (1945); Pym, Literary Notebook VIII (MS. Pym 47), 15 October 1955.

CHAPTER XVIII

1.   Holt, *ALTA*, p. 172.
2.   Literary Notebook IX (MS. Pym 48), 21 September 1956.
3.   Denton Welch, 30 August 1942, in *Journals*, ed. Michael De-La-Noy (2011), p. 8.
4.   Literary Notebook VII (MS. Pym 46), April 1955.
5.   Denton Welch, *Good Night, Beloved Comrade: The Letters of Denton Welch to Eric Oliver* (2017), p. 20.
6.   Literary Notebook IX (MS. Pym 48), 1956 (no specific date given).

CHAPTER XIX

1.   Literary Notebook XII (MS. Pym 51), 29 April 1958.
2.   David Cecil to BP (MS. Pym 148).
3.   Review clippings in MS. Pym 164.
4.   *AGB*, p. 12.

5. *AGB*, p. 207.
6. *AGB*, p. 213.
7. *AGB*, pp. 214, 270.
8. *AGB*, p. 277.

CHAPTER XX
1. Literary Notebook XI (MS. Pym 50), August 1957.
2. *NFRL*, pp. 1, 9.
3. *NFRL*, pp. 39–40.
4. *NFRL*, p. 116.
5. *NFRL*, p. 10.
6. *NFRL*, p. 191.
7. Literary Notebook VII (MS. Pym 46), May 1955.
8. *NFRL*, p. 38.
9. *NFRL*, p. 78.
10. BP to RS, 21 October 1960; RS to BP, 8 March 1961.

CHAPTER XXI
1. BP to RS, 16 March 1961.
2. Literary Notebook XVI (MS. Pym 55), 11 April 1961.
3. Literary Notebook XVI, 11–20 April 1961.

CHAPTER XXII
1. BP to PL (Letters from Barbara Pym to Philip Larkin, Bodleian Library, MSS. Eng. lett. c. 859–60), 1 March 1961.
2. PL to Norman Iles, 5 June 1943.
3. Anthony Thwaite (ed.), *Selected Letters of Philip Larkin 1940–1985* (1999), pp. 48, 69.
4. Andrew Motion, *Philip Larkin: A Writer's Life* (1993), p. 59.
5. Motion, *Larkin*, p. 59.
6. Motion, *Larkin*, p. 309.
7. Larkin's friend Monica Jones, quoted, Motion, *Philip Larkin*, p. 308.
8. PL to BP, 5 March 1961.
9. Literary Notebook IX (MS. Pym 48), 1 March 1956.
10. BP to PL, 23 September 1961.

11. BP to PL, 15 October 1961.
12. Published in Philip Larkin's second volume of verse, *The Less Deceived* (1955).

CHAPTER XXIII

1. Virginia Nicholson, *How Was It For You? Women, Sex, Love and Power in the 1960s* (2019), p. 11.
2. Macmillan, speech to South African Houses of Parliament, 3 February 1960.
3. *UA*, p. 17, first published by Macmillan (1982). Quoted from first paperback edition (Granada Publishing, 1983). Not in Virago Modern Classics.
4. *UA*, p. 26.
5. *UA*, p. 126.
6. *UA*, p. 72.
7. *UA*, p. 114.
8. *UA*, p. 185.
9. *UA*, p. 193.
10. *UA*, p. 194.
11. *UA*, p. 250.
12. Literary Notebook XVIII (MS. Pym 57), 24 March 1963.

BOOK THE SIXTH:
THE WILDERNESS YEARS

CHAPTER I

1. BP to RS, 8 February 1963.
2. Quoted, Nicholson, *How Was It For You?*, p. 123.
3. Private communication, Yvonne Cocking to the author.
4. BP to PL, 8 July 1963.

CHAPTER II

1. Literary Notebook XIX (MS. Pym 58).
2. BP to PL, 12 May 1963.

CHAPTER III

1. BP to RS, 15 December 1961.
2. RR to BP (MS. Pym 159), 7 January 1964.

CHAPTER IV

1. Literary Notebooks XVII–XXVIII (MSS. Pym 56–67).
2. Literary Notebook XVII, 22 March 1962.
3. Literary Notebook XVIII, 14 August 1963.
4. Literary Notebook XIX.
5. BP to PL, 16 February 1964.
6. BP to RS, 11 June 1963.
7. BP to RS, 11 January 1963.
8. BP to RS, 16 October 1963.
9. BP to RS, 16 October 1963.
10. BP to RS, 8 December 1963.

CHAPTER V

1. BP to PL, 12 May 1963.
2. PL to BP, 15 July 1963.
3. BP to PL, 23 August 1963.
4. PL to BP, 7 December 1963; BP to PL, 12 January 1964.
5. RR to BP, 7 January 1964.
6. Richard writes [19]65, but means [19]64.
7. BP to RS, 23 January 1964.
8. BP to RS, 23 March 1965.
9. BP to RR, 25 March 1964.
10. Literary Notebook XX (MS. Pym 59), 29 March 1964.
11. Literary Notebook XX, 1 May 1964.
12. BP to PL, 16 February 1964.
13. 'Faith Healing' in Philip Larkin, *The Whitsun Weddings*, published by Faber and Faber (1964), p. 15.
14. Larkin, *Whitsun Weddings*, p. 10.
15. PL to BP, 14 July 1964.
16. Literary Notebook XX, 12 May 1964.

CHAPTER VI

1. RR to BP, 4 September 1964.
2. RR to PB, 4 July 1964.
3. RR to BP, 6 August 1964.
4. Literary Notebook XX, 10 September 1964.
5. BP to RR, 30 June 1964.
6. BP to RR, 18 August 1964.
7. Literary Notebook XXI, 10 September 1964.
8. BP to PL, 14 September 1964.
9. BP to RS, 27 September 1964.
10. BP to RS, 27 September 1964.

CHAPTER VII

1. BP to RR, 4 October 1964.
2. BP to RR, 4 October 1964.
3. BP to RR, 4 October 1964.
4. Literary Notebook XXI, 11 October 1964.
5. Literary Notebook XXI, 28 November 1964.
6. RR to BP, 23 September 1964.
7. BP to RR, 5 January 1965.
8. RR to BP, 3 February 1965.
9. It is uncertain whether she sent the poem.
10. Literary Notebook XXII (MS. Pym 61), 20 February 1965.
11. RR to BP, February 1965.
12. Holt, *ALTA*, p. 211.
13. Literary Notebook XXII, 29 May 1965.
14. BP to PL, 16 February 1965.
15. Larkin, 'Toads', in *The Less Deceived*.
16. BP to PL, 16 February 1965.
17. Literary Notebook XXII, 16 June 1965.
18. Literary Notebook XXII, 1 July 1965.
19. Literary Notebook XXII, 17 August 1965.
20. PL to Charles Monteith, 8 February 1965, Thwaite (ed.), *Selected Letters*, p. 371.
21. BP to PL, 21 August 1965.
22. Literary Notebook XXII, 19 July 1965.

CHAPTER VIII
1. PL to Monica Jones, 3 March 1964, quoted, Motion, *Philip Larkin*, p. 343.
2. 'The True and the Beautiful: a conversation with Philip Larkin' (interviewer John Haffenden), *London Magazine*, vol. xx (1980), pp. 81–95.
3. All these insults are cited in Motion, *Philip Larkin*.
4. PL to Monteith, 15 August 1965, Thwaite (ed.), *Selected Letters*, p. 375.
5. PL to Monteith, 15 August 1965, Thwaite (ed.), *Selected Letters*, p. 376.
6. PL to BP, 30 August 1965.
7. Larkin to Monteith, 23 August 1965, Thwaite (ed.), *Selected Letters*, p. 376.

CHAPTER IX
1. Literary Notebook XXII, 24 August 1965.
2. Literary Notebook XXII, 22 June 1965.
3. BP to RS, 29 November 1965.
4. Literary Notebook XXII, 26 September 1965.
5. BP to RS, 4 January 1966.
6. Literary Notebook XXIII (MS. Pym 62), 10 March 1966.
7. Literary Notebook XXIV (MS. Pym 63), 8 July 1966.

CHAPTER X
1. Literary Notebook XXIV, June 1966.
2. BP to RS, 3 June 1966.
3. RR to BP, 31 May 1966.
4. Literary Notebooks XXIV, 8 July 1966.
5. BP to RS, 22 August 1966.
6. Literary Notebook XXIV, 23–25 September 1966.
7. BP to RS, 19 September 1966.
8. BP to RS, 20 October 1966.
9. Literary Notebooks XXIV, 26 October 1966.
10. BP to RS, 12 December 1966.
11. BP to RS, 30 December 1966.

12. BP to RS, 30 December 1966.

CHAPTER XI
1. PL to BP, 13 January 1967.
2. BP to PL, 7 December 1967.
3. BP to PL, 9 September 1968.
4. PL to BP, 17 October 1968.
5. BP to PL, 20 October 1968.
6. Betjeman, 'In Westminster Abbey', in his *Old Lights for New Chancels*, published by John Murray (1940).
7. PL to BP, 7 December 1963.
8. BP to RS, 30 December 1966.
9. BP to RS, 16 February 1967.
10. BP to RS, 7 June 1967.
11. BP to RS, 7 July 1967.
12. BP to RS, 9 August 1967.
13. Literary Notebook XXV (MS. Pym 64), 16 February 1967.

CHAPTER XII
1. Correspondence with publishers, MS. Pym 165.
2. *SDD*, p. 9. Originally published by Macmillan (1978); quoted from first paperback edition (Panther Books, Granada Publishing, 1980). Not in Virago Modern Classics.
3. *SDD*, p. 131.
4. *SDD*, p. 132.
5. *SDD*, p. 132.
6. *SDD*, p. 145.
7. *SDD*, p. 132.
8. *SDD*, p. 180.
9. *SDD*, p. 181.
10. Literary Notebook XXIII–XXVIII (MSS. Pym 62–67), entries between 15 February 1965 and 5 April 1969.
11. Literary Notebook XXVIII, 11 August 1969.

CHAPTER XIII
1. Literary Notebook XXVIII, 15 August 1969.

2. BP to PL, 10 December 1969.

3. BP to PL, 10 December 1969.

4. BP to RS, 6 November 1970.

5. PL to BP, 8 October 1969.

6. BP to RS, 11 December 1969.

7. Literary Notebook XXVII (MS. Pym 66), 17 July 1968.

8. Literary Notebook XXVII, 20 October 1968.

9. Literary Notebook XXVIII (MS. Pym 67), 27 May 1969.

10. Literary Notebook XXIX (MS. Pym 68), 26 January 1970.

11. BP to PL, 21 March 1970.

12. BP to PL, 21 March 1970.

13. Literary Notebook XXIX, 9 November 1970.

14. *SDD*, p. 140.

15. *SDD*, p. 141.

CHAPTER XIV

1. Robert Smith, 'How pleasant to know Miss Pym', *Ariel*, 2.4 (October 1971), pp. 67–8.

2. Literary Notebook XXIX, 9 November 1970.

3. Literary Notebook XXX (MS. Pym 69), 27 April 1971.

4. BP to RS, 1 May 1971.

5. BP to PL, 22 June 1971.

6. BP to PL, 22 June 1971.

7. PL to BP, 18 July 1971.

8. BP to PL, 7 November 1971.

9. PL to BP, 26 June 1971.

10. PL to BP, 18 July 1971.

11. BP to PL, 7 November 1971.

CHAPTER XV

1. PL to BP, 18 July 1971.

2. PL to BP, 22 March 1972.

3. *AQ*, p. 10.

4. Literary Notebook XXX (MS. Pym 69), 10 November 1971.

5. Literary Notebook XXXI (MS. Pym 70), 6 March 1972.

6. *AQ*, p. 135.

7. Literary Notebook XXXI, 6 March 1972.
8. Literary Notebook XXXI, 20 March 1972.
9. Literary Notebook XXXI, 19 April 1972.

CHAPTER XVI
1. BP to PL, 24 October 1972.
2. BP to PL, 24 October 1972.
3. BP to PL, 24 October 1972.
4. Literary Notebook XXXI, 2 October 1972.
5. BP to PL, 11 July 1973.
6. Literary Notebook XXXI, July 1972.
7. BP to RS; BP to PL, 19 July 1974.
8. Literary Notebook XXXIII (MS. Pym 72), 28 November 1973.
9. BP to PL, 16 October 1973.

CHAPTER XVII
1. PL to BP, 5 June 1974.
2. BP to PL, 19 July 1974.
3. BP to PL, 1 December 1974.
4. Literary Notebook XXXV (MS. Pym 74), 2 February 1975.
5. BP to PL, 15 April 1975.
6. PL to BP, 17 April 1975.
7. PL to Judy Egerton, 9 June 1975, *Selected Letters*, p. 525.

CHAPTER XVIII
1. Paul Binding interviewed by Ann Allestree, in *Barbara Pym: A Passionate Force* (2015), p. 112.
2. Literary Notebook XXXV (MS. Pym 74), 12 May 1975.
3. Literary Notebook XXXV, 28 July 1975.
4. Literary Notebook XXXV, 8 October 1975.
5. BP to RS, 11 January 1976.
6. BP to RS, 1 March 1976.
7. Literary Notebook XXXVI (MS. Pym 75), 17 February 1976.
8. Literary Notebook XXXVI, 17 February 1976.
9. BP to HH, 6 April 1976.
10. BP to PL, 8 March 1976.

11. Literary Notebook XXXVI, 30 July 1976.
12. BP to PL, 23 March 1975.
13. PL to BP, 10 April 1975.
14. Literary Notebook XXXVII (MS. Pym 76), 15 December 1976.

BOOK THE SEVENTH:
IN WHICH THE FORTUNES
OF MISS PYM ARE REVERSED

CHAPTER I

1. Literary Notebook XXXVII, 10–12 January 1977.
2. PL to BP, 27 September 1976.
3. BP to RS, 8 February 1977.
4. 'Reputations Revisited', *Times Literary Supplement*, 21 January 1977.
5. Allestree, *Barbara Pym*, p. 112.
6. 'How are the mighty fallen – according to the critics', *The Times*, 22 January 1977, p. 1.
7. Lord David Cecil to BP (MS. Pym 148), 29 January 1977.
8. Literary Notebook XXXVII, 22 January 1977.
9. Literary Notebook XXXVII, 14 February 1977.
10. BP to PL, 21 February 1977.
11. PL to BP, 22 February 1977.
12. Caroline Moorehead, 'How Barbara Pym was rediscovered after 16 years out in the cold', *The Times*, 14 September 1977.

CHAPTER II

1. BP to PL, 4 March 1977.
2. RL to BP, 18 March 1977.
3. PL to BP, 14 May 1977.
4. BP to RS, 18 June 1977.
5. BP to PL, 9 July 1977.
6. BP to PL, 21 August 1977.
7. Moorehead, 'How Barbara Pym was rediscovered . . .'.
8. Literary Notebook XXXVIII (MS. Pym 77), 22 September 1977.
9. David Cecil to BP, 18 October 1977.

10. PL to BP, 29 October 1977.
11. Literary Notebook XXXVIII, 21 October 1977.
12. PL to BP, 20 September 1977.

CHAPTER III

1. Literary Notebook XXX (MS. Pym 69), May 1971.
2. *QIA*, p. 8. First published by Macmillan in 1977; quoted from Picador Classic paperback edition (2015). Not in Virago Modern Classics.
3. *QIA*, p. 8.

CHAPTER IV

1. Review clippings in Correspondence with Publishers (MS. Pym 165).
2. RS to BP, 8 September 1977.
3. Review clippings in Correspondence with Publishers (MS. Pym 165).
4. Correspondence with publishers (MS. Pym 165).
5. BP to RS, 9 October 1977.
6. BP to PL, 9 November 1977.
7. BP to PL, 9 November 1977.
8. Literary Notebook XXXIX (MS. Pym 78), 23 November 1977.
9. BP to PL, 24 November 1977.
10. BP to PL, 29 January 1978.
11. BP to PL, 16 March 1978.
12. BP to PL, 16 March and 6 April 1978.
13. Literary Notebook XL (MS. Pym 79), 28 April 1978.
14. Literary Notebook XL, 6 July 1978.

CHAPTER V

1. BP to RS, 25 October 1978.
2. PL to BP, 17 June 1978.
3. BP to PL, 27 July 1978.
4. Clippings in Correspondence with Publishers (MS. Pym 164).
5. RS to BP, 23 August 1978.
6. Available at https://www.bbc.co.uk/sounds/play/p009mykr.

7. Von Arnim, *Love* (1925) and *Mr Skeffington* (1940).
8. PL to BP, 21 August 1978; BP to PL, 20 October 1978.

CHAPTER VI

1. Literary Notebook XL (MS. Pym 79), 17–19 August 1978.
2. Literary Notebook XXXV, 28 June 1975.
3. *FGL*, p. 2, first published by Macmillan (1980), with the dedication 'For my sister Hilary and for Robert Liddell this story of an imaginary village'; quoted from first edition. Not in Virago Modern Classics.
4. *FGL*, p. 13.
5. *FGL*, p. 9.
6. *FGL*, p. 33.
7. *FGL*, p. 87.
8. Larkin, 'An Arundel Tomb', in *Whitsun Weddings*, p. 46.

CHAPTER VII

1. Literary Notebook XLI (MS. Pym 80), 8 January 1979.
2. Literary Notebook XLI, 13 January–14 February 1979.
3. BP to PL, 15 March 1979.
4. PL to BP, 18 March 1979.
5. Literary Notebook XLII (MS. Pym 81), 23 March 1979.
6. Literary Notebook XLII, April 1979.
7. BP to PL, 1 May 1979.
8. Literary Notebook XLII, 18 May 1979.
9. Literary Notebook XLIII (MS. Pym 82), 3 June–24 June 1979.
10. BP to PL, 2 July 1979.
11. Literary Notebook XLIII, August 1979.
12. BP to RS, 18 October 1979.
13. *ALTA*, p. 277.
14. BP to PL, 28 October 1979.

EPILOGUE

1. PL to Anthony Thwaite, 21 January 1980, Thwaite (ed.), *Selected Letters*, p. 615.
2. Anderton, 'Barbara Pym', *Oldie Magazine*, January 2020.

3. 'The Novelist's Use of Everyday Life', lecture given in 1956 (MS. Pym 98, fols. 66–123).
4. 'The Novelist's Use of Everyday Life'.
5. RL, 'Account of his friendship with Barbara Pym', written February 1981 (MS. Pym 153, fols. 198–202).
6. RL, 'Account of his friendship'.
7. Larkin, 'An Arundel Tomb', the closing poem of *Whitsun Weddings* (p. 46).

AFTERWORD

1. *SDD*, p. 85. Robert Wyatt Ellidge recalled Pym's funniness when saying the word 'scones': https://www.albionbeatnik. co.uk/2016/12/13/tea-and-scone-with-barbara-pym/.
2. George Orwell, *The Lion and the Unicorn: Socialism and the English Genius* (1941), p. 11.
3. *SDD*, p. 120.
4. Readers wishing to venture into the territory of academic criticism might begin with the close reading of four novels in Deborah Donato, *Reading Barbara Pym* (2006), the social historical contextualisation by Orna Raz, *Social Dimensions in the Novels of Barbara Pym, 1949–1962: The Writer as Hidden Observer* (2007), and the varied collection of essays *'All This Reading': The Literary World of Barbara Pym*, edited by Frauke Elisabeth Lenckos and Ellen J. Miller (2003).
5. Barbara Pym's love of the eighteenth-century author Edward Young took her not only to his *Night Thoughts* but also to his *Conjectures on Original Composition* (1759), in which he wrote that truly original authors 'shine like comets' and that the greatest of them all, Shakespeare, 'mingled no water with his wine'. In *Some Tame Gazelle*, she combined the simile and the metaphor, describing her autobiographical heroine Belinda in a phrase that remains supremely appropriate to Barbara Pym herself.

Suggestions for Further Reading

Miss Pym's Works

Some Tame Gazelle (1950)
Excellent Women (1952)
Jane and Prudence (1953)
Less than Angels (1955)
A Glass of Blessings (1958)
No Fond Return of Love (1961)
Quartet in Autumn (1977)
The Sweet Dove Died (1978)
A Few Green Leaves (1980)
An Unsuitable Attachment (rejected 1963; published posthumously, 1982)
Crampton Hodnet (completed 1940; published posthumously, 1985)
An Academic Question (written 1970–72; published posthumously, 1986)
A Very Private Eye: An Autobiography in Diaries and Letters, posthumously selected and edited from her papers by Hazel Holt and Hilary Pym (1984)
Civil to Strangers and Other Writings, short stories and extracts from unpublished novels, edited posthumously by Hazel Holt (1987)

Miss Pym's World

Hazel Holt, *A Lot to Ask: A Life of Barbara Pym* (1990) was the first biography, written by her colleague at the Africa Institute, with the benefit of personal knowledge. A psychoanalytic approach was taken in Anne M. Wyatt-Brown, *Barbara Pym: A Critical Biography* (1992) and there are some fresh insights in Ann Allestree, *Barbara Pym: A Passionate Force* (2015), but the most valuable addition to Hazel Holt is Yvonne Cocking's splendid *Barbara in the Bodleian: Revelations from the Pym Archives* (2013).

My sense of Pym at Oxford was shaped by part 3 of L. W. B. Brockliss, *The University of Oxford: A History* (2016) and, for atmosphere, the research in my own *Mad World: Evelyn Waugh and the Secrets of Brideshead* (2009). My understanding of Pym's German experience owed much to *Travellers in the Third Reich: The Rise of Fascism through the Eyes of Everyday People* (2017), Julia Boyd's fascinating account of how other visitors were allured by what they saw there in the 1930s. Pym's realisation of the ugly reality was made possible by Lion Feuchtwanger's powerful novel *The Oppermanns* (English translation, 1934), which is still very much worth reading. It is also worth tracking down Bartlett Vernon, *Nazi Germany Explained* (1933) and the script of the radio-drama *Shadow of the Swastika* (1940).

Social histories helped me enormously in bringing Pym's world alive, notably Martin Pugh, *We Danced all Night: A Social History of Britain between the Wars* (2008); Lara Feigel, *The Love-charm of Bombs: Restless Lives in the Second World War* (2013); Rachel Cooke, *Her Brilliant Career: Ten Extraordinary Women of the Fifties* (2014); Virginia Nicholson, *How Was It for You? Women, Sex, Love and Power in the 1960s* (2019); and Janet H. Howarth, *Women in Britain: Voices and Perspectives from Twentieth-Century History* (2019).

Pym's beloved Julian Amery is brought alive in David Faber's excellent family biography, *Speaking for England: Leo, Julian and*

John Amery – The Tragedy of a Political Family (2005) and her loyal fan Philip Larkin in Andrew Motion, *Philip Larkin: A Writer's Life* (1993) – and many of his letters to her are included in *Selected Letters of Philip Larkin*, edited by Anthony Thwaite (1992). The ecclesiastical aspect of her novels is explored in the essays in *No Soft Incense: Barbara Pym and the Church*, ed. Hazel K. Bell (2004). This was published by the Barbara Pym Society, in the journal of which, *Green Leaves*, there is a wealth of Pymiana.

One of the great pleasures of entering Miss Pym's world is the discovery of the writers she loved. Aldous Huxley's *Crome Yellow* (1921) inspired her to become a novelist; Philip Larkin's *Jill* (1946) is set in an Oxford much like hers; John Betjeman's *Continual Dew* (1937) was her favourite volume of contemporary poetry – until the publication of Larkin's *The Whitsun Weddings* (1964). For Elizabeth von Arnim, readers should start with *The Enchanted April* (1922) or *Elizabeth and her German Garden* (1898) and then move on to *Love* (1925) and *Mr Skeffington* (1940), which share Pym's theme of an older woman falling for a younger man; for Ivy Compton-Burnett, *Pastors and Masters* (1925), *More Women than Men* (1933), or *Manservant and Maidservant* (1947); for Elizabeth Taylor, *Mrs Palfrey at the Claremont* (1971); for Denton Welch, *Maiden Voyage* (1943), *In Youth is Pleasure* (1945) and *The Denton Welch Journals* (1952), which Pym loved. Her taste for ephemera may be sampled in Logan Pearsall Smith, *All Trivia* (1945). A reading of Stevie Smith's *Novel on Yellow Paper* (1936) will allow for an appreciation of the parodies Miss Pym and Jock Liddell shared in their correspondence.

Robert Liddell was my great discovery during the research for this book. His study *A Mind an Ease: Barbara Pym and her Novels* (1989) is far from his best work – as we have seen, her mind was usually anything but at ease. His brief sketch of Taylor and Compton-Burnett, *Elizabeth and Ivy* (1986), is more rewarding, but it is the autobiographical fiction trilogy that is his masterpiece: *Kind Relations* (1939), *The Last Enchantments* (1948), so evocative of Pym's Oxford, and *Stepsons* (1969). And there is a not entirely generous portrait of Miss Pym herself in *An Object for a Walk* (1966).

Illustration credits

Bodleian card: courtesy of the Bodleian Library, Oxford

Sketch by Henry Harvey: courtesy of the Bodleian Library, Oxford

Julian Amery: Getty Images / Hulton Archive, photograph by Walter Bellamy

Hitler: United States Holocaust Museum, courtesy of Michael O'Hara

ARP poster: World War Two postcard by William Henry Barribal; Amoret Tanner Collection / Alamy Stock Photo

Capri: Creative Commons Licence, photograph by Berthold Werner

Manuscripts of *Young Men in Fancy Dress*, *A Record of the Adventures of the Celebrated Barbara M C Pym* and *Excellent Women*: courtesy of Tom Holt (the Estate of Barbara Pym), photograph by permission of the Bodleian Library, Oxford

Letter to Larkin: courtesy of Tom Holt (the Estate of Barbara Pym), photograph by permission of the Bodleian Library, Oxford

Last notebook: courtesy of Tom Holt (the Estate of Barbara Pym), photograph by permission of the Bodleian Library, Oxford

All other images courtesy of the Barbara Pym Society

Index